Fundamentals of

VOICE AND ARTICULATION

Fundamentals of
VOICE AND ARTICULATION

THIRTEENTH EDITION

Lyle V. Mayer

Boston   Burr Ridge, IL   Dubuque, IA   Madison, WI   New York   San Francisco   St. Louis
Bangkok   Bogotá   Caracas   Kuala Lumpur   Lisbon   London   Madrid   Mexico City
Milan   Montreal   New Delhi   Santiago   Seoul   Singapore   Sydney   Taipei   Toronto

Higher Education

FUNDAMENTALS OF VOICE AND ARTICULATION
Published by McGraw-Hill, a business unit of The McGraw-Hill Companies, Inc., 1221 Avenue of the Americas, New York, NY, 10020. Copyright © 2004, 1999, by The McGraw-Hill Companies, Inc. All rights reserved. No part of this publication may be reproduced or distributed in any form or by any means, or stored in a database or retrieval system, without the prior written consent of The McGraw-Hill Companies, Inc., including, but not limited to, in any network or other electronic storage or transmission, or broadcast for distance learning.
Some ancillaries, including electronic and print components, may not be available to customers outside the United States.

This book is printed on acid-free paper.

3 4 5 6 7 8 9 0 QPD/QPD 0 9 8 7 6 5

ISBN 0–07–283730–6

Publisher: *Philip A. Butcher*
Sponsoring editor: *Nanette Giles (Kauffman)*
Developmental editor II: *Jennie Katsaros*
Senior marketing manager: *Sally Constable*
Producer, Media Technology: *Jessica Bodie*
Senior project manager: *Jean Hamilton*
Production supervisor: *Carol A. Bielski*
Supplement associate: *Marc Mattson*
Senior designer: *Gino Cieslik*
Typeface: *10/12 Times Roman*
Compositor: *The GTS Companies / York, PA Campus*
Printer: *Quebecor World Dubuque Inc.*

Library of Congress Control Number: 2003106723

www.mhhe.com

For Marci, Jeff, Tracy,
Norman, and Isolde

Preface

A textbook should be judged by the results it gets, and *Fundamentals of Voice and Articulation,* in the years since its first edition was published in 1953, has worked successfully for an astonishing number of students and teachers. The book earns a space in the *Guinness Book of Records* for being on the market longer than any other textbook in the field of speech communication—approximately half a century.

The book is aimed primarily at people who want to improve their speech and voices. It can be used by the nonspecialist for whom a course in voice and diction/articulation might be the only contact with the speech communication area. It can be used as readily by the specialist—the communication arts or drama/theater major.

It has also been used successfully in many special, nonacademic, three-day seminars or weeklong crash courses in voice and speech improvement for businesspeople, executives, lawyers, doctors, and entrepreneurs. And it's been popular with individuals not enrolled in any kind of class, but who are working for vocal improvement "on their own."

Whatever the background of the student, the book's practical, nontechnical approach sets specific goals and targets for anyone interested in developing effective voice and speech habits. The student and the instructor are told in precise and "reader-friendly" language how to reach those goals and targets.

A lot of textbooks are harder to read than they must have been to write. This one, I sincerely hope, will be enjoyable.

Drill material and exercises, as always, have been updated, augmented, and enlivened. A few, having outlived their usefulness, have been consigned to the shredder.

There are numerous colorful and relevant quotations from contemporary celebrities, ranging from rock stars to Olympic champions, from movie and TV personalities to politicians. Noncontemporaries are represented, too, but in most cases their quoted wisdom is deliberately chosen from the less familiar.

Many of the exercises in the book, in one form or another, have been tested for several decades. They've worked successfully for thousands of human beings—the majority of them college students—but also major generals, grandmothers, baby boomers, nonboomers, and CEOs.

A wise, anonymous quotation says, "The most wasted day of all is the day on which we have not laughed." In other words, "He who laughs, lasts."

Drill material, even when it's serious, is lively. And much of it is fun. I am grateful to the anonymous genius who coined this one: "There's no fun in medicine, but there's lots of medicine in fun. Fun can help recharge our mental, emotional, and physical batteries. Fun can lead to longevity."

In my more than 45 years of teaching experience, I've rarely found a student who resisted humor in drill material, but I've known many students and instructors who dislike intensely the dreary and unimaginative material found in a majority of voice and articulation textbooks. Two examples: *Mary read the classified ads* and *John said "Hello" to Tiger, his cat.* This kind of stuffiness is guaranteed to put an average class into deep hypnosis within 15 minutes. And it certainly won't fire students with enthusiasm or foster voice and speech improvement. There are always, of course, individuals who object to any kind of humor in academia. George Saintsbury says it well: "Nothing is more curious than the almost savage hostility that humor excites in those who lack it."

Regardless of whether students want to work on their own or take the course, the book will help them acquire better voice and speech. In a sense, as one authority says, "All speech ought to be conversational."

THE 13TH EDITION

Chapter 1, "A Preview," addresses the not infrequently asked questions "Why should *I* take a course in voice and articulation? What's in it for me? What's the payoff?" It also analyzes the ingredients of effective voice and speech, and it offers a few suggestions and comments about stage fright, delivery, and listening.

Chapter 2, "Sound Off! The Beginnings of Voice," discusses good breathing habits and the mechanics and production of sound.

Chapter 3, "Put Your Best Voice Forward! Quality," details how a pleasant quality is developed, and it takes a head-on approach to such problems as breathiness, stridency, harshness, nasality, throatiness, and hoarseness.

Chapter 4, "Speak Up! Loudness," focuses on how to project your voice energetically while avoiding vocal abuse.

Chapter 5, "Articulate!" introduces the student to the subject of articulation and provides practical warm-up exercises for the articulatory mechanisms.

Chapter 6, "Conserve Your Consonants," describes the correct manner of producing all English consonants and of achieving clear, distinct, intelligible speech.

Chapter 7, "Varnish Your Vowels," concentrates on the correct production of all English vowels.

Chapter 8, "Discipline Your Diphthongs," suggests how to make acceptable diphthongs.

Chapter 9, "Be Varied and Vivid—Expressiveness," emphasizes acquiring a well-pitched and colorful voice and speaking with animation and spontaneity.

Appendix A looks at pronunciation and vocabulary and includes sound symbols, 149 commonly mispronounced words, and correct use of the dictionary.

Appendix B includes suggested checklists for every assignment given in the text. Students may use the checklists as guides and for help in self-evaluation. Instructors will find them valuable for pinpointing specific voice and speech problems.

Appendix C contains a voice and speech profile and analysis charts. The instructor may use these to evaluate students. Students may use them to appraise themselves or other speakers.

TO THE INSTRUCTOR

> The staggering number of exercises gives the instructor the power of selection. Most important, the instructor should take advantage of the book's variety and flexibility and *assign material on the basis of individual needs and differences.*

There are obviously far more exercises in the book than any one class will be able to or needs to cover. Nor is it possible to do all 18 assignments.

A comparison is in order: If you do your Christmas shopping in a large department store—Saks, Mervyns, or Macy's—you don't buy everything in the store. But the advantage over a small mom-and-pop operation is that you have a lot more stock to choose from.

I've used every possible combination of assignments. Here is a basic, suggested outline. It contains all of the essentials but permits options.

A. *Quality.* Choose one or more, as needed, from Assignments **1, 2, 3, 4,** or **5.**

B. *Loudness.* Assignment **6.**

C. *Consonants.* Choose one or more, as needed, from Assignments **7, 8, 9,** or **10.**

D. *Vowels and diphthongs.* Assignment **11** or **12.** Choose one or both, as needed.

E. *Expressiveness.* Choose one or more, as needed, from Assignments **13, 14, 15, 16,** or **17.**

F. *Spontaneity/final oral performance.* Assignment **18.**

One reviewer of a previous edition said, "This book is a pleasure to teach. It celebrates the joy of speech." I've tried to let those words guide me in preparing the new edition.

I'll conclude by stealing from myself. There is a paragraph from the preface of several earlier editions that I wish to repeat:

> Some time ago, a distinguished professor addressed a conference of educators. He caused some academic eyebrows to vault upward when he commented, "It's about time that writers of textbooks write for their students and stop writing to impress their colleagues."

That statement has also guided me in preparing the 13th edition.

TO ESL STUDENTS AND INSTRUCTORS OF ESL STUDENTS

This section will be of most interest to ESL students. Placing it at the end of the preface should not be misconstrued. It's not an attempt to isolate these students. It's simply a matter of expediency for all students. There are some colleges and universities in which few ESL students are enrolled. And in others, only a few ESL students are enrolled in Voice and Articulation courses.

IS ENGLISH YOUR SECOND LANGUAGE?

Then, welcome to American English.

There is an old joke: If you speak three languages, you're trilingual. If you speak two languages, you're bilingual. If you speak one, you're American.

Count your blessings. You're ahead of most of your American friends, because you're probably bilingual.

The chances are, however, that you have an accent. And you probably want to lessen or shrink it. You'd like to speak clear, intelligible English. You want to sound like Americans who have good speaking voices.

This textbook will help you.

Chapters 6, 7, and 8 deal with articulation, the making of speech sounds. The sounds will be divided into families. For example: **p, b, t, d, k,** and **g** are PLOSIVES.

Do you have difficulty with any of these sounds? If you do, you'll find useful information and exercises at the *end* of the section covering plosives. Similarly, if one or two of the glides or fricatives give you a hard time, check the ESL pages at the ends of those sections.

This special material is on designated and easily identifiable, highlighted pages.

Also, headings are printed in bold caps. Going back to the plosives, for example:

§ § § CONFUSING [p] AND [b]

Two things that most voice and articulation textbooks rarely mention to ESL students:

1. To improve your English, *think,* as much as possible, not in your native language, but in English. And this isn't easy!

2. Are you a glutton for punishment? Go to a few American movies, but sit through them two or three times. By the time you finish the third viewing, if rigor mortis hasn't set in, you'll comprehend a lot of dialogue that you may have missed the first time around. And you'll have a better feeling for the intonation and rhythm of our language.

Good luck!

SUPPLEMENTARY RESOURCES FOR INSTRUCTORS AND STUDENTS

The new edition of *Fundamentals of Voice and Articulation* offers resources that will help instructors to teach and students to learn.

An updated Instructor's Manual and Test Bank includes teaching strategies, 30 test questions for each chapter, and numerous practice exercises and activities.

A **Student CD-ROM,** packaged free with every copy of the book, includes:

- *Pronunciation Flashcards*—practice drills for the sounds presented throughout the book.
- *Video Clips*—six segments that illustrate the material covered in Chapter 2, *Sound Off! The Beginnings of Voice,* and Chapter 5, *Articulate!*
- Icons in the margins of the text direct students to the flashcards and video segments on the CD-ROM.

ACKNOWLEDGMENTS

I would like to thank the following reviewers for providing helpful suggestions: Jennifer Cochrane, Indiana University Purdue University at Indianapolis, Marcia Douglass, University of Maine, Barbara Tannenbaum, Brown University, and Peggy Johnson, Keene State University.

Brief Contents

Contents

Appendices

A PREVIEW

. . . People who have poor speaking voices—the kind that set your teeth on edge—are almost always unaware of this? We are our most enchanted listeners, and it's human nature for each of us to believe that nobody speaks as well as we do.

. . . Being tall, strong, and well-proportioned doesn't necessarily guarantee you a deep, rich, or booming voice? Movie star Tom Selleck confesses, "I don't have a six-foot-four voice."

. . . Political experts now agree that most successful candidates are elected not on the basis of *what* they say, but *how* they say it?

. . . The 10 most persuasive words in English, according to a Harvard study, are *you, money, free, easy, love, save, new, guarantee, health, sex?*

. . . Men are far more likely to dominate conversation than women? They do so by interrupting, changing the subject, or refusing to participate.

THE COURSE

If you decide to buy a new car, you must be prepared to invest quite a bit of money. Generally, before you close the deal, you listen to the salesperson at some length. This person spends quite a bit of time telling you not only about the outstanding features of the product, but also why you should own it. If you're a good buyer, you'll ask questions. You're tying up a substantial amount of cash, and you have a right to know all about the product.

If you're reading this page, it probably means you're enrolled in some kind of a course in voice and speech improvement. Perhaps you've elected the course; perhaps you're required to take it. Whatever, this course, like that new car, represents a significant investment of your money as well as your time.

As you read this sentence, are your experiencing the **WIIFM** syndrome? (**WIIFM:** What's In It For Me?) Probably.

Or maybe your first question is, "What will I be able to do after I finish the course that I can't do pretty well right now?"

Here are some answers.

What is a course in voice and articulation?

It's a course that deals with talking, conversation. It doesn't concern itself so much with *what* you say, but *how* you sound when you're saying it. It's a course that will help you talk more comfortably, efficiently, and effectively.

Do you realize how much talking you do? About 30,000 words a day, averaging four sounds per word: 120,000 sounds!

In general, do the people you talk to daily react favorably to your voice? Can they understand you easily? Can they hear you? Do they find your voice pleasant and agreeable? Do they find you animated and interesting to listen to?

Do I really need a course in voice and articulation?

The chances are excellent that you'll profit from this course. Most people will. Here are some interesting but alarming examples that explain why.

Thirty percent of 1,100 people, according to a research study at the University of Arizona, are unhappy with the sound of their voice.

Every spring, many companies and industries send representatives to college campuses to interview prospective employees. Eight large state universities and 10 smaller colleges recently asked various firms to state their reasons for not hiring the students they had rejected. In approximately two-thirds of the cases, the reason given was that the job seeker did not speak effectively during the interview. A General Motors vice president stated in a letter to me,

> I hire, fire, and promote people, and I find it quite appalling that the reasons I don't hire too many of them in the first place is not so much *what* they say during the interview as *how* they say it. I have very little time for mumblers—those with a mouthful of mush and a dumpling in the throat. And then there are the ones who come in with the Minnie or Mickey Mouse voices—so weak and thin that, even though I sit about 4 feet from them, I can't hear half of what they say (and my doctor tells me I have 20–20 hearing). Maybe worst of all is the hopeful young person with the harsh, raw, and grating voice. It is like running your fingernails up and down the chalkboard; it sets your teeth on edge.

Speech communication instructors contact and listen to many students each year. Over a period of years, the total figures may run into the hundreds. Most teachers agree that at least two-thirds of their students will benefit from a voice and articulation improvement course.

What about the postcollege years? You may spend approximately 5 percent or less of your life in college before you enter the professional world. Poor speech habits will definitely not increase your chances for success and advancement in your chosen occupation.

Listen to Dr. Arnold Aronson, head speech pathologist at the Mayo Clinic: "The higher one ascends the socio-economic scale, the greater the emphasis placed on pleasant, effective voices. With few exceptions, the greater the dependence on voice for occupational and social gratification, the more devastating the effects of a voice (or speech) disorder in a person."

I taught in a midwestern college for 25 years. We kept careful track of dozens of job-hunting graduates. This we learned: Students who had participated in dramatics and debate and who had taken one or more public speaking or voice and articulation courses landed jobs much faster than did other students. Many colleges have done follow-up surveys and found the same results.

The U.S. Department of Labor, Washington, D.C., says bluntly that for 8 out of 10 jobs, you have to be able to talk. Carhop or carpenter, data processor or doctor, nurse or nuclear physicist, lawyer or librarian, teacher or tambourine player, actor or archbishop, you had better plan to do a lot of talking—more than 11 million words a year. That's equivalent to 110 novels!

Recently a woman was hired by an employment agency in a large western city. Every day she called as many as 150 corporations, firms, or small businesses to seek job listings. She discovered that approximately one-third of the receptionists—those who provide the first business contact with a company—had unpleasant vocal traits or were totally unintelligible and mangled the names of the companies who paid their salaries. *Ears Ickle Armen,* she learned, was *Sears Optical Department.* The *Oh Noy Lassner Vision* was discovered to be *Owens-Illinois Glass Container Division.* These same Sloppy Joes and Josephines pepper their business dialogue with such gems as "Gimme yer name agin" and "Woncha hang on a mint?"

Do you travel by plane? Visit airports? How about some of the word-choppers who call flight departures? "Flifivoursev fo Norkn Scnekdy now reayfodepartr agate thireigh, concourB." Care to translate?

How a person says something rather than *what* the person says forms a lasting and almost permanent impression. Your voice is the sharp cutting edge of your personality. First impressions *do* count. As the old saying goes, you never get a second chance at a first impression.

We all want to have friends. We all want to be liked. We all want social approval. But many people persist in thinking that an unpleasant speaking voice always signifies a disagreeable personality. A shrill, strident, grating voice, for example, is supposed to belong to an individual who is tense or neurotic—a person to be avoided. A weak or too-soft speaking voice suggests that its owner has a cotton candy personality and is completely lacking in strength of character and guts. Such stereotypes are not always fair, of course, but nevertheless our listeners often jump to hasty conclusions about our personalities on the basis of listening to our speech for only a few minutes. Agreeable speech habits obviously increase our chances of social and professional success.

A popular columnist, an expert on etiquette and behavior, warns us, "If you are single, your speech may decide whether you will ever marry. If you are married, your speech may decide whether you stay that way."

A University of California researcher has determined that approximately 7 percent of any message is communicated with words, but almost 40 percent of any message is communicated by the voice—*the way we sound.*

Dr. Lillian Glass, a prominent Beverly Hills voice and speech consultant, who has worked with many actors, such as Julia Roberts and Dustin Hoffman, has decided that the way we talk is actually far more important than the way we look. She conducted an interesting experiment. The results are startling.

She selected two groups of people, 10 individuals to a group. Each group was to be judged on a scale of 1 to 10. They weren't told how or why they were being judged. One group consisted of people who were considered to be relatively attractive but who had poor speaking voices and speech: abrasive, nasal qualities and sloppy articulation. The jury rated this group a 2 (unattractive).

The second group consisted of people who were average-looking, but who had melodious voices and clear-as-a-whistle articulation. The same jury rated this group a 10 (attractive).

Beauty, it seems, isn't necessarily in the eye of the beholder. Much of it is in the ear of the listener.

This isn't a personality improvement course, but it is a course that improves personality. I've seen dozens of shy, quiet students blossom and open up.

After all, I've been talking for 18 years, more or less. If there's something wrong with the way I talk, why haven't I found out about it before now?

The truth of the matter is that you've been told quite a few things about your talking. Your parents started giving you advice when you were a year old: "Speak up!" "Don't mumble!" "Don't talk so fast." "Sh-h-h-h!" "Don't talk with your mouth full!" Like a lot of other parental advice, it may have gone quite unheeded, maybe because you heard it so often. And you probably reacted the same way to the advice of your teachers.

You should remember that your parents, siblings, friends, or spouses hear you a great deal. They become accustomed to the way you speak. You may be a terrible mumbler. You may have clogged speech, a galling, whiny, or one-half-decibel voice. The people closest to you, however, like you in spite of these faults. As far as your friends are concerned, they wouldn't be your friends if they continually harped at you about your faults.

Popular magazines bulge with advertisements that warn us about body odor, morning-after breath, gray teeth, zits, and dandruff. But bad speech habits? As the old advertisement says, "Even your best friend won't tell you."

Maybe my voice isn't as good as it should be, but I've been communicating successfully with other people for quite a few years. What's also important: I can certainly hear myself when I talk. Doesn't that count for something?

As one expert says, "Talking is like walking. Both are taken for granted. We know how to do both rather well, and we think we understand the relatively simple basic mechanisms of both."

Were you startled the first time you heard a tape of your own voice? "That can't be me," you said. "I don't sound like *that!*" Indeed, you don't sound like *that,* at least, not to yourself.

When you're speaking in a conversational situation, or even when you're speaking in front of the class, how *do* you hear yourself? Other people can hear you only via sound waves that reach their outer ears. To them, your voice is entirely airborne. You hear yourself partly by the same waves; but don't forget that your voice is also amplified by the bones in your skull. And you are, of course, much closer to the sound of your own voice than anyone else. Furthermore, not only are you used to the sound of your voice, you're fully aware of what you're thinking, so that as a rule you give little thought to how you sound as you speak.

The sad fact remains: You *do* sound like that!

This course will help you to cultivate an educated ear, an ear that not only listens to, but hears critically, the world of sounds—speech or otherwise—around you. In the process of accomplishing this, you will become a far better critic of your own voice.

Why is it that some people are born with good voices?

To be born with the *potential* for a great voice is certainly an advantage, but you don't have to own gold-plated vocal cords to make a success of your life. Abraham Lincoln, for all his backwoods ruggedness, had a rather high-pitched and reedy voice. Winston Churchill had a slight lisp. Bill Clinton has a croupy voice. Popular sexologist Dr. Ruth Westheimer has a little girl's pipsqueaky voice.

Speech is a learned skill. You learned to speak when you were a small child, just as you learned to walk. You imitated your parents, brothers, sisters, friends, and later, your teachers. The good voices you occasionally hear in TV, radio, movies, or plays were generally acquired by their owners only as the result of extensive work and training. Good voices are rarely acquired accidentally.

Who should not take this course?

A frequent comment in student course evaluations: "Don't take this course unless you're prepared for a lot of constructive criticism, both give and take. This course isn't just physically and emotionally challenging, it's sometimes painfully so."

Can I actually change my voice?

Definitely yes! Perhaps *improve* is a better word. Your Adam's apple won't suddenly get bigger or disappear. You can discover, however, ways and means of taking the basic equipment you already have and using it with greater efficiency. Golfers can better their strokes, sopranos can learn to hit high notes without screeching, and sprinters can shorten their running time. This course will help you—if you're willing to work hard—develop a voice that is more likable and appealing than your present speaking voice. This course may give your voice a little "class"—in other words, *refinement* and *polish*. Sound snobbish? It is. But wouldn't you rather travel first-class than economy class?

How do I go about improving my voice and articulation?

> We ain't as good as we should be;
> And we ain't as good as we're going to be;
> But we're better than we was!

The largest room in the world is the room for improvement! The most important thing is practice, practice, and then more practice! And remember this: Practicing isn't always exciting fun. Neither is dieting or bodybuilding. You won't notice any results immediately, but if you discipline yourself and hang in there, you will eventually.

The eye-popping performances of the Green Bay Packers and the Denver Avalanche are not spur-of-the-moment inspirations. They're the result of grueling, endless hours of practice long before the season starts.

Olympic gold medal winner Carl Lewis was asked how many years he'd spent developing his tremendous athletic skills. He replied, "The day I stopped crawling, I took up running."

Or as Itzhak Perlman, said to be the world's finest violinist, once told a class of beginners, "Before you march onto the stage at Carnegie Hall to tackle the Beethoven Violin Concerto, you'd better learn how to tune your instrument."

Experience has taught that few of us can make substantial progress with less than 30 minutes of daily practice. In many cases, 45 to 60 minutes would be better. It's a good idea to break up your practice into two or three quarter-hour sessions or half a dozen five-to-eight-minute periods rather than one long session.

Take your time! Be patient! You can't rid yourself of a vocal fault overnight or by doing one or two assignments. Change takes place slowly. Remember, you've been talking the way you do for at least 18—maybe more—years. And it'll take a while to modify or eradicate any bad speech habits that you might have.

Concentrate! Learn how to listen critically and objectively to yourself as well as to others. Take charge! You are your own best investment.

With intentional irony, somebody has said, "There is absolutely no substitute for a genuine lack of preparation."

Many students tape themselves daily, not just to prepare for classroom assignments, but also to monitor their own voices and check their progress. Excellent idea!

If, however, at any time you feel vocal strain or a sore throat developing, stop! And see your instructor.

WHAT KIND OF SPEAKING VOICE TURNS PEOPLE ON?

PLEASANT QUALITY

A top-notch speaking voice has a pleasing quality.

Quality *is the timbre, tone color, or texture of a voice.* If a clarinetist, a trumpet player, and a violinist stand behind a screen and play "Dixie" in the key of C at the same rate of speed and the same degree of loudness, you'll have no problem recognizing which is which. Each instrument has its own personality or timbre. Similarly, if you overhear two friends talking in an adjoining room, you can invariably tell one from the other.

As one expert says, "Like fingerprints, each of us has a one-of-a-kind voice."

You already know a great deal about yourself, but primarily from the inside out. It may come as a bit of a shock to you to be told that you come across to others as arrogant, cranky, sarcastic, or bitchy, especially when you really don't have the slightest desire to create that kind of an impression.

"There is no index of character so sure as the human voice," British Prime Minister Benjamin Disraeli once remarked.

Here is a list of undesirable vocal qualities:

Breathy	Feathery, fuzzy, and whispery. Breath seems to be escaping noticeably. The voice is almost always too soft and doesn't carry well. The late Marilyn Monroe had a downy, wafer-thin little voice. In most of her cozier scenes, Sharon Stone readily slips into breathiness. And one TV reviewer described an award-winning soap opera actor as "having a voice so soft that it sounds like a gas leak."
Strident	Hard, tense, brassy, and sometimes relatively high-pitched. The voice seems tight, as if it were produced by a pressure cooker. To some, Barbara Walters is acid and abrasive. ABC News Commentator Carole Simpson has springy articulation, but a steel-edged voice. Both Kelsey Grammer and David Hyde Pierce elect to use strident voices in their "Frasier" TV characterizations.
Harsh	Rough, raspy, gravelly, and sometimes quite low-pitched, reminding you of rusty hinges and creaky doors in slasher movies. Numerous actors use a barbed-wire voice to great effect playing Scrooge in Dickens's *A Christmas Carol.*
Nasal	Talking through the nose—a nasal clang. The voice has a foghornlike and sometimes a wailing or whiny quality. Singers of country music, such as George Strait and Dwight Yoakam, like it. Jay Leno is nasal.
Denasal	A cold-in-the-nose, stuffy quality. The voice sounds bottled up. Actors use this one to play plug-uglies or the boxer with the too-often-broken nose. Robert DeNiro uses it occasionally and Sly Stallone bases most of his characterization on denasality.
Throaty	Hollow, muffled, dullish. A voice-from-the-tomb quality. A throaty quality appeals to some actors playing the darker characters in slice-and-dice horror movies and the *Harry Potter* and *Lord of the Rings* films.
Hoarse	Noisy, scratchy, raw, strained. The voice suggests that its user either has laryngitis or needs to clear the throat. Ubiquitous election-year politicians often become hoarse.

Quite a few actors and entertainers owe some of their fame and fortune to rough, twangy, or screaky voices. Some of these voices are apparently natural, but in other cases they are deliberately acquired. Oscar-winning actors have admitted to using negative vocal traits to enhance their performances: a cigarettes-and-cognac quality or a soft, hoarse purr.

Do not, however, use most of these people as role models! Evidence shows that many of these unusual voices prematurely fail or "give out."

CLEAR ARTICULATION

A first-rate voice is distinct, intelligible, and easy to understand.

Articulation _involves movements of the lips, jaw, tongue, and velum (soft palate) to form, separate, and join individual speech sounds._

Articulation must be as sharp and incisive as a laser beam. (_Articulation_, _enunciation_, and _diction_, for all practical purposes, mean the same thing.)

Feeble articulation is our numero uno problem as far as voice and speech are concerned. Lazy lips! The word _mumbling_ is often used to describe careless, sluggish articulation. The more you gobble your words, the more indistinct you become. Mumblers don't open their mouths. Their lips, which have as much spring and bounce as two pieces of stale liver, never move. These wordwreckers drop or omit sounds:

> A reporter specializing in small businesses called a real estate broker.
> Receptionist:
> "Gummenendawanda."
> "Would you repeat that, please?"
> "Whoja wanna talkta?"
> "No one at your firm, thank you."
> Potential loss to firm—$5,000 in commissions.

Give me is heard as _gimme_.

Thinking becomes _thinkin'_.

Going to changes to _gunna_.

Understand turns to _unerstan_.

Or as Rambo tells it, _"I just gotta do what I gotta do."_

Garblers are first cousins of mumblers. They mangle sounds or add extra, unwanted sounds:

These, them, with are heard as _deze, dem, wit_.

Length, strength alter to _lenth, strenth_.

Athlete, across become _ath-a-lete, acrost_.

An _iggle_ is an _eagle_. A _paramour_ is a _power mower_. Arnjoos is _orange juice_. Orals are a baseball team.

The most saluted man in America? Richard Stans: "I pledge allegiance to the flag and to the republic for Richard Stans."

The only aquatic reptile to be honored in a hymn? "Lead On, O Kinky Turtle." ("Lead On, O King Eternal.")

APPROPRIATE LOUDNESS

An outstanding speaking voice is easily heard.

Loudness _refers to intensity (sound level), volume, projection, or force._

"What did you say?" Do your friends often ask you that? Maybe you're muttering. It's more likely that you're not talking loudly enough.

Ever attend a student government or a city council meeting? There are almost always a number of underprojectors at these sessions who insist on asking questions, making comments or speeches—and who simply can't be heard. Microphones and PA systems aren't always available or aren't functioning, and the would-be orators are greeted with choruses of "Louder! Louder! We can't hear you." And many individuals with vocal mufflers show up in classrooms—on both sides of the lectern, too.

You might have beautiful enunciation and still be unable to reach your listeners. A voice that is excessively faint or frail annoys most people. It also labels you as timid and weak-kneed.

EXPRESSIVENESS

A superfine voice is animated, expressive, and well-pitched.

Expressiveness _means vocal variety: the pitch level at which we speak, our vocal movements from pitch to pitch, our rate of speaking, phrasing, emphasis, and contrast. Overall, it refers to the successful communication of meanings and emotions._

A lively, vivacious voice suggests a colorful and energetic personality. A dead, ho-hum monotone too often indicates a dull, dreary personality.

One late Broadway producer chose his actors on the basis of how much animation and sincerity they could inject into two lines: *I hate you!* and *I love you!*

Are you a one-note speaker with little pitch variation? You can put your listeners to sleep. If you have no fire in your voice, you can't warm others. A too-fast speaking rate may prevent your message from being understood, and a consistently slow and draggy rate is boring. Without phrasing, emphasis, and contrast, your conversation or speeches will sound stuffy and pointless.

An excessively high-pitched voice can earn you the wrong kind of attention. A chirpy little voice, even if trapped in Julia Roberts's body, gets a negative response, as would a Michael Jackson voice emanating from an Arnold Schwarzenegger physique.

The pitch of your voice is often more significant than the words you're saying.

A voice of lower pitch is an advantage for both men and women. According to popular psychologist Dr. Joyce Brothers, "While pitch is probably more important in a woman's rise up the ladder of success, a male with a very high voice is going to have trouble being taken seriously. A high, thin voice is a distinct disadvantage to a man."

UNOBTRUSIVE PRONUNCIATION

Good speech doesn't attract undue attention to itself.

Good **pronunciation** *should be appropriate to the speaker, to the area in which the speaker lives, and to the speaker's audience.*

Oddly enough, a single mispronounced word not only stands out like a zit on the end of your nose, but can snap the thread of your listener's attention. After a recent inaugural speech by a new college president, most of his audience ignored what he'd said. They were much too busy discussing a handful of words that he'd mispronounced: *axe* (for *ask*), *ad MIR able* (for *AD mir able*), and *griev I us* (for *GRIEV us*).

DIALECT

Accent? Who, me?

You have one. Actually a better word is *dialect*.

Anything that is said in this book about accent or dialect is not intended as a put-down. Humorous examples are given, but there is a vast difference between humor and ridicule. If you've been told that your accent or dialect is quaint, or if people complain that it's hard to understand you, put your accent on a sliding scale and *modify* it.

The richness and diversity of American speech are astonishing.

The CEO of one of the largest hotels in the Southwest reports that the personnel in the main office come from half a dozen different geographical areas. The result, he stated, is a conglomeration of dialects that makes the office a fun place to work.

Some, but not all, citizens of the New York City area may walk through Central *Pock,* visit *Lon Guyland,* or spend time *boid* watching.

If you add a drop of mountain cheer to *right here* and come up with *ri-cher,* you've possibly spent some time in Maryland, Virginia, or West Virginia.

Visit the *What House?* You may be from any one of several Southern states.

As one TV comic has said, "You can always identify accents. South of the Mason–Dixon line everybody says *y'all*. North of it—*youse*."

Dialect *is a variety of language that is distinguished from other varieties of the same language. It is used by a group of speakers in a certain area who are set off from others geographically and socially.* Dialects constantly change. Why? Education, TV and radio, and migration. (The oil booms of the 1970s and 80s brought so many Northerners to Texas, for example, that one columnist remarked, "There are more New Yorkers in Houston than there are in all of Manhattan.") Still, there are at least four regional dialects in the United States.

General or Standard American

General or Standard American is spoken by approximately 140 million Americans. Boundary lines between various dialects are not sharp and rigid. In general, however, this dialect is most commonly spoken in the Midwest (as far south as the Mason–Dixon line), in the West, in Alaska, sporadically in Hawaii, and in parts of the East and the Southwest.

Bear in mind that General American is spoken in a large geographical area. The speech one hears in Boise is not identical to the speech in Bismarck or Beverly Hills. Detroiters don't sound exactly like Denverites. But they're all classified as speaking General American.

One city or area doesn't necessarily have "better" speech than another city or area. Because regional dialects are dissimilar doesn't mean that they're defective.

Nevertheless, a majority of outstanding educators and social and civic leaders use General American. Prominent network newscasters, commentators, and talk show hosts such as Tom Brokaw, Dan Rather, Katie Couric, Connie Chung, Oprah Winfrey, David Letterman, and Peter Jennings (with a dollop of Canadian color) use it.

Most movie and TV actors use it. General American is, as one dialect expert has said, "Classless but classy."

A colorful exception—Westerns. The casts in these shoot-from-the-hip Billy the Kid/Wyatt Earp sagas generally use a dialect that's a compromise between Texas Panhandle and Hollywood Hills.

Eastern

Differences in dialects are most apparent along the Atlantic Coast.

Eastern, specifically, is spoken by approximately 30 million people. It is heard in the Middle Atlantic states, although the dialects of New York City, Newark, and Baltimore are touch-and-go—unstable and not always easy to locate geographically. Some dialect authorities believe that New York City deserves its own category, and, for sure, some unique speech can be heard in Manhattan and its adjacent boroughs.

Apart from movies and TV shows about cops and mobsters, according to an article in the *New York Times,* "on the playgrounds and in the offices of daily New York life, the pungent dialect that brands New Yorkers in the popular American imagination seems to be fading into history." In other words, the Big Apple resident who tells you "I'm a Noo Yawkuh, and I tawk like this awl the toime" is becoming an endangered species.

New England

The New England dialect is spoken by approximately 15 million people. It includes Massachusetts, Rhode Island, Connecticut, Vermont, New Hampshire, and Maine. But here again, fishermen from Massachusetts and Maine accuse each other of having "accents." Bangor isn't Boston.

Southern

The Southern dialect is spoken by approximately 100 million people. It's used in the region roughly equivalent to the states of the Old Confederacy. It extends as far west as Arkansas and into sections of Texas. Both Bill Clinton and Ross Perot are labeled as southerners, but there are obvious differences in their dialects. In Kentucky alone, 17 different sub-dialects have been recognized.

No section of the United States has a monopoly on good or correct speech. Nor is there any reason why we should all sound alike any more than we should all look or dress alike. As one humorist wisely observed,

> If we all spoke the same, dressed the same, acted the same . . . this country would not be the unique place that it is, would not have the benefit of our spice and variety, and everybody probably would be in the Rotary Club.

An interesting feature story in a late-summer issue of a Fort Worth, Texas, newspaper gave advice to Texas preppies getting ready to go to exclusive eastern colleges. "Worried about your Texas accent?" asked the writer. "Do not—we repeat—*do not* attempt to get rid of it. They'll absolutely adore it back east."

If you speak with an accent or dialect, should you be proud of it?

Yes, but . . . fair or not, prejudices in favor of General American are very much with us.

New York newspapers advertise such courses as "Lose Your Brooklyn Accent." A Southern college offers a course called "How to Control Your Southern Accent."

In the past decade, Americans have become markedly more positive in their attitudes toward dialects that differ from their own. You can be from—or in the geographical area of—Boston or Bismarck, Dallas or Denver, Sacramento or St. Louis; *if your articulation is clear and crisp,* your dialect will not interfere with your ability to communicate successfully.

LISTENING OBJECTIVELY

Prick up your ears: Listen!

There's a big difference between hearing and listening. Even a duck can hear, but a duck doesn't listen.

We spend approximately 30 percent of each day talking, 45 percent listening. College students may spend more than 50 percent of their communication time listening: instructors, friends, parents, stereos, TV.

The problem is that most of us don't listen too well. Perhaps we hate listening. Listening is so commonplace that, like breathing and walking, we take it for granted. Unfortunately, you can't fake listening. It shows. The shocker: Most of us comprehend only 25 percent of what we hear!

Why?

There are several reasons.

The brain can handle 400 to 800 words per minute, but most of us talk at a rate of 125 to 175 words per minute. This makes it rather easy and much more fun to let the mind jump ahead of the speaker or take a leave of absence and wander a million miles away and daydream about other things.

You're now embarking on a voice and speech improvement program. *An important part of this program is learning how to listen carefully and objectively to the voices around you.*

You can't improve if you have no model to emulate but yourself. As you listen to others' voices, note their weak as well as their strong features. You won't be too surprised to discover that you may possibly share some of their positive vocal attributes as well as a few of the negative ones.

Are you a *passive* listener? When you listen with one ear to your TV, radio, passing sirens, or a boring lecture—that's *passive* listening. We all do it. Often it's justifiable.

But now you want to emphasize *active* listening. It's hard work. It takes a lot of energy and a ferocious sense of concentration.

Some universities offer semester-long courses in listening. If you can't afford that much time, here are six highlights that you can mull over in less than six minutes.

How to Improve Active Listening Habits

1. Don't concentrate exclusively on **what** is being said. Focus some of your attention on **how** it's being said.

    For example, is the speaker harsh, nasal, monotonous? Does he or she speak too rapidly, too softly? Does he or she freeze his or her lips when speaking and smudge the words?

2. Don't prejudge the speaker.

    For example, Delbert Drone may have mumbled his way through his first oral performance in your voice and articulation class, but he's in the course for the same reason that you are—to make improvement. He may sound a lot better in subsequent performances.

    Or if he's wearing purple socks, a diamond-studded nose ring, a Mohawk haircut, and a tattoo of Hillary Clinton on his left elbow, don't let these distract you from listening to his voice.

    If you're listening to a celebrity, you may have strong positive or negative feelings about the celebrity's personality. This can be a trap. Don't let your personal likes or dislikes influence your listening.

    Want to test your objectivity? Listen to and evaluate the voices of Howard Stern and Rush Limbaugh.

3. Listen with your entire body.

    Sit in a comfortably erect position, both feet on the floor. Don't slump.

4. Block out distractions.

    If it's possible, do your listening in an attractive environment. But if the room's too hot or too drafty, or the seats are too hard, ignore them as best you can.

    Learn to filter out extraneous noises: two people near you whispering and the passing fire truck.

5. Don't fake attention.

    We're all guilty. Perpetual head-nodders and eternal smilers may be daydreaming.

6. You can't listen well if you're doing *all* the talking.

    Occasionally, *zip those lips!*

If you can do all of these things, you'll soon become more sensitive to your own voice. *The first step toward improvement is self-awareness.*

You'll enjoy the following exercises, but they're tricky. Don't concentrate on *what* your subject is saying. Concentrate on *how* the subject is saying it. Become a human sponge. Absorb and size up every sound you hear.

1. Listen to a radio drama, or try this interesting experiment: Listen to a TV soap opera—preferably one with which you're not familiar—by closing your eyes or disregarding the picture. Concentrate intensely on the sounds of voices rather than the dialogue. Most soaps have stereotypes: the heavy; the Good Samaritan; the oily, philandering letch; the "other" woman; the decent and long-suffering spouse.

    Can you identify them by their vocal traits? Do you like or dislike them? Why?

2. *Listen to rather than watch* other programs such as talk shows, *60 Minutes,* interviews, and newscasts. Don't prejudge the speakers. Empty your mind of physical images or preconceptions. Rate and compare their voices. Why do you react favorably to some and unfavorably to others?

3. Listen to and appraise the voices of one or two of these individuals:

    a. A favorite professor.
    b. A professor you dislike.
    c. A close friend.
    d. An acquaintance you dislike.
    e. A clergyperson or a salesperson.
    f. Someone you know who has an unusual voice.
    g. A radio, TV, or movie personality.
    h. An actor or actress in a professional or collegiate dramatic production.

Analysis Charts 1 and 2, Appendix C, will help you evaluate voices.

RECORDING YOUR VOICE

Hear yourself as others hear you!

Tape your own voice. If time permits three tapings, do the first one at the beginning of the course, the second one midterm, and the final one at the end of the course.

(As previously noted, some instructors require their students to bring their own tape recorders to every class meeting. Many students work with recorders daily.)

For your tapings, use informal, conversational, and unrehearsed material. An interview with a classmate or the instructor or a brief impromptu chat are suggested.

An unrehearsed reading might be included. The following selections are examples of effective material. They contain all the sounds in the English language commonly found to be troublesome or temperamental.

a. When you get a hundred million people watching a single pro football game on television, it shows you that people need to identify with something. Pro football is like atomic warfare. There are no winners, only survivors. The football season is like pain. You forget how terrible it is until it seizes you again. Is it normal to wake up in the morning in a sweat because you can't wait to beat another human's guts out? Every time you win, you're reborn. When you win, nothing hurts. When you lose, you die a little. No one knows what to say in the loser's room. How you play the game is for college boys. When you're playing for money, winning is the only thing that matters. Fewer than three touchdowns is not enough, and more than five is rubbing it in. You're a hero when you win and a bum when you lose. That's the game. They pay their money, and they can boo if they feel like it. Hell, if football was half as complicated as some sportswriters make out it is, quite a few of us would never have been able to make a living at it.

b. Once there was a prince, and he wanted to marry a real princess. He traveled all around the world to find one, but always he found something wrong. There were princesses enough, but he found it difficult to tell whether they were real ones. One evening a terrible storm came along. Suddenly a knock was heard at the gate. It was a princess. But what a sight she was after the dreadful weather. The water ran down her hair and clothes. And yet she said she was a real princess.

"We'll soon find out," thought the old queen. She went into the bedroom, took all the bedding off the bedstead, and laid a pea at the bottom. Then she took twenty mattresses and laid them on the pea. On this the princess slept all night. In the morning she was asked how she had slept.

"Terribly!" said the princess. "Heaven only knows what was in the bed. It felt as though a huge rock was under that mattress. I am black and blue all over."

Nobody but a real princess could be as sensitive as that. So the prince married her, for now he knew that he had a real princess.

TOPOPHOBIA

What Are Our Greatest Fears?

Surveys conducted in the past two decades asked more than 3,500 Americans this question. The results:

10. Blind dates.
 9. Talking with someone in authority.
 8. Deep water.
 7. Spiders, insects, snakes.
 6. Heights.
 5. Flying.
 4. Financial problems.
 3. Job interviews.
 2. Dying
 1. Speaking before a group.

Not listed among common phobias are *pteronophobia* (fear of feathers) and *icthyophobia* (fear of meeting a fish).

Were you startled to find *speaking before a group* in the number one position? Probably not. There are many people who'd rather swallow Drano, have their fingernails pulled out, or spend 10 years in solitary confinement than give a speech.

Not a few professionals insist that speaking before an audience is the most stressful thing that people can do with their clothes on.

Topophobia is also known as *speech fright, state and trait apprehension, performance anxiety, podium panic, speech trepidation,* and, of course, *stage fright.*

If stage fright is the mortal enemy, then the best thing to do is to understand what it's all about.

Some Truths about Topophobia

- It's normal. It's natural. Almost everybody, even professionals, gets it.
- It's usually invisible and inaudible. Audiences can't see your churning stomach or hear your pounding heart.
- It does *not* indicate a personality defect or a mental quirk.
- It isn't necessary to completely eliminate it. Accept it and just try to get it under control.
- It can actually be beneficial to the speaker.
- It diminishes as you go along.
- It has never been listed as the cause of death.

Enrico Caruso, perhaps the world's greatest tenor, sang 607 performances at the Metropolitan Opera in New York. He once said, "I've never done a stage performance in my life without being knock-kneed with terror."

> I once asked former Texas Governor Ann Richards how she controlled stage fright. Her reply: "I visualize everyone in my audience sitting there stark naked."
>
> When asked the same question on national TV, comedian Carol Burnett responded, "I visualize everybody in the audience seated on the john."

The first time Jerry Seinfeld tried stand-up comedy in 1978, he froze. A month later he forced himself to try again and, as we like to say, a star was born.

While performing in a 1967 concert in New York, Barbra Streisand blanked out in front of 135,000 people. Her jangled nerves prevented her from performing in public for 27 years. And in spite of the $20 million she was paid for her Las Vegas comeback, she still gets jittery on performance days. She plays meditation tapes to calm herself.

What are the physical causes of stage fright? Adrenaline, released into your bloodstream, throws your heart into fast forward and raises your blood pressure. Your breathing rate increases. You get larynx lock, and your pounding heart sounds like the cannon used in Tchaikovsky's *1812* Overture. (Your classmates in the first row can't hear it, however.) All in all, it's like being strapped in the electric chair and given your choice of AC or DC.

All these phenomena—the increased flow of adrenaline, the increased heart rate, and the raised blood pressure—simply serve to make you think and react more rapidly and make you far more energetic and alert. You've shifted into high gear. You're psyched up! It's nature's way of preparing you to act in case of emergency. As far as performing in front of this class is concerned, there isn't one chance in a million that you'll ever come face to face with a genuine emergency, so don't worry about it.

Count your blessings. In most so-called public speaking courses, a certain amount of memorization is necessary. Even if you use notes, your instructor will harangue you not to read your speech word for word and to look at your audience 95 percent of the time. In this course, you will rarely if ever be asked to memorize anything. You will probably be reading most of your material. Nevertheless, be prepared!

Practice, rehearse, practice, rehearse! The more you practice your material outside the classroom, the sooner you will get stage fright under control. The more you rehearse, the sooner you will force excessive fear-energy to work *for* you rather than *against* you.

A Few Tips

- For your oral assignments, as much as possible, select, prepare, and work with material that you genuinely *enjoy*. You'll get a lively response from your audience, and this will also make *you* feel better.
- Think positively.
- When you go up to the front:
  Take a couple of deep breaths and RELAAAAAAX!
  Think, "I'm glad I'm here and I'm glad you're here."
  Give your audience the eye sweep. Look at the entire audience. You'll notice that no one is sneering at you.
  Think, "If I fumble or do something dumb with my voice, so what? That's why I'm here."
  Begin.

DELIVERY

And now that you're up front . . .

You'll spend some time behind that lectern up front. Good posture makes you look *and* sound better! Don't lean on the speaker's stand or drape yourself around it. Stand comfortably erect, but not rigid. Rock and roll is great for concerts, but not in the classroom. Stand still and don't be a weight shifter. And don't fidget with notes, hair, beard, clothing, or your car keys.

What are you supposed to do with your hands? It's only when you face an audience that you discover that each hand weighs 150 pounds. The best thing to do with them: Leave them right where they are at the ends of your arms, relaxed at your sides. With certain types of material, you may feel a gesture or two coming on. And when you're ready to do what comes naturally, your hands will be ready too.

Remember: Gesturing not only relaxes you, but audiences are definitely more comfortable with speakers who gesture.

Look at your audience!

Be so familiar with your material that you don't have to read it word for word. When you clasp or shake somebody's hand, you establish physical contact. *Eye clasp* is just as important. And to reemphasize, eyeballing your audience is also a marvelous antidote for stage fright. When you've finished, everybody in the class ought to feel that you've communicated with them personally for at least half of your presentation.

And avoid verbal fungi: *well, er, uh, cool,* and *you know.*

The Black Plague, which killed millions of 14th century Europeans, has made a comeback. The *Y'Know Plague* has struck millions of Americans, including two U.S. presidents, talk show hosts, and the celebrities they interview, among them Jim Carey, Arnold Schwartzenegger, and Tom Cruise. A U.S. senator has recommended that, y'know, colleges and universities, y'know, deny diplomas to, y'know, seniors who use this abomination. Y'know?

> Job interviews? Prospective employers are very firm in stating that they react negatively to earsores such as *you know, uh, cool,* and *okay.* Rid your vocabulary of them.

> To help your instructor get better acquainted with you, during the first week of the course complete the Voice and Speech Profile on p. 291, Appendix C.

WRAP-UP

1. Almost everybody can profit from a course in voice and articulation.
2. Many authorities believe that the way we talk is actually far more important than the way we look.
3. A course in voice and articulation is concerned with how you sound when you talk, rather than what you talk about.
4. People are seldom aware of their own vocal faults and are almost never aware of how their voices sound to others.

5. Practice is the single most important factor in voice improvement.

6. *Quality* refers to the timbre, tone, or texture of the voice. Undesirable vocal qualities include breathiness, stridency, harshness, nasality, denasality, throatiness, and hoarseness.

7. *Articulation* involves the movements of the lips, tongue, jaw, and velum to form, separate, and join individual speech sounds. Poor articulation is the most common speech fault.

8. *Loudness* refers to the intensity (sound level), volume, projection, or force of the voice.

9. *Expressiveness* refers to vocal variety: pitch level, vocal movement, rate of speaking, phrasing, emphasis, and contrast.

10. *Good pronunciation* is unobtrusive and appropriate to the speaker, the area in which the speaker lives, and the speaker's audience.

11. *Dialect* refers to one of the regional or social varieties of a single language. The United States has four main dialects: General American, Eastern, New England, and Southern. There are numerous subdialects. One dialect isn't necessarily better than another. Because regional dialects are dissimilar doesn't mean they're defective.

12. Objective listening, which is another way of defining *active* listening, is essential if you are to learn to judge your own speech habits accurately.

13. A series of physical phenomena—increased flow of adrenaline, increased heart rate, and raised blood pressure—are responsible for the stage fright that most speakers and performers experience. Stage fright is natural. Much practice will help you get stage fright under control.

14. Maintaining good posture and eye contact and avoiding verbal fungi (*uh, y'know, okay*) improve the way you look and sound.

chapter 2

SOUND OFF!
THE BEGINNINGS OF VOICE

WOULD YOU BELIEVE THAT

. . . The loud sounds that accompany enthusiastic kissing are made as you inhale? You also inhale as you sob. You exhale, however, as you laugh.

. . . The Adam's apple is so called because, according to folklore, a piece of the apple that Adam ate in the Garden of Eden got stuck in his throat?

. . . When you are silent, you do about 12 to 16 inhale–exhale cycles per minute? By practicing Yoga, a Hindu philosophy, you can train yourself to breathe only twice a minute. A brand-new baby breathes 35 to 40 times a minute.

. . . When jogging, you take in about 125 quarts of air a minute?

. . . When you sneeze, the force of the sneeze is equivalent to 150 miles per hour? A cough—400 miles per hour?

. . . If a surgeon looked at the larynxes of a great operatic tenor and a professional hog caller, he wouldn't be able to tell which was which?

. . . An 11-year-old Utah boy won a $500 prize from a major cereal manufacturer for being one of the five silliest kids in America? His accomplishment: belching his way through the entire alphabet.

THE PRODUCTION OF SOUND

Sound is an intriguing subject, but you wouldn't sit through a performance of *The Lion King,* Beethoven's Fifth Symphony, or Ruptured Spleen's rock version of "You Take Off My Edge" analyzing what you heard in terms of sound waves and vibrations.

Watch the video clip about "Respiration" on the CD

You're certainly aware, however, that the pleasant sounds come from a group of skilled musicians seated in the orchestra pit or on the stage who bow, pluck, or strike their instruments, or blow air into them.

All of this might remind you of a simple law of physics: *Sound has as its source an object that vibrates.*

What makes the object vibrate? The violinist runs a bow across the strings of a Stradivarius. The harpist plucks the strings of the instrument. The xylophonist strikes graduated wooden bars, and the French horn player, by blowing into a mouthpiece, sets into motion a column of air in about 12 to 16 feet of tubing.

But what about the speaker, actor, or singer who must produce sound without the aid of strings, bars, or metal tubing? These individuals have in their throats the most remarkable instrument of all—the larynx, or voice box.

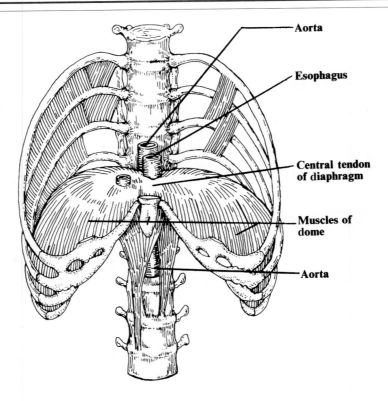

Aorta

Esophagus

Central tendon of diaphragm

Muscles of dome

Aorta

Figure 2.1 The diaphragm.

The larynx houses the vocal folds, or bands, and a flow of air sets them into vibration. To produce sounds successfully, you have to regulate and control this flow of air, which brings up the interesting subject of breathing.

THE NATURE OF BREATHING

You breathe about 20,000 times a day!

Now, take a deep breath.

You'll notice that your chest expands and lifts. What are you doing? You're making your body (and lungs) bigger. Air flows in. Inhalation, in other words. But when you breathe out, you make your body smaller in volume. Air flows out—exhalation.

The thorax, or chest, is a large, almost barrel-shaped container. At the rear is the spinal column (backbone). Attached to the backbone are 12 pairs of ribs. The 10 upper pairs are connected, directly or indirectly, by means of cartilage to the sternum (breastbone). The two lowest pairs, because they are not directly attached in front, are called free, or floating, ribs. It's obvious that the rib cage isn't a rigid structure and that the lower part is more flexible in outward movement. The whole thorax can be lifted and enlarged from front to back as well as from side to side.

Within the thorax are two large, cone-shaped lungs. They're not hollow sacs, but spongy, porous organs that, except for the heart and esophagus, almost completely fill the cavity. The base of each lung is in contact with the upper surface of the diaphragm.

Breathing does *not* consist of the lungs sucking in or pushing out air. The lung tissues are passive; actually, they serve as storage bins for air.

> Think of the diaphragm as a trampoline suspended from the bottom edges of the rib cage, or as a kind of launching pad.

Many muscles are involved with breathing. One of the most important is the diaphragm, which is a tough, double-domed muscle.

The diaphragm, along with the muscles in the lower chest area, plays an active and important part in inhalation. This muscular partition, which separates the chest and the abdominal cavity, isn't a solid, unbroken sheet. Openings in it permit the esophagus, various nerves, and an important blood vessel—the aorta—to pass through it (Figure 2.1).

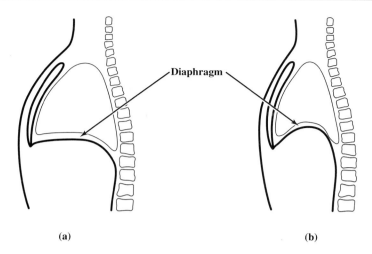

Figure 2.2 Changes in thoracic cavity and positions during (a) inhalation and (b) exhalation.

INHALATION

When you inhale, this is what happens:

- Your body needs air and your brain signals the diaphragm.
- As the muscles of your diaphragm tense and contract, the diaphragm moves downward and flattens slightly. (In normal respiration, the movement is less than an inch.)
- This downward movement pushes the organs of the abdomen against your relaxed abdominal wall, causing a slight outward bulge.
- Your ribs are raised upward and outward.

Your chest capacity is now increased in three directions: top to bottom, side to side, and front to back. Because of this increase in capacity, the air pressure within your lungs is decreased (a partial vacuum also is created in your chest), and air from the outside rushes in to equalize the pressure.

EXHALATION

This is what happens when you exhale, if you're not talking but are only breathing quietly:

- What goes in must come out, and again the brain alerts the diaphragm.
- The various muscles of your diaphragm relax, permitting the diaphragm to return to its arched position.
- Your abdominal organs, which have been under slight pressure, return to their relaxed, uncompressed position.
- As the muscles relax, your ribs move downward and inward because of the pull of gravity.

Inside your body there are 22 tons of atmospheric pressure trying to exit. Outside, there are approximately 22 tons of atmospheric pressure trying to enter.

These movements decrease the size of your chest cavity and compress the air in your lungs. The internal air pressure is now greater than that outside your body, and the air is expelled through your mouth and nose. This kind of exhalation requires no conscious control or awareness. It's basically a process of muscular relaxation rather than of tension.

When you're talking, however, exhalation must be consciously controlled. Greater pressure and push are involved.

- Four powerful sheaths of muscle that form the front wall of your abdomen contract and push in on the abdominal organs.
- In turn, the abdominal organs push up against your diaphragm.
- Your diaphragm then returns to its arched position.

These movements decrease the size of your chest cavity and, consequently, increase the pressure on the air within your lungs (Figure 2.2).

Table 2.1   Differences between Breathing to Live and Breathing to Speak

Breathing to Live (Nonspeech)	Breathing to Speak
Inhalation is active. The diaphragm plays an active role, which means that the diaphragm does most of the work.	Inhalation is active.
Exhalation is passive. The diaphragm plays a passive role.	Exhalation is active.
Breathing is comparatively shallow. Approximately one pint of air is involved.	Breathing is somewhat fuller and deeper, depending on the needs of the speaker (length of sentences to be spoken, increase in loudness). Approximately one to two quarts of air are involved.
Inhalation occurs at about the same rate as exhalation. Inhalation and exhalation occur smoothly and rhythmically, about 12 times per minute.	Inhalation occurs quickly between phrases. About one-sixth of speaking time is spent taking in air. Exhalation is generally slow and irregular. About five-sixths of speaking time is spent in letting air out as sounds are produced.

BREATHING TO SPEAK

Breathing to sustain life is primary and automatic—we're not always conscious of breathing. Only secondarily do we breathe to speak. In breathing for speech, we form intelligible vocal sounds (phonation) during the process of exhalation. (Try to speak intelligibly while inhaling and see what happens.) When we breathe to speak, we control the process of exhalation (Table 2.1).

BREATH CONTROL

In breathing to speak, then, an easy, natural, and flexible control of your exhalation will help you achieve effective vocal production.

Is there any method of breathing that will give you the right kind of control? A lot of gibberish has been written about so-called diaphragmatic breathing. It would be impossible to breathe normally without the diaphragm! Actually, it makes more sense to talk about **central–deep** breathing. Probably 95 percent of us breathe this way (Table 2.2). The other 5 percent use **clavicular–shoulder** breathing.

Central–Deep Breathing

Most of the expansion–contraction activities occur in the abdominal area. The majority of people with good speaking voices, as well as numerous fine singers, actors, speakers, and athletes use this kind of breathing because it promotes sensitivity, flexibility, ease, and comfortableness in the control of breathing.

Clavicular–Shoulder Breathing

Most of the movement involves the extreme upper chest and consists of raising and lowering the clavicles (collar-bones) and shoulders while breathing. Superior voices are found infrequently among individuals using this type of breathing, because it doesn't allow for sensitivity or flexibility of control. In certain extreme activities—the 100-yard dash and the Olympic swimming races—this method may, as a breathing supplement, enable an individual to take in additional oxygen. Under most circumstances, however, clavicular–shoulder breathing may hinder the development of good voice.

Table 2.2   An Evaluation of Breath Control Methods

Clavicular–Shoulder	Central–Deep
Breathing is shallow rather than deep. The movements of the upper chest are too meager to provide an adequate amount of air.	The *control* of the breath stream rather than the amount of air inhaled is of primary importance. Expansions and contractions in these areas are natural, unlabored movements. Greater ease of control is possible.
Inhalation may become too frequent. Speaking rhythm is apt to be jerky. The individual is forced to pause for breath too often and at places that chop phrases into awkward, meaningless chunks.	Inhalations will generally be less frequent. The speaker doesn't have to gasp for breath. Longer phrases can be used and jerky rhythms can be avoided.
Excessive tension is created in the upper chest, straining the vocal machinery. A grating, strident voice may result.	If most of the expansion and contraction movements are in or near the midregion of the body, the throat and larynx are likely to remain free of unnecessary tensions. Experience has shown that if an individual who has an unpleasant voice quality changes breathing habits by eliminating clavicular–shoulder breathing and adopting central–deep breathing, voice improvement generally results.

EFFICIENT BREATHING

Control of the breath must at all times be sensitive. In the following exercises, don't think of *Inhale* as a sharp command. Think of it as a gentle drawing in. Don't think of *Exhale* as a sharp command. Think of it as a gentle release.

To help you relax and develop sensitivity, try Exercises 1–4:

1. Flutter your lips by blowing air through them. (This is the kind of lip activity children perform when they're imitating racing cars or trucks.)
2. Gently release air from your lungs. As it flows out, it should sound like a soft, effortless *ffffff.*
3. Sigh three times:
   a. A small, relaxed sigh.
   b. A medium, happy sigh.
   c. A huge sigh of relief. (You're expecting an *F* in a math course, but receive a *B* instead.)
4. Exhale. Let the air flow out of your lungs. Pause, but don't tense up until you need to take in a new breath. Inhale. Let the air flow into your lungs. Repeat.

The following exercise will make you aware of the differences between efficient and inefficient breathing, and will help you acquire efficient habits in breathing to speak.

5. Stand comfortably erect and try each of the two methods of breathing. Deliberately exaggerate the movements involved. Which method of breathing seems the most natural and comfortable to you?
   a. Clavicular–shoulder: Get the feel of raising and lowering your collarbones and shoulders.
   b. Central–deep: Place your hands below and in front of your lower ribs. Inhale. Exhale.

If you seem to be using only central–deep breathing, your breathing habits are probably efficient. If you're using clavicular–shoulder breathing, however, try to eliminate it. Exercises 6–12 will help you get rid of extreme upper-chest breathing.

6. Place your hands on your upper chest with the thumbs aimed at your collarbone. Take a deep breath, and then count from 1 to 10. If you are aware of any pronounced movement of your shoulders, repeat the exercise and deliberately use the pressure of your hands to prevent this kind of movement. Repeat this procedure saying the months of the year: January through June, and then July through December.

7. Sit comfortably erect in an armless chair. Grab the bottom of the chair seat firmly. Your shoulders should not be able to rise. Inhale and exhale, concentrating on movements in or near the midregion of your body.

8. (Not for the faint of heart!) From a standing position, bend over and touch the floor—if you can! All the air should be out of your lungs. Concentrate on a column of breath as if it were a light entering your body. Slowly, slowly straighten up, inhaling, the light flooding your chest. As you're doing this, spread your arms up and out. Your lungs are full of air. Now begin to exhale. Move your arms back in, slowly bend your body forward until your fingertips touch the floor again. Your lungs are empty. Repeat several times.

9. At home, lie flat on your back. Place your right hand or a book on your abdomen, and place your left hand on the upper part of your chest. Breathe as naturally as possible. You'll notice a slow and regular expansion and contraction in the area under your right hand or the book and very little movement in the area under your left hand.

The following exercises are for general practice:

10. Stand comfortably erect. As you breathe, try to keep most of the movement in the center of your body. Place your hands on your waistline, the fingers extended to the front and the thumbs to the rear. Notice the general expansion in this area.

11. Press a book against your abdominal area below the ribs. Inhale. The expansion in this area should force the book out from ¾ to 1¼ inches. Exhale. The contraction permits the book to go back in. Get the feel of the action.

12. Inhale deeply and, keeping the ribs raised, count to 15, gradually letting the ribs descend between 15 and 20.

CONTROLLING EXHALATION

You make sounds, of course, as you exhale. It's especially important that you control your outgoing breath. Exhale frugally. Be a miser. You must ration, or dole out, your breath. Don't allow air to escape before you start to make a sound or word, between words or phrases, or within a word itself.

13. You should be able to read each of the following paragraphs in one breath. Try them.

   A dog is smarter than some people. It wags its tail and not its tongue. No matter which screw in the head is loose, it's the tongue that rattles. Everybody agrees that a loose tongue can lead to a few loose teeth.

   A bit of advice: Say nothing often. There's much to be said for not saying much. It's better to remain silent and be thought a fool than to open your mouth and remove all doubt. If you don't say it, you won't have to unsay it. You never have to take a dose of your own medicine if you know when to keep your mouth shut.

If you didn't succeed, the following exercises will help you gain control over your flow of breath:

14. Take a deep breath and release it slowly, making the sound s. Keep it even and regular, free of jerkiness and bumpiness. Try it with the sound f.

15. An interesting experiment: Hold a small, lighted candle about six to eight inches in front of your mouth. Sustain s and then try f. Keep your exhalation regular and constant. The flame shouldn't flicker and certainly shouldn't go out.

16. With the second hand of a watch to guide you, allow yourself about 35 seconds to count aloud to 50. Now try the count on one breath. (It *can* be done, but don't asphyxiate yourself!) Be sure that you don't allow breath to escape between numbers.

17. You'll notice that some words are relatively hissy, noisy, and wasteful of breath. The s in *six,* the *th* in *thirteen,* the *f*s in *forty-four,* for example, are the culprits, especially if you allow too much breath to escape on these sounds. Now repeat Exercise 13. If you avoid producing any "hissers," you'll probably be able to read both paragraphs in one breath. Repeat Exercise 16. You'll increase your count.

18. Let's travel. If you survived Exercise 16 and want to go for the gold, try this one. Be ultraconservative with your breath control. Read as many of the states as you can on one breath, but don't strain. Tip: States with the leakiest sounds are listed first. If you run out of breath by the time your reach Ohio, you'll never make it to Iowa.

Massachusetts	Hawaii	Arizona	Rhode Island
Mississippi	North Carolina	Texas	Wyoming
New Hampshire	South Carolina	Kentucky	Maryland
Washington	North Dakota	Nevada	Delaware
Wisconsin	South Dakota	Virginia	Oregon
Tennessee	West Virginia	Kansas	Illinois
Arkansas	Louisiana	Georgia	Montana
Missouri	Pennsylvania	Vermont	New York
Michigan	New Mexico	Colorado	Utah
Alaska	New Jersey	Idaho	Maine
Nebraska	California	Ohio	Iowa
Florida	Connecticut	Indiana	
Minnesota	Oklahoma	Alabama	

For home practice, select any of the exercises in this chapter that you believe will help you. Are you breathing efficiently? Your final target is to achieve easy and natural control of breathing. This means that you shouldn't be consciously aware of how or when you breathe as you read, speak in class, or talk to friends. Remember:

- Breath control must be coordinated with phonation (the making of speech sounds).
- It must never interfere with phonation. The outgoing breath must be used economically and not wasted.
- Breath control must be coordinated with phrasing. Inhalation must be accomplished quickly where a pause permits.

HOW YOU PRODUCE SOUND

A typical day: You have been up and around, presumably awake, for 16 hours. If you talk for 15 minutes of each hour, saying 150 words per minute, and if each word has 4 sounds, you will be producing about 144,000 sounds per day!

Where do these sounds come from?

You've been grunting and gurgling meaningfully since you were a few weeks old. But how often do you consider the fascinating organ in your throat that makes the grunts and gurgles, as well as the more cultivated sounds? When you do, you may refer to it as the voice box. It's the human sound box, but it's more correctly known as the *larynx*, and it's about the size of a large walnut.

Watch the video clip about "Phonation" on the CD

THE LARYNX

The larynx (and pronounce it **layer-inks,** not **lar-nicks**), about two inches high and one inch in diameter, is the principal organ of sound. It houses the vocal cords. It's a cylinder that functions as a kind of air valve by regulating the flow of air from your lungs, just as a faucet or a nozzle controls the flow of water from a pipe or hose.

In addition, the larynx serves in three other capacities:

- The larynx is generally closed when you swallow, which prevents liquids, food, or foreign matter—fishbones, for example—from entering your windpipe and then your lungs, perhaps choking you to death.
- If you swallow a fishbone anyway, or if too large a chunk of sirloin steak gets stuck in your throat, your larynx and lungs set up a cough reflex, producing a blast of compressed air to help expel the intruder.
- When your larynx is closed, air is trapped or impounded in your chest cavity. You must be able to hold your breath for any kind of strenuous work such as lifting bricks or swimming underwater, and for such biological necessities as bearing down (in excretion or childbirth).

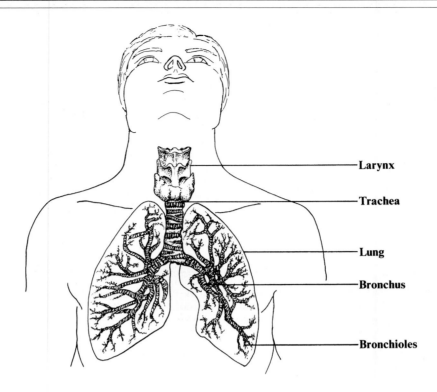

Figure 2.3 Frontal view of larynx, trachea, and lungs.

The Adam's apple or voice box is nothing more than the front and slightly bulging part of the larynx (it is more prominent in men than in women). Hum *m* or say *ah*. Place your thumb and forefinger on each side of your voice box. You'll feel a slight vibration. What is vibrating, and what causes the vibration?

All sounds must have a motivating force. Breath, of course, is the sum and substance of sounds you make in your throat. After the breath is expelled from your lungs via the bronchial tubes, it passes through the trachea (windpipe)— a flexible tube. At the top of the trachea, which is about four inches long and one inch in diameter, rests the larynx (Figure 2.3).

A long time ago Greek physicians decided that the two connected sides of the larynx resembled a shield. The word *thyroid* comes from the Greek word for "large shield," *thyreos.* This butterfly-shaped thyroid cartilage forms the outside wall of the larynx (Figure 2.4). With your thumb and forefinger you can partially trace the outline of the thyroid.

At the top and front of the thyroid, your finger will hit a small notch or depression. The vocal folds are also known as vocal bands, lips, or cords (but never chords!). *Folds* is probably a more accurate term than *cords* because when operating, they "fold" back and forth rather than twang, as a cord or a guitar string does. The folds are attached within the larynx just behind and below this tiny V-shaped notch. From there, extending shelflike back along each side wall of the thyroid, they slope slightly downward. At the rear, they are attached to two small, triangular, movable cartilages known as arytenoid cartilages, which have to do with the opening and the closing of the vocal folds.

THE VOCAL FOLDS

If you watch professional actors like Anthony Hopkins, Russell Crowe, Whoopi Goldberg, or Denzel Washington, you'll be deeply impressed with the powerful, rich sounds rolling out from them so effortlessly. One would almost be inclined to think that the owners of these golden voices have, by some miracle, giant pipe organs instead of small voice boxes hidden in their throats.

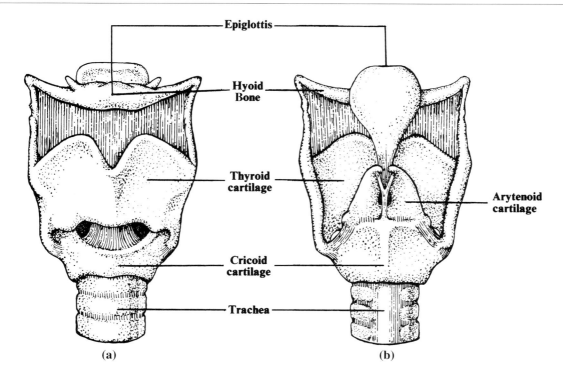

Figure 2.4 (a) Front view of the laryngeal cartilages;
(b) back view of the laryngeal cartilages.

It is incredible that voices such as these, as well as yours and mine, originate within the larynx and, more specifically, from a series of amazingly complicated movements by two tiny muscles commonly referred to as the vocal folds. Consider these facts:

- The average length of the vocal folds in males is about ⁹⁄₁₀ of an inch (although they can reach 1¼ inches in length). It's the larger, thicker, and longer vocal cords that give males their deeper voices.
- The average length of the folds in females is about ⁷⁄₁₀ of an inch.

The vocal folds are long, narrow, smoothly rounded flaps of muscle tissue. They've also been described as "blobs" of muscle, because they're difficult to depict. They're not sharp and taut, and they don't resemble rubber bands. The folds may be lengthened or shortened, tensed or relaxed. They may be drawn apart; they may be drawn together. The inner edges are composed of a glossy, pinkish, fibrous material, and they're covered with mucous membrane. If you're a heavy smoker, your vocal folds may appear to be pale red; if you have a sore throat or laryngitis, they're a flaming red.

During quiet breathing, the vocal folds are drawn apart, leaving an opening, the glottis, between them. Like a hole in a doughnut, the glottis is empty space, but it's defined by what surrounds it. In this relaxed position, the folds form a V shape, with the point of the V at the front.

How the Vocal Folds Produce Sound

Relaxed, the vocal folds are relatively quiet and immobile, but when you're speaking, these intrinsic muscles vibrate or flutter with incredible speed. If you hum middle C, the frequency of the vibration is approximately 256 cycles per second! What is the nature of this vibration?

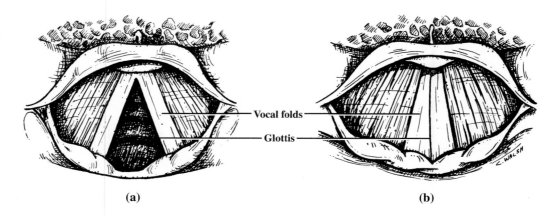

Vocal folds
Glottis

(a)   (b)

Figure 2.5 The vocal folds in position for (a) quiet breathing (glottis opened), and (b) phonation or vocalization (glottis closed).

Do you snore? Have a *uvulopharyngoplasty.* It's a surgical technique, a sure cure for snoring. If you're wary of surgery, become an astronaut. You can't snore in outer space because weightlessness lets the soft palate float.

When you were a kid, did you ever place two blades of grass between your fingers and blow on them to make them whistle? Or did you blow out air between slightly tensed lips to imitate the sound of a motorboat or a diesel truck?

If you ever studied a brass instrument such as a trombone or a trumpet, you may recall that your initial efforts were largely confined to vibrating or fluttering your lips rapidly (as you might have in producing the unpleasantly expressive Bronx cheer, except that while you were blowing into your mouthpiece, your tongue was entirely inside your mouth). In any case, these examples may give you a rough idea of how the vocal folds vibrate or flutter to produce sound.

This is how the vocal folds work:

- The vocal folds are apart during quiet breathing. Before sounds can be produced, the folds come together, somewhat like swinging-sliding doors, and completely close off the larynx (Figure 2.5).
- When the vocal folds are tightly closed, air pressure builds up beneath them.
- When this air pressure rises to a peak, it blows the vocal folds open, and puffs of air escape into the vocal tract.
- The vocal folds are elastic, and as the air pressure beneath them decreases, they spring back together.
- As soon as the vocal folds are closed, the pressure beneath them builds up once more, and again the vocal folds are forced apart.

This cycle occurs again and again. The successive escaping puffs of air set the edges of the vocal folds into vibration, and they, in turn, cause the column of air in the voice tract to vibrate. It is this vibration which, when heard by listeners, is recognized as sound.

In general, the faster the folds vibrate or flutter, the higher the pitch. The slower they vibrate or flutter, the lower the pitch.

Watch the video clip about "Resonation" on the CD

RESONANCE AND RESONATORS

A popular daytime TV program once presented a fascinating experiment in sound. Three musical instruments were displayed: a bassoon, a cello, and a trombone. Then "Twinkle, Twinkle, Little Star" was played on each instrument. Great dissimilarities of sound quality were noticeable among the three instruments. The bassoon, often used by composers for comic effects, growled. The rather plaintive cello had a husky richness. The brassy trombone was alternately brilliant and mellow.

The television audience was then asked to listen to a series of four special recordings of each instrument playing the same tune. The audience was also told that the sound had been tampered with. While listening to the first of these recordings, it was easy to tell that the bassoon had lost some of its growl, but it still sounded like a bassoon. The cello and the trombone, respectively, had lost some of their huskiness and brilliance, but not their identities. But when the fourth recording was played, the three instruments not only had lost all traces of their identifying characteristics, but they also sounded exactly alike! What had happened? In the first of the special recordings, a number of *overtones* had been eliminated. In the second and third recordings, more and more of the overtones had been erased until only the *fundamental* tone remained in the fourth recording.

Overtones? Fundamentals? Read on.

Resonance

As the cellist draws the bow over a string, the string is set into vibration. Tone that results from vibration over the full length of the string is known as the *fundamental.* It is the fundamental that tells us the pitch of the note.

Not only does the cello string vibrate over its full length, however, but it also vibrates simultaneously in halves, thirds, fourths, or fifths.

> Each of the vibrating segments of the cello string produces a pitch that is higher and weaker than the fundamental. These tones are known as *overtones.*

Thus, the tone that we actually hear isn't a pure, simple, or single tone. It's a composite type of tone, a blending together of a fundamental and overtones.

The vocal folds, being far more complex than cello strings, produce a greater number of different, simultaneous vibrations. The number and the relative strength of the overtones, in combination with the fundamental, help identify voices as well as instruments. As a simple example, very few overtones are produced in the piccolo or flute. The tone quality of these instruments is relatively pure and simple. That sometime musical clown, the bassoon, produces a good many overtones, however, and its tone quality is much more complicated and difficult to describe.

Resonators

If you remove a string from a guitar and stretch it tightly between two chairs, even John Williams could produce only limpid and chirpy musical scratchings and scrapings from the string. Strip the sounding board from your Steinway grand, and you can still sit down and play—but the lush, sumptuous tones would be missing, and your Chopin would sound as if it were being played on 88 tiny, tuned tin cans.

Some kind of soundboard or vibrator is needed to reflect and renovate the original tone or sound. The guitar string needs the body of the instrument. The piano keyboard and strings need their sounding board.

Resonance, then, refers to a process that includes

- Reinforcement and enrichment of sound. (It's something like what happens when you add speakers in a stereo.)
- Modification and blending (selection and emphasis) of particular groups of overtones. Different parts of the original tone are emphasized or built up, and other parts are damped or filtered out.

Reinforcement, enrichment, and *modification* are key words to our understanding of the resonating process. How are these brought about in the human voice?

THE HUMAN RESONATORS

If you could whisk yourself inside your larynx and listen to yourself speak, you would hear something like a series of buzzing noises. It would certainly not sound like the voice that you recognize as your own. The vocal folds need their soundboards, too: the throat, mouth, nasal cavities, and perhaps the chest.

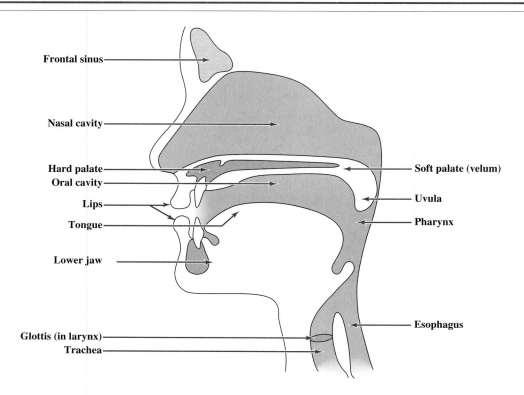

Figure 2.6 Section of head and neck showing resonance tract.

Sound begins with the vibration of the vocal folds in the larynx. The sound waves pass up through the cavities of the pharynx (throat), oral cavity (mouth), and nasal cavities (nose). These three cavities are the human resonators (Figure 2.6).

The sounds produced by the vocal folds are initially weak and thin. They are reinforced by being echoed, reflected, or bounced off the surface of the cavities approximately in the manner of sound magnified by a megaphone. Simultaneously, the sounds are enriched and modified by changes in the size, shape, and surface tensions of the throat and mouth. The nasal cavities may also be used or completely closed off. All of these changes and adjustments produce characteristics that identify an individual's voice quality.

The Pharynx (Throat)

Description

The pharynx is a trumpet-shaped, tubelike, muscular passageway, about five inches long, with soft side and rear walls, which extends from the tops of the larynx and the esophagus to the cavity behind the nasal passage.

Function as a resonator

An unnecessarily tight, constricted throat with tense, rigid walls will possibly emphasize and give prominence to the higher overtones and frequencies. The resulting vocal quality may be strident, harsh, or metallic.

Openness of the throat and relative relaxation of the constrictor muscles, walls, and surfaces emphasize and give prominence to the fundamental and lower overtones and damp out some of the higher overtones and frequencies. The resulting vocal quality may be relatively mellow, full, and rich.

The Oral Cavity (Mouth)

Description

The oral cavity is the most variable in size and shape of all the resonance chambers. It is bounded at the front by the lips and the jaws, below by the tongue, above by the hard and soft palates, and on the sides by the insides of the cheeks.

Function as a resonator

As the most versatile and the largest cavity resonator, the mouth acts as a balancer or as a kind of coordinator for the other resonators. The hard palate (arched roof of the mouth) probably acts as an efficient reflector of sound. On the other hand, the tongue and the soft, inner surfaces of the cheeks and the lips may have an absorbing or damping effect on certain overtones. The possibilities and the combinations are as complex as they are infinite. The vowel sounds, of course, are produced by changing the size and shape of the oral cavity. If you will compare the vowel [i] in *eat* with the vowel [a] in *calm,* you will feel the difference in the shape of your mouth. Most likely the vowel in *eat* makes greater use of certain overtones than the vowel in *calm.*

In a selective capacity, then, the oral cavity reinforces particular overtones, which are primarily responsible for the distinguishing characteristics of the vowel sounds.

The Nasal Cavity (Nose)

Description

The nasal cavity actually consists of two cavities. The dividing wall of thin bone and cartilage between the nostrils extends back to where the velum is joined to the hard palate.

Function as a resonator

The nasal cavity is the least versatile resonator and is primarily responsible for resonating in [m], [n], and [ŋ]. Its total contribution to resonance is somewhat limited, although it can have a damping or diminishing effect on many sounds.

RESONANCE AND QUALITY

The voices of both Bugs Bunny and ABC newscaster Peter Jennings have resonance, but (and we may all be quite thankful) Jennings's voice quality is vastly different from that of the famous cartoon character. Bugs Bunny's voice, in reality, came from the throat of a quite human and unrabbitlike gentleman, the late Mel Blanc, who provided the voices of many cartoon characters, human and animal.

But we shouldn't say that Jennings's voice has more resonance than Bugs Bunny's. Or we might say that Bugs has too much of the wrong kind of resonance. Actually, Blanc created the brassy voice of that pesky rabbit by deliberately interfering with and impeding resonance: He tightened the muscles of his mouth and throat. Similar techniques very likely produce the unforgettable voices of a couple of the raucous and gabby characters of TV's *The Simpsons.*

The individual sounds that identify the voices of Jennings, Bugs, and the Simpsons are characterized not by their resonance, but by their quality. In other words, *quality is the hearer's interpretation of resonance.* Thus one voice doesn't have more quality than another, but a different kind of quality.

After all is said and done, the human voice, as one expert has noted, "is a resonated, acoustically altered laryngeal 'buzz.' "

How, then, do you develop the appropriate kind of sound quality? The next chapter answers that question.

WRAP-UP

1. The chest cavity, or thorax, has 12 pairs of ribs attached to the spinal column (backbone). The 10 upper pairs are connected as well to the sternum, or breastbone. The two lowest pairs, which are not attached to the sternum, are called free, or floating, ribs.

2. The chest cavity is almost entirely filled by the two lungs, which are spongy and elastic air reservoirs. They are shaped something like cones that are narrow on top and wide at the bottom.

3. Lung tissues are passive. They neither suck in nor push out air.

4. The most important muscle of breathing is the diaphragm. It separates the chest cavity from the abdominal cavity. It is a thin but very tough muscle that resembles a dome or an upside-down bowl.

5. In inhalation, you breathe in by increasing your chest capacity. Your diaphragm flattens, pulling down the floor of your chest cavity. The air pressure in your lungs is now lower than the pressure outside your body, and air rushes into your lungs.

6. In exhalation, you breathe out by decreasing your chest capacity. Your diaphragm is pushed back up. The air pressure in your lungs is now higher than the air pressure outside your body, and air rushes out of your lungs.

7. The primary reason we breathe is to stay alive. Secondarily, we breathe to speak.

8. Life (nonspeech) breathing involves comparatively shallow breaths. You inhale about as fast as you exhale, approximately 12 times a minute.

9. Breathing to speak requires fuller and deeper breaths. Inhalation is quick. About one-sixth of your time is spent taking in air. Exhalation is slow. About five-sixths of your time is spent expelling breath as you speak.

10. Clavicular–shoulder breathing involves movements of the upper part of the chest. This method tends to provide shallow breathing, and it may lead to excessive tensions in the throat. The method is used infrequently by people with superior voices.

11. Central–deep breathing uses movements in the abdominal area. This method permits greater control, ease, and flexibility and is used frequently by people with superior voices.

12. The larynx, or voice box, is a structure of cartilage and muscle that sits on top of the windpipe. As the principal organ of sound, it houses the vocal folds, or bands.

13. The vocal folds, which average less than an inch in length, are made to vibrate by puffs of air coming up from the lungs and windpipe. The vibrating vocal folds act as a sound generator.

14. How slow or fast the vocal folds vibrate or flutter is determined by their length, their thickness or mass, and their tension when they start to vibrate. In general, the greater the number of vibrations of the folds, the higher the pitch. The fewer the vibrations of the folds, the lower the pitch.

15. The sounds produced by the vocal-fold vibrations are little more than weak buzzes or noises. These sounds have to be reinforced, amplified, modified, altered, and enriched by resonators before we recognize them as voice. The process is known as resonance.

16. Resonators are the soundboards that reinforce, modify, and enrich sounds. The three principal human resonators are the pharynx (throat), the oral cavity (mouth), and the nasal cavity (nose).

chapter 3

PUT YOUR BEST VOICE FORWARD! QUALITY

WOULD YOU BELIEVE THAT

. . . There is only one voice in the world exactly like yours: your own? Your voice is you; you are your voice. Many courts recognize voice prints as evidence that is as acceptable as fingerprints for identifying an individual.

. . . Although most opera stars are absolute fanatics about the care of their voices, Enrico Caruso, the world's greatest tenor, was not? He smoked two packages of superstrong Egyptian cigarettes daily.

. . . Most prostitutes, according to a serious study conducted by sociologists, have low, rich, melodious voices? The experts aren't quite certain why.

. . . If TV had been around during the times of Thomas Jefferson, one of our greatest presidents, it's possible that he wouldn't have been elected. Jefferson's voice was extremely soft. One critic described it as effeminate.

IS YOUR VOICE PLEASANT TO LISTEN TO?

Ten outstanding speaking voices, chosen by 100 speech and communication experts, are those of Sean Connery, James Earl Jones, Oprah Winfrey, Diane Sawyer, Whoopi Goldberg, Denzel Washington, George Clooney, Julia Roberts, Russell Crowe, and Senator Joseph Lieberman.

"We want to hear you, not your voice," someone has said. But your voice tells a lot about you. It's a key to your identity. It's your calling card, your trademark, your personal logo. It proclaims to the world what kind of a person you are.

One raspy-voiced folk-rock singer sued a producer who'd imitated his gravelly voice in a Doritos commercial and won $2.4 million. Entertainer Bette Midler sued a major automobile corporation for imitating her voice in several of its commercials. Specifically, her attorney noted, "to impersonate her voice is to pirate her identity." She won the case.

Quality is that certain something about voices that makes us rate a voice as first-rate or second-rate. People we respond to favorably often have agreeable voices. A pleasant voice suggests a pleasant personality. The people we avoid may possibly have voices that jar us or get on our nerves.

Thanks to movies and TV, we associate a certain kind of voice with a specific character type. We see a Woody Allen character—timid, anemic-looking—and we expect a wishy-washy, mousy voice to come out of him. If you watch a few episodes of *Law and Order, Sex in the City,* and *The Sopranos,* you'll hear an amazing assortment of vocal personalities, ranging from gruff to shrill, marshmallow-soft to raucous. Andy Rooney looks the way he sounds, or should we say that he sounds the way he looks?

Quality *is the texture or timbre of a sound or tone that distinguishes it from another tone having the same pitch, duration, and loudness.*

Even blindfolded, you could easily tell the difference between pieces of silk, flannel, and cashmere. Voices, too, have texture, and texture helps you tell one voice from another.

Metropolitan Opera star Dawn Upshaw, Barbra Streisand, and Reba McEntire, of less Olympian heights, have at least one thing in common: each of them is a soprano. Yet if each lady recorded "America, the Beautiful" in the same key, few of us would mistake one singer for another.

Likewise, if a trumpet player, a violinist, and a saxophonist played middle C and sustained the tone for the same length of time and at the same level of loudness, you'd have no problem recognizing which was which. And if a close friend phones you, you can generally identify the person at once. Perhaps there is a warmth and richness about this particular voice. Another friend's voice, however, may sound like a chain saw. A third friend who calls may sound breathy and whispery. All of these characteristics help you identify the quality—tone, color, or timbre—of the voice.

We may sometimes overlook the unpleasant vocal quality of a speaker who is highly persuasive, funny, or fluent, or we may become engrossed in *what* is being said rather than *how* it's being said. Most of the time, however, an unpleasant voice—occasionally described as a voice from hell—is a liability.

Two things determine voice quality:

- The production of the original tone by the vocal folds (*phonation*).
- The process of selection, reinforcement, and enrichment of this tone by the resonators (throat, mouth, and nasal cavities).

Certain aspects of your vocal quality, which are determined by the structure of your body, cannot be changed, but some features can be substantially improved.

Your vocal mechanism is an integrated, not an isolated, part of your body. In other words, things that affect you emotionally or physically may also affect, directly or indirectly, your speech processes. Simply stated, good emotional and physical health are generally necessary before you can produce effective voice. Rarely do you hear a great voice coming from a sickly, cadaverous body. The voice is an amazingly good index of the physical and mental health of a person.

NECESSARY AND UNNECESSARY TENSION

Are you stressed out? Are you worried or under pressure because of your *love life, looks, livelihood, teachers, tests, term papers, terrorists, fitness, friends,* or *family problems?* I can't do anything about your family problems, but I can help you learn how to relax and overcome some of the stress and strain.

Tension and stress not only are enemies of good health, but they can also seriously interfere with your resonance and vocal quality. The Wrought-Up Robertas and High-Strung Hirams of the world often produce voices to match: unattractive. That "voice from hell" again.

If you have a tight, constricted throat with rigid walls, for example, your voice may be strident, jarring, and rasping.

Openness of throat and relaxation of its walls and surfaces will help to promote a more mellow, velvety, and molasses-rich quality.

RELAXATION

Relax—let go completely! *It can't be done!*

As wit Evan Esar says, "Nowadays if you're too relaxed, you probably need a therapist."

Researchers now believe that a total lack of stress produces profound boredom, which can lead to serious mental illness.

If you didn't have some muscular tension, you couldn't walk, talk, or blow your nose. Could you bat a baseball or a tennis ball if your arms were totally relaxed? B. F. Skinner, Harvard psychologist, once said, "If everything goes right, there would be something wrong. You must have tension to stay alive."

Let go completely really means: Try to get rid of *unessential* tension in those muscles not needed to perform your task.

(And have you noticed? Tension, like yawning, can be contagious. If you're tense, the people around you may also get tense.)

Part of the difference between the professional and the amateur—be it an Olympic champion or a student of voice—is the ability to distinguish between tension that is necessary and tension that isn't. You're concerned with eliminating the undue tightness that hampers voice improvement. You're committed to finding the right kind of relaxation. But never confuse relaxation with inertia or laxness. Relaxation is *selective, conscious,* and *controlled.*

One of the most effective antidotes for tension, many authorities agree, is deep breathing. It supplies the body with extra oxygen. Subsequently, the body releases more endorphins, nature's most efficient tranquilizers.

The large muscles of the body are easier to get at and loosen, and you can't isolate and relax the relatively small muscles of your vocal equipment if the large ones are taut, so it's with these that we begin:

1. Transformation exercise: In an ancient myth, a god, displeased with an earthling, punished the offender by turning his flesh, inch by inch, into marble.

    (Obviously, don't try to hold the textbook in one hand as you practice Exercises 1–6. Your instructor will give you the gist of each exercise.)

    Stand with your feet apart, and, beginning with the toes, tense and tighten the muscles. Work your way up through your legs, hips, abdomen, chest, shoulders, arms, then your face and head, all the way through your scalp. Hold the statue posture for 5 to 10 seconds and release. Do this exercise three or four times.

2. While you're standing, have somebody raise one of your arms slowly and then release it. There should be no resistance, and your arm should fall limply to the side. Repeat, but this time offer some resistance, keeping the rest of your body relaxed. Gradually relax the resisting arm.

3. The *yu-u-uck!* exercise. Pretend that you've accidentally plunged your arm into a barrel of gunk or slime. It smells terrible. Shake your arm vigorously to get rid of the repulsive stuff. It helps to say *"Yu-u-uck!"* as you do this. Repeat, but this time the slime is on your legs, then your torso, and finally on your neck and head.

4. Stretch and begin to yawn. But rather than finishing the yawn, sigh deeply. The stretching part should be intense, but the yawn–sigh must be gentle.

5. Sit. Tighten your body. Then relax, allowing your head to fall forward and your arms to dangle loosely at your sides.

6. Rotate your shoulders four or five times—first the right, then the left. Then do both shoulders simultaneously.

Try Exercise 7 at home:

7. Select a quiet, comfortable room and lie down, face up on a sofa or bed. Loosen tight clothing. Unwind mentally. A background of soft music helps. Or relive a previously serene and soothing experience.
    a. Stretch and yawn. The stretching should be intense, but the yawning gentle.
    b. Purposely stiffen the larger muscles of your body and then let go. Repeat this pattern several times.
    c. Lie on your left side and rotate your right shoulder slowly and tensely. After a few seconds, relax the shoulder and continue to rotate it. Try the left shoulder.
    d. Extend your right arm rigidly into the air. Relax it and then let it fall limply. Try the left arm.
    e. Assume a fetal or near-fetal position. Bow your head forward, draw your arms and legs in toward your chin. Curl up. Tighten your entire body. Think of yourself as being absolutely compact and not much bigger than a basketball. Hold this tense position for six to eight seconds, then suddenly let your body go limp. Try to feel a wave of relaxation sweeping down from your forehead to your feet. Concentrate on removing any tensions around your forehead, eyes, mouth and jaw, neck, and back.

8. Now that you've removed the crinkles from the larger muscles, let's do the same for the smaller ones. These exercises will help you loosen the sound-producing mechanisms:
    a. Stretch your neck forward and downward, tensing your jaw and neck muscles. Let your head drop forward so that your chin touches your chest. Don't raise your shoulders as you tilt your head slowly to your right shoulder, to the left shoulder, and forward to the chest again. Repeat this pattern several times, maintaining muscular rigidity and tightness. Now repeat these motions, but this time gradually relax the jaw and neck muscles, and make a gentle humming sound somewhere deep in your throat.
    b. Say the following as though sighing. Stre-e-etch those vowel sounds: *aw-haw-arm-cot-caw-maw-palm-tall-mush-mum-sup.*

9. This tranquil material will help you unwind. Read it quietly, calmly, and slowly. Pro-o-o-long the vowels slightly. Concentrate on a general feeling of unbending and easing up. Think of moving a column of sounds from the basement to the penthouse of the voice.

    a. Soft heads do more harm than soft muscles.
    b. When it's dark enough, you can see the stars.
    c. What we have to be is what we are.
    d. The Arctic expresses the sum of all wisdom: silence.
    e. Those who want the fewest things are nearest the gods.
    f. What is life? It is the flash of a firefly in the night.
    g. Death tugs at my ears and says, "Live, I am coming."
    h. Let your speech be better than silence, or be silent.
    i. The idea of calm exists in a sitting cat.
    j. Why is the place where I want to be so often so far from where I am?
    k. Even if this is the dawn of a bright new world, most of us are still in the dark.
    l. One was asked, "What is hell?" The answer: "It is heaven that has come too late."
    m. People go to take sunbaths. Why have so few had the idea of taking baths of silence?
    n. When you are deeply absorbed in what you are doing, time gives itself to you like a warm and willing lover.

Relaxing Throat and Mouth

As you've discovered in the last couple of pages, general, overall bodily relaxation is the first step in developing a pleasant vocal quality. Now you can move to the next step.

Two conditions are necessary before you can build a satisfactory quality:

- *Your throat and mouth passageways must be relatively open, selectively relaxed, and free of unnecessary tension.*

- *Your lips and the jaw and, of course, your tongue must be agile and flexible.*

(One authority states that vomiting is the best way to achieve an open mouth. He's right, but the following are more decorous for a classroom workout.)

Tension in the throat may put your vocal cords on a collision course. These exercises will help you avoid such an accident. (Another thought: Many of the exercises are like bodybuilding for the larynx.)

10. Yawn deeply, heartily. Can you feel an openness in the back of the throat? Good. If you can't, repeat the yawning.

11. Carrying over the yawning feeling from the previous exercise, relax your lips and hum. (Hold each hum for about six seconds.)

    mmmmmm / / mmmmmm / / mmmmmm

    Repeat, holding each hum for about 10 seconds, but don't sneak in a breath during the pauses.

      Repeat again, this time using your hand to move your jaw back and forth as you hum.

12. "Freeze" or tense your throat and jaw muscles and then swallow. Holding this extreme tension for a few seconds, say *ah*. What happens to your vocal quality?

13. Say each italicized word with as much tension as possible. On the other words, be easy and open.

    a. Never *eat* the *last* cookie.
    b. *Keep* your eyes open *and* your mouth shut.
    c. Don't go to *sleep.* Too many *people* die that way.
    d. Set a *thief* to catch a *thief.*
    e. Sometimes in the dark, you *see* what you want to *see.*
    f. If you believe everything you *read,* better not *read.*
    g. Know *thyself,* but tell no one what thou *knowest.*
    h. Sometimes stress runs roughshod over your *life,* not to mention your *pantyhose.*

      Repeat drills a–h. This time—no tension on the italicized words. Read the entire sentence in an easy and relaxed manner.

14. By the simple expediency of relaxing your jaw, you can rid your whole body of a lot of stress and tension. As you say the columns of words in unison, flop your arms around like a rag doll.

who	now	odd	up	too
how	moo	oh	mush	oat
awl	rue	sue	call	loll
coo	saw	shawl	lass	sum

15. Expa-a-a-and your vowels and diphthongs as you read these with an open and relaxed throat. Concentrate on producing cream-of-tomato-soup sounds—smooth and rich.
    a. The day was like gold and sapphires.
    b. The river is a tide of moving waters.
    c. The lights were sown like flung stars.
    d. Come to us through the fields of night.
    e. Darkness melted over the town like dew.
    f. Come up into the hills, O my young love.
    g. The light was brown-gold like ground coffee.
    h. The soft rays of the sun beat the gentle earth.
    i. Froth and foam trickled through the thawing mash.
    j. The hush of dawn washed the murmuring brook in glowing pink.
    k. The blue gulf of the sky was spread with light, massy clouds.
    l. The quiet music of the stars nudged the heavy clouds of night.
    m. The mountains were said to be in labor, and uttered the most dreadful groans. People came together far and near to see what birth would be produced; and, after they had waited a considerable time, in expectation, out crept a mouse. [Aesop]

16. This exercise will help you develop agility and flexibility of your lips and jaw. Open your mouth as wide as you can on the initial sound in each word.

opera	owl	always	hour	awl
awful	oddly	ouster	army	ought
almond	otter	office	ostrich	auk
auger	oxen	alder	object	ocelot

17. You now know the feeling that accompanies relaxation of the throat, mouth, lips, and jaw. But don't be relaxed to the point of being soporific. If other words, as you say the following, don't allow yourself to sound as if you're talking in your sleep. Work for *relaxed energy*.
    a. Superglue is forever.
    b. Wear a hat when feeding seagulls.
    c. Your friends love you anyway.
    d. Why isn't *phonetic* spelled the way it sounds?
    e. I don't have a solution, but I admire your problem.
    f. You never really learn to swear until you learn how to drive.
    g. The mind is not a vessel to be filled, but a fire to be kindled.
    h. Everybody has a photographic memory. Some just don't have the film.
    i. If FedEx and UPS were merged, would they be called FedUp?
    j. How much deeper would the ocean be if sponges didn't grow in it?
    k. I honor my personality flaws, for without them I'd have no personality at all.
    l. If the No. 2 pencil is so popular, why is it still number two?
    m. Tell me what you need, and I'll tell you how to get along without it.

THE SOUND OF YOUR VOICE

The human voice is the most beautiful instrument in the world. The sound that touches the human being most is the voice of another human being.

Some 1,500 students in voice and articulation classes were asked to appraise the voices of Democrats and Republicans prominent in politics within the past decade.

On the donkey side of the ballot, the voices of Bill Clinton, Al Gore, and Joe Lieberman were most often labeled as *warm, edgy, silky, gritty.*

On the elephant side of the ballot, the voices of George W. Bush, Donald Rumsfeld, and Colin Powell were most often labeled *cellolike, growly, steely, coarse, oily.*

One suspects that the political persuasion of the listeners might just possibly have something to do with their choice of adjectives. What is *growly* and *dead* to Patrick is *creamy* and *enticing* to Patricia. Yet many of these terms do help us tag a certain kind of voice.

As previously noted, actors often deliberately use bizarre vocal qualities to aid in their characterizations. Without her whiny cackle, the Wicked Witch of the West would hardly be wicked.

Over the years, prominent movie critics have coined colorful phrases to describe these off-beat voices: "a lullaby voice," "the voice with the built-in purr," "a satin and steel voice," "cocoa-voiced," "terrier-voiced," and an "oilier-than-thou" voice.

But here are more specific terms widely used by voice experts (and you'll remember reading about some of these terms earlier in the book): *breathy, strident, harsh, vocal fry, nasal, denasal, throaty, glottal shock, hoarse.*

A word of caution: A lot of voices refuse to fit snugly into any given category. In a recent experiment, a student with a decidedly nasal voice was evaluated by six speech therapists. Three of them agreed that she was nasal, but the other three described her voice quality as strident. Similarly, three of the therapists found a harsh-voiced male to be just that, but the other three were convinced that he was throaty.

NOTE

Assignments in this section should be selected according to individual needs. If you can, tape yourself. Your instructor will help you identify any specific problems and will recommend exercises that will help you do a voice-lift. Occasionally we encounter students with no defects of quality.

THE BREATHY VOICE

DO YOU SOUND FUZZY, WHISPERY, OR FEATHER-EDGED? YOU MAY BE *BREATHY.*

If you have this woolly, hush-voiced quality, it's because when you're talking, you don't bring your vocal folds together firmly enough to form a tight seal, and unused air leaks between them. A breathy voice makes inefficient use of the air supply.

The breathy voice is a delicate, soft-textured voice, about one notch louder than a whisper.

Breathiness can suggest immaturity; a frail, puny personality; a total lack of credibility; or that you're in a chronic state of torpor.

Breathiness is less common among male voices, although many actors in soap operas, particularly in the steamier scenes, tend to produce voices that contain more soap suds than clear and solid tones. To some, a breathy male voice is regarded as effeminate.

ELIMINATING BREATHINESS

The answer is to get just the right amount of tension in your vocal cords. They should be neither too tight nor too relaxed. Don't try to be as limp and floppy as the Scarecrow of Oz. Inadequate tension may be responsible for the failure to bring the vocal cords together during tone production. Be aware of muscle adjustments in your throat. Exercises 18–26 will help you.

18. Sit like a robot in an armless chair. Grip the sides of the chair and tighten your body, especially your arms and shoulders. Say the pronoun *I* half a dozen times, using a strong voice. You'll feel some pressure in your throat and hear a firmer tone quality. Then substitute these sentences for *I*:

    a. Facts do not change. Feelings do.
    b. Soup should be seen but not heard.
    c. If you can't stand the heat, get out of the oven.
    d. The family that stays together probably has one car.
    e. If at first you're not believed, lie, lie again.

Try these exercises at home:

19. Hold a cold mirror about an inch and a half away from your mouth. Say *ah.* Check the mirror. Is it foggy? Probably. Wipe the mirror and try it again, this time saying *ah* much louder. Check the mirror. There should be less fogging. Repeat, using *oh, ow, ee, oo* sounds. Practice until you eliminate most of the condensation.

20. Remember Samson of biblical fame? Stand in an open door with the palms of your hands placed flat against each side of the door frame. Push as firmly as you can. You'll feel the increased tension of muscles in the abdominal and chest areas. Hold the position for five to six seconds (your vocal folds should now be closed), then release the pressure. Relax. Repeat the Samson exercise half a dozen times.

21. Repeat, but as you let go, count from 1 to 10. Make the numbers hard and robust. Do this several times.

22. As soon as your voice sounds strong and sturdy with the numbers, try these:

    a. Love teaches even people with two left feet to dance.
    b. Think before you speak. Then you won't.
    c. Blind dates are better than no dates at all.
    d. Do it now! Today will be yesterday tomorrow.
    e. What this country needs is more unemployed politicians.
    f. Why didn't Noah swat those flies when he had the chance?

23. As you rehearse the first sentence in each trio, exaggerate and use a breathy, smoky, and sighing quality. Make the second sentence louder, and eliminate *some* of the featheriness. The third sentence should be spoken in a firm voice. Do away with all traces of fuzz and fluff.

    a. The more the change, the more it is the same thing.
       As ye sew so shall ye rip.
       The lights went out, but where to?
    b. Advice to people who are single: stay.
       Saint: A dead sinner revised and edited.
       If love makes the world go around, why are we going into outer space?
    c. Man will always delight in a woman whose voice is lined with velvet.
       A fox is a wolf who sends flowers.
       The world is getting better every day—and then worse again in the evening.
    d. You can never be too skinny or too rich.
       Quit worrying about your health and it'll go away.
       A good line is the shortest distance between two dates.
    e. Some people speak from experience. Others—from experience—don't speak.
       If you're there before it's over, you're on time.
       A good rooster crows in any hen house.

f. Energy is beauty. A Rolls-Royce with an empty tank doesn't run.
   Self-love is the greatest of all flatterers.
   Fun is like life insurance: the older you get, the more it costs.
g. Money is always there, but the pockets change.
   Marriage is two people agreeing to tell the same lie.
   Start every day with a smile and get it over with.

24. Certain sounds are breathier and hissier than others: *s, f, th, h, sh,* and *p.* They're simply molded puffs of air. The problem arises if you carry over the hissy sound to a next-door vowel or consonant. In the word *shall,* for example, the feathery quality of *sh* shouldn't color the rest of the word: *all.* Deliberately, for negative practice and contrast, expand the underlined sounds in these words:

a.	say	him	fine	sham
b.	hill	hiss	kid	thin
c.	pad	show	sick	tall

    Repeat, but this time cut short each underlined sound. Don't draw it out.

25. Read these word clusters at a moderately loud level. Keep each word entirely free of breathiness. The third and fourth words in each group need special attention.

a.	I–die–sigh–high	f.	ale–bale–pale–sail
b.	am–dam–Pam–ham	g.	air–bare–tear–hair
c.	ow–bow–sow–how	h.	eyed–bide–side–hide
d.	at–bat–fat–sat	i.	all–ball–Paul–hall
e.	ode–code–mode–sowed	j.	Ike–bike–tyke–hike

26. Use full volume as you start these selections, but after you read a phrase or a line, gradually reduce the loudness until you hit a moderate volume. Keep out the vocal vapors.

    a. How come it's always the loudest snorer who falls asleep first? A woman can cure her husband's snoring by kindness, patience—or stuffing an old sock in his mouth.
    b. Be careful about marrying the man of your dreams, ladies. Fifteen years later you may find yourself married to a reclining chair that burps. [Roseanne]
    c. It's surprising how easy it is to tolerate people when you don't really have to. Always be tolerant with a person who disagrees with you. After all, he has a right to his ridiculous opinion.
    d. It's no secret that organized crime in this country takes in over $100 million a year. This is quite a nice profit, especially when you consider that the Mafia spends very little for office supplies.
    e. The boy called out "Wolf, Wolf!" and the villagers came out to help him. A few days afterward he tried the same trick, and again they came to his help. Shortly after this a wolf actually came, but this time the villagers thought the boy was deceiving them again and nobody came to his aid. A liar will not be believed, even when he speaks the truth. [Aesop]
    f. Let's have a merry journey, and shout about how light is good and dark is not. What we should do is not future ourselves so much. We should now ourselves more. "Now thyself" is more important than "Know thyself." Get high on now. Reason is what tells us to ignore the present and live in the future. So all we do is make plans. We think that somewhere there are going to be green pastures? Why? It's crazy. Heaven is nothing but a grand instance of the future. Listen, now is good. Now is wonderful. Enjoy now. [Mel Brooks]

Breathiness is often related to other voice problems. An inadequately loud voice, for example, is frequently breathy. If you have this type of voice, you should work on both problems simultaneously, and the exercises in Chapter 4 will be helpful. A voice that's improperly pitched, especially one that's excessively low, may occasionally be breathy. There's a serviceable and agreeable pitch level—the optimum level—for most of us, and if we use it, we'll generally not be breathy. See Chapter 9.

Assignment 1: Breathiness

Prepare and practice material to be read in class. Two to three minutes of material, 300 to 450 words, is typical, but your instructor may modify the amount of material and the time limits.

Your instructor may recommend specific material, but if you're on your own:

Please select interesting material (for future assignments as well). Informal prose is generally preferable to poetry. Choose something that is conversational and casual. Newspaper editorials or paragraphs from your microbiology and calculus textbooks are written in a more formal style for the eye rather than the ear. **Avoid these!**

You'll do a better job with an anecdote, a folk tale, the most unforgettable character you've ever met, or a personal experience: an embarrassing or frightening moment, an amusing job experience. Enjoy what you're doing! Have some fun! If you do, you'll get a good response from your listeners, and an enthusiastic reaction will encourage you and help you to perform better.

As you practice, use a relatively moderate level of loudness. Make your vowel sounds forceful and clear. Don't let breath escape between words or during pauses, and avoid blasting on voiceless sounds. When you perform before the class, do so in a voice that's free of breathiness and vocal fuzz.

Suggested Checklist for Assignment 1: See page 263, Appendix B.

THE STRIDENT VOICE

DO YOU SOUND BRASSY, PIERCING, OR STRAINED? YOU MAY BE *STRIDENT.*

Breathy voices don't always faze hearers, but listening to strident voices is something like having a root canal job without novocaine. It's ear-splitting, steely, and forced.

Does your voice sound blaring and abrasive even when you're not waspish or uptight? You can often *see* stridency! Talk to your mirror. Do the veins and muscles in your neck seem to knot or bulge? If they do, your voice may have all the raucous charm of an outraged parrot.

A strident voice can hurt your listeners' ears, although TV star Fran Drescher has parlayed an extremely strident voice into big money.

This high-pitched harshness generally results from excessive muscular tension in the throat. It's more characteristic of women's voices than of men's, although there are males who have this cawing-crow quality. And the gender issue, fair or not, is present. What might be termed "aggressive" in a male is apt to be described as "strident" in a female.

Howard Stern is hard-voiced. Paradoxically, the strident Kramer character on "Seinfeld" has a mashed potatoes kind of voice off-camera.

REDUCING STRIDENCY

Stridency is often related to one factor or a combination of several factors:

- Using too much of the wrong kind of loudness. Squeezing and rasping the tone out of the throat with no feeling of body support. How do you get that body support? Chapter 4 tells you.

- Speaking with a too-high pitch level. Chapter 9 helps you find a comfortable pitch level.

- Shallow breathing. Have you checked your breathing lately? Remember, clavicular breathing promotes throat tension. Deep breathing doesn't. If you need to, check Exercises 5–12 in Chapter 2.

- Unnaturally tight throat. Don't tie a square knot in your vocal cords. Review Exercises 8–15 in this chapter.

27. Locate the V-shaped notch at the top of your larynx. Say this sentence several times at a comfortably low pitch level: *She and he weeded the wiry seaweed.*

If you can't find the notch, you may be raising your larynx too high in your throat. Again, too much tension is the villain. Practice until you're able to lower the larynx to its normal position.

28. With your tongue on the floor of your mouth, start an easy, gentle yawn. Your throat area is reasonably relaxed. Whisper *ah* and hold for about five seconds. Gradually add voice to the whisper, and build it up to a moderately loud level. But don't allow a feeling of tightness to creep into your throat. Repeat with these sounds:
ee (meet) oh ah ow oo (moon) oi uh

29. In the following, the first word in each pair has more "relaxed" sounds. The second word has more "tense" sounds. As you do these, try to carry over the relaxation that you had on the first word into the second word:

awl–eel	call–keel	hop–heap
con–keen	bond–band	roughed–raft
sup–sap	swatch–switch	smock–smack
bird–beard	Paul–peel	top–tape

30. In these nonsense sentences, "tense" sounds that might promote stridency are placed near "relaxed" sounds that help alleviate stridency. The "tense" words are **bold-faced.** As you read, let all of the words float out of your mouth effortlessly and free of stridency.
   a. All **Enid** does is **sleep** calmly on **steel** cots.
   b. Art **eats** buns, **bananas,** lard, **beans, and** odd crawfish for his **daily** brunch.
   c. Rhonda **asked** Buzz **Beeson** to shove the **cab** into the **valley.**
   d. **Pete's** socks **and T**-shirts turned **green and** soft **lavender** in the **sealed** tub.
   e. The bombings in **Atlanta,** Augusta, **Athens,** Marlboro, **and Peaksville** must **cease.**

31. As you say the first sentence in each group, *be a tad strident.* (Don't overdo the stridency! A little bit goes a long way. If you have a sore throat, don't do it at all.)

But read the second sentence with a soft and hushed quality.

Now, for contrast, try the third sentence with a normal quality—no stridency, no breathiness.
   a. **(strident)** "Be yourself!" is about the worst advice you can give some people.
   (soft) People don't change. They just become more so.
   (normal) Why do they call it rush hour when nothing moves?
   b. **(strident)** I think the world is run by C students.
   (soft) Teeth placed before the tongue give good advice.
   (normal) The greatest of faults, I should say, is to be conscious of none.
   c. **(strident)** It doesn't matter if you're rich or poor, as long as you've got money.
   (soft) If your soul is in your belly, nobody can drive you out of your skull.
   (normal) Everything comes to one who waits—among other things, death.
   d. **(strident)** The main reason I want to stay alive is because it's good for my health.
   (soft) Never miss a good chance to shut up.
   (normal) Traffic warning sign: "Heads you win—cocktails you lose."
   e. **(strident)** If an atom bomb destroys the human race, will surviving turtles wear peopleneck sweaters?
   (soft) It is hard for an empty bag to stand upright.
   (normal) Don't borrow trouble. Borrow money, and trouble will come of its own accord.
   f. **(strident)** The main thing about being a hero is to know when to die.
   (soft) Conscience is the inner voice that warns us that someone may be looking.
   (normal) Don't read the small print. Sucker born every minute.

32. Inhale deeply and then sigh. After you've done this several times, vocalize the words here on the sigh. Start with a relatively high tone, and then glide downward to a low tone. Your vocal folds should become more relaxed as you lower the pitch.

well	law	full	show	shop
our	dart	fool	boy	prowl
who	boil	not	cart	doll
round	mellow	brawl	lodge	warm

33. Deliver these in a leisurely manner and stre-e-e-tch your vowels and diphthongs slightly, but avoid extreme exaggeration. Pay careful attention to breathing and pitch level. Work for proper relaxation, an unconstricted throat, and, of course, a vocal quality that isn't caustic or strident.

   a. In heaven they will bore you. In hell you will bore them.
   b. Any jackass can kick down a barn. It takes a carpenter to build one.
   c. If fortune turns against you, even jelly breaks your tooth.
   d. Night is the time of love, of strange thoughts, of dreams.
   e. Don't shout for help at night. You might wake the neighbors.
   f. A penny saved is a penny earned. So what?

THE HARSH VOICE

DO YOU SOUND ROUGH, RASPY, OR BASSOON-VOICED? YOU MAY BE *HARSH.*

This type of voice is gruff and husky. Harrison Ford has a Papa Bear bass growl kind of voice. A few of the exotic creatures in the *Star Wars* series have voices like a Jeep skidding in gravel.

> The reality shows, in which a group of people is isolated in a wilderness area, have become popular in the early years of the millennium.
>
> Some of the contestants have candidly admitted that they voted to oust one of their colleagues because the person had a harsh and grating voice.

A harsh voice is invariably low-pitched. In a sense, then—*what strident is to the female voice, harsh is to the male voice.*

The owners of these corrosive voices sometimes create the impression that they're cold and unsympathetic individuals—downright "meanies." Movie and TV heavies like Robert DeNiro and Brian Dennehy and the miscellaneous pushers, pimps, and sleazoids who inhabit most cops-and-robbers car-chase thrillers make use of a human hacksaw voice as one way to create their tough-guy characterizations.

Oddly enough, a guttural voice occasionally identifies a lazy and careless individual and, now and then, an ill-at-ease person—one who seems to be afraid of the sound of his or her own voice.

REDUCING HARSHNESS

What causes harshness?

- Not enough energy in your speech. Many people with harsh voices have improved substantially by speaking more energetically (and louder).
- A too-low pitch level. Sometimes it's necessary to raise the habitual pitch level (the pitch level most frequently used) two to four semitones. See Exercises 1–12 in Chapter 9.
- Permitting your tongue to hump up in your throat. Pulling back the tongue muffles the sound and also contributes to mealy-mouthed articulation.
- Burying your chin in your neck while speaking. If you do this (once again have a dialogue with a mirror and check that chin position), you're pulling the voice box down into an abnormally low position.
- Too much relaxation of the throat.
- Too much tension in the throat area. To assure openness of your throat and mouth passageways and flexibility of your jaw, review Exercises 8–17 in this chapter. If you're still harsh, Exercises 34–37 will put you on the right track.

34. Raggedy Ann–Raggedy Andy: Be a rag doll and lower the upper part of your body so that your shoulders almost rest on your knees. Let your head flop around and your arms dangle loosely at your sides. Do you feel comfortably relaxed?

Now sit up, but keep the same easy, relaxed feeling that you had a second ago.

35. Do a rerun of Exercise 34, but this time while in the sitting-up phase, hum *n* quietly. Hum on various pitches, taking a breath between each change of pitch and holding the hum for 5 to 10 seconds.

36. Repeat the humming, but now do it louder and with more relish. Can you *feel* the difference?

37. Lower your pitch a tone or two as you speak the first sentence in each group. Let the words fall back into your throat, and speak with as little gusto as possible. Sound exhausted! You'll find yourself simulating a grating, growly quality.

    The second sentence: Raise your pitch one or two tones and read in a *relatively* strong voice, but don't overdo!

    The third sentence: Use a normal quality, with no trace of harshness. Concentrate on the second and third sentences in each group.

    a. Love shows that God has a sense of humor.
       Etiquette: Learning to yawn with your mouth closed.
       A critic is one who knows the way but can't drive the car.
    b. An alarm clock is a device that makes you rise and whine.
       Bumper sticker: Born free. Taxed to death.
       For Christmas, why not give the gift that keeps on giving? A female cat.
    c. All sins cast long shadows.
       Millions of Americans aren't working, but thank heaven they've got jobs.
       It's easier to float a rumor than to sink one.
    d. Never take any advice, including this.
       Sign in a liquor store: "Preserve wildlife. Throw a party!"
       You're making progress if each mistake you make is a new one.
    e. A road sign in Texas: "Drive like hell, and you'll get there."
       Blessed are the teenagers, for they shall inherit the national debt.
       Carrots are good for the eyes. Have you ever seen a rabbit with glasses?
    f. Adam and Eve ate the first vitamins, including the package.
       Fate makes our relatives. Choice makes our friends.
       There is nobody who is not dangerous for someone.
    g. Silence gives consent, or a horrible feeling that nobody's listening.
       Living well is the best revenge.
       If a person thinks he can or can't, he's probably right.
    h. Age doesn't matter unless you're a cheese.
       Average: The poorest of the good and the best of the bad.
       He has what it takes to be an honest politician—a fear of getting caught.

VOCAL FRY

DO YOU SOUND LIKE GREASE IN AN OVERHEATED FRYING PAN? YOU MAY HAVE *VOCAL FRY.*

Here's an odd vocal foible—an offshoot of harshness—that one hears now and then. You don't have to be consistently harsh to be a victim of the "Irksome Quirk"—as it's so aptly nicknamed. At the end of a phrase or sentence, if you drop the pitch of your voice down into the cellar, the final sound is a gypsy croak—a noise from the back of the vacuum cleaner. It sounds something like bacon frying. Or if you try to carry on a conversation while lifting a 200-pound weight, you'll sound like this.

Sometimes the "fry" has to do with poor breath control. If your air supply is depleted, the last few words of a thought or phrase may be squeezed out of your throat with a popcorn-popping quality.

The drop in pitch that most of us use at the end of a sentence may be accompanied by this vocal fry quality. Its occasional appearance needn't alarm you, but a persistent basement buzz saw rumble might indicate excessive tension of your vocal folds.

REDUCING VOCAL FRY

(Review breath-control Exercises 13–18 in Chapter 2, and relaxation Exercises 1–17 in this chapter.)

38. With energy and enthusiasm, read the following at a fairly high pitch, higher than you'd normally use. *Hear* what you're doing and also get the "feel" of it.
    a. You're a good example of why some animals eat their young. [Jerry Seinfeld to heckler]
    b. Any person who can sleep at night with a pint of ice cream in the fridge has no soul.
    c. "You Spread Your Love Around Like Peanut Butter and Now You're in a Jam." [Country music title]
    d. Some people do and some don't.
       Some will and some won't. Some can and some can't.
       Some is and some ain't. I is. [Darryl Dawkins, former NBA player]
    e. Sneeze on Monday, sneeze for danger.
       Sneeze on Tuesday, kiss a stranger.
       Sneeze on Wednesday, sneeze for a letter.
       Sneeze on Thursday, something better.
       Sneeze on Friday, sneeze for sorrow.
       Sneeze on Saturday, joy for tomorrow.

    Dropping your pitch one or two tones, repeat the sentences. Monitor yourself carefully to prevent the frizzle from sneaking back into your voice.

39. Start each of these words on a fairly high pitch, and then slide your voice downward. When you've reached the lowest level you can—without the crackle—prolong the vowel or diphthong.

die	how	who	lie	do
roe	they	me	lay	doe
maw	why	sea	no	play
boy	new	low	buy	too

    Repeat, but do the opposite of what you just did. Slide your voice upward on each word. As you begin, let your voice fall back into your throat and rumble. Raise the pitch slowly, and as soon as you hear and feel the disappearance of the growling quality, hold the vowel or diphthong sound for a few seconds on that particular pitch level.

40. Say each of the commands forcefully and on one pitch. You'll notice that the rumble disappears.

Quiet!	Jump!	Go!	Now!
Stay!	Stop!	Faster!	Quit!
Hide!	Slower!	Don't!	Run!

41. Read these. The first sentence in each pair is loaded with front vowel sounds and the so-called tongue-tip consonants in which the front part of your tongue is most active. To say them clearly and sharply, you'll have to move your tongue quite far forward. Exaggerate this forward tongue movement, and aim for sturdy, untarnished sounds. Slightly more forceful projection will also help you eliminate vocal fry.

    As you read the second sentence in each pair, concentrate on maintaining the same degree of brightness and vigor. Work also for crispness of articulation.
    a. If I had my life to live over again, I would have eaten less cottage cheese.
       The dog is the god of frolic.
    b. We can't all be heroes because somebody has to sit on the curb and clap as they go by.
       People who know how much they're worth generally aren't worth very much.
    c. Six feet of earth makes us all of one size.
       I wonder what language truck drivers use now that everybody's using theirs.
    d. If George Washington were alive today, he'd turn over in his grave.
       Most people are too busy earning a living to make any money.
    e. People who have little to do are great talkers. The less we think, the more we talk.
       The wish is father to the thought.
    f. Some people are so fond of ill luck that they run halfway to meet it.
       Make the most of the best and the least of the worst.
    g. Fool me once, shame on you. Fool me twice, shame on me.
       There are more warmed-over ideas than hot ones.

    h.   He who laughs has not yet heard the bad news.
           The trouble with country music is that it doesn't stay there.
    i.   The fellow who brags about how smart he is wouldn't if he were.
           It's time to go on a diet when you start puffing going down stairs.
    j.   Ideas are funny things. They don't work unless you do.
           Never get mad at people for knowing more than you do. It's not their fault.

Assignment 2: Stridency, Harshness, and Vocal Fry

If your voice is strident, prepare quiet and reflective material. Devote some of your practice period to the procedures suggested in Exercise 31. Read a line or two (no more) in a relatively strident manner. Read several lines in a breathy voice. Then reread the entire selection several times, using a quality that is free of stridency.

If your voice is harsh, or if you have vocal fry, prepare material that is lively and spirited. If you write your own material, be sure that you include many front-vowel words (*me, it, bed, take*) and tongue-tip consonant words (*tip, day, night*). In your classroom presentation, avoid exaggerating as you read, and avoid harshness or vocal fry.

Suggested Checklist for Assignment 2: See page 265, Appendix B.

THE NASAL VOICE

DO YOU SOUND LIKE A FOGHORN? DO YOU TWANG OR WHINE THROUGH YOUR NOSE? YOU MAY BE *NASAL.*

"A country singer," Dolly Parton says, "is a person who sings through his nose by ear."

As a matter of fact, if country singers stopped singing through their noses, their careers would be over.

Two voice specialists have made fascinating studies of how people react to certain vocal characteristics. A *nasal* voice, reports one, is often associated with immaturity, lower-than-average intelligence, and general dullness of personality. The other expert reports that individuals with these high, strangulated *nasal* voices are often perceived as sarcastic and cold.

Nasality is a loose word. The bottom line: There are two kinds—*too much* and *too little*. First, let's talk about hypernasality—the *too much* kind.

42.   With your thumb and forefinger, pinch your nose, closing off your nostrils and say: *Television is what gives you something to do when you aren't doing anything.* Feel the vibrations in your nose—especially on *m, n,* and *ng?*

      Place a few bits of facial tissue on a piece of cardboard, and place the cardboard directly under your nose. Without pinching your nose, read the test sentence again. What happens to the pieces of tissue?

or

      Put a clean mirror in a freezer compartment for a few minutes. Then place the mirror under your nostrils and read the test sentence again, not holding your nose. There should be small clouds on the mirror.

      Once again, pinch your nose and say: *Hollywood's all right. It's the pictures that are bad.* You should feel no vibrations. If you do, you're talking through your nose. You have *too much* nasality.

      Do the tissue trick again. The pieces of tissue shouldn't move. Or . . .

      With a cold, clean mirror reread the test sentence, not holding your nose. This time, there should be no cloudy spots on the mirror. If there are—you're nasal.

Three of our most pleasant and musical sounds are *m, n,* and *ng* (as in *sing*). They're also the only three legitimate nasal sounds in the English language.

Want proof? The sounds *m, n,* and *ng* must be directed through your nose. Hum *m* for a few seconds and then pinch your nostrils with thumb and forefinger. You'll cut off the sound.

Now sing *aw* for a few seconds and then pinch your nostrils. It makes no difference. *Aw* can be produced with the nasal passages closed off.

How do you produce a nasal consonant? The breath stream must be blocked at some point in your mouth, and your velum must be lowered and relaxed. If these conditions are present, tone will be directed through your nasal passages.

When you say *ah* and permit the velum to hang relaxed and slightly open, however, your nasal passages act as supplementary resonators, and in this capacity they may accentuate the overtones of other vowels, diphthongs, and consonants as well as *ah*. In recent research, high-speed motion picture X rays indicate that some speakers with normal voices leave the velum partially lowered during the production of vowel and diphthong sounds. The degree to which the velum is lowered or raised for the production of nonnasal sounds obviously varies from individual to individual.

What causes *excessive* nasality?

- Your tongue humps up in the rear of your mouth. Sound is blocked from coming out of the mouth. It backfires and is directed through your nose.

- Your jaw is too rigid, and your teeth are clenched or nearly closed. The sound gets trapped in your throat.

- Dilapidated articulation and talking too softly *increase* nasality. A wider mouth opening, talking louder, and crisper articulation will help you *decrease* nasality.

- Excessive relaxation of the velum.

REDUCING NASALITY

> Barbara Walters is possibly the only celebrity who is simultaneously nasal *and* strident. But, as one of her talk-show rivals says, "She makes lots of money."

If you're excessively nasal, listen to a tape of your voice and try to identify the vowels and diphthongs that you nasalize. You may even notice the nasality on certain consonants other than *m, n,* and *ng*. Perhaps your instructor or a classmate can imitate your vocal quality. Listen carefully to the voices of various personalities in movies, radio, and TV, and pick out the voices with too much nasality. If your nasality is caused by a pulled-back tongue, a narrow mouth opening, or a rigid jaw, review Exercises 8–17 in this chapter.

43. Watching yourself in a mirror, open your mouth widely and say *aw–ng, aw–ng, aw–ng*. What happens to the velum? To produce *aw*, you must raise the velum. To produce *ng*, you must lower the velum. (See Figure 3.1). Repeat the exercise until you get the feeling of this action.

44. Start to sound *b,* building up air pressure behind closed lips, but then let the air escape through your nose for *m*. Can you feel the action of the velum? Repeat this procedure, using *d* and *n* as a combination and then *g* and *ng*.

45. In this exercise nasal and nonnasal sounds are listed in alternate order. Practice saying them until you can differentiate clearly between them:

    m–aw–n–ee–ng–i–m–oh–n–eh–ng–oo–m–b–n–d–ng–g

46. In these exercises, don't let your vowels become unduly nasal:
    a. Hold *aw* briefly, pause, and then add the nasal sound. Repeat without the pause.

       aw . . . m   aw . . . n   aw . . . ng
       awm   awn   awng

    b. Follow the pattern of Exercise 46*a*, but place the nasal at the beginning.

       m . . . aw   n . . . aw   ng . . . aw
       maw   naw   ngaw

    c. Place the nasal sound between the vowels.

       aw . . . m . . . aw   aw . . . n . . . aw   aw . . . ng . . . aw

    d. Place the vowel between the nasals.

       m . . . aw . . . m   n . . . aw . . . n   ng . . . aw . . . ng

47. The first sentence of each pair here is saturated with nasal sounds. As you read them, try to ricochet the tones through your nose. There are no nasal sounds in the second sentence of each pair; exaggerate the nonnasal quality as you read.
    Repeat until you can *feel* and *hear* the difference.

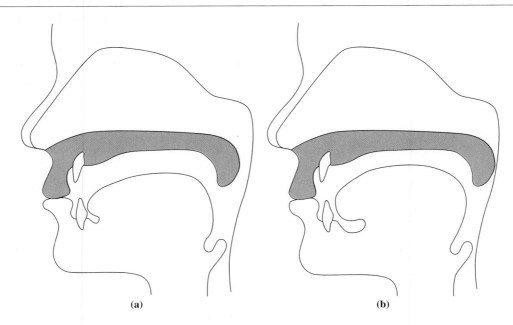

Figure 3.1 (a) Position of velum in production of the nasal consonants *m, n, ng;* (b) position of velum in production of oral sounds (for many individuals, the velum is completely raised).

    a. Don't be so humble. You're not that wonderful.
        I have a perfect cure for a sore throat. Cut it. [Alfred Hitchcock]
    b. I base most of my fashion taste on what doesn't itch. [Rosie O'Donnell]
        He who laughs, lasts.
    c. A rich person is nothing but a poor person with money.
        The best way to get praise is to die.
    d. The devil and me, we don't agree. I hate him and he hates me.
        Without red cells, blood would bleed to death.
    e. A censor is a person who knows more than he thinks you ought to.
        If you drive a car, I'll tax the street. If you try to sit, I'll tax the seat.
    f. Other people's sins are before our eyes. Our own are behind our backs.
        Politics is like football. If you see daylight, go through the hole.
    g. Here's a marvelous rule I recommend: Never practice two vices at once. [Joan Collins]
        Bill Cosby to a heckler: "If your IQ rises to thirty, sell!"
    h. One reason I don't drink is that I want to know when I'm having a good time. [Brooke Shields]
        Whoever gossips to you will gossip about you.
    i. Some people are like musical glasses. To produce their finest tones, you must keep them wet.
        If exercise is so good for us, why do star athletes retire at 35?

48. These selections contain no nasal consonants. As you read them, have somebody listen to you. Practice until you're free of unpleasant nasality.
    a. Several years ago I heard a preacher who was powerful good. I decided to give his church every dollar I had. But he refused to quit. A little bit later I decided to keep the bills but just give a few loose quarters. A quarter hour later I decided to keep the quarters too. A half hour later he stopped; the plate was passed. I was so exhausted that I took out five dollars out of sheer spite. [Mark Twain]

b. Friday was always a good luck day for Jack, a poor woodchopper. This particular Friday, he was overjoyed to discover a huge oak tree. "That tree is so large," he told his wife, "that we'd have wood to build a great house for a duke." "Why the delay?" she asked. "Cut it!"

He dashed back to the oak. He raised his axe. "Stop!" said a voice. A tree sprite appeared. "Please save the tree. It's where I live. If you do, I'll give you three wishes. Whatever you ask for is yours."

Jack spared the tree. His wife was furious. "Just for that, you idiot, you'll go without supper." "I wish I had a fat, juicy sausage," he said. A beautiful sausage appeared.

His wife was baffled, so he told her about the three wishes. Said she, "What a jackass you are to waste a wish. I wish that stupid sausage were stuck to your face."

It was, too.

He pulled as hard as he could, but the sausage stayed where it was. "I'll have to use the last wish. Let the sausage fall off."

It dropped off.

The couple, poor as ever, at least had a delicious sausage for their supper.

ASSIMILATION NASALITY

"Watch those nosy nasal neighbors," as one student put it, "or you'll turn into a nasal drone."

Pronounce *nan* and *lap*.

You'll notice that the vowel *a* is more nasal in *nan* than it is in *lap*. The three nasals, *m, n,* and *ng,* have a tendency to carry over and strongly affect neighboring vowels. Too much of this can give your voice a nasal aura.

Say *nan* again. Your velum must be lowered for *n,* raised for *a,* and lowered again for final *n.* Efficient, prompt control of the velum is essential.

49. Read the following word pairs. Words to the left contain no nasals. Words to the right do. Stress or round out the vowels and hang on to the nasals briefly. But be careful not to jump the gun by allowing the words to become excessively nasal.

fat–fan	Ed–end	yet–net	bay–nay
tip–tin	big–bin	sick–sing	buy–my
row–no	lake–make	Vic–vim	Pat–Pam
dog–dawn	Polly–Molly	wade–wane	sack–sang

50. As you read the first column of words, prolong the nasal consonants as indicated. Pause slightly and then say the vowel or diphthong.

As you read the second column, don't prolong the nasal sounds, but pause briefly before you say the final sound. With the third column, eliminate the pause.

mmmmmmm / / y	m / / y	my
mmmmmmm / / e	m / / e	me
mmmmmmm / / oo	m / / oo	moo
nnnnnnn / / ight	n / / ight	night
nnnnnnn / / ail	n / / ail	nail
nnnnnnn / / o	n / / o	no

51. Run through the following word pairs. Avoid nasality in the second word of each pair. You must raise the velum *immediately* after you sound the nasal in the first word. Carry over the nonnasal quality into the second word, exaggerating lip and jaw motions.

might–bite	nut–but	may–day
nest–best	mat–bat	knack–back
moat–coat	nix–tricks	mace–face
maze–daze	narc–ark	moo–Sue

52. Exaggerate the nasal quality the first time you read the following. Repeat, but avoid nasality that lingers from a nearby *m, n,* or *ng.*

   a. Rambo: "Pain don't count."
   b. When angry, count to 10. When very angry, swear.
   c. The only way to look younger is not to be born too soon.
   d. A tax refund is the next best thing to being shot at and missed.
   e. When one burns one's bridges behind one, what a nice fire it makes.
   f. I'd leave a man for a movie, but I'd never leave a movie for a man. [Elizabeth Taylor]
   g. There are moments when everything goes well. Don't be frightened. It won't last.
   h. If you don't want to work, you have to earn enough money so that you won't have to work.
   i. If anything can go wrong, it will. In 1895 there were two automobiles in Michigan, and they collided.
   j. I think it can be stated without denial that no man ever saw a man he would be willing to marry if he were a woman.

THE DENASAL VOICE

DO YOU SOUND STUFFY, COLD-IN-THE-HEADISH, DEHYDRATED? YOU MAY BE *DENASAL.*

We've talked about the *too much* kind—excessive nasality. Now let's talk about the *too little* kind—hyponasality or denasality.

"Good bawdig. Sprig has cub, ad I have a bad cold id by dose."

Ever sound like that? Your case of sniffles is temporary, of course, but once in a while we hear a voice that always sounds blocked and congested.

Many actors who play the cretinous goons and mafiosi in "fuzz and footpad"—better known as "cops and robbers"—movies and TV shows automatically adopt the denasal quality. Like its opposite, excessive nasality, *denasality* generally suggests that its owner's IQ is in the 50–80 range.

Sylvester Stallone, in his *Rocky* movies, deliberately worked for the broken-nose, bottleneck effect. That's great for playing a punch-drunk boxer. Otherwise, denasality can seriously hamper understandability of speech.

Denasality happens if a small amount of air or no air at all enters the nasal passages as you talk. Sometimes a barrier is responsible. Enlarged adenoids, swollen tonsils, allergies, a broken nose, or a deviated septum will give you this nasal roadblock. (The septum is the thin wall that divides your nasal cavity into two passages.)

Possibly surgical repair or medical treatment is needed. Unfortunately, even after such treatment, some individuals remain denasal. A little vocal retraining will generally solve the problem.

CORRECTING DENASALITY

53. Hum *m, n,* and *ng* (as in *sing*) up and down the scale. You'll feel the vibrations and tinglings on your lips and in your nasal passages.

   You won't feel any ripples in your nose as you say the first word in each pair below. But as you say the second word, prolong *m, n,* and *ng,* and you'll feel prickling sensations there.

bay–May	dell–Nell	bag–bang
bad–mad	day–nay	rug–rung
bail–mail	dill–nil	big–bing
bake–make	door–nor	log–long

54. Read these words twice, the first time slowly and the second time rapidly. In both readings, make the nasal consonants as prominent as you can.

an	lime	noon	moll	length
sign	bone	mat	bend	strength
aunt	rhyme	moon	chin	finger
mom	plain	dawn	bring	ring

55. Speak each of these sentences twice. The first time, stretch the nasal sounds so that you're definitely aware of nasal tremors.

Can you make the tone quality of the vowels and diphthongs as vibrant and ringing as it is on *m, n,* and *ng*? The second time: Don't exaggerate, but be certain that *m, n,* and *ng* have normal nasality and that your vowels and diphthongs also have a bit of luster.

a. Punk rock isn't dead. It just smells funny.
b. A comic says funny things. A comedian says things funny.
c. Slasher movie axiom: You can always find a chain saw when you need one.
d. Every man, woman, and child has at least one scheme that won't work.
e. Some are bent with toil, and some get crooked trying to avoid it.
f. Never take the advice of someone who hasn't had your kind of trouble.
g. Do unto yourself as your neighbors do unto themselves and look pleasant.
h. We didn't all come over on the same ship, but we're all in the same boat.
i. Classical music is the kind that we keep thinking will turn into a tune.
j. Today's trying times in about 20 years will have become the "good old days."
k. Today if you invent a better mousetrap, the government comes along with a better mouse.

Assignment 3: Nasality and Denasality

If you're excessively nasal, prepare two short selections. The first one should contain no nasal consonants (*m, n, ng*), but the second one should contain a moderate number of nasals. Listen to yourself carefully as you practice. If possible, have someone else listen too.

If denasality has been one of your problems, select material that is loaded with nasals. Practice with this suggestion in mind: Exaggerate the nasals somewhat but try to make the vowels and diphthongs as bright and vibrant as the nasals.

When you do your assignment in class, concentrate on ease and naturalness.

Suggested Checklist for Assignment 3: See page 267, Appendix B.

THE THROATY VOICE

DO YOU SOUND MUFFLED, TRAPPED, ZOMBIELIKE? YOU MAY BE *THROATY.*

No pun is intended, but *guttural* is a fine choice of word because a scraping voice seems to grind its way up from a vocal gutter.

Throatiness and harshness are kissing cousins. There are obvious similarities, but there are also differences. Most throaty voices sound harsh, but not all harsh voices sound throaty.

This is the voice-from-the-tomb quality—a heavy echo bouncing off the back wall of a cave. It almost sounds as if its owner has a physical obstacle in the mouth that prevents the voice from coming out.

Not surprisingly, when TV comedies want to portray a character as a dummy, a booby, or a nerd, the actors often use this sooty, throaty quality.

Outside the entertainment world, this dammed-up kind of voice can be objectionable to listeners because it generally lacks carrying power. It sounds swallowed and thick. The peculiar clogged quality attracts attention, if not necessarily approval. (Throatiness has also been described as "vocal constipation.") Occasionally, throatiness sounds like vocal fry. A throaty voice can also be harsh, as well as denasal.

To some, a throaty voice hints that its owner is lazy, indifferent, or even callous.

If you can "see" a strident voice, you can also "see" a throaty voice. The throaty person often likes to bury his chin in his neck, and a hollow, rumbling voice-in-the-sewer-pipe sound emerges.

"Keep your chin up," in other words, is fine advice in more ways than one. *Check your chin position in a mirror.*

REDUCING THROATINESS

(Review vocal fry Exercises 38–41 and denasality Exercises 53–55.)

56. Read these sentences three times. The first time, pull your chin back against your neck. The second time, go to the other extreme. Tilt your head back quite far, and raise your chin high. The third time, strike a compromise posture. Your chin should be in a normal position. Your throatiness should disappear. If you're still having problems, repeat the techniques suggested for the second and third readings, but omit the first, chin-against-the-neck position.

   a. Easy doesn't do it.
   b. Never give advice. Sell it!
   c. When you want salt, sugar won't do.
   d. A piano is a piano is a piano. [Gertrude Steinway]
   e. By the time we've made it, we've had it.
   f. If you touch a sleeping sea snake, you'll feel eel at ease.
   g. One thing this country needs is fewer needs.
   h. Oh, no! Not nuclear war! What about my career?

57. With your chin in a normal position, read the following. Push all of the sounds toward the front of the mouth. Think of it as bouncing them off your incisors.

   a. What Adam and Eve started, atom and evil may end.
   b. We are near waking when we dream we are dreaming.
   c. You can't steal second base and keep one foot on first.
   d. Classified ad: Waveless waterbed for sale. No surfers, please.
   e. Feeling bad makes me look bad, but knowing that I look bad makes me feel worse.
   f. That polar bears mate at all is remarkable, considering that both parties have such cold feet.

58. Is your tongue position correct?
   If your tongue is consistently pulled too far back or humped up toward the rear of the mouth, some of your important vowel sounds will be murky and inky. Try the sentences below three different ways:
   First, retract the tongue. Pull it back as far as you can, and read the sentence. You'll notice that some of the sounds will be greatly distorted.
   Second, move your tongue slightly forward as you read.
   Finally, push your tongue far forward. Definitely get the feeling that most of the activity involves the front part of the tongue.

   a. Of soup and love, the first is best.
   b. Fame is all right if you don't inhale.
   c. Office hours are from 12 to 1 with an hour off for lunch.
   d. Forgive your enemies, but never forget their names.
   e. We don't all think alike. In fact, we don't all think.
   f. He who hesitates is not only lost, but miles from the next exit.

59. The first sentence in these pairs is chock full of sounds that have warmth and sparkle—front vowels and tongue-tip consonants. You'll find it easy to avoid throatiness while reading this material.
   The second sentence in each pair is studded with dark and dusty sounds—sounds that lack sheen.
   Try to transfer at least some of the brightness and the feeling of the front-of-the-mouth production that you had with the first sentence. Repeat the exercises until you're able to read all of the material with a luminous quality.

   a. Travel folder: A trip tease.
      Never trouble trouble till trouble troubles you.
   b. The tongue of man is a twisty thing.
      What do you call a doughnut if you put the doughnut hole back in?
   c. Men who never get carried away should be.
      Two can live as cheaply as one, but it costs twice as much.
   d. Deed: Past tense of do. "Macbeth deed the bloody did."
      A true artist is one who won't prostitute his art except for money.

e. The first and greatest commandment: Don't let them scare you.

   I must say that I hate money, but it's the lack of money I hate most.

f. Isn't it a bit unnerving that doctors call what they do "practicing" medicine?

   A budget tells us what we can't afford, but it doesn't keep us from buying it.

g. Washing your car and polishing it all up is a never-failing sign of rain.

   Prayer of the modern American: "Dear God, I pray for patience, and I want it right now."

h. Rain is much nicer than snow because you don't have rain plows piling up rain in eight-foot piles.

   If dogs could talk, perhaps we'd find it as hard to get along with them as we do with people.

i. Middle age is when you're sitting home on Saturday night and the telephone rings and you hope it isn't for you.

   I hate small towns because once you've seen the cannon in the park there's nothing else to do.

j. Tax reform: When you take the taxes off things that have been taxed in the past and put taxes on things that haven't been taxed before.

   If you live to the age of a hundred you have it made, because very few people die past the age of a hundred.

Assignment 4: Throatiness

If you're throaty, prepare material that contains many of the front vowels. (In the following words, front vowels are underlined: m*e*, *i*t, d*a*te, *e*gg, h*a*t.) Also include words that contain tongue-tip consonants: *t*in, *d*og, *l*ad, *n*ot. Run through your material a few times, using the procedures described in Exercise 56. Spend most of your time practicing the material as you plan to do it in class, *without* the two extremes of the chin-against-the-neck or the chin-raised-high.

Suggested Checklist for Assignment 4: See page 269, Appendix B.

GLOTTAL SHOCK

DO YOU MAKE EXPLOSIVE GRUNTS ON YOUR FRONTAL VOWELS? YOU MAY HAVE *GLOTTAL SHOCK*.

Read aloud the following sentences, inserting a slight pause between the words:

Andy and Opal invited Eve to the eerie island in April.

Ask Ann and Arthur to open the old apple with an axe.

The owl eyed the eel and ate the olive in August.

If you notice a raspy little bark or a sharp staccato click on the vowels at the beginning of each word, you may have glottal shock (also known as glottal attack, click, or stroke). In one sense, glottal shock is the opposite of breathiness, in which breath is allowed to escape before initial vowels are begun. In glottal shock, however, the glottis is closed firmly *before* the vowel is sounded. The subglottal breath pressure builds up, and the breath finally explodes its way through, blasting the vocal folds apart. Part of the problem in overcoming glottal shock, then, is a matter of timing and coordination. The air stream must begin to flow as the vocal folds are ready to receive it.

REDUCING GLOTTAL SHOCK

Glottal shock gives the impression that the owner is antsy and high-strung.

Frequently, a tense, strained throat and larynx are responsible for glottal shock. If the vocal folds are closed completely and too tensely as phonation (the production of vocal tones or sounds) begins, the blast will generally be pronounced. As an example, tense your throat muscles and repeat the same three sentences, deliberately attempting to start each word with a glottal shock. Repeat these until you are able to hear this attack.

Now perform the following exercises.

60. Start *aw* on a whisper, but gradually begin sound with the softest and gentlest tone you can make. Be especially careful that when your voice changes from a whisper to a vocal tone there's no clicking sound or rasp. Hold the nonwhispered sound for five or six seconds and then repeat. Try with *oo, ee, oh, a* (as in *ask*).

61. Try these, working for an easy, relaxed attack.

    a. ha–ha–ha–ha–ha–ha–ha–ha
    b. ho–ho–ho–ho–ho–ho–ho–ho
    c. he–he–he–he–he–he–he–he
    d. hi–hi–hi–hi–hi–hi–hi–hi
    e. hoo–hoo–hoo–hoo–hoo–hoo–hoo–hoo

    Repeat these syllables, dropping the *h*.

62. As you drill with these word pairs, you'll notice that it's easy to produce a clickless vowel if it follows *h*. Try to keep this easy, "doing-what-comes-naturally" approach as you say the second *h*-less word in the following pairs:

Hal–Al	holly–Ollie	ham–am	hoe–owe
hold–old	hill–ill	hunk–unk	hair–air
hide–I'd	honk–onk	hope–ope	hun–un

63. As you read aloud or speak conversationally, you tend to link or blend words together in phrases or clusters. Read the words in each of the columns. Don't permit a break between the phrases in the second and fourth columns. For example, *an* and *apple* in the second column should be blended together just as the syllables are in *Annapolis* in the first column. Avoid glottal shock.

Annapolis	an apple	tiara	tee are
thrash	three ashes	trio	tree oh
theater	the account	beatify	be at
Newark	new ark	Neanderthal	knee and

64. Read each of these phrases in one continuous and uninterrupted flow of breath. Be cautious with the attack on the initial vowel.

    a. in–an–open–alley
    b. evening–April–air–is–elegant
    c. add–an–owl–and–an–ogre
    d. Enid–eats–onions–and–omelettes
    e. oats–and–apples–are–extra
    f. I–am–in–agony
    g. ill–in–old–office
    h. odes–in–October–are–awesome

65. Trying negative practice, read each of the following twice. On the first reading, sound the (h) as indicated:

    (h)Anybody who says that life (h)is (h)a bowl (h)of cherries (h)is bananas.

    On the second reading, drop each (h):

    Anybody who says that life is a bowl of cherries is bananas.

    But pay close attention to the frontal sounds and work for easy, shockless attacks. Don't chop off the words. Blend or link them together without interruption.

    a. Professionals built the *Titanic*—(h)amateurs, the (h)ark.
    b. (h)I (h)owe, (h)I (h)owe, so (h)it's (h)off to work (h)I go.
    c. Wherever (h)I climb, (h)I (h)am followed by (h)a dog called (h)ego.
    d. (h)It (h)is (h)only possible to live happily (h)ever (h)after (h)on (h)a day-to-day basis.
    e. There (h)aren't (h)any (h)embarrassing questions—(h)only (h)embarrassing (h)answers.
    f. (h)A word (h)isn't (h)a bird. (h)If (h)it flies (h)out (h)and (h)escapes, you'll never catch (h)it (h)again.
    g. (h)I (h)often feel (h)I'll just (h)opt (h)out (h)of this rat race (h)and buy (h)another chunk (h)of Utah. [Robert Redford]
    h. (h)Always try to (h)excel but (h)only (h)on weekends.

Assignment 5: Glottal Shock

Prepare material in which most of the words begin with vowels or diphthongs. You may use nonsense material. As you practice, link the words together, but be certain that the initial words are free of glottal shock.

Suggested Checklist for Assignment 5: See page 271, Appendix B.

THE HOARSE VOICE

DO YOU SOUND RUSTY AND RASPING? YOU MAY BE *HOARSE.*

This voice is raw, husky, gruff, and rust-encrusted. Hoarse people don't talk—they croak! A hoarse voice has been described as a voice with acne, and it's often called a "smoker's voice," even if its owner is a nonsmoker.

A major cable network employs an unseen announcer who previews and introduces programs. He has an extremely irritating voice—simultaneously breathy and hoarse.

Hoarseness due to a bad cold or sore throat will generally disappear. There isn't much you can do about it, but throat specialists frequently prescribe vocal rest—*cut your talking.*

Persistent hoarseness may result from organic defects or structural abnormalities. Nodes, polyps (benign, noncancerous growths—something like small knobs—on the vocal cords), or malignant tumors may be responsible for trouble. Surgical treatment is generally required for these more serious defects.

> If your voice is affected by chronic hoarseness, see a physician.

WRAP-UP

1. Quality of voice is the texture, tone color, or timbre that characterizes your voice and nobody else's. It's the distinctive sound of one voice that distinguishes it from all other voices.

2. It's human nature to judge others by how they sound. Right or wrong, we tend to associate a certain type of voice with a certain type of person.

3. Quality is determined by the production of the original tone by the vocal folds. As the tone passes through the throat, mouth, and nasal cavities, it's altered and modified, reinforced and enriched. The shape, size, and tension of these resonators determine the sound the listener hears.

4. Vocal quality is a surprisingly reliable indicator of the physical as well as the emotional health of a person.

5. Relaxation and good vocal habits usually go hand in hand, but only the right kind of selective relaxation. Such advice as "Let go. Relax completely!" really means "Relax those muscles not needed to perform your task" or "Try to get rid of unnecessary tension."

6. There are many popular, colorful terms to describe vocal qualities. The most specific, relevant, and widely used terms are *breathy, strident, harsh, vocal fry, nasal, denasal, throaty, glottal shock, hoarse.*

7. Certain vocal qualities may be difficult to label. What strikes some listeners as nasal may be described by others as strident.

8. A breathy voice sounds whispery and fuzzy. If the vocal folds aren't sufficiently together during speech, unused air escapes. A breathy voice is inefficient and weak. It may tag its owner as lazy, extremely shy, or sickly.

9. A strident voice is harsh, brassy, and high-pitched. It's more frequently associated with women's voices than with men's. It generally results from excessive muscular tension in the throat.

10. A harsh voice is husky and guttural. It's often low-pitched and more often associated with men's than with women's voices. Not speaking loudly enough, using too low a pitch level, or relaxing the throat excessively may produce harshness. With some people, however, too much tension of throat muscles, rather than laxness, causes this hacksaw quality.

11. Vocal fry is the voice quality that results if the pitch of the voice drops at the end of a phrase or sentence and the voice is allowed to weaken. The final sounds have a growly, bacon-frying, popping sound. Poor breath control and excessive tension of the vocal folds may be responsible.

12. The nasal voice is often described as talking through the nose. Excessive relaxation of the velum is a major cause of this bottled-up vocal quality of too much nasality.

13. In assimilation nasality, the nasal consonants *m, n,* and *ng* exert a strong influence on neighboring vowels. The velum must move rapidly in a word such as *man.* If it doesn't, the vowel sound will also be directed through the nose.

14. Denasality—too little nasality—produces a stuffed-up nose or muffled sound. A physical problem such as enlarged adenoids or a broken nose can promote denasality.

15. The throaty voice sounds swallowed, thick, and dull. It may also have a hollow, voice-from-the-tomb sound. Burying the chin in the neck while speaking, incorrect tongue position, and an excessively low pitch range all contribute to throatiness.

16. Glottal shock, a raspy little click on vowels at the beginning of words, is often caused by a tense, strained throat. If the vocal folds are closed too firmly or too tensely before the initial vowel is pronounced, the breath blasts the folds apart.

17. The hoarse voice is harsh, husky, and raspy. Acute hoarseness may be caused by a simple sore throat. Chronic (persistent) hoarseness may result from abnormal growths on the vocal folds.

chapter 4

SPEAK UP! LOUDNESS

. . . There is documented evidence of permanent deafness striking rock musicians who perform an average of about 12 hours a week for one year?

. . . You don't have to yell to lose your voice? Whispering also strains the voice. And if you're a telephone addict and have a tendency to cradle the phone between your shoulder and neck as you're talking, you can easily strain your voice.

. . . The word *decibel* is derived from the inventor of the telephone, Alexander Graham Bell? Loudness or intensity of sound is measured in units known as *bels*. A decibel is $\frac{1}{10}$ of a bel.

   A whisper measures 20 decibels

   Ordinary conversation—40–60 decibels

   Symphony orchestra (playing Wagner full blast)—100 decibels

   Pain and danger level—120 decibels (several rock groups have been measured at 141 decibels!)

. . . New Year's Eve and Super Bowl Sunday are the two worst days of the year for vocal strain? Pathologists suggest that if you participate, substitute whistling for yelling and apple juice with lemon for vodka.

APPROPRIATE LOUDNESS

"Sorry, can't hear you!"
"What did you say?"
"Would you speak a little louder, please?"
"Huh?"

How often do people say these things to you?

So you turn up your volume. You project. Or maybe you just think you do. How well *does* your voice carry?

As mentioned in Chapter 1, *loudness* refers to the intensity of sound vibrations and to the amount of energy and force that are applied to the vocal folds as they are set in motion. Loudness increases as air pressure beneath the vocal folds increases.

For many students, urban living has meant growing up in an environment of apartments, condominiums, and nearby neighbors. Youngsters who from ages 2 to 20 are constantly being shushed by well-intentioned parents and other adults become, in time, intimidated enough to reduce their loudness levels and speak in vocalized whispers. Another bad habit launched.

Let's consider Lisa in the back row of the classroom. As far as she's concerned, she's physically unable to talk any louder. Possibly she has a mental block. *She doesn't want to hear herself any louder.* Her own value system and her own personal code of behavior dictate that a quiet, soft speaking level is ideal and that loudness has something to do with aggressive, sometimes even obnoxious, behavior. Lisa simply doesn't feel comfortable speaking loudly to a group of people. Extroverts are always loudmouths, thinks Lisa. Sometimes they are.

And then there's 28-year-old Professor Dovetonsils, who has a PhD in political science from what is perhaps the most prestigious university in the country, Phi Beta Kappa, glowing references.

Two days after class started, the dean's office was inundated with student complaints. (One of the young instructor's classes, 15 minutes into his lecture, even did a mass exodus.) Although he was constructed like an NFL athlete, Dr. Dovetonsils (so named by his students) could not be heard in the classroom.

He was sent to our department for help. I had him read aloud in a small auditorium, but he seemed unable to speak above a whisper.

His background explained a lot. Wealthy, socially prominent parents, luxury apartment living. They taught their son that gentlemen do not raise their voices, and he grew up in a hush-hush atmosphere. This, plus the fact that his alma mater did not teach speech communication courses. ("We don't teach courses in walking," as one of their faculty once told me, "so why would we teach courses in talking?")

It took three weeks to help Dr. Dovetonsils find a strong, focused, well-projected speaking voice.

> A Florida judge ordered a well-known rock band to pay thousands of dollars to a woman who claimed her hearing was severely damaged after attending a rock concert by this band. Similar cases are pending against other rock groups.

Something else bugs the Lisas and the Dovetonsils (and they may react by turning down their own volume). Noise pollution: the blaring, raucous world around them, enough to reach 10 on the headache scale.

And another factor that concerns all of us. Are we getting lazier or are we merely being spoiled? Probably a combination of both. Surrounded by electronic wizardry, we can now tap keys, press buttons, ring bells, and let our computers do our talking for us. At this point, loudness is the least of our concerns.

A person who can't be heard is wasting the listener's time. Communication is a two-way street. If A can't hear what B is saying, there is no effective verbal communication.

It's impossible for you to judge your own levels of loudness. Your voice is amplified by the bones in your skull, and it always seems as loud as World War II to your own ears. Anyway, you know what you're thinking, so why shouldn't you know what you're saying?

Talking too softly suggests that you're an insecure person, unsure of yourself. It signals to your listeners that you don't genuinely believe in what you're saying. What's worse, it causes others, weary of straining to hear you, to tune out.

You're not being asked to develop loudness merely for its own sake. Loudness must be adequate for the situation, but it must also be tempered and varied.

VOCAL ABUSE

Whatever time of the year it is when you read this page, the chances are that you are in the football, basketball, hockey, or baseball season.

Maybe you're going to a game this weekend. Plan to do some yelling? Lots of luck! What you'll probably find yourself doing is going from loud to louder to loudest! Swept along by the enthusiasm of the crowd, we find ourselves shouting at the top of our lungs. A prominent vocal therapist has a few words of warning:

> Cheerleaders stand to lose more than their voices. Most of them damage their vocal folds, and this can lead to a host of professional or personal problems. Nobody can scream for two or three hours without doing a lot of damage.

Likewise, many rock singers are doomed to short professional careers. Vocal abuse does irreparable damage to their vocal machinery, and they are soon "washed up" and disappear from the charts.

Gargling is one of the worst things you can do for a sore throat, according to studies by throat specialists at the University of California. Throat-clearing doesn't help matters either.

What then? Drink lots of water to keep throat tissues moist.

In prolonged yelling, the vocal folds are slammed together, and this can result in vocal nodules.

In more than one sense, the noisemaking is half the fun of attending a sports event. Now and then, however, some of us report to classes or work the following Monday morning with a vocal "hangover." The throat is raw and inflamed, and the voice—what is left of it—is unpleasantly hoarse. It hurts to talk. When this happens, we generally attribute our sore throats to excessive yelling, shrug it off, and assume that in a day or two most of the hoarseness will disappear. Vocal hangovers are by no means confined to sports enthusiasts. Lawyers, teachers, actors, and speakers—more often the green, inexperienced novice than the seasoned professional—become victims of acute hoarseness. If this happens often enough, the novice may also be committing vocal suicide.

Yet thousands of individuals don't develop hoarseness, even though their occupations tax the larynx. How about Broadway stars who must get their voices across to a theater audience as often as eight times a week? How about election-year politicians and their door-to-door, stump-to-stump campaigning? How about teachers who must often lecture several hours daily in good-sized classrooms? Athletic coaches? Announcers? Ministers? Salespeople? Receptionists?

Seldom do these individuals come down with vocal hangovers. The logical conclusion, then, is that it's quality rather than quantity of loudness that leads to hoarseness.

STRENGTHENING THE VOICE

What factors are involved in developing an adequately loud voice?

Articulation

A person with a weak voice often doesn't open the mouth widely enough in speaking. The voice doesn't carry because, in a sense, it doesn't have much chance to get out of the mouth in the first place. Maybe it's true that convicts are sometimes forced to communicate with each other in this ventriloquist, not-moving-the-lips fashion, but it's poor practice for anyone else (unless you're planning a career of crime).

As an experiment, try the old tongue twister *Peter Piper picked a peck of pickled peppers* in three different ways:

- Say it as if your lips were glued together and your jaw wired shut.
- Say it with normal lip and jaw activity.
- Exaggerate lip and jaw activity. Open your mouth as wide as you can.

Can you feel and hear the difference?

If your class has already gone through the chapters on articulation, then you should know all about how to open your mouth and let the sounds come out. You should be an expert by now. But in case you haven't worked with Chapters 5–9, or if you feel in need of a little brushup, practice Exercises 1–6 in Chapter 5.

Proper Pitch Level

"Speak Low" is a smart song title, and it's good advice if you're lucky enough to own a naturally deep voice.

But it's not so good if you're trying to produce the voice-from-the-mummy's-tomb and speaking at a level that's too low for you. Or if you're a soprano who lets your voice soar into outer space—you may be speaking (or squeaking?) at a pitch level that's too high for you. If you have a loudness problem and believe that it has to do with your pitch level, investigate Chapter 9, Exercises 1–12.

Even if you're using your best pitch level, do you still permit your pitch to jump upward five or six tones when you read or speak with considerable loudness? The resulting sound is generally terrible. And talking this way can also be dangerous to the speaker. Remember the comment about vocal suicide?

Maximum Use of Resonance

Loudness, in part, results from the reinforcement of the original tone by the resonators. Openness of throat and freedom from undue muscular constrictions are important in developing loudness. If you need to, review Exercises 10–14 in Chapter 3.

> Elementary, middle school, and high school administrators agree unanimously that most teachers who are poor disciplinarians have feeble or whispery voices.

A burly and seasoned drill sergeant whose job it was to teach potential drill instructors once told me, "I don't tell 'em anything scientific about shoutin' commands. I just tell 'em to pack the tone from the guts. And it works!"

It probably does, too.

To put it more delicately, however, the sergeant was advising his students to get their propulsive power from their midregions. The strength and vitality that produce loud, firm tones *come from the muscles of breathing, mostly in the middle areas of your body,* and not from the muscles of your throat.

Clear Tone Quality

The individual whose voice is breathy, harsh, or hoarse may also have a problem getting the voice across. In particular, a breathy voice is generally a weak voice; a weak voice is generally a breathy voice. Which came first—the chicken or the egg? Of one thing you can be certain: If you're deliberately trying to be soft-voiced, wasted breath will help you reach your goal.

Conscious Control of Rate and Articulation

"Speak slower!"

Marvelous advice, and most of us pay as much attention to it as we do to "Drive carefully!" If you're told to slow down while talking, what you probably do is put longer pauses *between* words and phrases. (Try producing a loud pause and see what comes out.)

As far as loudness is concerned, what "Speak slower!" really means is slowing down *on* the words. Point up your vowels and diphthongs by ha-a-a-anging onto and stre-e-e-etching them. They are the sounds that cut through.

Say *Stop.* You can make a lot more of the right kind of noise on the *o* than you can on the *st–p.* Try it.

To emphasize: Athletic, crisp articulation is essential for a bright, thrusting tone and lean, clarion projection.

Sufficient Energy and Animation

> "Power," said Secretary of State Colin Powell, "isn't what seems to make things happen, but the voice that orders those things to happen."

Shy, bashful individuals aren't always the only ones unable to make themselves heard. Vocal laziness, not to mention indifference, hinder good projection. Another complication. The minute vocally lazy persons are urged to speak loudly enough, they protest, "But I'm screaming!" But, *to their hearers,* they're not screaming.

If your emotional and physical health is good, you'll have excellent projection if you speak with more force and energy. Your entire body must respond! A well-projected voice doesn't merely reach its hearers—it penetrates them. Research indicates that strong, dominant personalities tend to have more forceful and energetic voices. Passive personalities apparently are more slack-voiced.

Animation and power are there for the asking if you have something to say, a purpose in saying it, and, above all, a strong desire to say it.

A former student is now a district attorney in a large city. He's required to speak in a courtroom almost every day—without a mike. Says he, "I refuse to scream, but I do use my voice as a weapon. I've found that the more aggressively I project and beam my voice at the judge and jury, the more convictions I get."

Nevertheless, it's only fair to mention that there are limitations to the amount of loudness individuals can produce. Exceptions notwithstanding, small-bodied people can't always produce big, bellowing voices—and may not need such voices.

WHAT YOU'RE SAYING, WHERE YOU'RE SAYING IT, AND THE SIZE OF YOUR AUDIENCE

Nature of Material Being Presented

Material that expresses relatively strong and forceful emotions or ideas (happiness, elation, rage, anger, conviction) is often more effective if relatively loud levels are used. Material that expresses sadness, despair, profundity, moodiness, or sincerity is frequently more effective if relatively quiet levels are used.

What level of loudness would you use for the following?

- Once upon a midnight dreary, while I pondered, weak and weary.

- Almighty God! I know not what course others may take, but as for me, give me liberty or give me death!

Room or Area: Size and Acoustics

When a room is packed with people, furniture, and heavy drapes, loudness has to be increased because these items absorb sound waves.

For the right tonal impact, voices must compete with the cubic footage of the performing space, not to mention all surrounding noises—*and win!*

Speaking to an audience in an auditorium that seats 2,000 or to a few friends in a small living room are two entirely different situations. Everybody knows that. Yet some speakers who find themselves in an unfamiliar room or area make no effort to adjust their volume, and without the aid of a mike they can't be heard. Rather than laziness, their problem is a lack of experience or an inability to adapt to circumstances.

Audience Size and Proximity (Nearness)

> Many of us are annoyed by people who speak too loudly, but according to a recent Gallup communication survey, 80 percent of us are most annoyed by people who speak too softly.

You shouldn't have to turn up your volume in a Coke, coffee, or Coors conversation with three friends in a booth to the same extent that you do if you're talking to 30 or 300 people in a large hall. The nearness of the audience is also important. To a partner five feet away, you can pitch a baseball with a mere flick of the wrist. If the partner is standing 50 feet away, more energy and strength are required.

Everyone should be capable of audible speech without electronic amplification. There are obvious exceptions. If you're addressing the Republican National Convention, you'll have to use amplification. But remember that Lincoln delivered the Gettysburg Address, and Christ, the Sermon on the Mount, without the aid of mikes and speakers. And, contrary to certain popular religious paintings, Christ delivered the sermon from a *sitting position!*

LEVELS OF LOUDNESS

In some of these exercises, we'll experiment with three levels of loudness:

- Soft (avoid whispering).
- Medium loud.
- Loud.

1. As a sergeant in charge of a firing squad, you're about to give the commands *Ready! Aim! Fire!* three times. The first time, you're standing next to your squad. The first level of loudness will work. The second time, you're standing about 10 yards from your squad—second level of loudness. The third time, you're standing about 20 yards away—third level. As you give the commands three times, don't try to control the pitch levels, and on the third one, let the sound "blast."

As a result of this negative practice *(and don't try it more than once!),* you'll certainly feel or hear several things: a "leaping larynx," which means an upward swoop in pitch; a strangled and strident vocal quality on level three; and a possible slight irritation in your throat. All of these are highly undesirable elements in achieving loudness.

2. Begin *ah* softly, and then increase it to your loudest tone of good quality. Hold the tone for a few seconds, and then decrease it to your softest tone of good quality. Repeat several times, keeping the pitch constant. Try it at the three levels of loudness.

3. As you go through the following, make every **bold-faced** word substantially louder than the adjacent words. What happens? Your pitch tends to swoop upward on the emphasized word. **Don't let this happen.** Keep your pitch constant.

   a. Life is something to **do** when you can't get to **sleep.**
   b. Virus is a **Latin** word used by **doctors,** meaning, "Your guess is as good as **mine.**"
   c. No **marriage** is perfect. Even **Adam** and Eve raised **Cain.**
   d. I was so much older **then.** I'm younger than that **now.** [Bob Dylan]
   e. We all make **mistakes,** but luckily we **don't** always **marry** them.
   f. The **more** you see of **television,** the **more** you like it **less.**
   g. Many a folksinger **sings** with feeling, but they don't **always** feel as **bad** as they **sound.**
   h. The three most **common** types of **parking** are double, **illegal,** and **no.**

4. Musicians are concerned with signs and symbols as well as notes. The sign < indicates a gradual increase in loudness or intensity (a crescendo). The sign > indicates a gradual decrease in loudness or intensity (a decrescendo).

   Let's apply these signs to short sentences. This is how they would look.

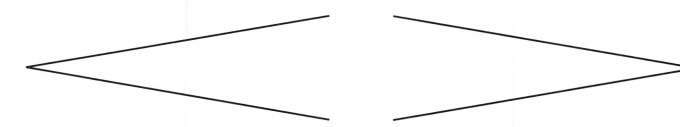

STEP OUT OF THE CAR, PLEASE!   YOU DON'T MEAN THAT!

Using these patterns, read the sentences in the left column in a *crescendo.* Read the sentences in the right column in a *decrescendo.*

As you practice:

Keep your pitch level constant.

Avoid tightening your throat.

Think of the support coming from the muscles of breathing.

   a. How many times must I tell you?   Don't call us. We'll call you.
   b. Don't ever speak to me again.   You won't get by with this.
   c. One of us has to go.   Now, on the other hand.
   d. Please sit down now.   Oh, I give up.
   e. Get set, go.   Turn around, please.
   f. You have the right to remain silent.   Anything you say will be used against you.

5. In reading each of these commands at the three levels of loudness, inhale deeply and quickly. Give them some clout. Say them briskly, but keep the throat as relaxed as possible. Notice the sudden contraction of your abdominal muscles as you project the phrases.

   a. Bug off!   d. Eyes right!   g. Order arms!
   b. Hands up!   e. All aboard!   h. Get lost!
   c. Company, halt!   f. On the double!   i. Play ball!

Exercises 6 and 7 are coming up.

Staying in? If you've been reasonably comfortable with Exercises 1–5, you might be ready for a little change. Keep this uppermost in mind: Loudness is a *relative* term.

As a little switch, let's go for four levels of loudness. Flex your vocal muscles.

- *soft*
- medium loud
- LOUD
- **VERY LOUD**

6. Four columns of words appear below. Read across the columns. Say the same four words on one breath. Read the words in the first column (in italics) softly, in the second column (regular print) medium loudly, in the third column (small capitals) loudly, and in the fourth column (capitals) very loudly.

    A little bodily activity will help you. Make fists, and as you say the word, punch out straight ahead of you. The louder the word, the bigger your punch. Sound silly? Of course it does. But it works. Try it.

    | *hey* | hey | HEY | HEY |
    | *no* | no | NO | NO |
    | *sit* | sit | SIT | SIT |
    | *leave* | leave | LEAVE | LEAVE |
    | *out* | out | OUT | OUT |
    | *die* | die | DIE | DIE |
    | *ho* | ho | HO | HO |

7. Drill with these short sentences. The instructions in parentheses preceding each sentence in section *a* suggest a loudness level.

    a. **(Telephone conversation: quiet)** I'll see you in five minutes.
       (Casual, face-to-face) That prof's a rough grader.
       (Vigorous) You know better than that!
       (Belt it out!) I refuse to listen to you!

    As you read these sentences, repeat the pattern suggested in *a:*

    b. I have no idea where she is.
       Let's go on a picnic tonight.
       He always cheats in tests.
       I've never been so mad.
    c. Sorry, but I'm busy tonight.
       Sorry, but I'm busy tonight.
       Sorry, but I'm busy tonight.
       Sorry, but I'm busy tonight.
    d. I haven't seen you in months.
       Why is that card up your sleeve?
       I don't care what you think.
       I don't care what anyone thinks.
    e. Do you know what I saw today?
       They used to go together.
       There's a serial killer loose on this campus!
       Don't bother me. Leave me alone!
    f. I don't watch TV anymore.
       I heard that she was seriously ill.
       Politics? Yuck! This country's a mess!
       I'll never wait for you again.
    g. I'm getting a new roommate.
       Isn't the food around here terrible?
       You've said that a hundred times.
       Listen to me: We're all through!

h. I'm going to level with you.
    What can I do about it?
    Go away!
    He's got a gun!
i. Why are you staring at me like that?
    Why are you staring at me like that?
    Why are you staring at me like that?
    Why are you staring at me like that?
j. Honey, wake up, there's a burglar in the basement.
    I don't want to tell you again.
    It's all over. You're under arrest!
    I smell smoke. Let's get out of here!
k. Do you hear something ticking in that case?
    Come along. The boys downtown want to talk to you.
    What do you mean—you lost it?
    If it's the last thing I ever do, I'll get you for this!
l. There's something you ought to know.
    Don't move until I tell you to.
    You're the last person in the world I'd suspect.
    Don't touch! It's a live wire!
m. What's that scratching at the door?
    Whatever it is—don't open that door!
    I'm not afraid of anything. I'm opening the door!
    He-e-elp!
n. We can't go on like this.
    We can't go on like this.
    We can't go on like this.
    We can't go on like this.

Vitalize Your Vowels, Dust Off Your Diphthongs

Earlier in the chapter you were advised to *point up* your vowels and diphthongs by stre-e-etching them. They are the sounds that carry and project.

8. Say the following as vigorously as possible. This is an artificial device, but the hyphens will remind you to le-e-engthen and pro-olo-ong your vowels and diphthongs. Exaggerate.
    a. Whe-en i-in dou-oubt, do-on't.
    b. Ou-out, da-amned spo-ot, ou-out, I say-ay!
    c. Show-owing u-up i-is ni-nety perce-ent o-of li-ife.
    d. E-even the-e be-est fa-amily tree-ee ha-as i-its sa-ap.
    e. Whe-en I-Irish e-eyes a-are smi-iling, wa-atch yo-our ste-ep.
    f. I-if you-ou ca-an la-augh a-at i-it, you-ou ca-an li-ive wi-ith i-it.
    g. Go-old! Go-old! Bri-ight a-and ye-ellow-ow, ha-ard a-nd co-old!
    h. Loo-ook too-oo this-is day-ay! Fo-or i-it i-is the ve-ery wa-ay o-of li-ife!
    i. May-ay the de-evil cha-ase you-ou e-every day-ay o-of yo-our li-ife a-and ne-ever ca-atch you-ou.
    j. Two-o he-eads a-are be-etter tha-an o-one exce-ept i-in he-ead o-on colli-isions.
    k. I-if you're a-angry, spea-eak. You'll ma-ake the be-est spee-eech you'll e-ever regre-et.
    Repeat *without exaggerating,* but make your vowels and diphthongs spirited and springy. Be sure that they carry.

9. *The blond fox of Oz said, "Gosh!" as he squashed the kumquat.*
    Nonsense? Of course! But you can have some fun with it. What's the point? After all, we don't communicate with each other using gobbledygook.
    The point: Practicing nonsense material, you'll quickly discover that loudness alone won't put it over. Once again you'll be compelled to fatten your vowels and diphthongs and, above all, to tackle your consonants with force and energy.

Your primary target with the jabberwocky here is the gusty and robust projection of speech sounds. Forget about meanings!

Read these as dynamically as you can:

a. Did Kay rake wires and tar toes with omens?
b. Cobblers often knock Tom the jock on Wanda's yacht.
c. Have you been picking your ears with a ballpoint pen?
d. Wells of soda gurgled toward doghats and green oxen.
e. Olive, the odd otter, sat on the oblong palm at the opera.
f. Ong gnawed the eggnog in Sergeant Saul's ominous vault.
g. Don Juan coughed as he drank the frosted rainwater in the rotunda.
h. Audrey and Austin waltzed in Grandpa's long johns in the Austrian Alps.
i. A hundred muggers threw marshmallows at Bonnie, the fluttering paperhanger.
j. Advice offered to clients by a car rental agency in Tokyo: "When passenger of foot heaves into sight, tootle the horn. Trumpet him melodiously at first but if he still obstacles your passage, then tootle him with vigor."

Obviously we don't spend our lives communicating with people through the use of nonsense sentences. But maybe this exercise has made you more sensitive to the need for sprightly, bouncy articulation in order to project intelligibly. Can you carry over this awareness into non-nonsense material, some of which is conversational? It's not always the public speaker who fails to project; it's often the person in private or everyday conversation.

10. This material demands a thunderous, window-rattling intensity. As you work with these lines, here are some DON'Ts and DOs.

DON'T let your voice take off like a skyrocket.

DO speak at a suitable pitch level and stay there.

DON'T get your support from your throat.

DO get your pushing power from your midregion.

DON'T tighten up.

DO loosen up.

DON'T compress the stressed vowels and diphthongs.

DO expand them.

a. Boot, saddle, to horse and away!
b. Damn the torpedoes! Full steam ahead!
c. A horse! A horse! My kingdom for a horse!
d. Arm! Arm! It is the cannon's opening roar!
e. Ye crags and peaks, I'm with you once again!
f. Roll on, thou deep and dark blue ocean, roll!
g. Cry "God for England, Harry and Saint George!"
h. Forward, the light brigade! Charge for the guns!
i. Don't fire until you see the whites of their eyes!
j. The anchor heaves! The ship swings free! To sea, to sea!
k. Heave at the windlass! Heave all at once, with a will!
l. A Yankee ship and a Yankee crew! Ye ho, ye hoo! Ye ho, ye hoo!
m. Ring, happy bells, across the snow. The year is going, let him go.
n. The sea! The sea! The open sea! The blue, the fresh, the ever free!
o. Fifteen men on the dead man's chest. Yo-ho-ho, and a bottle of rum!
p. Ha, ha, ha, you and me. Little brown jug—how I love thee!
q. Free at last! Free at last! Thank God Almighty, we are free at last!
r. Come live, be merry, and join with me to sing the sweet chorus of "Ha, ha, ha!"
s. March we along, fifty score strong! Strong-hearted gentlemen, singing this song!
t. Blow, winds and crack your cheeks! Rage! Howl! You cataracts and hurricanes, spout!
u. Is this a dagger I see before me, the handle toward my hand? Come, let me clutch thee!

PSYCHOLOGICAL CONTRAST

Your vocal thunder has to be sufficiently high powered so that your listeners can hear you, but it also has to be varied and tempered. You have to learn when to purr and when to roar and what to do in between. An orchestra never plays so loudly that it blasts the audience out of the concert hall; it never plays so quietly that the audience can't hear it; but its 110 instrumentalists do vary their volume.

Obviously, you'll need to use something close to the fourth level of loudness if you call out to a friend a block away. In a telephone booth, however, the first level will do. But what of the speaker in a large room? Must he use the fourth level exclusively? By no means. It would be unnecessary and extremely monotonous.

In reality, dealing with loudness in terms of four levels is an artificial device. There are probably 40 or perhaps 400 levels. In other words, the nuances and shadings are endless.

The following are some suggestions that will help you vary your loudness.

11. Talk at a relatively low level of loudness for a minute or two. Then, at a key word or punch line, raise your volume to a near-shout. This will jolt your listeners.

    For example, as you read the following material, start close to Level 1, and pause when you get to the pause marks: / /

    Read the final phrases, after the pause, in the vicinity of Levels 3 or 4.

    a. I was—I am Mary of Scotland—and I came to you for mercy. This you have denied me. You tore me from my people. You cast me into a prison. However, let us forget all the cruelties I have suffered. You will never use the power you have to kill me. I give up all claims to your throne. You've done your worst. You have destroyed me. My sins were human. Can as much be said of yours? You did not inherit virtue from your mother. We know only too well what brought the head of Anne Boleyn to the block! If there were justice, you would be kneeling here before me because I am your lawful queen./ /The English have been cheated by a juggler! A bastard—yes, a bastard, soils the British throne. [Schiller, *Mary Stuart*]

    b. I can see him there . . . he grins . . . he is looking at my nose . . . that skeleton. What's that you say? Hopeless? Why, very well! But a man does not fight merely to win! No no . . . better to know one fights in vain! You there! Who are you? A hundred against one! I know them now, my ancient enemies! Falsehood! Prejudice! Cowardice! What's that? Surrender? No! Never, never!/ /Yet in spite of you, there is one crown I bear away with me, and tonight when I enter before God, my salute shall sweep all the stars away from the blue threshold! One thing without stain, unblemished, unspotted . . . and that is . . . my white plume! [Rostand, *Cyrano de Bergerac*]

12. Read the selections in Exercise 11 again. Start with Level 3 or 4 and just before getting to a major point (after the pause) drop your volume to a near-whisper, a subdued Level 1. Your hearers may even lean forward, feeling that they're being taken into your private confidence.

13. Tricks have a somewhat mechanical basis. A good conversationalist or speaker doesn't concentrate on four levels of loudness. These techniques, when used judiciously, will help.

    The selections here are not marked in any way. No guidelines are given. As you read, forget about gimmicks. Can you achieve loudness that is ample? Diverse and different?

    (The following story from Stephen E. Lucas, *The Art of Public Speaking* © 1983, the McGraw-Hill Companies, was told in a student speech about child abuse. It is reproduced here by permission of the McGraw-Hill Companies.)

    a. Neighbors had reported Jonah's mother several times for beating him unmercifully. One evening, she beat him with a broomstick for failing to clean up his room, the living room, and the kitchen. After knocking him unconscious, she put him on the back porch and left to go partying at 9:00 P.M. At midnight, hearing moans, the neighbors investigated and found Jonah on the back porch, alone and uncovered in 30-degree weather. He was rushed to the hospital but died two hours later. Apparently he had regained consciousness at one point and reentered the house, for police found a note on the kitchen table. It read:

        Mom,

        I'm sorry for not cleaning up. I love you.

        Jonah

b. The world's richest man, King Midas, was also the greediest. He prayed to Bacchus, "I'm poor. Give me gold!"
    The god replied, "Your wish is granted."
        A delighted Midas sat down to dine. The food and wine he put to his lips turned into gold. His little daughter climbed up onto his lap and turned into a gold statue.
        "Bacchus!" cried the king. "You are a monster!"
        The angry god changed Midas's ears into those of an ass. The king was so humiliated that he hid his hairy ears under a cap. Only the royal barber knew Midas's secret. And he was sworn to silence. But one day he could stand it no more and he dug a hole in the field and spoke his secret into it. He filled up the hole, but in the spring reeds grew there, and every time they were stirred by a breeze, they whispered to the whole world, "King Midas has asses' ears! King Midas has asses' ears!"

c. My dear husband, how can you say a thing like that about me? How could I have done anything wrong when I was with you—the man I married? I would never stoop to the behavior you're accusing me of. Is it your idea to catch me in adultery? You never will! What's more, you're probably thinking I'll shrug this off just like so much water under the bridge. I will not! And keep your hands off me! I'm saying good-bye now. Keep your part of the property, and please return mine at once! [Plautus, *Amphitryon*]

d. I don't deny the charges. I admit them. I buried my brother's body. If it's a crime, then it's a crime that God commands! What I can't stand is meekly submitting to my brother's body being unburied. You smile at me. If you think I am a fool, maybe it is because a fool condemns me! You find me guilty of treason? I have defied you. And for this I am being dragged off by force. I shall never marry. I shall never bear children. I'm to be buried alive! I just want to ask what moral law I have broken? I have done no wrong. I have not sinned before God. But if I have, I will know the truth in death. [Sophocles, *Antigone*]

e. My Lords, you cannot, I venture to say, you cannot conquer America. What is your present situation there? We do not know the worst, but we know that in three campaigns we have done nothing and suffered much. You may swell every expense and strain every effort; you may traffic and barter with every pitiful German Prince who sells and sends his subjects to the shambles of a foreign country. Your efforts are forever vain! For it irritates the minds of your enemies to overrun them with the sordid sons of plunder! If I were an American as I am an Englishman, while a foreign troop was landed in my country, I never would lay down my arms!—never! never! never! [William Pitt (1777)]

f. I'm shuddering all over, but I just can't go away. I'm afraid to be quiet and alone. I was born here. My grandparents lived here. I love this old house. My husband . . . died in this room. My boy . . . my only son . . . was drowned here. Oh, don't be so rough on me, Peter. I love you as though you were one of us. I'd gladly let you marry Anna—only, you do nothing. You're simply tossed from place to place. Strange, isn't it? And you must do something with your beard to make it grow longer. You look so funny. [Chekhov, *The Cherry Orchard*]

g. The knife, where's the knife? I left it here. It'll give me away! What is this place? I hear something . . . something that's moving! But now it's quiet . . . so very quiet! Marie, Marie . . . why are you so pale? Where did you get those red beads that you are wearing around your neck, Marie? Did you earn them with your sins? Your sins made you black, Marie, and I made you pale. But the knife, the knife! There! I've got it. Now, into the water with it! Ha, it'll get rusty! Nobody will ever find it! But why didn't I break it first? And am I still bloody! I've got to wash myself. There's a spot, there, and there's another. [Buechner, *Woyzeck*]

h. Do you want me to prove that none of you is completely sane? If you are sane and rational, you would have control over your own mind, right? Yes. Now I want all of you to concentrate real hard and think of an elephant. Okay. Start visualizing. Think about the elephant's size, color, that long trunk, those big floppy ears. Do you have a picture of an elephant in your mind? And now: Do *not* think of an elephant for the next five seconds as I count to five. Can you do it? Here goes. One . . . two . . . three . . . four . . . five. Did anyone succeed in *not* thinking of an elephant? Just as I thought: Everyone of you has a crinkle in the cranium, a pimple in your personality. Remember: One out of every four people in this country is mentally unbalanced. Think of your three closest friends. If they seem okay, then . . . you're the one!

i. Why are we so violent? Why do most of us enjoy violence so much? Everybody in his life, everybody here has at least once kicked, slapped, or scratched another human being. And don't deny it. (And did you notice how much better you felt after you did it?) A Chicago paper recently took a survey. They interviewed college couples—those going steady or sharing an apartment. More than 50 percent admitted that they had used violence on each other, and not just those big, hairy guys on the poor, helpless girls. There were a surprising number of cases in which those poor, helpless girls beat up on those big, hairy guys. Maybe it all goes back to what we watch on TV. One week of evening TV alone will bring you an average of 84 killings and 372 other acts of violence. Have you hugged someone today?

j. Don't talk to me about the Count. By the time I left the house he was dead. It was an accident. He fell into the lake. He drowned. But I haven't come here to talk about him, but to tell you that I am going . . . to die. Of love. That's how it is! I loved her so, and I love her still. I'm dying of love, I tell you! If you knew how beautiful she was . . . when she let me kiss her. It was the first time I ever kissed a woman. I kissed her alive. Yes, alive. And she looked as beautiful as if she had been dead! [From *Phantom of the Opera*, the novel by Gaston Leroux]

k. Listen to me, Sancho. Ever since you joined up with that crazy knight, you've been impossible. You're out in the world battling imaginary giants and dragons. You believe they really exist, don't you? Your fly-brain is upside down. And you actually think that old lunatic, Sir What's-His-Name? is going to find some god-forsaken island for you to be governor of? Look, you fat jackass, if by any chance that demented fool finds you an island, don't forget me and your daughter. Remember, she wouldn't drop dead if a decent husband came her way. But you bring home the money, Sancho, and leave the marrying part to me. Go ahead and govern your damned island and strut around all you like, but you'd better understand one thing, Governor. Neither my daughter nor I is going to stir one step from this village! Not one blessed step! Now be on your way! [Cervantes, *Don Quixote*]

l. She was there, lifeless and inanimate, thrown across the bed, her head hanging down and her bloodless and distorted features half covered by her hair. I rushed toward her and embraced her, but the coldness of the limbs told me that what I now held in my arms had ceased to be the Elizabeth I had loved and cherished. The murderous mark of the monster's grasp was on her neck, and the breath had ceased to issue from her lips. While I hung over her in agony, I happened to look up. I saw at the open window a hideous figure, gigantic in stature, its face concealed by long locks of hair, its skin the color of a mummy's. A loathsome grin was on the monster's face. He seemed to jeer, as with his fiendish finger he pointed towards the corpse of my wife. Drawing a pistol, I fired, but he jumped to the ground. I choked with rage. I was answered by a loud and fiendish laugh, and I felt as if all hell surrounded me with mockery and laughter. [Mary Shelley, *Frankenstein*]

m. I wish that lightning would split my head open. What use do I have now for living? I only want to die. My husband throws me aside. And our children! And takes a new wife! Oh, we women are wretched creatures! A man, when he's tired of his home, goes out of the house and puts an end to his boredom. But we don't dare do that! Men like to say that we have a peaceful time living at home while they fight the wars. How wrong they are! I'd rather fight in three battles than bear one child! But now in misery I'm cast out of this land and forced to exile. Where am I to go? Home? No! I betrayed my father, I murdered my own brother. I'm hated by my friends. And the children? I will not stand by and watch them roam the earth as beggars. They're his children too. I know my task. I must steel my heart and take the sword. I will not falter. I'll kill the children! [Euripides, *Medea*]

n. He's after me! He's going to kill me! And you, Doctor Van Helsing, you say that you'll save me? Why, you poor puny moron! You measure your brains against his? You don't know what you're dealing with! You're a stupid fool. The entire police force in London couldn't stop the Master from doing what he wants to do. The Master is angry! He promised me eternal life and live things, live things, big ones, not flies and spiders. But blood to drink, always blood and plenty of it! I must obey him but I don't want to be like him . . . I am mad, I know, and evil, too, for I've taken lives, but they were only little lives. I'm not like him. And why did I betray him? For a woman. But I made him angry, and now he'll kill me. And I won't get any more live things to eat. There'll be no more blood! [Stoker, *Dracula*]

o. There is no sound. I hear nothing. Why doesn't this man cry out? If some man came to kill me, I'd cry out. I'd struggle! Strike, Executioner, Strike! I hear no sound. There's a terrible silence! Ah, something has fallen to the ground. Excellent! Send soldiers down to bring me the head of this man . . . the head of John! Ah, when you were alive, you wouldn't let me kiss your mouth. Oh, but I'll kiss it now, John! But why don't you look at me, John? Why are your eyes closed, John? And your mouth? You say nothing, John. Well, then. I'm still living and you are dead. And your head, your head belongs to me! I am thirsty for your beauty! I am hungry for your body! Nothing can quench my passion! Ah, I've kissed your mouth, John, I've kissed your mouth! There was a bitter taste on your lips. No! It was the taste of love! [Wilde, *Salome*]

p. I stops this cuckoo backstage. Wearing a mask. Got this lady with him. Talking on the phone. That lady looked a little familiar. I'm not sure. But she was scared as a rabbit in a fox's mouth. He was using her as a sort of shield, you know. Kept her in front of him. Says he hasta go onna stage. I says, "No way. You got no business here this hour of the night." And he says, "Don't interfere." So just as I reach for my piece, guess what this creep does. Without no warning he pulls out this axe from inside his jacket. And hits me on the shoulder. An axe. Can you believe it?

q. Many years ago, in this palace, a scream rang out, and down through the decades that shriek has found refuge in my heart. My country was conquered, and Princess Ling, my ancestress, was dragged away by a man like you, a stranger in the cruel night, and her voice was stilled. She was murdered. And that's why I refuse to marry foreign princes. But I don't just turn them away. No. I summon the executioner, and I have their bloody heads. How many I've seen die for me. And I despised them. But then you came to me and I feared you. In your eyes I saw the light of heroes. In your eyes I saw victory. I hated you for it. And I loved you for it. Prince, do not seek victory. Go, stranger, with your secret. Go, go, go. [Puccini, *Turandot*]

Assignment 6: Loudness

Prepare material that lends itself to vibrant, dynamic projection. A narrative, especially one that contains dialogue, is often effective for this type of assignment. Read it with enough overall loudness to be heard in a reasonably large room, but work for as much contrast and variety in loudness as you can.

or

Divide your material into three sections and present it using three levels of loudness (medium loud, loud, very loud). Or divide it into four sections and present it using four levels (soft, medium loud, loud, very loud). *Suggested Checklist for Assignment 6: See page 273, Appendix B.*

If possible—

    a. Practice your material in a large room or auditorium.
    b. Present the assignment in a large room or auditorium.

When you do your assignment, position yourself as far away from your audience as you can. If you project with focused energy and precision, your classmates will understand every word you say, regardless of the volume level you're using.

WRAP-UP

1. Loudness refers to the intensity of sound vibrations and to the amount of energy and force that are applied to the vocal folds as they are set in motion. Loudness increases as air pressure beneath the vocal folds increases.

2. Loudness is measured in decibels—a decibel being a unit to express the intensity of a sound wave.

3. Loudness is also referred to as intensity, volume, force, strength, and projection.

4. Some individuals are too soft-spoken, underprojected, and, at times, impossible to hear. The reasons:
    a. Concerned parents may continually have hushed their normally noisy children.
    b. Personal value systems may identify a loud voice as a sign of an extrovert or an aggressive person.
    c. Excessive competition from the noisy environment frustrates many people. They compensate by speaking quietly.
    d. Shyness or insecurity may encourage a speaker to adopt a hushed and whispery manner of talking.

5. Excessive yelling or shouting is vocal abuse. It can damage the vocal cords.

6 The following conditions will help you achieve adequate loudness:

    a.   Open your mouth. Tight lips and a frozen jaw will block the sound. Sharp and crisp articulation is a forerunner of satisfactory loudness.

    b.   Don't let the pitch of your voice zoom skyward like a rocket. Work within a comfortable pitch range.

    c.   Support the tone. Think of the energy and power being concentrated in the middle of your body.

    d.   Speak slower. Don't squeeze your vowels and diphthongs. They have better carrying power than many of the consonants.

    e.   Be alert! Be animated!

7. The amount of loudness you need also depends on

    a.   What you're talking about. If you need to be forceful or persuasive, you may want to turn up the volume. If you want to be meditative or romantic, you may want to turn down the volume.

    b.   The size and acoustics of the room or area in which you're talking.

    c.   Your audience: How many? How near?

8. Projection gives thrust, precision, and intelligibility to sound. The speaker has a strong desire to communicate. A projected voice is beamed to listeners. It does more than reach them; it penetrates them.

9. Loudness is relative, and it must always be varied and subtle. Contrast is important. The range of loudness extends from very soft soft to very loud loud.

chapter 5

ARTICULATE!

ARTICULER! ARTICULAR! ARTICOLARE!
ARTIKULIEREN! ARTICULARE! KANKETSU NI
HYOGEN SURU! YATAMAKKAN!*

WOULD YOU BELIEVE THAT

. . . The trickiest tongue twister in the English language is not *Peter Piper picked a peck of pickled peppers?* It's this one. Try it: *The sixth sick sheik's sixth sheep's sick.* Not far behind is the oldie, *rubber baby buggy bumper* and, surprisingly enough, a two-worder: *toy boat.* How fast can you say it?

. . . The most powerful orator of all times, Demosthenes, was a weak, awkward, and skinny youth? He stuffed pebbles in his mouth not only to slow himself down, but also to improve his articulation and volume. He enjoyed giving speeches above the roar of the sea, and he ran up and down hills, declaiming at the top of his voice.

. . . German is a wonderful language in which to practice your consonants? The German word for the royal Bavarian beer-tax collector is *Koeniglichbayerischeroberbiersteuer-haupteinkissierer.* Try it.

. . . The Hawaiian alphabet has only 12 letters?

ARTICULATION

WHAJASAY?

Joe and Ed in this scene are not rejects from *Aliens, Part III*. They're from Zap, North Dakota, and one of them is a fisherman. Can you translate?

Joe: Hiyed.

Ed: Lojo. Whatimezit?

Joe: Boutaquar nine.

Ed: Whajasay?

Joe: Quarnine. Howzt gon?

Watch the video clip about "Articulation" on the CD

---

*In case you're worried, all of these words mean *articulate* in, respectively, French, Spanish, Italian, German, Latin, Japanese, and Arabic.

Ed: Nasaha.

Joe: Whasamatta?

Ed: Jescopla bites.

Joe: Gotanthin col a drink?

Ed: Gottajug lemade. Wansome?

Joe: Nah, Godago.

Ed: Wazzarush?

Joe: Gotpoinment adenis. Se yamorrow.

Ed: Tekedezy.

Joe: Gluk!

> Do you understand all the messages you hear on answering machines? Do your friends understand the messages that *you* leave on their machines?

Joe and Ed are afflicted with a tiresome and commonplace verbal disease: indistinct, mushy speech. It's goulash! More formally, it's referred to as poor articulation.

Articulation *is the process by which individual speech sounds are produced by the tongue, lips, teeth, and soft palate modifying the outgoing breath stream.*

I use the term *articulation* in its broadest sense. It means the same thing as *diction* and *enunciation*. (Some prefer to use the word *enunciation* only in reference to the production of vowels and diphthongs.) All of these terms refer to clarity, intelligibility, and distinctness of speech.

Sharp, lucid speech is generally a reliable indication of the mental and physical alertness of the individual, so how did the gentlemen get this way? Laziness? Apathy?

Nervous tension and problems of health and hearing, of course, contribute to gummy, dilapidated speech. What about environment? If Joe's and Ed's parents, their playmates, and their teachers have contaminated speech and sludgy articulation, it tells us why Joe and Ed mutilate their speech.

Only about 3 people in 100 have good or superior articulation. More than one-third speak so indistinctly that they are in need of some kind of special help.

Startling? Yes, indeed—considering how much of all the communicating that we do is oral! And all listeners like to hear neat and brisk sounds, because it obviously makes the job of listening easier.

Are You a Mumbler?

If your speech is muddy or slushy, it won't be easy to convince you that your articulation needs overhauling. People are rarely conscious of their speech habits, and if their attention is called to them, they may shrug off the problems. After all, they're always intelligible to themselves. Even if they couldn't hear themselves, they'd still know what they were thinking. As one of these mushmouths once said to me, "Mebbe issa consadence, but se'ral m'bes frens are gittin deaf. They kin ne'er unerstan anathin I sayn keep askin me ta r'peat alla time."

He had never heard his recorded voice. I taped him. When we played it back, at first he was aghast, then furious. Mr. Mumbles accused me of either hexing his tape or sneaking in somebody else's voice.

> Pop star Rickie Lee Jones, says one critic, has diction that dissolves. She sings "and when the day is through" so that it sounds like "ah en uh ay ih ooooh."
>
> A speech by Keanu Reeves at a recent Oscar awards ceremony was described by one reviewer as "sounding like slurped oatmeal."

I arranged for two of his friends to be present as witnesses and then taped him again. It took the three of us to persuade him that what he'd heard was truly himself. He enrolled in a voice and articulation course, and in 16 weeks tidied up his articulation.

Good articulation requires precision, but a precision that isn't excessive. Natural articulation avoids either of two extremes: sloppiness and artificiality. It's neither *undercooked* nor *overcooked*. It's simply speech that is as clear and sharp-edged as it is apparently easy and unforced. It doesn't distract the listener.

Sharp enunciation or diction doesn't mean that one must make every word shimmer like a sword blade. Articulation that calls attention to itself is generally undesirable.

OVERLAPPING SPEECH (ASSIMILATION)

Always bear in mind that you speak most often in phrases and sentences and not in disconnected words. Your language tends to flow along smoothly. It's fluid and supple. Words seemingly melt or blend into one another.

Would you really say at lunch, for example (pause where you see the double vertical lines),

Please | | pass | | the | | salt | | and | | pepper.

Probably not. The chances are you'd say,

Pleasepassthesalt'n'pepper.

Overlapping, connected speech isn't a slow-moving, old-fashioned freight train—an open space between each boxcar. Instead, it's a slick Amtrak streamliner.

Speech sounds are rarely given their full value in overlapping or interconnected speech. One sound modifies and colors its neighboring sounds in a word. Sounds are strongly influenced by their "environment." The process is also known as *assimilation* or *coarticulation*. Assimilation helps to make sounds and sound combinations easier to pronounce, because it facilitates the various movements of the articulators. Assimilation, because it telescopes sounds, reduces the travel time between sounds, increasing the speed and overall efficiency of articulation.

Your speech organs take the easiest route through a group of words. It's easier to say

izzybusy?	than	is		he		busy?
bustop	than	bus		stop
what'r'ya doing?	than	what		are		you		doing?
wouldja lika cupatea?	than	would		you		like		a cup		of		tea?

If overlapping is common and necessary in our speaking, what was wrong with the way Joe and Ed were talking? These two mumblemouths were overlapping to the *n*th degree.

If you say "Jeat?" instead of "Did you eat?," "Fyull" for "if you'll," and "T'sup?" for "What's up?" your overlapping is extreme. If assimilation is practiced to such a degree that it interferes with intelligibility, it's wrong.

Everyday conversational speaking permits more overlapping than formal situations. Don't forget, as you set to work with the material in this chapter—connected speech is natural and smooth-flowing. The word *articulation*, after all, also means *joined.*

THE ARTICULATORS

> Film critics and not a few moviegoers have complained that in many of the Arnold Schwarzenegger–type action movies, about half of the dialogue is incomprehensible. When actors are engulfed in explosions and raucous special effects, they are forced to substitute inarticulate shrieking for intelligibility.

You form and sculpt speech sounds by the movements of your

- LIPS, which pout and protrude, squeeze and stretch, relax and rebound. They pucker: *weep, wool, oats.* They touch: *pill, beet, man.* They spread: *cheese, he, eel.*
- FRONT TEETH, which help out when your tongue or lower lip touch them. Say *Velma, cook the veal very thoroughly.* You'll feel your lower lip or your tongue tip contact your upper teeth.
- LOWER JAW, which opens and closes in varying degrees. Drops on *awl* and *calm,* but is almost closed for *oven* and *few.*
- TONGUE, which flattens, flits, narrows, and furrows; stretches and spreads; pushes and pulls. Ever watch the darting tongue of a chameleon? Your tongue's movements, if not quite as visible, are almost as spectacular. If you say *da-da-da* as fast as you can, the way a baby might babble, the tip of your tongue is moving about eight times a second! Notice the variety of tongue positions as you say *think, these, bust, buzz, fool, show, noon, suit.*
- VELUM. As you say the words *my, nine, ring,* the velum (soft palate) lowers like a curtain (the word *velum* comes from the Greek word for *veil*). This diverts the breath stream into the nasal cavities on the three nasal sounds: [m], [n], [ŋ].

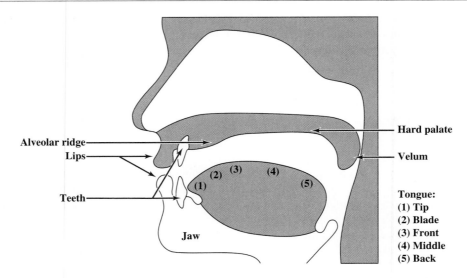

Figure 5.1 Organs of articulation.

All the articulators are shown in Figure 5.1.

Returning a moment to Joe and Ed, we will assume that their articulators are normal. What is it about their organs of articulation that makes their speech so sloppy?

You've observed and heard the slack-jawed person who speaks with limp lips. Joe and Ed are excessively lax and loose-lipped.

At the risk of almost certain assassination, I nominate David Duchovny of *The X-Files* for the most spongy-lipped and leaden-jawed actor in a major TV program. He has raised garbled and watery articulation to an art form.

EXERCISES FOR THE ARTICULATORS

Here are some setting-up exercises, or articulatory push-ups, that will help you limber up your articulators.

Exercises for the Lips

1. The Push-Pull Exercise: Push your lips out as far as you can, and then pull them back tightly into an extreme smiling position. Repeat.
2. Exaggerate lip movements as you say
   a. too–tee–too–tee–too–tee–too–tee
   b. bee–boo–tee–too–bee–boo–tee–too
   c. wee–way–wee–way–wee–way–wee–way
   d. mro–mro–mro–mro–mro–mro–mro–mro
   e. Television has proved that people will look at anything rather than each other.
   f. Our slogan is WYSIWYG—pronounced *wizzy-wig:* What you see is what you get.
   g. "Whistling with the Wind" was one of Walt Weber's wildly popular winners.
   h. If this is coffee, please bring me some tea. If this is tea, please bring me some coffee. [Abraham Lincoln]
   i. Here's to one and only one and may that one be she Who loves but one and only one and may that one be me.
   j. A bigamist is a man who wants to keep two himself.
   k. If at first you don't succeed, destroy all evidence that you tried.
   l. Tom, the tubby tuba tooter, told Tim to take time out to travel to Toronto.

Exercises for the Jaw

3. Drop your jaw easily as if you were going to say *aw*. Move the relaxed jaw from left to right with your hand.

4. Exaggerate jaw movements as you say
   a. taw–taw–taw–taw–taw–taw–taw–taw
   b. goo–gaw–goo–gaw–goo–gaw–goo–gaw
   c. gee–gaw–goo–gaw–gee–gaw–goo–gaw
   d. Cars and bars mean stars and scars.
   e. Not all who auto ought to.
   f. In the long run we are all dead.
   g. Noah's wife—Joan of Ark.
   h. Laws, like the spider's web, catch the flies and let the hawks go.
   i. Automobiles continue to be driven at two speeds—lawful and awful.
   j. Sign in a car on an out-of-the-way parking lot: "Attention, car thieves—this car is already stolen."
   k. Doctors are busy playing God when so few of them have the qualifications and, besides, the job is already taken.
   l. Dog for sale: Eats anything and is fond of children.
   m. There's so much comedy on TV. Does that cause comedy on the streets?

Exercises for the Tongue

5. Double your tongue back against your soft palate as far as you can. Then thrust your tongue firmly against the inside of your left cheek and then against the inside of your right cheek.

6. Exaggerate tongue movements as you say
   a. bead–bad–bird–bud–boom–boom
   b. teen–tune–ten–tone–tam–Tom
   c. A fool and his money are soon parted.
   d. Be advised: Training your child is always a matter of pot luck.
   e. If you want to get fat, don't eat fast. If you want to get thin, don't eat—fast.
   f. Your IQ shows you are not what you think you are, but what you think, you are.
   g. Nowadays early to bed and early to rise probably means that the television set isn't working.
   h. If it isn't broken, fix it until it is.
   i. Today is the tomorrow you wondered about yesterday.

Exercises for the Velum (Soft Palate)

7. Watch yourself in a mirror as you yawn. Note that your velum rises. Repeat the yawn.

8. Still observing yourself in the mirror, make the sound *aw*. Be sure that your soft palate is raised high. Repeat. Say *m*. Your soft palate is now lowered. Repeat.

9. Try to feel the contrasting actions of the soft palate as you say
   a. aw–m–aw–m–aw–m–aw–m
   b. n–aw–n–aw–n–aw–n–aw
   c. b–m–b–m–b–m–b–m
   d. ee–m–ee–m–ee–m–ee–m

10. Be certain that your soft palate is lowered for *m, n,* and *ng*, but is in a relatively higher position for all other sounds as you read these sentences:
    a. There is no glory in outstripping donkeys.
    b. Before the telephone, there were no teenagers.
    c. Half of being smart is knowing what you're dumb at.
    d. They say that marriages are made in heaven. So are lightning and thunder.
    e. There are two kinds of folk singers: Those who can sing and don't and those who can't sing and do.
    f. Being unable to sleep at night is wonderful. It encourages thinking, including thinking about not thinking.
    g. Maybe there is an afterlife, but nobody knows where it's being held.
    h. Any book worth beginning is a book worth reading.
    i. Only one person in two billion will live to be 116 or older.

SOUND FAMILIES

There are three major sound families: *consonants, vowels,* and *diphthongs.*

CONSONANTS

"Consonants can be made either by stopping the breath or by disturbing it, making it explode, or making it buzz or hum," Charlton Laird writes in his delightful book, *The Miracle of Language.*

In making **consonants,** *the lips, front teeth, lower jaw, tongue, or the velum must interfere with, obstruct, or modify the outgoing breath stream to produce a sound or noise.*

Or as one student wrote, "Consonants are the clinks and clangs, huffs and puffs, plinks and plunks of our language." Consonants are "closed" sounds.

Consonants make for clearness and intelligibility in our speech. They act as dividing units and frequently separate vowel sounds. Consonants are the skeleton, and vowels the flesh of our speech. Almost 65 percent of all English sounds are consonants, and about 35 percent are vowels.

Problems and defects of articulation involve consonants far more often than vowels.

VOWELS

Say *ah-h* as you do when the doctor checks your throat. You've made a vowel sound, and you noticed that there was virtually no obstruction of the breath stream as you formed the *ah.*

Now make these sounds: [p] and [z]. You have to set up an obstacle course inside your mouth to block the airstream in order to produce consonants. *Vowels are made with more or less open mouth and without blocking the airstream.* Vowels are voiced and nonnasal. Vowels are free from fricative noises.

Vowels are "open" sounds.

Vowels can be sung. (You can't sing plosives.) Vowels give the language carrying power and beauty. The consonants may provide beginnings, middles, and endings of words. They're often the boundary markers of speech. When we talk about intelligibility, crispness, and distinctness of speech, we're primarily concerned with consonants.

"Consonants," said Alexander Graham Bell, "constitute the backbone of the spoken language—vowels, the flesh and blood."

Vowels, it's been said, provide the emotional atmosphere of words; consonants, the intellectual.

Compare Figure 5.2, which shows the articulators in a consonant position, with Figure 5.3, which shows the articulators in a vowel position.

DIPHTHONGS

How now, brown cow? Check your *ow* sound!

Say the words slowly, and you'll discover that the two vowels you're merging in each word are [ɑ] as in *ah* + [ʊ] as in *book.* Now meld [ɑ] quickly with [ʊ], and you'll make the diphthong [ɑʊ].

A **diphthong** *is a rapid blending together of two separate vowel sounds within the same syllable.*

However, a diphthong isn't always represented by two letters in everyday spelling. The *i* in *night* is also a diphthong. Say the sound in slow motion, and you'll hear both vowels: [ɑ] as in *ah* + [ɪ] as in *it.*

Blend the two rapidly and you'll produce [ɑɪ].

Problems pertaining to dialects ("accents") involve vowels and diphthongs more often than consonants.

VOICED AND VOICELESS SOUNDS

All vowels are voiced, but, oddly enough, your vocal folds do not vibrate with 10 of the consonants, the *voiceless* sounds. Fifteen consonants, however, are *voiced.* This means that your vocal folds are vibrating.

How can you tell the difference?

Place your fingertips lightly against your Adam's apple. Pronounce the sounds in Column 1. (Say the sound, not the name of the letter.) You'll feel no movement or vibration because your vocal folds aren't working. They're resting. The result is that *t, p, k, s,* and *f* are only little, molded puffs of air, *voiceless* consonants.

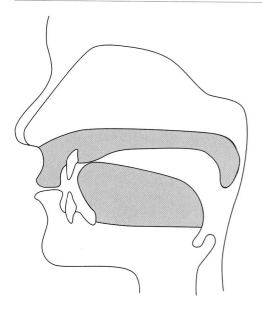

Figure 5.2 The consonant [n] as in *nun*.

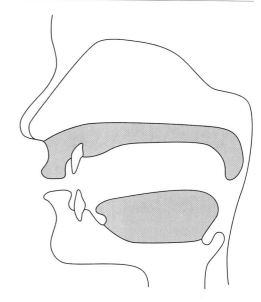

Figure 5.3 The vowel [ɑ] as in *calm*.

But as you run through the *voiced* consonants in Column 2, you'll feel some movement and vibration. For *d, b, g, z,* and *v,* your vocal folds are working and producing extra sound to accompany the puffs of air. They're *voiced* consonants. Three-quarters of all speech sounds are voiced.

Column 1	Column 2
t	d
p	b
k	g
s	z
f	v

Now try these word pairs. The **bold** letters in the left columns are *unvoiced*. The **bold** letters in the right columns are *voiced*.

fuss–fu**zz**	co**p**–co**b**
hi**t**–hi**d**	**sh**ock–**J**acques
fat–**v**at	pi**ck**–pi**g**
e**tch**–e**dge**	**th**igh–**th**y

SOUNDS AND SYMBOLS

How many different ways can you pronounce *u* in this nonsense sentence?

S<u>u</u>rely, b<u>u</u>sy st<u>u</u>dents b<u>u</u>ry th<u>u</u>gs and then b<u>u</u>y f<u>u</u>rs.

The sentence contains seven different *u* sounds!

A young German once wrote a jingle to help his German friends who were struggling to learn English:

Gear and tear, but wear and tear . . .
Meat and feat, but sweat and great.
(That last word rhymes with freight and weight.)
Quite different again is height
Which sounds like bite, indict, and light . . .
Crew and blew and few, but sew,
Cow and row, but sow and row . . .

It's no wonder that English spelling is a highly unreliable guide to pronunciation and that English spelling is the world's most awesome mess, as a Columbia University professor declared.

English! It's a glorious language—the language of Shakespeare, Lincoln, and Churchill—but it *is* loaded with eccentric spellings. (Speaking of Shakespeare, he spelled his own name 20 different ways!)

In what other language can *manslaughter* and *man's laughter* be spelled the same way?

The Italian language has 27 sounds and an alphabet of 27 letters.

In German, you have to learn to pronounce an *a* only once, unlike English where an *a* can represent seven different sounds, as in "Father takes a pleasant bath with soap."

At this point, the only logical way to represent the almost 50 sounds of American English is to use an alphabet of symbols in which each symbol represents one distinct sound and one sound only.

> Almost 50 different sounds are found in the English language, but the English alphabet provides symbols for only 26 sounds—five vowels (a, e, i, o, and u) and 21 consonants.

THE INTERNATIONAL PHONETIC ALPHABET (IPA)

In *My Fair Lady*, Professor Higgins gets the plot rolling when he attempts to copy down and then mimic the cockney dialect of Eliza Doolittle, the flower girl.

> Ow, eez ye-ooa san, is e? Wal, fewd dan y' de-ooty bawmz a mather should, eed now bettern to spawl a pore gel's flahrzn than ran awy athath pyin. Will ye-oo py me f'them?
> (Oh, he's your son, is he? Well, if you'd done your duty by him as a mother should, he'd know better than to spoil a poor girl's flowers and then run away without paying. Will you pay me for them?)

Professor Higgins is a phonetics expert, and he remarks that phonetics is the science of speech. More accurately, **phonetics** *is the study of the sounds of spoken language.*

Table 5.1   Consonants: Identical Phonetic and Dictionary Symbols

Phonetic Symbols	Dictionary Symbols	Key Word	Examples
[p]	p	pig	pen, paper, slip
[b]	b	bet	bag, robber, lab
[t]	t	tip	tow, pretty, at
[d]	d	din	day, meddle, lid
[k]	k	kin	choir, liquor, pick
[g]	g	gone	ghost, dagger, plague
[f]	f	fell	phony, differ, tough
[v]	v	vain	vat, driver, live
[s]	s	sin	scene, mister, nice
[z]	z	zone	zany, sizzle, has
[h]	h	him	hall, who, ahead
[l]	l	late	look, holly, soul
[r]	r	ran	wreck, glory, near
[w]	w	win	want, away, quiet
[m]	m	mad	my, hummer, hymn
[n]	n	nod	nail, manner, sign

The most widely used alphabet, the International Phonetic Alphabet, is a universal alphabet. It contains hundreds of symbols. If you learn the entire alphabet, you can write out phonetically any language on earth from Afghan to Zulu. For this course, however, you can get by with learning fewer than 50 symbols. A reasonable degree of familiarity with these symbols will aid you in identifying precisely the sounds you hear and make.

Each symbol represents a *phoneme*—a basic unit or sound family. As an example, the *d* sound in *dog* and in *bad* is a phoneme. Actually you can't produce the same *d* in both words any more than nature produces two identical snowflakes, but you can recognize and understand both sounds as *d*. There is such a thing as a typical *d*.

You'll need to recognize 43 phonemes. Twenty-five are consonants and 18 are vowels and diphthongs. Learning the IPA symbols isn't difficult. *You're already familiar with 16 of the IPA symbols for consonants,* since they're the same as the diacritical markings, or symbols, used to indicate pronunciation in dictionaries. These 16 IPA symbols and their dictionary equivalents are shown in Table 5.1. (A more detailed presentation of dictionary symbols can be found in Appendix A.)

The IPA symbols for the remaining nine consonants may not be so familiar to you. Some of the symbols are modifications of familiar letters, and two symbols are borrowed from the Greek alphabet and the Old English alphabet. These phonetic symbols, along with their corresponding dictionary symbols, are shown in Table 5.2.

The vowel symbols represent 14 vowels (see Table 5.3) and five diphthongs (see Table 5.4).

Table 5.2 Consonants: Different Phonetic and Dictionary Symbols

Phonetic Symbols	Dictionary Symbols	Key Word	Examples
[θ]	th	thrill	think, ether, bath
[ð]	t̸h	them	they, father, bathe
[ʃ]	sh	shell	shed, machine, mush
[ʒ]	zh	beige	casual, vision, rouge
[tʃ]	ch	chain	chum, righteous, catch
[dʒ]	j	gem	jilt, soldier, edge
[hw]	hw	while	where, somewhat, which
[j]	y	yes	yet, union, beyond
[ŋ]	ŋ or ng	ring	king, banker, singer

Table 5.3 Vowels: Phonetic and Dictionary Symbols

Phonetic Symbols	Dictionary Symbols	Key Word	Examples
[i]	ē	tee	eat, meet, be
[ɪ]	i	it	if, sieve, pity
[e]	ā	fate	ape, gauge, weigh
[ɛ]	e	bet	ebb, many, steady
[æ]	a	sad	at, plaid, rang
[ɑ]	ä	ah	alms, far, sergeant
[ɔ]	ô	jaw	all, brought, saw
[o]	ō	obey	oasis, vocation, omit
[ʊ]	o͝o	put	look, would, wolf
[u]	o͞o	tool	ooze, fruit, who
[ɝ–ɜ]	ûr	murder	ermine, herd, deter
[ɚ]	ər	ever	perform, singer, error
[ə]	ə	ahead	among, carnival, banana
[ʌ]	u	cut	under, sum, flood

Table 5.4   Dipthongs: Phonetic and Dictionary Symbols

Phonetic Symbols	Dictionary Symbols	Key Word	Examples
[ɑɪ] or [aɪ]	ī	r<u>i</u>de	<u>i</u>sle, wh<u>i</u>le, d<u>ie</u>
[ɑʊ] or [aʊ]	ou	n<u>ow</u>	<u>ou</u>t, h<u>ou</u>se, s<u>ow</u>
[ɔɪ]	oi	b<u>oy</u>	<u>oy</u>ster, n<u>oi</u>se, j<u>oy</u>
[eɪ]	ā	d<u>ay</u>	<u>a</u>le, pl<u>a</u>ne, aw<u>ay</u>
[oʊ]	ō	g<u>o</u>	<u>o</u>de, t<u>o</u>ll, sn<u>ow</u>

When placed above and to the left of a syllable, this mark (ˈ) indicates that the syllable is to receive the principal or primary emphasis or accent. *A stressed syllable is generally louder, longer, and slightly higher pitched than an unstressed syllable.* A stressed syllable is the most important part of a word.

ˈdʌblɪn (Dublin)

diˈtrɔɪt (Detroit)

When placed below and to the left of a syllable, this mark (ˌ) indicates that the syllable is to receive a secondary accent—one that is weaker than the primary accent.

ˌmɪs ə ˈsɪpɪ (Mississippi)

ˈækrəˌbæt (acrobat)

NOTE
If you're using the diacritical marking system, the stress mark (') is placed to the right of the syllable that is to receive the heavier emphasis.

WRAP-UP

1. Articulation is the process by which individual sounds are produced by the tongue, lips, teeth, and soft palate modifying the outgoing breath stream.
2. Articulation means clarity, intelligibility, and distinctness of speech. In a general sense, it's the same thing as *enunciation* and *diction.*
3. Overlapping speech (also known as assimilation or coarticulation) is fluid, connected speech. It telescopes sounds, increasing the smoothness and overall efficiency of articulation. It's easier to say *I'll beat'ya ina game of Dungeons 'n' Dragons* than to say *I will beat you in a game of Dungeons and Dragons.*
4. Speech sounds are formed, molded, separated, and joined by the movements and contacts of the most important articulators: the lips, the front teeth, the lower jaw, the tongue, and the velum.
5. The lips pucker as in the first sound in *will,* touch together as in *pipe,* and spread as in *pizza.* The lower lip contacts the upper teeth as in *vim.*
6. The front teeth assist enunciation as the tip of the tongue touches them, as in *Thanks, Thelma,* or as the airstream hits them, as in *Save Sally.*
7. The lower jaw drops as in *awe* and *palm* but is almost closed for *dew.*
8. The tongue is the most active, versatile, and important of the articulators. Run through these words and note the variety of tongue positions: *then, fuzz, feet, should, soon, tuck.*
9. The velum (soft palate) lowers and blocks the oral cavity, forcing the breath stream through the nasal cavities on the three nasal sounds: [m], [n], [ŋ].
10. Consonants: The lips, front teeth, lower jaw, tongue, or the velum must interfere with, obstruct, or modify the outgoing breath stream to produce a sound or noise.

11. Vowels: Made with a more or less open mouth and without blocking the airstream.

12. A diphthong is a rapid blending together of two separate vowel sounds within the same syllable.

13. Consonants are voiceless or voiced. For **voiceless** sounds, the vocal folds are at rest and do not vibrate:

    [p]   [θ]   th
    [f]   [ʃ]   sh
    [s]

    For **voiced** sounds, the vocal folds are moving and vibrating:

    [b]   [ð]   th
    [v]   [ʒ]   zh
    [z]

14. The English alphabet has 26 letters, but there are almost 50 different sounds in our language. Forty-three of these sounds and sound combinations can be represented by the symbols of the International Phonetic Alphabet (IPA). Twenty-five are consonants. Eighteen are vowels and diphthongs.

chapter 6

CONSERVE YOUR CONSONANTS

. . . Tongue twisters, once regarded as children's games, are making a comeback? Many Broadway actors warm up before going onstage with "Twixt Trent and Tweed. Gig-whip. Gig-whip. Gig-whip." Simple? Try it.

. . . The 10 most beautiful words in the English language are *chimes, dawn, hush, lullaby, luminous, melody, mist, murmuring, tranquil, golden?*

. . . The 10 ugliest words in the English language are *gripe, crunch, jazz, schizoid, mugged, plump, jerk, screech, cacophony, flatulent?*

. . . Dogs don't bark "bow-wow" or "woof-woof" in foreign languages? In French, it's "oua-oua," in Russian—"gav-gav." Dutch canines say "waf-waf"; in Japan—"wan-wan." Cows "moo" and crows "caw" in all languages, however.

. . . More English words begin with *s* than any other letter? *C* is the second, *p* is third. Oddly enough, there are more *z* sounds in English than *s* sounds.

CONSONANTS

Consonants, as you already know, are produced by interfering with or blocking the outgoing breath stream. Consonants are *closed* sounds. (See Table 6.1.)

Articulate [b] as in *bob.* You deliberately close the lips to obstruct your breath and then suddenly pop them open.

Vowels are *open* sounds. For a comparison, articulate [æ] as in *ask.* Notice the difference in the positions of your articulators.

(**Note:** *In Chapters 6, 7, and 8, you will encounter this symbol: §. An explanation follows.*)

§ **indicates sounds that are influenced by dialects.**

For example, in our treatment of the [r] phoneme, you will find this heading:

§ **Intrusive [r]**

This refers to the fact that some residents of the New England area may tack this particular sound onto a word where it doesn't belong: potat*er* and Cub*er* for potato and Cuba.

§§§ **Indicates sounds that may be troublesome for some ESL students—nonnative speakers of English.**

Again, in our treatment of the [r] phoneme, you will find this heading printed in **BOLD CAPS:**

§§§ **SUBSTITUTING [l] FOR [r]**

This refers to the fact that speakers of many Asian languages substitute [l] for [r].

Information about specific problems, along with appropriate exercises, is located on designated pages.

Table 6.1   Classification of Consonants by Place and Manner of Articulation
(Dictionary symbols are listed to the right of phonetic symbols only if they differ from the IPA symbols.)

Place of Articulation	Plosives		Glides		Nasals		Fricatives		Affricates	
	Voiceless	Voiced	Voiceless	Voiced	Voiceless	Voiced	Voiceless	Voiced	Voiceless	Voiced
Lips (bilabial)	p pal	b boy	hw why	w we		m me				
Lower lips and upper teeth (labiodental)							f for	v van		
Tongue and teeth (interdental)							θ th thin	ð t͞h them		
Tongue tip and upper or lower gum ridge (alveolar)	t tie	d do		l let		n no	s sick	z zoo	tʃ ch chair	dʒ j jail
Tongue blade and hard palate (linguapalatal)				r red j y you			ʃ sh shall	ʒ zh azure		
Back of tongue and soft palate (velar)	k kid	g gag				ŋ rung				
Space between vocal folds (glottal)							h ham			

PLEASE NOTE
The material on these designated pages will be particularly helpful to ESL students, but it isn't intended to be exclusive. Non-ESL students will also find many of the discussions and particularly the exercises and drills useful.

PLOSIVES [p] [b] [t] [d] [k] [g]

The **plosives** (also known as *stops* or *stop-plosives*) are made by briefly blocking the outgoing airstream and thus building-ing up air pressure. The velum is raised, preventing the escape of air through the nose. Then the tongue is dropped or the lips are opened suddenly, and the built-up air is released with a little explosion.
There are six plosives in English:

Is it a coincidence that so many quick-action verbs end in voiceless plosives? Think of pop, clip, snip, rap, slap, whip, cut, slit, hit, dart, crack, smack, whack, strike, peck.

Voiceless	Voiced
[p]	[b]
[t]	[d]
[k]	[g]

In the following sections they are considered in pairs, according to their places of articulation.

$\begin{bmatrix} p - b \end{bmatrix}$

pie, maple, cap   bait, able, tab

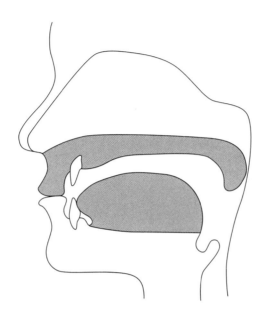

VARIOUS SPELLINGS	**[p]**	**[b]**
	gh as in HICCOUGH	b as in BONE
	p as in PINE	bb as in CABBAGE
	pp as in HAPPY	pb as in CUPBOARD

Classification   lips (bilabial)
[p] voiceless
[b] voiced

Piddling Pursuit

Phonetic   pə'lis ɑr nɑt ɔl bæd gɑɪz. 'nobɑdɪ ɪz ɔl bæd gɑɪz.

Diacritic   mī pâr'ənts po͝ot ə līv ted'i bâr in mī krib.

How to . . .
  Tongue   Relaxed.
  Lips and Jaw   Press your relaxed lower and upper lips together. Your teeth should be slightly parted. Compress the breath within your mouth, then part your lips suddenly, dropping your jaw. The air bursts out in a light pop.

WARMER-UPPERS [p]

Initial	Medial	Final
page	ample	burp
pail	apart	flop
palm	apron	gyp
Pam	captain	jeep
patch	dapper	mope
peach	Japan	skip
pink	lapel	sleep
pole	purple	slurp
pool	supper	stop
puff	topple	type
penny	tepee	whip
pickle	vapor	yelp

WARMER-UPPERS [b]

Initial	Medial	Final
bass	label	blurb
beach	lobby	crab
bear	saber	cube
blame	crumble	fib
blur	flabby	flub
bomb	trombone	glib
bore	barbell	grub
bough	eyeball	herb
bull	nobody	knob
burst	October	stab
Bette	fabulous	strobe
·beggar	February	vibe

Faults and Foibles

      A. Flabby articulation

      B. Omitting [p] and [b] sounds

§§§ **C. CONFUSING [p] AND [b]**

§§§ **D. CONFUSING [v] AND [b]**

Now for the details. Choose as needed.

A. Flabby articulation

"Clean up with a *damn* sponge" is the wind-up of a popular TV commercial in which an attractive lady is demonstrating a carpet cleaner. She obviously means *damp,* but that's not what we hear.

      Don't be a sound snipper! It's only too easy to chop off the final [p] and [b]: sleep, crab, pipe, tube.

      They're even more apt to be obliterated if they follow another consonant: chirp, bulb, trump, verb.

1. If you want clean and neat [p] and [b] sounds, be sure that your lips make solid contact with each other as you shape the plosives. Don't forget—these two sounds should be crisp, but they're not nuclear blasts.

   a. Don't rob Peter to pay Paul.
   b. Exurb: A suburb of a suburb.
   c. Rub-a-dub-dub. Three men in a tub. How kinky.
   d. Talk is cheap except when talking to a traffic cop.
   e. Stop crime at its source. Support planned parenthood.
   f. Sound sleep is the sleep you're in when it's time to get up.
   g. A bachelor is a person who takes a nap on top of a bedspread.
   h. A pinch of probably is worth a pound of perhaps.
   i. Bumbling bank bandit bears badge of blunder. [newspaper headline]
   j. If you count sheep two at a time, you'll fall asleep twice as fast.
   k. A harp is a nude piano.
   l. When you stop struggling, you stop living.
   m. It's just a job. Grass grows, birds fly, waves pound the sand. I beat people up. [George Foreman]
   n. Books tell us that barracuda rarely eat people, but very few barracuda can read.
   o. On November 17, 1837, the *Boston Blazer* reported that Vernon Barton, aged 97, was married to Betty Burns, 105. Both were found dead in bed the following morning.

What if a word ends in a plosive and the next word begins with one?

rob Peter	slammed doors
hot dog	bake caramel

Do you explode the first plosive separately? Not necessarily. Hold the final consonant of the first word and release it into the first consonant of the next. But don't get lazy and turn the adjacent sound into mush!

B. Omitting [p] and [b]

One of the most abused words in our language? *Probably.* Most people say *probly* or, worse, *proly.* Running a close second is *numer* for *number.* (The same people say *ho-fully* for *hopefully.*) Some regional speech inserts [b] where it doesn't belong. *Family* becomes *fambly.*

Although we can understand these warped versions, they imply sloppiness. What is responsible for most demolished [p] and [b] sounds? Comatose lips and general lukewarm activity, and both result from carelessness and indifference.

2. Snappy, vigorous articulation is needed for the sentences below. Your lips must be locked together for [p] and [b] and then opened quickly.

   a. Stay humble or stumble.
   b. Keep it simple, stupid. [Israeli Air Force maxim]
   c. We are the people our parents warned us about.
   d. The creep took the jeep to the chop shop.
   e. The glib snob decided not to snub the mob.
   f. The person with push will pass the person with pull.
   g. Dapper Mable wasn't able to play the purple trombone in Japan.
   h. On the keyboard of life, always keep one finger on the ESCAPE key.
   i. It's sad when a person has a head like a doorknob. Anybody can turn it.
   j. Some battle their way to the top. Others bottle their way to the bottom.
   k. Last night I dreamed I ate a 10-pound marshmallow, and when I woke up the pillow was gone.
   l. Never work before breakfast. If you have to work before breakfast, get your breakfast first.

m. No human being believes that any other human being has a right to be in bed when he himself is up.
n. Student blooper: King Solomon had 300 wives and 700 porcupines.
o. Betty Botter bought a pound of butter. "But," she said, "this butter's bitter. If I put it in my batter, it will make my batter bitter. But a pound of better butter will make my batter better." So Betty Botter bought a pound of better butter, and it made her batter better.

§§§ C. CONFUSING [p] AND [b]
For discussion and relevant exercises, see page 92.

§§§ D. CONFUSING [v] AND [b]
For discussion and relevant exercises, see page 92.

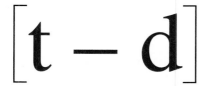

time, cattle, mat   **darn, noodle, hid**

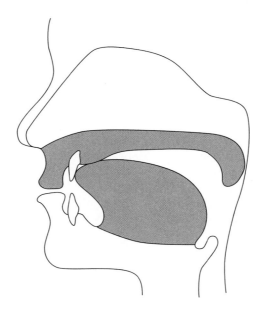

VARIOUS SPELLINGS

[t]	[d]
bt as in DEBT	d as in DIM
ght as in LIGHT	dd as in RUDDER
pt as in RECEIPT	ed as in RAINED
t as in TAKE	ld as in COULD
th as in THAILAND	
tt as in BATTLE	

Classification	tongue tip and upper gum ridge (lingua-alveolar) [t] voiceless [d] voiced
Piddling Pursuit	
Phonetic	dɛd mɛn dont bɑɪt.
Diacritic	det iz bet′ər ƫan deth.
How to . . .	
Tongue	Press the tip of your tongue against your upper gum ridge. The tongue is somewhat tensed. The sides should touch the upper molars. The air stream is momentarily dammed up. Now drop your tongue tip quickly.
Lips and Jaw	The lips are unrounded and relaxed, but as you drop your tongue, lower your jaw a little bit. Breath will be released in a small burst.

WARMER-UPPERS [t]

Initial	Medial	Final
tap	total	feet
tell	until	fruit
tick	attic	height
Todd	kitty	kite
tooth	metal	loot
town	tattoo	next
tree	Arctic	pint
trip	subtle	route
tuck	between	shoot
tune	mattress	sleet
twinkle	painting	wit
Thomas	writing	import

WARMER-UPPERS [d]

Initial	Medial	Final
Dan	adder	plod
dark	edict	rude
deaf	faddist	wide
dell	garden	Judd
dope	hadn't	load
drip	leader	board
drum	puddle	spade
dude	shadow	Swede
Dwight	shudder	sword
dental	udder	crawled
donor	wedding	raided
diaper	indent	meathead

Faults and Foibles

    A. Omitting [t] and [d] at ends of words

    B. Omitting medial [t] and [d]

    C. Substituting [d] for [t]

    D. Omitting [t] if followed by [s]

    E. Omitting or mispronouncing [əd]

§§§ **F.** **DENTALIZING [t] AND [d]**

§§§ **G.** **SUBSTITUTING [t] FOR FINAL [d]; OMITTING [t] AND [d] AT ENDS OF WORDS**

Now for the details. Choose as needed.

A. Omitting [t] and [d] at ends of words

If [t] and [d] occur in final positions, they're often omitted, especially if they're preceded or followed by other consonants. You'll say *jus, fac,* and *frien* instead of jus*t*, fac*t*, and frien*d*.

3.   Make your final plosives crystal clear and audible in these:

    a.

crept	just	world	ground
moist	crossed	sold	fad
pelt	quart	heard	crazed
raft	fact	hand	athlete

    b.   The future isn't what it used to be.

    c.   Don't go to bed mad. Stay up and fight.

    d.   Why isn't there mouse-flavored cat food?

    e.   Don't bite the hand that has your allowance in it.

    f.   Crime wouldn't pay if we let the government run it.

    g.   I don't get even, I just get older.

    h.   The only way to get rid of a temptation is to yield to it.

    i.   Backward, turn backward, O Time, in your flight, and tell me just one thing I studied last night.

    j.   They also serve who stand and wait, but they get no tips.

    k.   I get so tired of putting my cat out at night. I wish he'd stop playing with matches.

    l.   People can't live on bread alone. They must also have credit cards.

    m.   Part of the secret of success is to eat what you want and let the food fight it out inside.

B. Omitting medial [t] and [d]

Read this: *Dinty couldn't interrupt Betty's interview with the painter.* If you swallowed or omitted those middle plosives, you may have sounded something like this: *Din'y cou'n't in'errupt Be'ys in'erview with the pain'er.*

    nt combinations are particularly treacherous, because *n* and *t* are formed in similar fashion and the [t] is apt to be swallowed by the [n].

4.   Now let's restore these sounds. Give each middle [t] and [d] a brief but solid tap. Remember, you don't have to explode medial plosives separately, but be sure that they're present.

    a.

fatter	after	intake	intelligent
enter	data	couldn't	hadn't
wouldn't	biting	entertain	pardon
potato	shouldn't	whittle	understand

    b.   History is the short trudge from Adam to the atom.

    c.   Often it seems such a pity that Noah and his party didn't miss the boat.

    d.   There ought to be a better way of starting the day than having to get up.

    e.   If I only had a little humility, I'd be perfect. [Donald Trump]

    f.   One thing is absolutely certain about the unexpected. It's never what you expect.

    g.   No matter how hard you try, you can't baptize cats.

    h.   There are 2 million interesting people in New York and only 78 in Hollywood. [Neil Simon]

    i.   If you have an electric toothbrush and still get cavities, it may be a weak battery.

C. Substituting [d] for [t]

Did you know that a Corot landscape is *priddy?* A 25-cent piece is also called a *quarder?* If [t] occurs in the medial position and especially if it's preceded and followed by voiced sounds, there's a common tendency to substitute [d].

5. For contrast, do these word pairs. The words on the left need an energetic [t] in the middle. Be sure it's there, and be sure it's the *voiceless* [t] and not the *voiced* [d]. And don't make it too prominent.

a.
matter–madder	bitter–bidder	seating–seeding
latter–ladder	debtor–deader	wetting–wedding
batter–badder	rater–raider	writer–rider
daughter–dodder	rutty–ruddy	mutter–mudder

b. Comedy writer: Laughter drafter.
c. Little things please little minds.
d. H_2O is hot water, and CO_2 is cold water.
e. Harry Potter's daughter is a better batter than Artie Cotter.
f. It's better to be beautiful than good, but it's better to be good than ugly.
g. Do you get hotter faster in South Dakota than in North Dakota?
h. You're well adjusted if you can make the same mistake twice without getting nervous.
i. My parents had only one argument in 45 years. It lasted 44 years.
j. It's your attitude, not your aptitude, that determines your altitude. [Jesse Jackson]
k. Gangster "Pretty Boy" Floyd insisted that he had started out in life as an unwanted child, but by the time he was 24 he was wanted in 18 states.

D. Omitting [t] if followed by [s]

If [t] is preceded or followed by [s], it is commonly omitted. In general [s-t-s] combinations are tricky.

Result: *fists* [fɪsts] may sound something like *fiss* [fɪs]

vests [vɛsts] may sound something like *vess* [vɛs]

6. To correct this fault, pronounce [s-t-s] slowly and carefully as separate sound units. When you're certain that you're forming a sharp, clear [t], pronounce the sounds in a connected manner. As you practice the following, be sure that the [t] is not omitted when it occurs in difficult sound combinations.

a.
waists	masts	rusts	pastes
gifts	acts	busts	erupts
posts	lists	dusts	tastes
crusts	wrists	bastes	lasts
chests	trusts	boosts	cysts

b. Nowadays students have to pass more tests to get into college than their parents did to get out.
c. Hosts always post lists of guests.
d. When the going gets tough, the smart get lost.
e. The guts carry the feet, not the feet the guts. [Cervantes]
f. Hermits hide lots of gifts in crypts.
g. Mists and gusts drove the ghosts to their roosts.
h. The hosts' jests about the winter blasts were greeted with toasts.

E. Omitting or mispronouncing [əd]

If *-ed* [əd] is used to form the past tense of a verb, it's sometimes omitted or mispronounced.

If *-ed* is preceded by [t] or [d], it's generally pronounced as a separate syllable:

hunted is pronounced *huntud* [ˈhʌntəd]

skidded is pronounced *skiddud* [ˈskɪdəd]

If -ed is preceded by a voiceless sound, it's pronounced as [t]:

> *whipped* is pronounced *whipt* [hwɪpt]
>
> *asked* is pronounced *askt* [æskt]

If -ed is preceded by a voiced sound, it's pronounced as [d]:

> *nagged* is pronounced *nagd* [nægd]
>
> *filled* is pronounced *fild* [fɪld]

> Students from Liberia, Nigeria, and some other African nations may drop the -ed altogether.

> Result: *planned* is pronounced *plan*
>
> *belted* is pronounced *belt*

7. Pronounce the -ed endings correctly in the following material. Be sure that -ed doesn't entirely disappear.

    a. | | | | |
       |---|---|---|---|
       | lurched | matted | hoed | iced |
       | edged | razzed | trapped | drowned |
       | shaded | loved | rammed | ranted |
       | crashed | attacked | fitted | debauched |

    b. A penny saved is a penny taxed.
    c. One who is born to be hanged will never be drowned.
    d. The person who is all wrapped up in himself is overdressed.
    e. The crowd razzed the wretched player as the batted ball crashed into the dugout.
    f. I phoned my dad to tell him I had stopped smoking. He called me a quitter.
    g. A reckless driver is called a lot of names before he's finally called "the deceased."
    h. A jury reported back to the judge, "We just don't want to get involved."
    i. Men are nicotine-soaked, beer-besmirched, whisker-greased, red-eyed devils. [Carrie Nation, temperance agitator, 1903]

§§§ F. DENTALIZING [t] AND [d]

For discussion and relevant exercises, see page 93.

§§§ G. SUBSTITUTING [t] FOR FINAL [d]; OMITTING [t] AND [d] AT ENDS OF WORDS

For discussion and relevant exercises, see page 93.

[k – g]

kin, act, make   gum, rugged,
                      lag

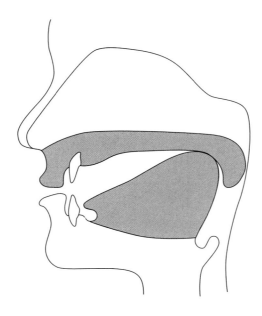

VARIOUS SPELLINGS

[k]	[g]
c as in COD	g as in GONE
cc as in OCCULT	gg as in JOGGER
ch as in HEADACHE	gh as in GHOUL
ck as in DOCK	gu as in GUARD
k as in KITE	gue as in PROLOGUE
kh as in KHAKI	x as in EXIT
qu as in QUIT	
que as in OPAQUE	
x as in FAX	
xc as in EXCITE	

Classification

back of tongue and soft palate (linguavelar)
[k] voiceless
[g] voiced

Piddling Pursuit

Phonetic

me ðə gʊd lɔrd dɪˈlɪvɚ ʌs frʌm ˈgulɪz, ˈgostɪz, ˈgɑblɪnz ænd θɪŋz ðæt go bʌmp ɪn ðə nɑɪt.

Diacritic

giv tə ə pig wen it grunts, and ə chīld wen it krīz, and yo͞ol hav ə fīn pig and ə bad chīld.

How to . . .	
Tongue	Press the back of your tongue against your soft palate (toward the rear of your mouth). Build up air pressure behind the tongue and then lower it abruptly.
Lips and Jaw	Lips are unrounded and relaxed, but as the tongue lowers, the jaw also drops, producing a small blast.

WARMER-UPPERS [k]

Initial	Medial	Final
call	anchor	brick
car	bacon	cork
chord	beaker	disk
clam	biscuit	fork
clod	bunker	hook
coach	echo	irk
curb	liquid	Luke
kipper	require	plaque
quash	success	stroke
Kansas	wicked	tank
quantum	exercise	awake
kangaroo	Alaska	historic

WARMER-UPPERS [g]

Initial	Medial	Final
gap	sugar	crag
gall	begged	Doug
gas	chugged	egg
gauze	finger	frog
ghost	giggle	hog
gouge	ragged	mug
grim	stagger	rig
guess	bagpipe	rogue
guilt	tangle	slug
ghetto	agony	vague
gorilla	dignify	wag

Faults and Foibles

    A. Flabby articulation

    B. Faulty pronunciation of the letter *x;* omitting [k] in *cc* spelling.

§§§ **C. CONFUSING [k] AND [g]**

Now for the details. Choose as needed.

A. *Flabby articulation*

Be certain that the back of your tongue makes light but firm contact with the soft palate. If you can *feel* this action, you won't turn these two craggy plosives into mush or sounds that resemble fricatives.

8. Try these:
    a. Never give a sucker an even break.
    b. The brick in the bag gave him a crick in his neck.
    c. Neither an egg nor an ego is any good until you break it.
    d. Television is the plug-in drug.
    e. Why keep a dog and bark yourself?
    f. I keep a rock garden, but last week six of them died.
    g. Vice shows itself in the eyes; crime in the back of the neck.
    h. Cells let us walk, talk, and think, and realize that the bathwater is cold.
    i. I can't think why mothers love them. All babies do is leak at both ends.
    j. If you're scared of the orthodontist, you've got a mental block about the dental doc.
    k. Three gray geese in the green grass grazing. Gray were the geese, and green was the grazing.
    l. What an opera singer needs most: a big voice, a big chest, a big mouth, and a big ego.
    m. There are two kinds of statistics: the kind that you look up and the kind that you make up.

B. Faulty pronunciation of the letter x; omitting [k] in cc spelling

The strange spelling that is given to a sound that is actually a [ks] or a [gz] may sometimes confuse us and account for faulty mispronunciations of words containing these sounds.

Problem words are ones such as *exert* and *extra.* In *exert,* the correct sound for *x* is [gz]: [ɪgˈzɜ·t]. In *extra,* the correct sound for *x* is [ks]: [ˈɛkstrə].

Two simple rules will help you distinguish *x* words that require the [gz] pronunciation and *x* words that take the [ks] pronunciation.

If the vowel sound following the *x* is stressed, the *x* will be pronounced [gz].

exactly [ɪgˈzæktlɪ]   *exempt* [ɪgˈzɛmpt]

If *x* is followed by a pronounced consonant or if it is found in the final position, it will be pronounced [ks].

excite [ɪkˈsaɪt]   *box* [bɑks]
expect [ɪkˈspɛkt]   *fix* [fɪks]

Other troublemakers are words such as *accept* that contain the *cc* spelling. A common fault is to omit the [k] sound in these words

Result: *accelerate* is incorrectly pronounced as [æˈsɛləret] instead of correctly as [ækˈsɛləret]

accessory is incorrectly pronounced as [æˈsɛsərɪ] instead of correctly as [ækˈsɛsərɪ]

The following sentences are crammed with [k] and [g] sounds, but the kaleidoscopic spellings don't always warn you that the two plosives are lurking in the background.

> Occasionally *k* is an unwelcome visitor. In a recent episode of a TV thriller, the lead actor said, "You say *ek-scape* is impossible? I'll tell you how we'll *ek-scape.*"

9. Be sure you form these sounds correctly. Remember: Back of tongue against soft palate. Hear and feel these plosives correctly too.
    a. With foxes we must play the fox.
    b. Who excuses himself, accuses himself.
    c. "All My Ex's Live in Texas." [Country music song title]
    d. How to succeed: Dress for success instead of excess.
    e. Learn to accept yourself. Then you can accept anybody.
    f. A Cadillac is what a doctor buys not to make house calls in.
    g. There are two good finishes for cars: lacquer and liquor.
    h. People who squawk about their income taxes can be divided into two classes: men and women.
    i. It's predicted that sexy love scenes will soon be banned in movies and TV. Sex will be rated "ex."
    j. Excessive speed on the access road caused the accountant's accident.

§§§ C. CONFUSING [k] AND [g]

For discussion and relevant exercises, see page 94.

[p–b]

§§§ C. CONFUSING [p] AND [b]

If your first language is German, Russian, Arabic (and this includes Iran, although Iranians speak Persian), Chinese, Korean, Vietnamese, or Spanish, you may confuse [p] and [b].

If the initial sound of the word is [p], a [b] is sometimes substituted, or an initial [b] might be replaced with [p]. The voiceless [p] is commonly substituted for the voiced [b] in the final position too.

> Result: *pay* [pe] and *bike* [baɪk] become *bay* [be] and *pike* [paɪk]
>
> *cab* [kæb] becomes *cap* [kæp]
>
> *knob* [nɑb] becomes *knop* [nɑp]

Remember that [p] is voiceless, but [b] is voiced. There will be, of course, a greater emission of breath with the voiceless [p].

10. For contrast practice these, differentiating clearly between the lightweight voiceless [p] and the heavyweight voiced [b].

    a.

pun–bun	rip–rib	bore–pore	cob–cop
putt–butt	cap–cab	pot–bought	dip–dib
pig–big	ape–Abe	back–pack	gab–gap
pin–bin	nip–nib	pet–bet	rope–robe

    b. The pot called the kettle black.
    c. Seize opportunity by the beard, for it is bald behind.
    d. Porcupines may not be popular pets, but they do have their points.
    e. The first bubble gum to be invented, named "Blibber-Blubber," appeared in 1906. It flopped.

§§§ D. CONFUSING [v] AND [b]

If you have a Spanish or German language background, or if your first language is Japanese or Korean, you may possibly replace [b] with [v], an error that generally results if the lips are not completely closed for [b].

11. As you practice these words and sentences, be certain that your lips are firmly closed for [b]. When you articulate [v], however, your lower lip should touch the edges of your upper front teeth.

    a.

sober	vie–buy	lib–live	bat–vat
habit	vale–bale	dove–dub	vex–Bex
ribbon	vow–bow	jibe–jive	berry–very
table	vile–bile	give–gib	voom–boom

    b. Bob, help Velda vacuum the velvet belt.
    c. Rain before seven—fine before eleven.
    d. If you have no money, be polite.
    e. A man in love mistakes a pimple for a dimple.
    f. It's a sad truth that everybody is a bore to somebody.
    g. Things don't turn up. They must be turned up.
    h. A prune is a plum that has seen better days.

[t–d]

§§§ F. DENTALIZING [t] AND [d]

As you already know, pressing the tip of the tongue against the upper gum ridge will produce a good, clear [t] or [d]. A few people, especially those whose first language is Spanish or Italian, place the tongue tip on the back of the upper front teeth. A slushy sound results, and [t] and [d] may resemble [ts] and [dz]. This is known as *dentalization*. Dentalization is fine for the [θ] in *th*in but not for the [t] in *t*in.

Do you make slushy, wet [t] and [d] sounds? This will happen if you place your tongue tip on the back of your upper teeth.

Result: *tin* and *did* sound more like *tsin* and *dzid*.

12. Press the tip of your tongue against your upper gum ridge, about a third of an inch behind your teeth. You'll produce tidy and dry [t] and [d] sounds. Work for a brisk upward movement of your tongue as you read these. "Trippingly on the tongue"—advice from Shakespeare—is still appropriate.

    a. teal–deal   tan–Dan   teen–dean
        ten–den   Tim–dim   toll–dole
        toe–doe   talk–dock   till–dill
        tore–door   tog–dog   tub–dub

    b. If you drink, don't drive. Don't even putt.
    c. Don't slam the door. You might want to go back.
    d. What can be done at any time is never done at all.
    e. The sins you do two by two you must pay for one by one.
    f. Lead us not into temptation. Just tell us where it is. We'll find it.
    g. I'm a champion. I play in the low 80s. If it's any hotter than that, I won't play.
    h. If you don't get everything you want, think of all the things you get that you don't want.

§§§ G. SUBSTITUTING [t] FOR FINAL [d]; OMITTING [t] AND [d] AT ENDS OF WORDS

If you substitute [t] for [d], you'll say

> [hɛt] for *head* [hɛd]
> [hɪt] for *hid* [hɪd]

And your first language might have been one of these: Arabic, Chinese, German, Japanese, Russian, Slavic (especially Polish).

If you drop final [t] and [d], you'll say

> [fæs] for *fast* [fæst]
> [plæn] for *planned* [plænd]

And your first language may have been one of these: Chinese, Japanese, Korean, Liberian, Nigerian, or Vietnamese.

Remember: [t] is voiceless. It's a quiet whiff of air.

[d] is voiced. It should sound like a minigrunt in your throat.

13. Check yourself carefully as you run through these:

    lend–lent–lend–lend
    mend–meant–mend–mend
    tend–tent–tend–tend
    rend–rent–rend–rend
    penned–pent–penned–penned
    send–sent–send–send

14. Here is material with [t] and [d] in various positions and sound combinations. You'll find it helpful to exaggerate somewhat as you practice. Eventually, of course, you'll want to strive for ease and naturalness as you articulate [t] and [d] sounds that don't call attention to themselves.

    a. You are what you eat. Be a hot tamale.
    b. You can lead a horse to water, but you can't make him float.
    c. I'm not afraid to die. I just don't want to be there when it happens.
    d. The husband who boasts that he never made a mistake has a wife who did.
    e. Judging by the divorce rate, a lot of people who said, "I do"—didn't.
    f. I'm better than I was, but not quite as good as I was before I got worse.
    g. The minute you toot your own horn, somebody will disconnect your battery.
    h. It's all right to hold a conversation, but you should let go of it now and then.
    i. The law can make you quit drinking, but it can't make you quit being the kind that needs a law to make you quit drinking.
    j. A guy asked the meat cutter at the supermarket if he had any veal. A lady standing nearby turned to him and said sharply, "Has it ever occurred to you where that veal comes from when you're eating it?" The man pointed to a carton of eggs in the woman's cart and replied, "Has it ever occurred to you where those come from when you're eating them?"

[k–g]

§§§ C. CONFUSING [k] AND [g]

Spanish, Russian, Indian, Chinese language background? You may be switching [g] with [k] or vice versa. You possibly pronounce *local* [ˈlokl] as *logal* [ˈlogl] and *pig* [pɪg] as *pick* [pɪk]. It isn't difficult to straighten them out. Don't forget that [k] is *voiceless*—a bantam breeze. There is no sound in your throat as you produce it. But [g] is *voiced*. It's a small grunt.

15. Keep your [k] and [g] sounds—they're described as *throaty* consonants—relatively light and clean-cut, and avoid producing a heavy, muddy sound.

    a. game–came   snigger–snicker   bag–back
        God–cod   stagger–stacker   nag–knack
        gate–Kate   lagging–lacking   sag–sack
        goat–coat   logging–locking   brig–brick
    b. "Bah!" said Scrooge. "Humbug!"
    c. The biggest dog was once a pup.
    d. Hard work never killed anybody, but why take a chance?
    e. The chicken came before the egg, because no supreme being would want to sit on an egg.

If your first language is Vietnamese, Korean, Chinese, or Japanese, you may find [k] and [g] in *x* [ks-kg] combinations bothersome.

Do you turn *excite* [ɛkˈsaɪt] into [ɛˈsaɪt]?

Do you turn *exact* [ɛgˈzækt] into [ɛzˈæt]?

Don't forget:

If the vowel sound following the *x* is stressed, the *x* will be pronounced [gz].

If *x* is followed by a pronounced consonant, or if it is found in the final position, it will be pronounced [ks].

16. Don't think about the rules as you practice these. If you get hopelessly stuck, review the rules. Then try again.

    exam   extra   exit   exert
    except   excel   excuse   exceed
    exist   explode   exclude   exotic
    exult   expand   exhaust   exuberant

GRAB BAG: PRACTICE MATERIAL FOR THE PLOSIVES

The plosives are the forgotten underdogs of all the sound families. Too often these useful sounds are aborted or annihilated. They shouldn't be. The plosives are the "drumbeats" of our language. One writer has compared them to snare drums, bass drums, cymbals, tom-toms, and timpani.

17. The material coming up contains all six plosives—[t], [d], [p], [b], [k], [g]—in a variety of positions and sound combinations.

THE TRIPLE PLAY
Do each sentence three times.
First time: Exaggerate your medial and final plosives considerably. Make them pop like a balloon.
Remember, this is for practice purposes only.
Second time: Use moderate exaggeration. Your medial and final plosives should be medium-loud pops.
Third time: No exaggeration. *Be natural.* Relaaax! Tap your plosives with a feather, but tap them!

or you may prefer

THE QUADRUPLE PLAY
First time: No exaggeration. Be natural, and so on.
Second time: Use moderate exaggeration, and so on.
Third time: Exaggerate considerably, and so on.
Fourth time: No exaggeration. Be natural, and so on.

---

a. Big toe: A device for finding furniture in the dark.
b. Fewer marriages would skid if more who said "I do" did.
c. If you worry about missing the boat, remember the *Titanic*.
d. What's Irish and stays outside all winter? Patio furniture.
e. Garbage bags do not make good parachutes.
f. I have always thought of a dog lover as a dog that was in love with another dog.
g. It's possible to like country music and not spit tobacco.
h. I'd give my right arm to be ambidextrous.
i. If a cat spoke, it would say things like, "Hey, I don't see the problem here."
j. I'm a real timid person. I was beaten up by Quakers.
k. "You Stomped on My Heart and Squished That Sucker Flat." [Country music song title]
l. I was so ugly when I was born that the doctor slapped everybody.
m. Lord, help me not be a perfectionist. (Did I spell that correctly?)
n. Why does the Psychic Hotline have to ask for your credit card number?
o. The company that prints those wallet cards that read I AM A DEVOUT CATHOLIC. IN CASE OF ACCIDENT, CALL A PRIEST has expanded its line to include a card that reads I AM A DEVOUT ATHEIST. IN CASE OF ACCIDENT, GOOD-BYE.
p. Writes a father, "I used to read my son to sleep in the hope that it would teach him proper English. But I gave up. One night as I walked in, he pointed to the book and said, 'What did you bring that book that I don't want to be read to out of up for?'"
q. The skunk sat on a stump. The skunk thunk the stump stunk, but the stump thunk the skunk stunk.
r. Jonah proved that you can't keep a good man down.
s. You are what you eat, but who wants to be a Brussels sprout?
t. Tired of being a conformist? Try this. Get on a crowded elevator on a top floor. And instead of facing the front, face the rear. Smile broadly. I did this recently, and in a second or two, somebody at the rear of the car whispered in a loud voice, "Better press the stop button. We've got a real fruitcake in here."

Assignment 7: Plosives

Prepare material that contains many examples of the six plosives—[t], [d], [p], [b], [k], [g]—in various positions and sound combinations. If you've found one or two of them to be unusually troublesome, be certain that your material is loaded with them. You may find it easier to write your own material. Nonsense material is generally acceptable, but emphasize simplicity. As you practice, try the Triple or the Quadruple Play.

Plosives are the *snap, crackle,* and *pop* sounds of the consonant families, but remember that normal, connected speech is natural speech.

or

Many classes have opted for a more specific format. These are suggestions only, and they may also be adapted to subsequent articulation assignments.

Part 1: Prepare eight sentences, 12 to 15 words per sentence.

Two sentences should be loaded with [p] and [b] in various positions, particularly final positions.

Similarly, two sentences should be loaded with [t] and [d].

And two sentences should be loaded with [k] and [g].

Two scramblers: Sentences loaded with all six plosives in various positions.

Part 2: Prepare and practice a short, short story, a joke, or a brief anecdote approximately 50 to 75 words in length. (Drill 17*t,* page 95, is an example.)

Suggested Checklist for Assignment 7: See page 275, Appendix B.

GLIDES (SEMIVOWELS) [L] [R] [W] [J]

To practice your diction, use the Pronunciation Flashcards on the CD

A **glide** *is a sound produced by a continuous gliding movement of the articulators from the position of one sound to that of another.* The glides have been described as vowels in motion.

There are four glides in English:

[l]	[w]
[r]	[j]

When you say [r], [w], or [j], for example, your tongue is in motion as these sounds are being formed.

Make the [w] sound in *well.* Hold it for a few seconds, as if you were going to say the whole word in slow motion. You'll discover that [w] really sounds like the *oo* [u] in *moon* [mun]. Now move into the *ell.* What's your tongue doing? Moving or gliding, as it were. Even your lips and jaw are in motion—a smooth, continuous gliding motion.

96 Chapter 6

[W]

way, aware

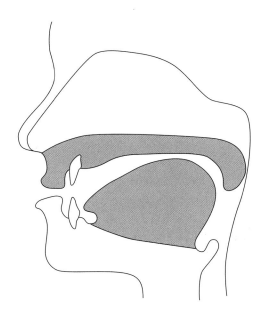

VARIOUS SPELLINGS

o as in ONCE   w as in WIN

u as in QUICK   wh as in WHY (optional)

Classification   lips (bilateral)

[w] voiced

Piddling Pursuit

Phonetic   sʌm wɪt wʌns sɛd ðæt ə prəˈfɛsɚ ɪz ə ˈwɔkɪŋ ˈtɛkstbʊk waɪrd fɔr saʊnd.

Diacritic   fish, tə tāst rīt, must swim thrē tīmz—in wô′tər, in but′ər, and in wīn.

How to . . .

    Tongue   The back of the tongue should be arched toward the soft palate. An excellent [w] can be produced with little or no movement of the tongue.

    Lips   Round and protrude your lips as you would to produce *oo* as in *moon*. It's the rapid widening of the lips that gives [w] its character. (The tongue and lips change into the position for whatever sound follows.)

    Jaw   Slightly lowered, then also moves into the position of the vowel that follows.

WARMER-UPPERS

Initial	Medial
wag	quill
one	swoop
wend	award
waltz	beware
wow	cobweb
wings	everyone
wire	highway
wiggle	inquest
Waldo	sandwich
wonder	thruway
willow	unwell
Wyoming	anyone

Faults and Foibles

    A. Weakening [w]

    B. Flabby [w]

§§§ **C. CONFUSING [w] WITH [v] OR [f]**

Now for the details. Choose as needed.

A. Weakening [w]

The *qu* spelling in such words as *quit, Quaker,* and *queen* doesn't indicate the presence of [w], but the sound is present in every English word that begins with *qu*. Notice the phonetic spelling of these words.

    [kwɪt]   [ˈkwekɚ]   [kwin]

    There's a tendency in careless speech to weaken the [w] sound in [kw] and other sound clusters: *quaff, dwindle, tweak.*

    Similarly, many speakers slight [w] if it begins the second syllable of a word: *always, backward, houseware.*

18.   Be sure that the sound is firm as you practice this material. Don't forget to round and push out the lips for [w].

    a.

quad	quilt	quick	awkward	unaware
quaint	quart	quantity	woodwork	unwind
quality	quite	quell	reward	byway
language	dwarf	twelve	twin	twilight

    b.   You are what you throw away.

    c.   Wisdom is knowing when you can't be wiser.

    d.   Wanda quivered quietly as she paid a quarter for the quail.

    e.   What word can be pronounced quicker by adding a syllable to it? Quick.

    f.   Those who escape temptation always leave a forwarding address.

    g.   Quickly got—quickly lost. Quite quoteworthy.

    h.   Quakers will not quarrel and quibble when quizzed.

    i.   This is the way the world ends, not with a bang but a whimper. [T.S. Eliot]

B. Flabby [w]

Chronic mumblers will generally produce anemic and puny [w] sounds. This glide isn't a difficult sound to make, but if the lips are allowed to hang like two pieces of limp liver, a clear [w] can't be produced. Lip movement must be vigorous, rapid, and forceful. Amateur ventriloquists try to avoid material loaded with [w] at the beginnings of words.

19. A student has labeled [w] as the "osculating" consonant. Extreme lip puckering and protrusion are required—a position that also comes in handy during the act of osculating (kissing). Let those lips bulge on all [w] sounds:

   a. Oaths are but words, and words but wind.
   b. The time you enjoyed wasting wasn't wasted.
   c. Said Will Rogers, "Nothing you can't spell will ever work."
   d. My wife and I were happy for twenty years. Then we met. [Henry Youngman]
   e. The longest word in the world is "a word from our sponsor."
   f. Postcard from Waikiki: The weather is here. Wish you were beautiful.
   g. Wyoming winter weather was wicked as wild storms whacked and walloped the West.
   h. Always give the public what they want, even if they don't want it.
   i. Laugh and the whole world laughs with you. Cry and your mascara runs.
   j. I will not eat oysters. I want my food dead—not sick, not wounded—dead.
   k. When I was born, I was such a big baby that the doctor was afraid to slap me. [Arnold Schwarzenegger]
   l. One good thing about prison is that one never has to wonder what to wear.
   m. The poor wish to be rich, the rich wish to be happy. The single wish to be married, and the married wish to be dead.
   n. At a dinner party, one should eat wisely, but not too well, and talk well, but not too wisely.
   o. A few weeks ago we went to a well-known German restaurant. The appetizer made us queasy, and the wurst was yet to come.
   p. If a woodchuck could chuck wood, how much wood would a woodchuck chuck if a woodchuck could and would? But if a woodchuck could and would chuck wood, no reason why he should. How much wood could a woodchuck chuck if a woodchuck could and would chuck wood?

§§§ *C. CONFUSING [w] WITH [v] OR [f]*

For discussion and relevant exercises, see page 112.

 or

whip, somewhere

Classification	lips (bilabial)
	an [h] approach to [w]; a fricative glide
Piddling Pursuit	
Phonetic	hu rɪˈmɛmbɚz hwɛn ˈtuθpest wəz hwaɪt?
Diacritic	ə hwāl iz ōn′li här pōōnd′ hwen it spouts.

How to . . .

Your lips assume the rounded position for [w], but the initial part of the following gliding movement is accompanied by the voiceless [h].

WARMER-UPPERS

Initial	Medial
wheeze	anywhere
whip	awhile
whir	bobwhite
whist	buckwheat
whoa	bullwhip
whoop	cartwheel
whistle	elsewhere
whittle	flywheel
whiskey	nowhere
whisper	overwhelm
whither	somewhat

Faults and Foibles

How do you handle these word pairs?

where–wear

whet–wet

whacks–wax

The vast majority of us pronounce *where/wear* the same way: [wɛr]

If you're a stickler for precision, you may want to pronounce that [h] in *wh* words. If so, you'll have to sound the [h] before, not after, the [w]. A thousand years ago in Old English, most of the present-day words beginning with *wh* were spelled with the two letters reversed and pronounced that way: *hwaer* (where).

Many speakers, readers, and actors concerned with finesse do pronounce *wh* words with the [h] sounded first (as if the everyday English spelling were *hwere, hwet, hwacks*).

But if you listen carefully to good speakers and well-trained voices, you'll discover that the [h] in *wh* combinations is disappearing from pronunciation rather rapidly. In other words, [hw] seems to be an endangered species. However, let's be reasonable. It's neither incorrect to use it, nor is it incorrect to drop it. Use it if you will.

> If you're into career speech and are planning to enter a profession that depends primarily on oral communication—acting or radio and TV announcing, for example—you may want to cultivate the [hw] phoneme. At least, you should be able to put it on hold.

20. For those who want to work on this sound, make a distinction between the *wh* combinations and the single *w* in the following:

    a. | | | |
       |---|---|---|
       | whether–weather | where–wear | whet–wet |
       | wheel–weal | whale–wail | whir–were |
       | when–wen | what–watt | whey–way |
       | whine–wine | whish–wish | why–y |

    b. The worst whistlers whistle most.
    c. It is a good answer which knows when to stop.
    d. The one who gives while he lives knows where it goes.
    e. What is the world to a man when his wife is a widow?
    f. If you don't know what you want, what you probably want to do is sleep.
    g. What is moral is what you feel good after, and what is immoral is what you feel bad after.
    h. I keep six honest servants. Their names are What, Why, When, How, Where, and Who.
    i. Behind the big question: What is life? is another important question: What's for dinner?
    j. Which witch whined when the wine was spilled on the wailing whale?
    k. It matters not whether you win or lose; what matters is whether *I* win or lose.
    l. Whiskers improve with age, but age doesn't improve with whiskers.

1

**lake, elbow,
pal**

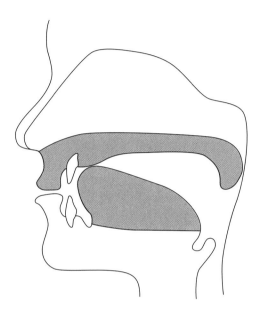

VARIOUS SPELLINGS

l as in LAB   ll as in ALLOW

Classification

tongue and upper gum ridge (lingua-alveolar)
[l] is voiced

Piddling Pursuit

Phonetic

ə fʊl ˈbɛlɪ ˈniðɚ fɑɪts nɔr flɑɪz wɛl.

Diacritic

ə kat iz a nib′lər ho͞o kan ēt wun mēl ə dā—ôl dā.

How to . . .
    Tongue

Place the tip of your tongue lightly but firmly against your upper gum ridge or roof of your mouth. The tongue is tense. Keep the sides of it down to allow the breath stream to escape laterally.

    Lips   Unrounded and relaxed.
    Jaw   Dropped slightly.

WARMER-UPPERS

Initial	Medial	Final
lark	fleece	apple
laugh	plump	bawl
lawn	Allen	bowl
length	ballad	cool
lid	believe	cruel
loose	crawling	kneel
lunch	gallows	pearl
Laura	jelly	pill
lemon	public	quail
llama	sailor	style
lover	squealer	twill
lucky	elderly	wrestle

Faults and Foibles

    A. Muffling [l]

    B. Omitting or swallowing [l]

§§§ **C. CONFUSING [l] AND [r]; SUBSTITUTING ANOTHER SOUND FOR FINAL [l]**

Now for the details. Choose as needed.

A. Muffling [l]

If [l] is a tail-ender, found at or near the end of words, as in *gall* and *galled,* it's a dark [l]. A dark [l] in itself certainly isn't incorrect, but if it's so dark that it's muffled and gluey, it'll probably hinder intelligibility. You'll make a too-dusky [l] if your tongue tip doesn't contact the gum ridge.

21.   To help you hear as well as feel the difference between a clear [l] and a dark [l], read the following. The first word of each pair begins with a clear [l]. Be sure that the back of your tongue is held relatively low. The second word ends with a dark [l]. Your entire tongue should be pulled farther back in your mouth than it is for a clear [l]. The back portion of your tongue is also higher for the dark sound than for the clear one.

        Say the final, dark *l*'s as if the words were spelled *seallll, tellll, dillll.* A good [l], somebody has said, should sound like "honey being spooned from the mouth."

lean–seal	lag–gal	lock–call	Luke–cool
let–tell	lot–tall	lime–mile	lick–kill
lid–dill	lip–pill	lead–deal	lame—male
late–tale	loot–tool	lost–stall	lope–pole

B. Omitting or swallowing [l]

Don't slight [l] if it's followed by another consonant: *help, silk, wolf, film.*

    Do you say *bid, code,* and *jade* for *build, cold,* and *jailed?* If you do, you're blotching or bleaching that important [l] sound.

22.   Caution: Your tongue tip *must* make proper contact with the gum ridge as you form [l] in the following:

    a.

wealth	twelve	jailed	revolve	dolphin
self	helm	shelve	malt	alb
Ralph	scald	alm	pelvis	pelf

    b.   A hothead seldom sets the world on fire.

    c.   Be wisely worldly, but not worldly wise.

    d.   You know how cannibals are. You're a little late for dinner and all you get is the cold shoulder.

    e.   It helps that the Dallas police have black belts in karate.

f.   I know a man who gave up smoking, drinking, rich foods, girls, and silk shirts. He was healthy right up to the time he killed himself.

g.   The cow is of the bovine ilk. One end is moo, the other milk.

h.   Driving the car helps you see the world, but how you drive determines which world.

23.   Do you say *aw* right for *all* right, baseb*a* for baseba*ll?* Then you're diluting or eliminating that final [l]. *Don't!* As you read these, don't let those tail-end [l] sounds droop or lurk in the back of your throat. *Push* them forward! Give them a bit of glitter.

a.   Any fool can make a rule.

b.   Hot tempers will mean cool friends.

c.   If it works well, they'll stop making it.

d.   Tip to young male drivers: Forget the girl and hug the road.

e.   Baseball is 90 percent mental. The other half is physical. [Yogi Berra]

f.   Conscience is the still, small voice that makes us feel still smaller.

g.   Internal Revenue Service: The world's most successful mail-order business.

h.   Next year, 3 million kids will turn 16, and 7 million parents will turn pale.

i.   Since it's better to speak well of the dead, let's knock them while they're still alive.

j.   Surely it's better to tell the truth behind people's backs than to never tell it at all.

k.   In college football, the real triple threat is one who can run, kick, and pass all his exams.

l.   There's no fool like an old fool who marries a young fool.

m.   If a woman says she'll call you, it means as soon as she gets home. If a man tells you he'll call, it means before he dies.

§§§   *C.   CONFUSING [l] AND [r]; SUBSTITUTING ANOTHER SOUND FOR FINAL [l]*

For discussion and relevant exercises, see page 112.

[r]

run, crime, fair

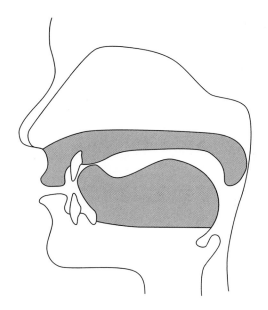

VARIOUS SPELLINGS

r as in RAID   rr as in CHERRY
rh as in RHUBARB   wr as in WROTE

Classification

tip of tongue behind upper gum ridge (linguapalatal)
[r] is voiced

Piddling Pursuit

Phonetic

ɑɪd ˈræðɚ bi əˈlɑɪv rɔŋ ðɛn dɛd rɑɪt.

Diacritic

rimem′bər, nō mat′ər wâr yo͞o gō, t͟hâr yo͞o är.

How to . . .
  Tongue

One manner of production: Bring the tip of your tongue close to the gum ridge and turn it back slightly toward the middle of the hard palate.
Another manner of production: Tense and raise the central portion of your tongue slightly toward the hard palate. Lower the tongue tip and draw it back somewhat from the lower teeth.

   Both of these are starting positions. As soon as the sound is begun, let your tongue glide or move to the position necessary to make the following sound.

  Lips and Jaw

Round your lips a bit and lower your jaw slightly, but the exact position of your lips and jaw also depends largely on the vowel that follows.

WARMER-UPPERS

Initial	Medial	Final
rain	brag	hair
rant	chrome	liar
ray	carrot	lure
red	describe	mere
rhyme	Henry	moor
rush	horrible	near
wren	marry	scare
write	narrow	tear
wrought	oral	umpire
really	syrup	affair
revenge	April	career
robot	squirrel	guitar

A *gremlin* in our language?

The [r] sound is a genuine mischief-maker. It's pesky and mercurial—and it's also controversial.

Run through these five words, and you'll come up with five entirely different [r] sounds: *rim, turn, matter, four* (some easterners pronounce it as *fo-wa*), *fire* (in some southern speech, the [r] disappears completely at the ends of words—it floats off to the nearest magnolia tree—as in *fah-yuh*).

The section of the country in which you live may strongly influence your [r] sounds.

Faults and Foibles

    A. Flabby [r]

    B. Substituting [w] for [r]

§   **C. Regional [r]**

§   **D. Intrusive [r]**

§§§ **E. SUBSTITUTING [l] FOR [r]; SUBSTITUTING [ɑ] FOR [r] OR [ɝ] IN THE FINAL POSITION**

Now for the details. Choose as needed.

A. Flabby [r]

A lazy, lifeless tongue will do much to destroy a clear and identifiable [r]. Let your lips be lazy, but your tongue needs to toil. [r] requires a frisky, "pole-vaulting" tongue.

A little extravagance is called for here.

Before you sound the initial [r] in such words as *red* and *right,* make the sound of *er* [ɝ] as in *ermine* and *fern.*

To make *er:* Raise the middle portion of your tongue toward the roof of your mouth. If this seems unnatural to you, simply make sure that the front of your tongue is higher than the back. Some individuals point the tip of the tongue upward; others curl it slightly backward.

24.   Do each of the words and sentences in this exercise twice. In the first reading, make an exaggerated *er* [ɝ] sound before the initial [r]:

Er-round the er-rough and er-rugged er-rock the er-ragged er-rascal er-ran.

The second time, keep the same tongue position on the initial [r] which is used on the *er* [ɝ] sounds, but cut the preliminary *er* quite short.

   a.
rent	rim	rail	ripe
rift	wren	rant	rock
raw	wrack	run	rink

   b.   A rose is a rose is a rose is a rose. [Gertrude Stein]

   c.   Hair transplant: Reseeding for the receding.

d.   A reckless driver is seldom wreckless for very long.
e.   Weathermen are never wrong. It's the weather that's wrong.
f.   Running for money doesn't make you run fast. It makes you run first.
g.   A problem teenager is one who refuses to let his parents use the car.
h.   The road to ruin is always kept in good repair.
i.   If the left side of our brain controls the right side of the body, then only left-handed people are in their right mind.
j.   Where do forest rangers go to get away from it all?
k.   Depend on the rabbit's foot if you will, but remember that it didn't work for the rabbit.

If [r], like its in-law [l], appears at or near the end of a word, there may be a tendency to swallow it. What's worse, many of the preceding sounds may also drop into the back of the throat.

25.   If your tongue is in a reasonably correct position for the [r] sound in the following, it may actually be encouraging you to gargle the tail-ender r's. A little extra lip and jaw activity comes in handy here. Also, it helps to concentrate on deliberately achieving a brighter sound on [r] and its neighbors.
a.   All men are born truthful and die liars.
b.   Carl Dort, the network's weather forecaster, was far out in predicting that February would be fairly fair.
c.   There is no cure for birth or death except to enjoy the interval.
d.   Is it weird in here or is it just me?
e.   Never lend your car to anyone to whom you have given birth.
f.   I'm going to give my therapist one more year, then I'm going to Lourdes. [Woody Allen]
g.   There are only two kinds of liars in car accidents—both drivers.

[r] *often blends with a next-door neighbor.*

prom, **br**ake, **fr**eight, **cr**ab, **gr**ab, **tr**ap, **dr**ill

A couple of little tricks will help you handle these blends quite readily.

[pr, br, fr] *blends*

As you've noticed, [p] and [b] require rather strong lip activity. But remember—and this is not as tricky as it may seem—the tongue articulates [r] in these blends at the same time that the lips articulate [p], [b], and [f]. In other words, before you have finished making the [p], [b], and [f], the [r] sound has already begun.

26.   Run through these words. You should find it quite easy to avoid flabby r's.

pride	brought	freak
prank	brick	frill
prod	brunt	fright

[kr, gr] *clusters*

Again, the initial consonant must virtually overlap with the [r]. This very close blend isn't difficult to form if the [r] is articulated with your tongue pulled back as it would be if [k] and [g] were being sounded.

27.   Don't hold the initial sounds too long as you practice the following:

cross	crate	grill	grace
crust	crack	grim	groom
crude	creek	grade	gripe

[tr, dr] *clusters*

The [r] that most of us produce in words such as *try* and *drip* is still another kind of [r] and with a personality of its own. Friction noises can sometimes be heard with this sound, and in its manner of production it's similar to the fricative family.

28. Lower the tip of your tongue just enough to produce the [t] or [d]. Then retract it quickly with the tip of your tongue near but not in actual contact with the gum ridge. Incidentally, many individuals find it easy to produce a successful [r] if the tongue touches the gum ridge lightly.

trim	dram	treat
trod	dreary	droop
trout	draft	tray

29. As you say these sentences, avoid two common faults: Don't make the [r] blends conspicuous—too noisy or sustained. And don't insert a sound resembling *uh*—the schwa [ə]—between an initial consonant and the [r]. When this is done, such words as *try* and *grant* become *tuh-ry* and *guh-rant*.

   a. Gripe: a ripe grape.
   b. Grinning Granny fed the green grapes to grumbling Grandpa.
   c. Never have children, only grandchildren.
   d. Dr. Livingstone I presume—full name of Dr. Presume.
   e. I think crime pays. The hours are good and you travel a lot. [Jerry Seinfeld]
   f. Is it progress or improvement if a cannibal uses a knife or fork?
   g. When angry, count to 10 before you speak. When very angry, count to 100.
   h. Frankly, if it weren't for P. T. Farnsworth, the probable inventor of television, we'd still be eating frozen radio dinners.
   i. The best month to get married in is Marembruary.
   j. You can drop human beings anywhere and they'll thrive. Only the rat does as well.
   k. College football should be played by instructors instead of students. There would be a great increase in broken arms and legs.

B. Substituting [w] for [r]

30. If you find that you're substituting *w* for *r*, here's how to convert to *r*: Keep your lips immobile, don't raise the back of your tongue, and emphasize movements of the *front* of your tongue as you make *r*.
   And don't forget: Pucker those lips on [w] and let the front of your tongue rest quietly.

   a.
wad–rod	way–ray	wide–ride	wig–rig	trice–twice
wade–raid	wane–rain	woo–rue	weed–reed	trill–twill
won–run	woe–roe	will–rill	watt–rot	crick–quick

   b. Rock and roll is the hamburger that ate the world.
   c. The secret is always to let the other person have your way.
   d. While waiting for the whales, Ronda and Wanda waded near the Wabash rails.
   e. It's a rare person who doesn't want to hear what he doesn't want to hear.
   f. Even if you're on the right track, you'll get run over if you just sit there.
   g. If it took six days to create the world, why should it take four weeks to get a loan?
   h. When you go into court, you're putting your fate into the hands of people who weren't smart enough to get out of jury duty.
   i. The reason why worry kills more people than work is that more people worry than work.
   j. Rock-a-bye, Baby,
   In the tree top.
   When the wind blows,
   The cradle will rock.
   When the bough breaks,
   The cradle will fall.
   Down will come baby,
   Cradle and all!
   k. Who put that cradle in the treetop in the first place?

§ C. Regional [r]

"You can't fool all the people all the time. Once every four years is enough."

How true! Every four years we watch and hear the two major political parties nominate candidates. There is enough hell-bubbling pageantry and speech-making for everybody. Most interesting to some of us, however, is the wonderful conglomeration of dialects or "accents."

The senator from South Carolina who tells the convention that a rogue nation could easily launch a *nucleah wah* is just as colorful as the chairperson, who identifies herself as a native *Noo Yawkuh,* with an absence of recognizable [r] sounds. But the visiting governor of Iowa hangs on to the [r] in R-R-R-Republican as though his life depends on it. (That hard, midwestern [r] has been nicknamed the "snarling [r].")

And a delegate from Boston may inform you that when he's home, he always *pahks his cah in Hahvahd Yahd.*

(As a loyal, lifelong Bostonian once told me, "Oh, but we do pronounce our *r* sounds. We just pronounce them differently.")

Are we saying that [r] is *never* heard in New York or in some New England or southern states? Not at all. Most residents of these locales pronounce their *r*'s if they're followed by vowels: *rap, trunk, barometer.*

Who has the correct [r] sound? All of them, as long as they're intelligible.

If [r] follows a vowel and occurs in or near the final position of a word, such as *far* and *dark,* and if you use General American dialect, you'll probably articulate the [r] with definite [r] coloring:

far = [fɑr]

dark = [dɑrk]

Some New Englanders and easterners:

far = [fɑ]

dark = [dɑk]

Some southerners:

far = [fɑə]

dark = [dɑək]

Maybe you have no problem with this variation of the [r] family. Let your instructor advise you. If you're told that your [r] sound is too hard and prominent or is accompanied by unpleasant friction noises, you may be curling the tongue tip back excessively as well as prolonging the sound. As you read the drill material, try to get the feel of your tongue activity and position. The tongue tip should not curl back on itself.

31. If your [r] sound is weak and pallid or is otherwise conspicuous for the area in which you live, raise the central portion of your tongue, and point the tip in the direction of the gum ridge. It may help if you prolong the [r] sounds briefly as you read the following:

   a. | fear | queer | leer | bare |
       |------|-------|------|------|
       | rare | mar | poor | floor |
       | liar | start | port | mire |
       | air | bored | barn | sire |

   b. Every ass loves to hear himself bray.
   c. Too many people pick a quarrel before it's ripe.
   d. I'd rather be strongly wrong than weakly right.
   e. A good question to ask ourselves: What kind of a world would this be if everybody were just like me?
   f. There's no harm in talking to yourself, but try to avoid telling yourself jokes that you've heard before.
   g. There is neither here nor there—nor elsewhere.
   h. They who drink beer will think beer.
   i. Where are the germs that cause *good* breath?
   j. Why is a carrot more orange than an orange?

§ D. Intrusive [r]

A friend from Boston may want to discuss the problems that America*er* has with Cub*er* and Kore-*er.*

This is the *intrusive r*—an *r* sound where, some feel, it doesn't belong. It's common in parts of New England and in the New York City area.

Hardly a criminal offense, it often provides amusement for outsiders. The [r] is inserted between two words if the first one ends with a vowel and the second one begins with a vowel. This seems to ease the transition between consecutive vowels. Thus we hear *sofa-***r** *in the living room, idea-***r** *of his, law-***r** *of the state.* Speakers who use the intrusive [r] may also hook it on the end of a single word: *potate***r** [pə ˈtet ɚ] for *potato* and *arear* [ˈɛri ɚ] for *area.*

Those who use General American or Southern dialect rarely use the intrusive [r], although in various sections of the country we hear *hor*spital for *hospital.* And some natives of the nation's capital insist that they live in *Warshington,* not *Washington.*

32. If you have a New England or an Eastern dialect, you may be inserting this extra [r] sound. If you want to eliminate it, practice the following. Let somebody listen to you. Work until the tacked-on sound disappears.

   a.
area	pizza	vanilla	Jonah
plaza	Atlanta	Manila	mesa
tufa	Maria	tuba	Bora Bora
Leah	cabana	plasma	panda

   b. Never eat Chinese food in Oklahoma or Montana.
   c. Trust in Allah, but tie your camel. [Arab proverb]
   d. Ada ate tortillas and raw oysters in Alaska and Canada.
   e. Dinah visited the arena to feed a banana to the panda.
   f. Joshua and Martha are moving to North Carolina or Georgia.
   g. Dairy slogan: Drinka pinta milka day.

§§§ E. SUBSTITUTING [l] FOR [r]; SUBSTITUTING [ɑ] FOR [r] OR [ɚ] IN THE FINAL POSITION

For discussion and relevant exercises, see page 113.

[**j**]   **Phonetic**

Diacritic Y

yodel, cube

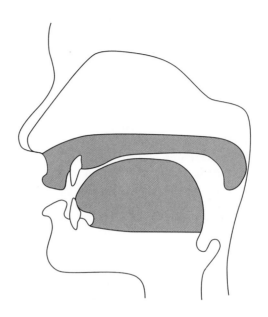

VARIOUS SPELLINGS

eu as in FEUD   j as in HALLELUJAH
ew as in PEW   u as in USEFUL
i as in MILLION   y as in YELL
ie as in PREVIEW

Classification   front of tongue and hard palate (linguapalatal)
[j] is voiced

Piddling Pursuit

Phonetic   ɪf ju θɪŋk ju kæn, ju kæn. ɪf ju θɪŋk ju kænt, jʊr rɑɪt.

Diacritic   ad′vərtīzing iz wut tûrnz ə yôn in′to͞o ə yûrn.

How to . . .
    Tongue   Place the tip of your tongue close to or let it touch the lower front teeth. Then lift the front part of your tongue to a position near the hard palate. Shift the tongue rapidly into the position for whatever vowel follows.
    Lips   Parted, slightly spread.
    Jaw   Narrowly open. Then it moves into position for the following sound.

WARMER-UPPERS

Initial	Medial
yarn	cute
yeast	fuel
ewe	view
youth	Houston
yacht	lawyer
union	amuse
yellow	canyon
unique	onion
usual	refuse
yogurt	senior
yesterday	stallion
eulogy	trillion

Faults and Foibles

    A. Confusing [u] and [ju]

§§§   **B. SUBSTITUTING [dʒ] FOR [j]**

A. Confusing [u] and [ju]

What differences in pronunciation do you hear between the vowel sounds in each of these word pairs?

    food–feud   cool–cue

    boot–butte   booze–abuse

    who–hue   spoon–spew

You can hear *oo* [u] in all of the words, but in the words to the right you hear an extra sound inserted just before the [u]. This sound, of course, is [j] or a sound closely resembling it. Together, [j] and [u] form a combination sound that is pronounced exactly like the common pronoun *you.*

When do you use [u], and when do you use [ju]? As a rule, when the spelling of a word uses *oo,* such as in *boot, loot, food,* and *mood,* do not use [ju]. The simple vowel [u] is also generally used when preceded by [s], [z], [l], or [θ].

When [u] follows other consonants, however, there is almost as much inconsistency as there is controversy about preference. The person who declares that "It is the *duty* [d-you-ty] of each *student* [st-you-dent] to read the *newspaper* [n-youz-paper] on *Tuesday* [t-youz-day]" is, it seems to me, working rather hard to achieve precision and finesse. Of course, if your education or environment dictates the use of [ju] in such words, there is probably nothing wrong with your doing so. The conclusion that can be made about [ju], when its use is optional, is probably the same as about the *h* in certain *wh* combinations: Its use seems to be fading.

33.   In these sentences when [ju] is required, pronounce it accordingly. When it's not required, let your own personal sincerity be your guide.

    a.   Said a Houston humorist, "Home is the place where dutiful teenagers go to refuel."

    b.   You are unique: You are the first you that ever was.

    c.   The union said that the barbecue was useless and confusing.

    d.   Is it stupid to muse and view the future of curfews with amusement?

    e.   She knew that it was her duty to cut coupons out of the duke's newspaper.

    f.   The puny student was aroused to fury when the ice cube was dropped on the new uniform.

    g.   When stupid people do something they are ashamed of, they always argue that it's their duty.

    h.   The pure air in the fuel tube was humid.

    i.   A university is not engaged in making ideas safe for students. A university is engaged in making students safe for ideas.

    j.   Luke's attitude toward the nuclear institute changed when he amused himself by planting tulips.

§§§ B. SUBSTITUTING [dʒ] FOR [j]

For discussion and relevant exercises, see page 114.

§§§ C. CONFUSING [w] WITH [v] OR [f]

If your native language is Scandinavian, German, Polish, Russian, Indian, Chinese, Hindi, or Pakistani, you might be confusing [w] with [v] or [f].

win becomes [vɪn] or [fɪn]

Compare the rounded lip position used for the English [w] with the positions for [v] and [f].

For [v] or [f]: The lower lip is held lightly against the edges of the upper front teeth.

For [w]: The lips mustn't touch the teeth.

Another little tip: As you pronounce the words beginning with [w] in the following material, first say the *oo* of *moon*, hold for two seconds, and then glide into the next sound. For example: *oo-ail* (wail), *oo-ell* (well).

34. Watch yourself in a mirror as you say:

a.			
vail–wail	vary–wary	vest–west	fade–wade
veal–weal	vault–Walt	vine–wine	fin–win
vane–wane	veld–weld	vaunt–want	food–wooed
vet–wet	vent–went	vee–we	fell–well

b.   First thrive and then wive.
c.   Will Velma Weber give Wilbur's western vest to the Veep?
d.   Seven days without laughter makes one weak.
e.   "If You Can't Live without Me, Why Aren't You Dead Yet?" [Country song title]
f.   The perfect lover is one who turns into a pizza at 3 A.M.
g.   Vinnie vowed to wow Winnie with her waltz through the vaults.
h.   Everybody wants to live a long time, but nobody wants to get old.
i.   Did the Berlin Wall fall because the Communists forsook their vile wiles?
j.   What, never? No, never! What, never? Well, hardly ever.
k.   Vincent Winston whispered, "Vaughn wandered with Wendy toward Venice."

[l]

§§§ C. CONFUSING [l] AND [r]; SUBSTITUTING ANOTHER SOUND FOR FINAL [l]

If you're from Cambodia, China, Japan, Korea, Laos, or one of the Indonesian countries, it's possible that you say something close to

crash for *clash*

labbit for *rabbit*

boi-oo for *boil*

These Asiatic languages don't contain sounds that are exactly like the English [l] and [r]. They do, however, contain a consonant that has some of the characteristics of both—hence the confusion.

For anybody who needs to work on this aspect of English pronunciation: Remember that for [l] the tip of your tongue must touch the upper gum ridge. Don't substitute lip movement for tongue movement on your [l] sounds. *Keep lip activity to an absolute minimum.*

For [r] raise the central portion of your tongue. Point the tip upward, but don't let it contact the gum ridge or the hard palate immediately above the gum ridge.

35.   With these differences in mind, practice this material:

a.

lamb–ram	Rhine–line	lewd–rude	toy–toil
lope–rope	rack–lack	rile–Lyle	fie–file
lip–rip	roan–loan	brink–blink	me–meal
lag–rag	rim–limb	blight–bright	may–mail

b.   Telling your troubles is swelling your troubles.
c.   Do not cram the clams into the crock near the clock.
d.   The heated lead turned red as the glow began to grow.
e.   Cleo hauled the long load of blue brew down the wrong road.
f.   People who don't like cats were probably rats in an earlier life.
g.   Lily Ringling arrived alive even though she'd lost Mr. Luby's rubies.
h.   Life can only be understood backward, but it must be lived forward.
i.   Frankie and Johnny were lovers;
     Oh, Lordy, how they could love.
     Swore to be true to each other,
     True as the stars above.
     He was her man, and he done her wrong.

[r]

§§§   E.   SUBSTITUTING [l] FOR [r]; SUBSTITUTING [ɑ] FOR [r] OR [ɚ] IN THE FINAL POSITION
Speakers of most Asian languages substitute a sound that resembles our [l] for [r].

frost [frɔst] sounds something like [flɔst]

raw [rɔ] is fairly close to [lɔ]

Similarly, many of these same speakers substitute [ɑ-ɔ] for [r] or [ɚ] in final positions.

paper [ˈpepɚ] becomes [ˈpepɑ]

care [kɛr] becomes [kɛ-ɑ]

Caution: For [l]—the tip of your tongue touches the gum ridge.
For [r]—your tongue should be retracted, curled up, and not touching the gum ridge or the palate.
The [ɑ-ɔ] substitutions—you can avoid these if you remind yourself that for [r] the tongue almost executes a "back-flip," but that for [ɑ] it's lazy, dormant, almost flat on the bottom of your mouth.

Acceptable [r] sounds

36.   Whatever the nature of your [r] sounds, be certain they're not so quirky and nonconformist that you're hard to understand. The sound should never be lengthened or deafening. Most important, if your [r] stands out like a beacon light, practice until you can produce a suitable [r] sound.

This material contains [r] in many combinations and positions.

a.

lung–rung	lid–rid	clam–cram	caw–car
load–road	claw–craw	glade–grade	pa–par
lime–rhyme	Blake–brake	ma–mar	ya–yar

b. Never chew your pills.
c. Laugh and the world laughs with you. Cry and you get all wet.
d. Rumor isn't always wrong.
e. Money is round. It rolls away.
f. Two wrongs do not make a right.
g. Except when I'm wrong, I'm always right.
h. Laugh before breakfast, you'll cry before supper.
i. Times are especially trying for those who aren't trying.
j. Early to rise, early to bed, makes one healthy, wealthy, and dead.
k. He promised me earrings, but he only pierced my ears. [Arabic saying]

§§§ B. SUBSTITUTING [dʒ] FOR [j]

Some persons with Scandinavian backgrounds may confuse [j] with [dʒ]. Thus one whose first language is Norwegian, Swedish, Danish, or Icelandic may say

yoke [jok] for *joke* [dʒok]

yune [jun] for *June* [dʒun]

(The Scandinavian influence shows up at a North Dakota zoo that has a pair of yaks. He's called Yak and she's called Yill.)

It will help to remember that for [j] the front part of your tongue is raised high toward, but not in actual contact with, the hard palate. For [dʒ], the tip of your tongue is pressed rather firmly against the gum ridge and then moves downward rapidly.

Another little trick: Say *i* as in *it*. Hold the *i* sound, then push your tongue forward, but don't let it touch the gum ridge.

Now say *yam, yet, year* as though they were spelled *iiiiyam, iiiiyet, iiiiyear.*

37. Using the *i* approach, try these:

yen	young	yank
yellow	Yuma	yoga

Do these without the *i* approach:

a.

yak–Jack	year–jeer	yo–Joe	yet–jet
yoke–joke	yaws–jaws	yip–gyp	yard–jarred

b. Jill yawns whenever Jane yearns for Jerry.
c. Jealousy is all the fun you think they had.
d. Joe dropped the yo-yo into the yam-flavored jam.
e. I was married by a judge. I should have asked for a jury.
f. June will yell if Jake Yates drops the yoke on her jacket.
g. He doesn't care a jot if the yellow jewels fall off John's yacht.

GRAB BAG: PRACTICE MATERIAL FOR THE GLIDES

This material contains all of the glides in a variety of positions and sound combinations.

38.   Practice for clear and accurate articulation of sounds, but avoid exaggeration.

   a.   When one will not, two cannot quarrel.
   b.   A marriage is a friendship recognized by the police.
   c.   A quorum means enough people are there to start a quarrel.
   d.   If you want to live wisely, ignore sayings—including this one.
   e.   A fairy tale is a horror story to prepare children for the newspapers.
   f.   A wedding is just like a funeral except that you get to smell your own flowers.
   g.   Acting is hell. You spend all your time trying to do what they put people in asylums for.
   h.   As the hen said when she stopped in the middle of the highway, "Let me lay it on the line."
   i.   If Robin Hood were alive today, he'd steal from the poor because the rich carry only credit cards.
   j.   You don't fall trees. You fell them. However, if you fell them, you're not a feller, but a faller.
   k.   Until you've walked a mile in another man's moccasins, you can't imagine the smell.
   l.   The lion and the calf shall lie down together, but the calf won't get much sleep.
   m.   Wear short sleeves. Defend your right to bare arms.
   n.   Sign in health food specialty shop: Closed due to illness.
   o.   When Lincoln said you can't fool all the people all of the time, the cloverleaf highway hadn't been invented yet.
   p.   If high heels were so wonderful, men would be wearing them.
   q.   Highway sign near Walla Walla, Washington: "Thirty days hath September, June, and November—and anyone exceeding the speed limit."
   r.   From *Weekly Farm News:* "Nebraska bachelor wants wife. Must be interested in farming and own tractor. Please enclose picture of tractor."
   s.   Funerals are very expensive. That's why people rarely have them until the last minute.
   t.   "Ronnie, where have you been?" Dr. Lowell screamed when Ronnie finally answered the phone. "Sorry, but I have bad news for you and what's worse, I have terrible news."
   Ronnie groaned. "Bad news and terrible news? All right—bad news first."
   "Well," said Lowell, "the bad news—you've got only 24 hours to live."
   "Hell's bells! Then what could the terrible news possibly be?"
   Lowell responded quickly, "I've been trying to call you since yesterday."

Assignment 8: Glides

Prepare material that contains all of the glides in various positions. (Remember that [w] and [j] do not occur as glides in final positions.) Be sure that there's an abundance of those glides that you've found troublesome. You'll recall that [l] and [r] are two of the trickiest sounds in our language. The glide [w] is relatively easy for most people, but if you've been criticized for having flabby articulation, it would be a particularly good sound for you to emphasize in this assignment. When you practice by yourself, the Triple and the Quadruple Play are fun, but when you do your assignment in class, be sure that your glides are accurate, natural, and not unnecessarily noticeable.

or

Part 1: Prepare eight sentences, 12 to 15 words per sentence. Two of them should be loaded with [w] in initial and medial positions. Two should be loaded with [l] in final positions. Two should be loaded with [r] in various positions. Two scramblers: All the glides, including [hw] and [j] in various positions.

Part 2: Prepare and practice a short, short story, a joke, or a brief anecdote, approximately 50 to 75 words in length. (Drill 38*t* above is an example.)

Suggested Checklist for Assignment 8: See page 277, Appendix B.

NASALS [m] [n] [ŋ]

To practice
your diction,
use the
Pronunciation
Flashcards
on the CD

Hold [ɑ] as in *calm* for a few seconds, and then pinch your nostrils quite firmly. What happens? Nothing.

Now hang on to [m] as in *hum* for a few seconds, and pinch your nostrils. What happens? Everything. You can't make [m] if your nasal passages are stopped.

[m], [n], and [ŋ] are known as nasal consonants because they are directed mostly through the nose rather than the mouth. The soft palate (velum) lowers, hanging something like a curtain, and diverts the breath stream through the nasal cavities as you say the nasals in *my, nine, ring.*

Pronounce [m], [n], and [ŋ] singly and place a finger on one side of your nose. Feel the vibrations? The nasals are voiced, of course.

Want to see your soft palate in action? Watch yourself in a mirror and say [ɑ]—*aw.* Your soft palate will rise. Say [m], and even though you can't see your soft palate perform with this sound, you'll sense that it's lowered. Say *aw-m-aw-m-aw-m* and you'll be able to feel the contrasting actions of the velum.

The nasals not only have superb carrying power, they can be prolonged almost indefinitely. And they're not difficult to make. This probably explains why they're so often taken for granted.

**miss, amber,
balm**

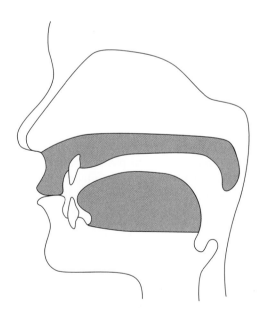

VARIOUS SPELLINGS

gm as in PHLEGM   mb as in LAMB
lm as in PSALM   mm as in SWIMMER
m as in MAY   mn as in CONDEMN

Classification   lips (bilabial)
voiced

Piddling Pursuit

Phonetic	ɑɪ æm piŋk. ˈðɛrfɔr, ɑɪ æm spæm.
Diacritic	run′ing iz ən abnôr′məl akt eksept′ frum en′əmiz and tə t̪ḫə bath′ro͞om.

How to . . .
Tongue	Relaxed and lowered.
Lips	Closed gently, relaxed. Teeth slightly parted.
Soft Palate	Lowered to allow tone to pass through the nasal passages.

WARMER-UPPERS

Initial	Medial	Final
mall	alms	atom
Mars	army	bomb
mask	cement	calm
mat	comic	comb
monk	complain	slam
mend	empty	foam
mayor	farmer	forum
mellow	Tammy	hymn
middle	thumbnail	limb
minnow	tumult	overtime
music	warmth	regime
Myrna	terminal	diaphragm

Faults and Foibles

    A. Disappearing [m]

§§§ **B.** **CONFUSING [m] WITH [n]**

Now for the details. Choose as needed.

A. Disappearing [m]

One of the most obvious of the consonant family, [m] is easy to make. It's also one of the first sounds that you learned. Now and then, however, and especially in careless and hurried speech, the [m] may lose its identity or disappear entirely. This happens most commonly when [m] is followed by another consonant.

    Result: *lamp* [læmp] may sound something like *lap* [læp]

          humble [ˈhʌmbl̩] may sound something like *hu'bl* [ˈhʌbl̩]

39.   Your missing [m] can be restored if you're careful to make a gentle but complete closure of your lips.

    a.
seemly	doomlike	hymnal	pumpkin
sometime	gemlike	ramp	tomcat
I'm trying	lumber	climbed	screamed
whimper	company	employ	themselves

    b.   Compete, don't envy. When in doubt, mumble.

    c.   Most mumblers grumble about the mangled speech in many TV commercials.

    d.   Amber Romney grumbled about the rumlike drink and the clam dip.

    e.   A lamp doesn't complain because it must shine at night.

    f.   If you can't remember a joke, don't dismember it.

    g.   I prefer the word *homemaker* because *housewife* always implies that there may be a wife someplace else.

    h.   Why do "slim chance" and "fat chance" mean the same thing?

i. When a man points a finger at somebody else, he should remember that four of his fingers are pointing at himself.

j. Simple Simon met a pieman. Said Simple Simon to the pieman, "Are your crusts made with butter or margarine?"

Basically a pleasant and mellifluous sound, [m] should be given its full value. *Don't prune it.* It will enrich the sound of your speech.

40. Read these sentences three times. The first time draw out the [m] for three or four seconds. On the second reading, hold it for about two seconds. The third time: No exaggeration, but don't lop it off.

a. Spank: To impress upon the mind from the bottom up.

b. Did you ever have the measles, and if so, how many?

c. What is mind? Doesn't matter. What is matter? Never mind. [Bertrand Russell]

d. A camel looks like a horse that was planned by a committee.

e. If there is no hell, many ministers are obtaining money under false pretenses.

f. Sign in store window: Semiannual after-Christmas sale.

g. As the cow said to the Maine farmer, "Thank you for a warm hand on a cold morning."

h. Oh! Susanna, Oh, don't you cry for me. I've come from Alabama with a banjo on my knee. [Stephen Foster]

i. Every person is a fool for at least five minutes every day. Wisdom consists in not exceeding the limit.

j. The best way to keep children home is to make the home atmosphere pleasant—and let the air out of the tires.

k. The main thing wrong with most monthly budgets is that there's always too much month left at the end of your money.

l. The chief problem about death is the fear there may be no afterlife. Maybe I don't believe in an afterlife, but I am bringing a change of underwear.

m. Married men make the best husbands.

n. Age: Mind over matter. If you don't mind, it doesn't matter.

§§§ *B. CONFUSING [m] WITH [n]*

For discussion and relevant exercises, see page 125.

n

not, doughnut, bone

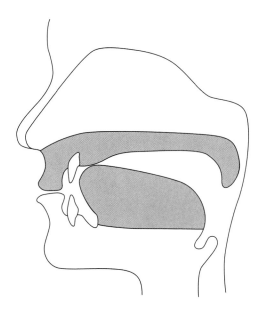

VARIOUS SPELLINGS

gn as in GNAW   nn as in SUNNY
kn as in KNIGHT   pn as in PNEUMATIC
n as in NINE

| **Classification** | tongue and upper gum ridge (lingua-alveolar) |
| | voiced |

Piddling Pursuit

Phonetic   nɑʊ ænd ðɛn ˈsʌmθɪŋ wɪl mek ju ˈkwɛstʃən jʊr ˈvæljuz, bʌt jul sun gɛt ˈovɚ ɪt.

Diacritic   ə pûr′sənz rīt tə smōk endz wâr t̶ẖə nekst pûr′sənz nōz biginz′.

How to . . .
   Tongue   Press the tip of your relaxed tongue against your upper gum ridge as you would for [d] or [t]. The sides of your tongue may touch the inner edges of your teeth.
   Lips   Opened slightly, unrounded, and relaxed.
   Jaw   Dropped slightly.
   Soft Palate   Lower your soft palate so that the air can exit through your nasal passages.

WARMER-UPPERS

Initial	Medial	Final
gnarl	money	barn
gnome	peanut	bin
knack	tennis	brown
knife	couldn't	hone
neck	include	phone
night	intend	scene
nil	lightning	train
nape	opener	rotten
nuke	Wednesday	wooden
normal	canary	machine
nasal	unpleasant	mention
nobody	personality	champagne

Faults and Foibles

    A. Disappearing [n]

A. Disappearing [n]

Like its cousin [m], [n] is repeatedly bruised and battered. When [n] precedes another consonant, it may be dropped altogether or transformed to an [m].

    government, Infantry, can meet, handbag

become

    goverment, imfantry, cameet, hambag

41.   Remind yourself that [n] is a tongue tip–upper gum ridge sound.

    a.

stand	tenth	unpin	lunch
Sunday	ninety	consider	happened
tension	infer	gigantic	unbound
concoct	ungainly	monstrous	environment

    b.   Handsome is as handsome does.
    c.   I was sane once and didn't like it.
    d.   We cannot unthink unless we are insane.
    e.   Nonsense is good only because common sense is almost unheard of.
    f.   You live only once—but if you work it right, once is enough.
    g.   One reason the Ten Commandments are so short and clear is that Moses didn't have to send them through the United Nations.
    h.   There are moments when everything goes well. Don't be frightened. It won't last.
    i.   I'm not just a gardener, I'm a plant manager.

In final and medial positions, [n] is often too thin and slim. Like [m], it's a gratifying sound, and it adds a bit of color and music to your speech. [n] has been likened to the sound of a violin.

42.   Repeat the process suggested in Exercise 40, page 118. When you get to the third step, give [n] its maximum rather than its minimum value.

    a.   I love mankind. It's people I can't stand.
    b.   A celebrity: A person known for his well-knownness.
    c.   The dangerous age is any time between 1 and 99.
    d.   One who dines with the devil should have a long spoon.
    e.   "Ow!"—one of the first words spoken by children with older siblings.
    f.   Tombstone near Old Phoenix: "John Kelly, Saloon-Keeper. This one is on me."

g. Accidents happen every hunting season because both hunter and gun are loaded.
h. There are three seasons in Minnesota: Last winter, this winter, and next winter.
i. If your parents didn't have any children, there's a good chance you won't have any.
j. The only person who makes money following the races is the one who does so with a broom and shovel.
k. Have as many enemies in front of you as you can handle, but never leave one behind you if you can help it.
l. It is futile to build a fence around a cemetery, for those inside can't come out and those outside don't want to get in.
m. Oinks: Only income, no kids.
Sinks: Single income, no kids.
Pinks: Paltry income, no kids.
Winks: What income? No kids.

[ŋ] **Phonetic**   Diacritic ŋ — ng

**link,
ding-a-ling**

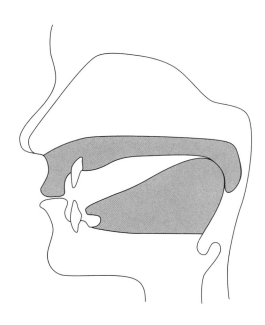

VARIOUS SPELLINGS

n as in SINK	ng as in THING
nc as in UNCLE	ngue as in MERINGUE

Classification   back of tongue and soft palate (linguavelar)
                         voiced

Piddling Pursuit

Phonetic   ˈsɪŋɪŋ ˈlɛsənz ɑr lɑɪk ˈbɑdɪbɪldɪŋ fɔr jur ˈlærɪŋks.

Diacritic   hol′iwo͞od iz līk bē′ing nō′wâr and tôk′ing tə nō′bodi əbout′ nuth′ing.

How to . . .

Tongue	Raise the back of your tongue so that it touches the lowered soft palate. The tongue tip rests behind the lower front teeth. The position of your tongue is very much like that used for [k] and [g].
Lips	Open and unrounded.
Jaw	Moderately dropped.
Soft Palate	Lower your soft palate so that the air can exit through your nasal passages.

WARMER-UPPERS

Initial	Medial	Final
	rink	hang
	brink	string
	sphinx	wing
	bingo	tongue
	banker	betting
	English	kissing
	fingertip	lusting
	mangle	rapping
	single	courting
	tangle	darling
	thinker	willing
	anxious	flapping

Faults and Foibles

A. Substituting [n] for [ŋ]

§§§ **B. ADDING** *ng-click* [ŋg]

§§§ **C. CONFUSING** [ŋ] **AND** [n]

Now for the details. Choose as needed.

A. Substituting [n] for [ŋ]

He: You dancin'?

She: You askin'?

He: I'm askin'.

She: I'm dancin'.

The misguided souls who talk this way are victims of articulatory herpes. Substituting [n], as in *sin*, for final [ŋ], as in *sing*, won't necessarily make your speech incomprehensible, but it will label your way of talking as flawed and careless.

> In their more casual press conferences, three U.S. presidents were or are *–ng* abusers.

Educated and cultured people may pronounce *Tuesday* as *tooz-day* ['tuzdɪ] instead of *t-youz-day* ['tjuzdɪ], and they may pronounce *when* as *wen* [wɛn] instead of *hwen* [hwɛn]. Very few intelligent listeners will criticize. But those who persist in saying *comin', goin', thinkin', sleepin'* may be askin' for trouble. They'll generally attract the wrong kind of attention to their speech, not to mention unfavorable criticism.

College graduate job seekers, otherwise well qualified, have been rejected at interviews because their speech was marred by this particular mannerism. One CEO of a large corporation was specific. "An *–ng* dropper has as much chance of getting a job with this firm as a candidate who comes to the job interview wearing a baseball cap backward."

This fault is known as "dropping the g"—a totally inaccurate description, by the way, because there is rarely a [g] plosive in most [ŋ] sounds.

Most sportscasters and jocks are unfamiliar with [ŋ]. Over a 10-year period in Denver, Colorado, sportscasters were monitored daily. Sixteen out of 17 consistently substituted [n] for [ŋ]. Of the jocks being interviewed, 140 out of 150 were guilty.

Most country music artists would rather die than sound a final [ŋ]. Popular singer George Strait, for example, was once at the top of the charts with his recording of "If You Ain't Lovin' You Ain't Livin'." And Gary Stewart does "She's Actin' Single and I'm Drinkin' Double."

Why do so many people cheat on the [ŋ] sounds?

- Laziness. [n] is a much easier sound to make than [ŋ].
- They're not aware that they're doing it.
- They don't want to be "different" from others.

43. Say slowly [n-ŋ-n-ŋ-n-ŋ-n-ŋ].

Notice the basic difference in tongue position between the two sounds?
[n] is formed with the front part, the tip, or the point of your tongue.
[ŋ] is shaped with the back of your tongue.
Remember this distinction as you practice these:

> I had a chance to appear on the David Letterman show a few years ago. He asked me to critique his speech. I commented that he was an "ng-dropper." His reply? "So does everybody else on TV." My rebuttal: "Everybody else? Such as Tom Brokaw, Diane Sawyer, Peter Jennings, Jane Pauley, Dan Rather?
> Letterman shrugged his shoulders.
> I haven't been asked back.

a.
sin–sing	lawn–long	gun–gung	tan–tang
run–rung	hun–hung	gone–gong	ton–tongue
sun–sung	thin–thing	pin–ping	win–wing
ban–bang	bin–bing	pan–pang	ran–rang

b. Read this nonsense material slowly. (Note: Read *across* the columns, from left to right.) Concentrate on the difference between the articulation of [n] and [ŋ].

Get the feel of [n] as a *tip-of-the-tongue* sound and of [ŋ] as a *back-of-the-tongue* sound.

fan	fang	fan–in	fang–in	fang–ing
sin	sing	sin–in	sing–in	sing–ing
ban	bang	ban–in	bang–in	bang–ing
gon	gong	gon–in	gong–in	gong–ing

The person who insists on saying *wearin'* for *wearing* would have no problem at all if asked to pronounce only the last four letters of the word. He or she would certainly say *ring* rather than *rin.*

Exaggerate as you practice this material. The words are divided in a purely mechanical fashion. Wherever you see two diagonal lines, pause for a second or two, eliminating any kind of vocal sound.

c. ring / / ring / / ring: fear / / ring   soar / / ring   hear / / ring
   ring / / ring / / ring: bar / / ring   sour / / ring   pour / / ring
   ring / / ring / / ring: mar / / ring   stir / / ring   star / / ring

d. Now, eliminating the pause that divides the word, connect the two syllables and say them rather rapidly. Are you able to make a firm [ŋ] at the end of each word?

fearing	soaring	hearing
barring	souring	pouring
marring	stirring	starring

44. Contrast negative with positive practice. Be sure that you can feel [n] as a tip-of-the-tongue sound and [ŋ] as a back-of-the-tongue sound. [ŋ], in other words, is a *throaty* sound.

   a. A *rollin* eye, a *rollin* heart.
   aa. A *rolling* eye, a *rolling* heart.
   b. If your ear's *burnin,* someone's *talkin* about you.
   bb. If your ear's *burning,* someone's *talking* about you.
   c. Don't knock *knockin.* It opens many doors.
   cc. Don't knock *knocking.* It opens many doors.

    d.   A boat that isn't *bein* rocked isn't *movin.*

  dd.   A boat that isn't *being* rocked isn't *moving.*

    e.   Friends are lost by *callin* often and *callin* seldom.

  ee.   Friends are lost by *calling* often and *calling* seldom.

    f.   *Havin* great success too soon is like *eatin* the *frostin* before the cake is baked.

  ff.   *Having* great success too soon is like *eating* the *frosting* before the cake is baked.

45.   The nasal [ŋ] is found only in central or final positions. As you work with this material, be supercautious. Don't let [n] weasel its way in and take over for [ŋ].

    a.   In teaching, the greatest sin is to be boring.

    b.   Gambling: The sure way of getting nothing for something.

    c.   Art is about making something out of nothing and selling it. [Howard Stern]

    d.   Acting is merely the art of keeping a large group of people from coughing.

    e.   The cost of living is going up, and the chance of living is going down.

    f.   I'm living so far beyond my income that we may almost be said to be living apart.

    g.   Some folks get what's coming to them by waiting; others, while crossing the street.

    h.   Health nuts are going to feel real stupid someday lying in hospitals dying of nothing.

    i.   There is no fun in having nothing to do. The fun is having lots to do and not doing it.

    j.   Having read so much about the bad effects of smoking, they decided to give up reading.

    k.   Some people spend the day complaining of a headache, and the night drinking the wine that gives it.

    l.   If things always have a way of getting better, why is it that funeral parlors are doing such excellent business?

    m.   Unhappiness is being trapped on a rainy highway with a slow-moving truck in front of you and a fast-moving truck coming up behind you.

    n.   A digital clock is something they have in an office so you can tell how long you must wait before you can start stopping work by stalling until.

    o.   Thanks to jogging, more people are collapsing in perfect health than ever before.

    p.   I got a burning yearning for learning after a bronco threw me on my head one day. That's when I realized what a long, hard road cowpunching is. [Cowboy poet Paul Patterson]

    q.   Retreating and beating and meeting and sheeting,
        Delaying and straying and playing and spraying,
        Advancing and prancing and glancing and dancing,
        Recoiling, turmoiling, toiling, and boiling,
        And gleaming and steaming and streaming and beaming,
        And rushing and flushing and brushing and gushing,
        And flapping and rapping and clapping and slapping,
        And curling and whirling and purling and twirling,
        And thumping and plumping and bumping and jumping,
        And dashing and flashing and splashing and clashing,
        And is never ending, but always descending,
        All at once and all o'er, with a mighty uproar,
        And this way the water comes down at Lodore. [Robert Southey]

§§§ *B. ADDING ng-click [ŋg]*

For discussion and relevant exercises, see page 125.

§§§ *C. CONFUSING [ŋ] AND [n]*

For discussion and relevant exercises, see page 126.

[m]

§§§ B. CONFUSING [m] WITH [n]

If Spanish is your first language, you may substitute [m] for [n] or vice versa.

from [frʌm] becomes [frʌn]

lane [len] becomes [lem]

[m] Say it. Your tongue is relaxed on the floor of your mouth. Lips are closed.
[n] Say it. The tip of your tongue rests against the gum ridge. Lips slightly open.

46. Monitor your tongue and lip positions as you do these word pairs:

a. map–nap   met–net   nail–mail
    mill–nil   mod–nod   knoll–mole
    mitt–knit   knack–Mack   knob–mob

Don't worry about tongue and lip positions as you do these. Read them as if you were talking to somebody.

b. Sometimes the devil is a gentleman.
c. One man's meat is another man's poison.
d. No bees, no honey, no work, no money.
e. Men may meet but mountains never.
f. To become a champion, fight one more round.
g. If you wish to grow thinner, diminish your dinner.
h. Never put off until tomorrow what you can do the day after tomorrow.

[ŋ]

§§§ B. ADDING *ng-click* [ŋg]

Say *singer, linger.*

Both words have [ŋ]. Did you notice, however, that [ŋ] is not pronounced the same way?

In *singer,* the [ŋ] is simply the nasal sound we've been working on. There is no plosive [g] in the word. You say *sing*-er [ˈsɪŋɚ].

In *linger,* however, the [ŋ] is a combination of the nasal [ŋ] and the plosive [g]. You say *ling-ger* [ˈlɪŋgɚ].

No wonder, then, that we sporadically have trouble with [ŋ]. Fiendish English spelling doesn't help either. To add to the turmoil, in certain foreign languages and dialects, [ŋ] is almost invariably followed by a [g] or a [k].

Individuals whose language backgrounds include Yiddish, Russian and other Slavic languages, Spanish, Hungarian, or Italian—even though they may be American-born—often add the villainous "Long GUY-land click."

gong becomes *gong-G* or *gong-K*

ring becomes *ring-G* or *ring-K*

How can the hard [g] be purged?

Your sense of hearing and feeling will help. You'll remember that the back of your tongue is raised against the velum or soft palate to make [ŋ]. Say *sing* and you'll feel the contact.

Say *sing* again, but this time listen quite conscientiously to the nasal sound, extend it a few seconds, and as you're holding [ŋ], pull your tongue away from the velum. If this is done, you won't add the hard [g].

47. Read this material slowly, always drawing out the [ŋ]. Don't forget to pull your tongue away from the velum *during* the production of the sound rather than *after*. You'll eliminate the click.

a.
thing	sing	ring	sting
bang	long	bong	hang
wrong	rang	clang	king
lung	wing	young	throng

b. The bells of hell go ting-a-ling-a-ling
    For you and not for me.
  For the angels sing-a-ling-a-ling,
    They've got the goods for me.
  O death where is thy sting-a-ling-a-ling?
    O grave thy victory?
  The bells of hell go ting-a-ling-a-ling
    For you and not for me. [American Salvationist Hymn]

48. Now that you've been told how to remove the after-click, let's put it back in! You do *not* use it with such words as *long, young,* and *strong*. But you *do* use it with the comparative and superlative forms:

longer [ˈlɔŋgɚ]   *longest* [ˈlɔŋgəst]
stronger [ˈstrɔŋgɚ]   *strongest* [ˈstrɔŋgəst]

If you find [ŋ] within the root or the middle of a word, it's generally pronounced with the click: [ŋ-g].

finger	monger	kangaroo	English
fungus	anger	mingle	tingle
hunger	single	angry	bungle
jingle	jungle	angle	extinguish

And to spoil the fun—the exceptions:

gingham, Washington, hangar, strength, length

Even outstanding speakers slip on these pesky and temperamental sounds. When in doubt, consult your dictionary.

§§§ C. CONFUSING [ŋ] AND [n]

If you pronounce

ban [bæn] as [bæŋ]
fan [fæn] as [fæŋ]

perhaps Spanish was your first language.
  If you pronounce

sing [sɪŋ] as [sɪn]
thing [θɪŋ] as [θɪn]

perhaps Japanese, Korean, Russian, or Vietnamese was your first language.
  Remember?

[n] is a front-part-of-tongue sound.

[ŋ] is a back-part-of-tongue sound.

49. Back up and select drills from Exercises 43–45. It's important that you *feel* as well as hear the difference as you practice the material.

GRAB BAG: PRACTICE MATERIAL FOR THE NASALS

Don't neglect your nasals! Nourish them!

As a reminder:

[m]: your lips must be firmly closed.

[n]: the tip of your tongue must be placed against your upper gum ridge.

[ŋ]: the rear of your tongue must make contact with your velum.

50. The Triple Play works beautifully with these sounds. And at the third level—even without the overplaying—make [m], [n], and [ŋ] glisten. Above all, be accurate.

   a. Two wrongs are only the beginning.
   b. Dentistry means drilling, filling, and billing.
   c. If I've learned one thing, it's always be nice to snipers.
   d. You know that the vacation is over when gun stores start having back-to-school sales.
   e. The male mind does not believe in medical treatment, except in certain such clear-cut situations as decapitation. [Dave Barry]
   f. We all learn by experience, but some of us have to go to summer school.
   g. What this country needs is a good five-second television commercial.
   h. My mother loved children—she would have given anything if I'd been one.
   i. The most important words in the English language seem to be *I, me, mine,* and *money.*
   j. Forgive me my nonsense as I also forgive the nonsense of those who think they talk sense.
   k. Basically my wife is immature. I'd be home in the bath and she'd come in and sink my boats.
   l. If you drive with one arm, you end up either walking up a church aisle or being carried up it.
   m. Nobody will ever win the battle of the sexes. There's just too much fraternizing with the enemy.
   n. Commencement speaker in Michigan: "My advice to young people going out into the world today—don't go!"
   o. Man wanted to work in dynamite factory. Must be willing to travel.
   p. Is it true that cannibals don't eat clowns because they taste funny?
   q. As I learn to trust the universe, I no longer need to carry a gun.
   r. Drink to me only with thine eyes. It's cheaper that way.
   s. An oxymoron is a figure of speech that uses seeming contradictions. Examples: *resident alien, found missing, legally drunk, military intelligence, honest politician, clearly misunderstood, diet ice cream.*

Assignment 9: Nasals

Prepare material containing numerous nasal consonants: [m], [n], [ŋ]. If you've had no special difficulty with these sounds, stress them slightly as you practice to bring out their pleasant quality, but avoid gross exaggeration. If you've found any of them troublesome—and [n] and [ŋ] in certain words, especially the latter as a final sound, are often faulty—work for sounds that are accurate and correct.

or

Part 1: Prepare eight sentences, 12 to 15 words per sentence. Two of them should be loaded with [m] in various positions, two loaded with [n] in various positions, and four loaded with [ŋ] in final positions.

Part 2: Prepare a short, short story, a joke, or an anecdote, approximately 50 to 75 words in length. (Drill 50s is an example.) Tell your story rather than reading it word for word. Do it naturally without exaggeration.

Suggested Checklist for Assignment 9: See page 279, Appendix B.

FRICATIVES [f] [v] [θ] [ð] [s] [z] [ʃ] [ʒ] [h]

To practice
your diction,
use the
Pronunciation
Flashcards
on the CD

Say *sizzle*. You'll notice that you're putting obstructions in your mouth that interrupt the outgoing breath stream. The air is forced through a small, narrow opening or slit. A friction noise is produced.

The fricatives have been described as the fizzers, hissers, buzzers, and blasters of the consonant tribe. If improperly produced, they *can* be noisy and offensive. Never allow yourself to expel too much air on the fricatives. These sounds have excellent carrying power. They can be sustained. But they should always be "underdone" rather than "overdone." (Dictionary symbols are shown to the right of bracketed phonetic symbols when the two differ. In the sections that follow, dictionary symbols will be shown on the right side of the page when they differ from phonetic symbols.)

Voiceless	Voiced
[f]	[v]
[θ] th	[ð] t́h
[s]	[z]
[ʃ] sh	[ʒ] zh
[h]	

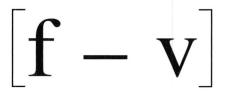

**fat, afford,
staff**

**van, never,
have**

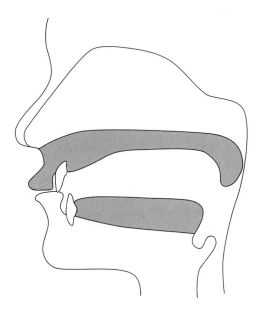

VARIOUS SPELLINGS

[f]
f as in FIN
ff as in SUFFER
gh as in TOUGH
lf as in CALF
ph as in PHOTOGRAPHER

[v]
f as in OF
ve as in SHELVE
v as in VIM
vv as in FLIVVER

Classification	lower lip and upper teeth (labiodental)
	[f] voiceless
	[v] voiced

Piddling Pursuit

Phonetic	ə prəˈfɛsɚ mʌst hæv ə ˈθiəri æz ə dɔg mʌst hæv fliz.
Diacritic	ɪf īv ōn′li wun līf, let mē liv it az ə blond.

How to . . .

Tongue	Rest your tongue on the floor of your mouth. The tongue tip is near or touches the lower front teeth.
Lips	Raise your lower lip, drawing it inward, and place it lightly against the front edges of your upper teeth. Force out air between the lower lip and upper teeth.
Jaw	Almost closed.

WARMER-UPPERS [f]

Initial	Medial	Final
farm	affair	chef
fast	afraid	cough
feed	awful	graph
fell	defeat	half
flip	jiffy	lymph
ford	laughter	off
frame	muffle	rough
freeze	refund	surf
fluid	soften	belief
future	twelfth	enough
pharmacy	telephone	giraffe

WARMER-UPPERS [v]

Initial	Medial	Final
vile	avoid	Eve
vault	convent	dive
very	David	groove
veto	devil	leave
valley	eleven	prove
vehicle	gavel	salve
Venus	having	slave
viper	nervous	above
vodka	rival	concave
vowel	shovel	naive
vanilla	waver	olive

Faults and Foibles

    A. Omitting or blurring [f] or [v]

§§§ **B. SUBSTITUTING [f], [p], OR [b] FOR [v]**

Now for the details. Choose as needed.

A. Omitting or blurring [f] or [v]

A lotta people have a lotta free time.

A lot of people also love to carve up that poor, impotent little word *of.* True, it's runty and inconspicuous, but that doesn't justify squashing it. *Of,* although spelled with an *f,* is pronounced with a *v.* Don't hit that [v] too hard, however. If the word following *of* begins with a voiceless sound (glass of *sh*erry, full of *p*ep), your [v] sound should be softened.

51. Go over this material slowly a few times, and then gradually increase your speed to a normal rate. Be conscious of the lip-to-teeth articulation as you make a *v* at the end of each *of.*

    a. | full of people | bunch of girls | full of smoke |
        | bag of peanuts | tired of him | one of those |
        | lots of money | rows of seats | box of candy |
        | half of those | can of soup | pat of butter |

    Bear in mind that a clean-cut [f] or [v] depends mostly on the activity of the lower lip. If your lip is protruded or drawn back too far, you'll be producing fuzzy fricatives. Your lower lip *must* make an easy contact with the bottom edge of the upper teeth as you articulate these fricatives. And don't spurn or slaughter those *of*'s.

    b. | fact | valve | fluff | dove |
        | fair | suffer | cover | above |
    c. Smoking is one of the leading causes of statistics.
    d. Van Frank doesn't love money, but he is very fond of it.
    e. Never, never laugh at live dragons.
    f. I've never been drunk, but I've often been overserved. [Robin Williams]
    g. I don't eat snails. I prefer fast food.
    h. It isn't the cough that carries you off. It's the coffin they carry you off in.
    i. You can sort of be married, you can sort of be divorced, you can sort of be living together, but you can't sort of have a baby.
    j. There are Ten Commandments, right? Well, it's sort of like an exam. You get 8 out of 10 right, you're just about top of the class.
    k. Advice to people who have fallen in love: Fall out.
    l. "Half a leaf is better than none," as Eve said to Adam.
    m. Change is predictable, except from vending machines.

§§§ B. SUBSTITUTING [f], [p], OR [b] FOR [v]

For discussion and relevant exercises, see page 144.

[θ – ð] Phonetic

Diacritic th – t̶h̶

thin, wealthy,   **their, mother,**
ninth   **lathe**

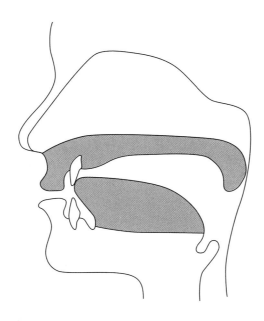

VARIOUS SPELLINGS	θ	ð
	th as in THANKS	th as in THEM
		the as in SEETHE

Classification   tongue tip between teeth (linguadental)
                       [θ] voiceless
                       [ð] voiced

Piddling Pursuit

Phonetic   ðɛr ɪz no sʌtʃ θɪŋ æz ə ˈprɪtɪ gʊd ˈɑmlɪt.

Diacritic   az t̶h̶ə fo͞ol thingks, so͞ t̶h̶ə bel klingks.

How to . . .
  Tongue   Relaxed and relatively flat. Place the tip lightly against the back or edges of your upper front teeth. **Or** thrust the flattened tongue tip slightly between your teeth so that the upper side makes a soft contact with the lower edges of the upper teeth. Drive the breath stream between your tongue tip and the teeth.
  Lips   Parted.
  Jaw   Relaxed, slightly opened.

WARMER-UPPERS [θ]

Initial	Medial	Final
thaw	depths	bath
theme	athlete	birth
thief	ether	growth
third	breathy	moth
thistle	plaything	sixth
thorn	ruthless	south
thought	toothbrush	teeth
thrill	withheld	warmth
thunder	youthful	wrath
Thursday	bathrobe	wreath
theater	pathetic	zenith
thimble	enthusiastic	fortieth

WARMER-UPPERS [ð]

Initial	Medial	Final
that	breathing	bathe
the	brethren	clothe
thee	clothing	lithe
their	farther	loathe
then	heathen	scathe
they	leather	scythe
this	neither	smooth
those	rhythm	swathe
thou	smoothy	tithe
though	southern	wreathe
thyself	weather	writhe
therefore	another	soothe

Faults and Foibles

    A. Confusing voiceless [θ] and voiced [ð]

§ **B. Substituting [t] and [d] for [θ] and [ð]**

§§§ **C. SUBSTITUTING [s] AND [z] FOR [θ] AND [ð]**

Now for the details. Choose as needed.

A. Confusing voiceless [θ] and voiced [ð]

Spelling never tells you which is which. Your ear does, however. It's no problem hearing the difference between the two sounds. There seems to be a trend toward using the lighter voiceless [θ] at the expense of the heavier voiced [ð]. It requires less effort.

    Actually, most of the time we use the right sound in the right place. Our built-in radar tells us which is which. Even so, we occasionally confuse them.

    Rules are almost always spoiled by the exceptions, but here are a few that may help:

Use the voiceless [θ] if—

- *th* follows a voiced consonant: *tenth, panther, warmth.*

- Verbs, nouns, adjectives begin with *th: thicken, thunder, thorough.*

Use the voiced [ð] if—

- A word ends in *the: teethe, sheathe, tithe.*
- A word ends in *ther: hither, brother, lather.*
- Pronouns, adverbs, conjunctions begin with *th: them, thus, though.*

52. As you go over these drill sentences, make sure that you hear *and* feel the difference between [θ] and [ð]. The voiceless [θ] is only a gust of air—no rumble. The voiced [ð] is always accompanied by a minirumble and a vibration in your throat.

    a.   Nothing is certain but death and the IRS.
    b.   Things are not as bad as they seem. They're worse.
    c.   When you get there—Death Valley—there's no there there.
    d.   What, oh what, is thought? It's the only thing, and yet nothing.
    e.   My mother and father are cousins. That's why I look so much alike.
    f.   The person who thinketh by the inch and speaketh by the yard should be kicketh by the foot.
    g.   The trouble with some people is that they don't think until they hear what they've had to say.
    h.   A sixth of the population celebrates the Fourth of July by buying a fifth on the third.
    i.   Many things are opened by mistake, but none so often as the mouth.
    j.   They who talketh about what they knoweth will also talketh about what they knoweth not. [Francis Bacon]
    k.   In California everybody goes to a therapist, is a therapist, or is a therapist going to a therapist.
    l.   He who driveth a car and looketh upon a woman loseth a fender.

§ *B. Substituting* [t] *and* [d] *for* [θ] *and* [ð]

Some native-born Americans, mostly easterners, permit the tongue to make too firm a contact against the edges of the teeth. A sound something like [t] or [d] will result.

You may have heard about the Bronx-born Hollywood star who achieved immortality with his delivery of the line "Yonduh lies duh castle of muh fadduh."

Hollywood makes movies in cycles. Gangster movies—*GoodFellas, Godfather III,* and *The Untouchables*—often reappear on your TV screen. You'll recall that some of the bad boys couldn't say *these, them,* or *mother.* They used a Brooklyn Mafia–Chicago mobster dialect that turned [θ] and [ð] into *dese, dem, mudder.*

Regardless of your birthplace—Boston or Bosnia; Paris, Michigan, or Paris, France—if you're having problems with [θ] and [ð], practice the following exercises.

53. Try sticking out the flattened tip of your tongue between your teeth on [t] sounds. For [t], however, don't let your tongue protrude, but place the tip of it against your upper gum ridge.

    a.   thrust–trust–thrust–thrust
        thread–tread–thread–thread
        three–tree–three–three
        through–true–through–through
        thug–tug–thug–thug

And now try this:

    b.   Extend your tongue so that the broad part of it touches your upper front teeth. Force out air as you gradually retract your tongue until the tip reaches the upper teeth. When you make a healthy sound, try the material in this exercise. Be certain that the contact is gentle for good [θ] and [ð] sounds, but solid for [t] and [d].

thin–tin	oath–oat	death–debt	mother–mudder
thought–taught	thank–tank	three–tree	their–dare
thigh–tie	theme–team	author–otter	breathe–breed
through–true	worthy–wordy	lather–latter	those–doze

    c.   Let not your tongue cut your throat.
    d.   The Lord giveth and the IRS taketh away.
    e.   The best throw with the dice is to throw them away.
    f.   Listen or thy tongue will keep thee deaf. [Native American proverb]
    g.   After the first death, there is no other. [Dylan Thomas]
    h.   Let me keep myself open to other people's ideas, wrong though they may be.

i.   Don't let your mouth get in front of your mind.

j.   The road to good intentions is paved with hell.

k.   I believe that I am in hell. Therefore, I am there. [Arthur Rimbaud]

l.   A person with a little learning is like the frog who thinks its puddle a great sea.

m.   Miss Diss said this: "Thanks for putting the tanks near the three trees."

§§§ C. SUBSTITUTING [s] AND [z] FOR [θ] AND [ð]

For discussion and relevant exercises, see page 144.

[S – Z] Phonetic

say, rusty,   **zap, fizzer,**
nice   **jazz**

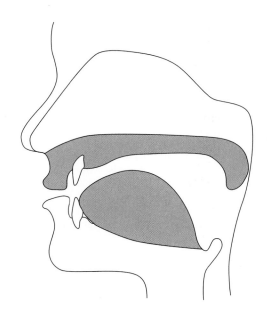

VARIOUS SPELLINGS	[s]	[z]
	c as in CITY	s as in FLEES
	ce as in ACCENT	se as in NOSE
	ps as in PSYCHO	ss as in POSSESS
	s as in SIGHT	x as in XENIA
	sc as in SCENE	z as in ZANE
	sch as in SCHISM	zz as in FUZZ
	ss as in LASS	
	x as in FIX	
	z as in BLITZ	

Classification   tip or blade of tongue, gum ridge (lingua-alveolar)
                                    [s] voiceless
                                    [z] voiced

Piddling Pursuit

Phonetic   ʌv ɔl ðə θɪŋz aɪv lɔst, aɪ mɪs maɪ maɪnd ðə most.

Diacritic   ə sûr'mən iz sel'dəm az long az it sēmz.

How to . . .
(There are two or possibly three ways to produce a satisfactory [s].)

Tongue	Think of [t]. Now retract your tongue a little bit so that it doesn't touch the gum ridge. Raise the sides of your tongue. The sides should lightly touch the middle and back upper teeth. Point your tongue toward the cutting edges of the front teeth. Position the tongue tip approximately a quarter inch behind the upper teeth. Direct a thin stream of air down a shallow groove in the middle of the tongue. (Some speakers produce an acceptable [s] by aiming the tongue tip at or gently touching either the upper or the lower gum ridge.)
Lips	Slightly open and spread.
Jaw	Almost closed.

The most troublesome and the most frequently defective sound in our language is probably [s]. (Whatever is said here about the articulation of [s] generally applies also to [z].) Producing an acceptable [s] sound requires not only a keen sense of hearing, but also rather precise adjustments of the articulators.

WARMER-UPPERS [s]

Initial	Medial	Final
sag	icy	bus
sip	bracer	crease
scent	blossom	cross
psalm	receive	dice
strum	whistle	fleece
Scrooge	Esther	floss
psych	lonesome	grass
saddle	decimal	lice
circle	excellent	mix
superb	sassafras	toss
schedule	Tennessee	kicks
science	Massachusetts	amiss

WARMER-UPPERS [z]

Initial	Medial	Final
Zak	causeway	boys
zip	cozy	buzz
zinc	design	fleas
Zeke	hazard	fuse
Xerox	lazy	fuzz
Zelda	nozzle	his
zombie	pleasant	please
Zurich	razor	rise
xylophone	resign	whose
Zanzibar	resume	arouse
zodiac	sneezing	dispose
zoology	whimsy	suppose

Faults and Foibles

    A. Overemphasizing [s] and [z]

    B. Omitting or distorting [s] in clusters: *str, skr, sts, sks*

§§§   **C. MISPRONOUNCING [s] AS THE FINAL LETTER OR SOUND**

PLEASE NOTE

Native speakers may also mispronounce a final [s]. To avoid repetition, the discussion and relevant exercises will be listed only once. See page 145.

Now for the details. Choose as needed.

A. Overemphasizing [s] and [z]

Hissers? Fizzers? Breath guzzlers? These two fricatives are one-sound cyclones.

    Listen to a group of people recite material in unison—responsive readings by a congregation are a fine example—and you'll hear waves of hisses that belong in a snake pit.

> Fine speaking voice notwithstanding, Sean Connery has a defective, slurpy [s] sound. Robert DeNiro also has a prominent, thick [s].

    A majority of hissers are probably articulating the sound correctly. What they're doing incorrectly is simply producing too much of it. Even a respectable, normal [s] is rackety and turbulent. If you're making an [s] that sounds like a tornado, reduce your breath pressure. *Don't* emphasize the sound. *Don't* hang on to it. Usually [s] should be cut short, touched lightly and briefly, but not allowed to vanish entirely.

54. For contrast and to help you hear the difference between a good, skimpy [s], and a long, fat [s], read these word pairs aloud. Build up the [s] in the first word of each pair as the spelling indicates. Make it sound like a minor monsoon.

In the second word of the pair, tap the sound as if touching a hot stove, and hurry on to the following vowel sounds. Stress the vowels instead.

    a. s-s-s-s-see–see   s-s-s-s-sad–sad
        s-s-s-s-so–so   s-s-s-s-saw–saw
        s-s-s-s-say–say   S-S-S-S-Sue–Sue

Work for an unobtrusive [s] and [z]. Don't blow them to smithereens. Condense and compress. Make them quiet.

b.	Sam	zone	zigzag	hiss	fizz
	sort	Zulu	using	face	has
	sod	zany	music	lass	craze

    c. Worry is as useless as sawing sawdust.
    d. Say it simply or simply do not say it.
    e. Sometimes it's worse to win a fight than to lose.
    f. If swimming is so good for your figure, how do you explain whales?
    g. There's an old southern saying: If it isn't busted, why fix it?
    h. Scratch the surface, and if you're lucky, you'll find more surface.
    i. It's what the guests say as they swing out of the driveway that counts.
    j. The noblest of all dogs is the hot dog. It feeds the hand that bites it.
    k. Don't sweat the small stuff because it's all small stuff.
    l. Cats are smarter than dogs. You can't get eight cats to pull a sled through snow.
    m. My boss and I have an understanding: I don't try to do his job, and he doesn't either.
    n. Please be careful about calling yourself an expert. An ex is a has-been, and a spurt is a drip under pressure.
    o. Many a man owes his success to his first wife and his second wife to his success.
    p. Vodka is colorless, odorless, tasteless, and too much of it leaves you senseless.

B. Omitting or distorting [s] in clusters: str, skr, sts, sks

> What's the hardest-to-pronounce short word in the English language? *Sixths.* If you say it this way: S-I-K-S, it's easy, but it's wrong. Now say it this way: S-I-K-S-TH-S, and you're right. (But try it rapidly and see what happens.)

Asks is a surprisingly tricky little word. No wonder you occasionally hear "The teacher *axe* questions." By itself [s] is a pesky sound, but hook *tr, kr, ks,* or *ts* onto it, and your tongue has to perform double somersaults to get the sound out of your mouth.

55. [str]: If you're in a rush to get to the [t], you'll flatten your tongue too soon. *Street* [strit] may sound like *shtreet* [ʃtrit].

Reading across the line, say the first word with a complete pause, as indicated. Say the second with no pause. In each one make the [s] sharp and short, and make a brisk [t] and a clear [r].

s | | trike–strike	s | | traw–straw	s | | tring–string
s | | trut–strut	s | | trip–strip	s | | trive-strive
s | | troll–stroll	s | | tray–stray	s | | trength–strength

56. [skr]: If you target the [k] too quickly you'll inadvertently raise the back of the tongue. *Scrap* [skræp] becomes *shkrap* [ʃkræp].

Using the procedure suggested in Exercise 55, try these. The [k] needs to be brittle.

s | | cratch–scratch	s | | cruple–scruple	s | | cript–script
s | | cram–scram	s | | crimp–scrimp	s | | crub–scrub
s | | crod–scrod	s | | crag–scrag	s | | creech–screech

57. [sts]: If you drop the [t] altogether you'll say *fiss* [fis] instead of *fist* [fist]. By now you know all about plosive [t]. Try the double pauses below and restore it.

ghos | | t | | s–ghosts	bus | | t | | s–busts	las | | t | | s–lasts
hos | | t | | s–hosts	mis | | t | | s–mists	thirs | | t | | s–thirsts
cas | | t | | s–casts	lus | | t | | s–lusts	nes | | t | | s–nests
lis | | t | | s–lists	mas | | t | | s–masts	cys | | t | | s–cysts

58. [sks]: If you omit the first [s], you'll say *flaks* [flæks] in place of *flasks* [flæsks]. Don't overlook the first [s] in each cluster.

mas | | k | | s–masks	dis | | k | | s–disks	flas | | k | | s–flasks
bus | | k | | s–busks	ris | | k | | s–risks	whis | | k | | s–whisks
bas | | k | | s–basks	mus | | k | | s–musks	des | | k | | s–desks
tas | | k | | s–tasks	hus | | k | | s–husks	fris | | k | | s–frisks

59. Here are some "scramblers." Read them slowly and carefully. Each cluster has a medial plosive. Are you sounding each [t] and [k]? Two of the clusters begin and end with [s]. Touch the fricatives as though you were plucking a harp string, but don't smear them.

After you've read the material slowly, repeat and try a conversational rate.

a. Paul Stratton strolled down the Stratford Street.
b. Scrooge screamed when the streaked ghost scraped its chains.
c. To show strength, scrawny knights wore masks in their jousts.
d. The hosts frisk everybody and then empty all flasks into casks.
e. If Strom scraps while playing Scrabble, will he scream and scrawl afterward?
f. Sam jests when he insists that lobbyists and Marxists are ideal guests at roasts.
g. A widow had this descriptive inscription put on her late husband's tombstone: "Rest in peace—until we meet again."

§§§ C. MISPRONOUNCING [s] AS THE FINAL LETTER OR SOUND

For discussion and relevant exercises, see page 145.

[ʃ – ʒ] Phonetic   Diacritic Sh – Zh

shall, insurance, smash   **Jacques, fusion, massage**

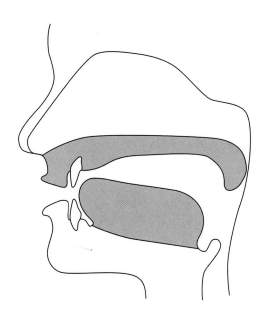

VARIOUS SPELLINGS	**[ʃ]**	**[ʒ]**
	c as in OCEAN	j as in JEAN (French)
	ch as in CHAMPAGNE	ge as in ENTOURAGE
	ci as in SOCIAL	s as in TREASURE
	s as in SUGAR	si as in PERSIA
	sc as in CONSCIENCE	z as in AZURE
	sch as in SCHNAPPS	
	sh as in SHELVE	
	ss as in ISSUE	
	ti as in RATION	

Classification   tip or blade of tongue behind gum ridge (linguapalatal)
[ʃ] voiceless
[ʒ] voiced

Piddling Pursuit

Phonetic   lɑɪf—ə ˈplɛʒɚ? Its ˈæʃɪz tu ˈæʃɪz.

Diacritic   shel′i selz bāzh sē-shelz tōō zhä-zhä.

How to . . .	
Tongue	Draw your tongue back slightly farther for [ʃ] than for [s]. Flatten the tongue somewhat. Point the tip toward the lower front teeth or the upper gum ridge. The sides should touch the inner borders of the upper back teeth. Direct the airstream over a relatively wide but shallow central passage rather than through the narrow groove that characterizes [s].
Lips	More protruded and puckered for [ʃ-ʒ] than for [s-z].
Jaw	Similar to the [s] position, although it might be a hairline lower.

WARMER-UPPERS [ʃ]

Initial	Medial	Final
shave	anxious	bash
sham	assure	brash
sure	cashew	brush
shill	cashier	flush
schwa	mention	Irish
shadow	Oshkosh	quash
Chopin	precious	quiche
Charlotte	pressure	smush
shoulder	tension	swoosh
charlatan	conscientious	Wabash
chaperone	fuchsia	varnish
Chicago	shish kebab	mustache

WARMER-UPPERS [ʒ]

Initial	Medial	Final
[ʒ] in initial positions	usual	loge
occurs mostly in words	vision	beige
of foreign origin.	regime	rouge
genre	measure	collage
jeté	lesion	corsage
jour	abrasion	garage
Zsa Zsa	adagio	mirage
	amnesia	prestige
	conclusion	barrage
	derision	camouflage
	evasion	sabotage

Faults and Foibles

§§§ *A.   SUBSTITUTING [s] FOR [ʃ] AND [z] FOR [ʒ]*

For discussion and relevant exercises, see page 146.

[h]

happy, inhale

VARIOUS SPELLINGS

h as in HELP   wh as in WHEN

j as in NAVAJO

Classification	glottis (glottal) [h] voiceless
Piddling Pursuit	
Phonetic	hi hu hæz no hɛd nidz no hæt.
Diacritic	t̸ẖə hâr iz rēl. its t̸ẖə hed t̸ẖats ə fāk.

How to . . .

No movement of the lips, jaw, or tongue is required to produce this soft, throaty sound. The vocal folds are brought closely enough together to restrict the outgoing breath. This makes an audible friction noise. The articulators are relaxed and more or less preset in position for the vowel sound that follows. The outgoing breath stream produces a slight, whispery noise before the succeeding sound is vocalized.

WARMER-UPPERS

Initial	Medial
hair	Ohio
hip	ahoy
hymn	exhale
who	foxhole
whole	overhaul
honey	perhaps
Jose	rehearse
Horton	somehow
hamster	unholy
Hannibal	hubba hubba
hydrogen	brouhaha
helicopter	exhibition

Faults and Foibles

§§§ *A. Omitting [h]*

For discussion and relevant exercises, see page 147.

AFFRICATES [tʃ] [dʒ]

An affricate is a closely and rapidly blended combination of a plosive and a fricative. The two sounds merge; you don't completely finish the plosive and then begin the fricative.

The tongue momentarily blocks the breath as it does for the plosives, but then the tongue quickly assumes the fricative position and the impounded air is released somewhat explosively.

To practice your diction, use the Pronunciation Flashcards on the CD

[tʃ – dʒ]   **Phonetic**   **Diacritic**   Ch – j

chuck, capture,   jail, bludgeon,
such   binge

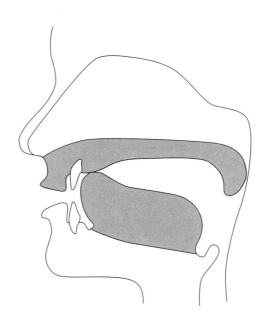

VARIOUS SPELLINGS	**[tʃ]**	**[dʒ]**
	c as in CELLO	dg as in EDGE
	ch as in CHURCH	di as in SOLDIER
	tch as in LATCH	dj as in ADJOIN
	te as in RIGHTEOUS	du as in GRADUATE
	ti as in SUGGESTION	ge as in ORANGE
	tu as in NATURE	gg as in EXAGGERATE
		j as in JUDGE

Classification   tongue tip and upper gum ridge plosive combine with tongue blade and front part of palate fricative (lingua-alveolar)
[tʃ] voiceless
[dʒ] voiced

Piddling Pursuit

Phonetic   dʒʌst bɪˈkɔz ju hæd ə ˈlɑʊzɪ ˈtʃɑɪldhʊd ɪz no ɛkˈskjus tə bɪ ə ˈlɑʊzɪ ə ˈdʌlt.

Diacritic   mun′i not ōn′li chānjəz handz, it chānjəz pē′pəl.

How to . . .

Press the tip and blade of your tongue quite firmly against the gum ridge. The sides touch the teeth. Then let the body of your tongue assume a position similar to that for [ʃ]. As the tip lowers quickly, the lips protrude slightly, and the jaw drops. A modified explosion, less sharp than that for [t] or [d], will be heard.

WARMER-UPPERS [tʃ]

Initial	Medial	Final
chap	actual	bench
chief	armchair	birch
chum	bachelor	glitch
charm	belching	itch
cheer	catches	lunch
chafe	denture	munch
chaw	hatchet	pouch
China	hitchhike	preach
cheetah	marching	slouch
cheddar	feature	witch
champion	ritual	wrench
chocolate	satchel	attach

WARMER-UPPERS [dʒ]

Initial	Medial	Final
gee	adjust	fringe
germ	agent	range
gin	digit	Madge
jeer	dungeon	siege
juice	enjoin	sponge
jury	fidget	surge
gentile	gadget	average
jealous	gorgeous	bandage
Gypsy	legion	cabbage
jewel	major	carriage
jockey	regent	cartridge
genius	surgeon	marriage

Faults and Foibles

    A. Overemphasizing the affricates

§§§ **B.** **SUBSTITUTING OTHER SOUNDS OR CONFUSING THE AFFRICATES**

Now for the details. Choose as needed.

A. Overemphasizing the affricates

If [tʃ] or [dʒ] are defective, generally only the fricative portions of those sounds are at fault. However, some individuals tend to exaggerate the plosive qualities of [t] and [d]. By the time they get to the fricative portion of the affricate, they're making minor vocal hurricanes.

Don't try to explode the [t] and [d] separately. Your tongue tip must be pressed against the upper gum ridge, not on the teeth, at the beginning of the affricate. Then drop the tongue away from the gum ridge, but never let it protrude between the teeth.

During all of this, your tongue should be relatively relaxed.

60.   Be sure that your affricates are sharp and relatively delicate rather than heavy and stressed as you read this material:

    a.

chill	birches	hitch	gist
choke	nature	lunch	giblet
cheap	richer	adjust	gigantic

    b.   Every Jack has his Jill

    c.   Mushrooms are spongy fungi.

    d.   Diet tip: To indulge is to bulge.

    e.   An engagement is an urge on the verge of a merge.

    f.   Generally speaking, it's dangerous to generalize.

    g.   It's better than riches to scratch where it itches.

    h.   Jenny enjoys junk food such as Jelly Belly jelly beans.

    i.   Longevity: An achievement to which there is no shortcut.

    j.   They say judgment comes from experience, but experience comes from poor judgment.

    k.   Don't ask if a person has been through college. Ask if a college has been through a person.

    l.   The key to everything is patience. You get the chicken by hatching the egg—not by smashing it.

  m.   Do you ever feel that life is just a bowl of cherries and that you're just a plate of Brussels sprouts?

    n.   Chimney sweeps are poorly paid, which proves that grime doesn't pay.

    o.   If you have an itch for success, keep on scratching.

    p.   Unruly bleacher creatures screech if players are benched.

    q.   Julie jilted Jungle Jim when he joined the bungee jumpers last January.

§§§   B.   SUBSTITUTING OTHER SOUNDS OR CONFUSING THE AFFRICATES

For discussion and relevant exercises, see page 148.

[f – v]

§§§ B. SUBSTITUTING [f], [p], OR [b] FOR [v]

If your first language is Arabic, Chinese, German, Japanese, Korean, Spanish, or Tagalog (the principal language of the Philippines), you may tend to make these substitutions.

live [lɪv] becomes [lɪf], [lɪp], or [lɪb]

love [lʌv] becomes [lʌf], [lʌp], or [lʌb]

(If you've come to the United States from Central Europe, you may also substitute [w] for [v]. *University* becomes *University*. Review the material dealing with the [w] *glide* earlier in this chapter.)

For [f–v] confusion: You'll be able to feel as well as hear the difference. [f] is a voiceless air puff—no vibration in your throat as you make the sound. [v] is voiced—there'll be a minicommotion in your Adam's apple.

For [p/b–v] confusion: [p–b] are plosives, of course, and to make them you must press your lips together. To sound [f–v], however, you must feel the *inner* part of your lower lip touching your upper teeth.

61. Distinguish carefully between the voiceless [f] and the voiced [v] in this material. Don't substitute plosives for fricatives. And don't let [f–v] vanish if they're in the middle of words.

    a.
ban–van	pal–Val	lubber–lover	fife–five
dub–dove	pet–vet	define–divine	cape–cave
base–vase	pan–van	folly–volley	saber–saver

    b. Is life worth living? That depends on the liver.
    c. Rainbow before seven, fine before eleven.
    d. You haven't lived until you've died in California.
    e. Never exaggerate your faults. Leave that for your friends.
    f. Better to have loved and lost a short person than never to have loved a tall.
    g. Shakespeare said that the evil men do lives after them. On TV this is called a rerun.
    h. Facts about the average American: First puppy love—age 13; first serious love—age 17; number of times in love—7.
    i. If your fiancé does something that bothers you before you're married, it will bother you twice as much after you're married.

[θ – ð]

§§§ C. SUBSTITUTING [s] AND [z] FOR [θ] AND [ð]

Remember the Tower of Babel incident in the Bible? "And the Lord said, 'Let us go down and confuse their languages, that they may not understand one another's speech.'"

And to compound the confusion, the Lord also saw to it that in the 5,000 spoken languages, only a handful of them contain [θ] and [ð] sounds. English, Greek, and Castilian Spanish, for example.

A listing of all the languages that don't have these sounds would fill several pages. Let's generalize. In most European, West African, and Asian (including Middle Eastern) languages, the sounds don't exist. [s] and [t] do, however, and that's why they're often substituted.

If your roots are in Germany or Japan, you may substitute [s] for [θ] and [ð].

If your roots are Italian, French, Hispanic, or German, you may be substituting [t] for [θ] and [ð].
Review your [s], [t] and [θ–ð] sounds.

A brief recap:

[s]: Think about [t], but pull your tongue back a little and raise the front of the tongue.

[t]: Press the tip of your tongue against the upper gum ridge.

[θ–ð]: Stick out the flattened tip of your tongue between your teeth.

62. Feel the difference in tongue positions as you run through these:

sat–tat–that	sin–tin–thin	song–tong–thong
sew–toe–though	sot–tot–thought	see–tea–thee
sums–Tums–thumbs	sign–tine–thine	sick–tick–thick
sigh–tie–thy	sink–tink–think	sank–tank–thank

63. If you're reasonably happy with [θ–ð], do these skimble-skambles. For two or three minutes, try not to think about tongue positions.

    a. "Staying single," said Thelma Thingle, "gives me a tingle."

    b. Put that tacky Thackeray novel on the sable table.

    c. A thinker doesn't tinker with a sinker.

    d. "Thanks," said Tor Thor as he sank the tank.

    e. The team's theme was printed on the seams.

[S – Z]

§§§ C. MISPRONOUNCING [s] AS THE FINAL LETTER OR SOUND

How is the final *s* pronounced when it's added to a noun or a verb?

If English is your second language, this *s* can baffle you. Not surprising, because it bewilders many native-born citizens who've been speaking English all of their lives.

In such words as *buys, boys, loves, dolls, runs, pencils, hides,* the final sound is pronounced as [z] because the sound immediately preceding it is *voiced.* It is easier for the vocal folds to continue vibrating the final sound. When you sound each of these words, articulate a [z] sound rather than [s] because a voiced sound precedes the final [s]:

lids	robs	fills	bathes	loves	shows

In such words as *hits, spoofs, pipes, decks, sifts,* the final sound is pronounced as [s] because the sound immediately preceding it is *voiceless.* It's only air! It's easier for the vocal folds to remain at rest for the final sound.

When you say each of these words, articulate [s] because it's preceded by a voiceless sound:

bats	laps	kicks	baths	huffs	escapes

In such words as *bosses, fizzes, churches, edges,* the final sound, if preceded by most fricatives, is pronounced as [ɪz] or [əz], and the ending actually becomes an extra syllable:

wishes	passes	judges	smashes	scratches

64. Try to do the following without thinking about the rules. Go back and check the rules only if you encounter a problem.

    a. Wishes can never fill a sack.

    b. Excuses are whines turned inside out.

    c. Where books burn, humans will later burn.

    d. People in phone booths rarely have short conversations.

    e. What this country needs is more open minds and fewer open mouths.

f. Newspapers carry good news and bad news. The ads are the good news, and the rest is the bad news.

g. About speed reading: "I read *War and Peace* in 15 minutes. It's about Russia."

h. The schlemiel always lands on his back and bruises his nose. [Yiddish proverb]

65. This material contains [s] and [z] in a variety of positions and combinations. As you practice the material, don't forget—they're *not* plosives. Don't let them sound like nuclear blasts. Fricatives should be pint-sized and knife-edged, but don't disregard them.

And, finally, is your tongue position correct? That [t] position will help you with most [s] and [z] sounds.

a. Ask me no questions and I'll tell you no fibs.

b. Assassination is the extreme form of censorship.

c. Even the best-running cars have some jerks in them.

d. More homes are destroyed by fusses than by funerals or fires.

e. Classical music is music composed by famous dead foreigners.

f. Gossip is when you hear something you like about someone you don't.

g. The secret of success is to start from scratch and keep on scratching.

h. He is such a decent, honest guy that he'd steal a car and keep up the payments.

i. The first screw to get loose in your head is the one that holds your tongue in place.

j. The first sign of maturity is the discovery that the volume knob also turns to the left.

k. In times like these, it always helps to recall that there have always been times like these.

l. Politically correct way to say someone is stupid: He doesn't have all his cornflakes in one box.

m. It is with narrow-souled people as with narrow-necked bottles; the less they have in them, the more noise they make in pouring out.

n. The fool says, "Don't put all your eggs in one basket." But the wise person says, "Put all your eggs in one basket—and *watch that basket!*"

o. Swan swim over the sea;
Swim, swan, swim.
Swan swim back again;
Well swam, swan.

[ʃ – ʒ]

§§§ A. SUBSTITUTING [s] FOR [ʃ] AND [z] FOR [ʒ]

Students who come to the United States from China, Japan, Korea, Vietnam, or any of the Malaysian countries may make these substitutions.

66. Watch yourself in a mirror as you articulate [s–z] and [ʃ–ʒ] again and again. Note the obvious differences in the positions of the articulators. It's especially important that you feel the difference of greater tongue retraction and lip rounding for [ʃ–ʒ] than for [s–z].

As you do these, you'll have no difficulty hearing the difference between the sounds. Because of a broader groove in the tongue, [ʃ–ʒ] have a more inflated, looser sound than [s–z].

a.
sack–shack	crass–crash	rues–rouge	puss–push
suit–shoot	lass–lash	bays–beige	muss–mush
sin–shin	lease–leash	lows–loge	seer–sheer

b. **Caution:** Don't forget that [ʒ] must be voiced.
leisure	explosion	prestige	version
camouflage	Asia	occasion	casual
collision	entourage	confusion	decision

c. To make pleasures pleasant, shorten them.
d. Your vision of treasure on the azure shore is only a mirage.
e. Television is all sight and sound and no vision.
f. A sharp tongue and a dull mind are usually found in the same head.
g. Did Shane hide the negligee in the garage when the invasion began?
h. Confessions may be good for the soul, but they're bad for the reputation.
i. What we need today is a transmission that will automatically shift the blame.
j. Shiny silk sashes shimmer when the sun shines on the shop sign.
k. She sells seashells on the seashore.
   The shells that she sells are seashells, I'm sure.
   So if she sells seashells on the seashore,
   I'm sure that the shells are seashore seashells.

§§§ A. OMITTING [h]

Individuals with non-English backgrounds—French, Italian, Russian, and Spanish—and those with a cockney English dialect, and some Australians may omit [h]. The absent [h] is more likely to call attention to itself if the sound occurs in a prominent stressed syllable.

If *Helen is happy because Harry is home* comes out as *'Elen is 'appy because 'arry is 'ome,* the absence of [h] is conspicuous.

Some Spanish speakers articulate [h] as a kind of guttural, throaty *"ch"* sound, something like the final consonant in the German *ach—*Ba*ch.* (We don't have it in English.)

67. All that's needed for a respectable [h]: a slight whispery noise, but don't let it sound as if you're clearing your throat.

Initial and medial [h] should be sounded but not emphasized in this material.

a. old–hold   odd–hod   it–hit   ahead
   at–hat   is–his   ope–hope   behave
   ill–hill   am–ham   as–has   anyhow
b. Unhappy Horace inhabited the unheated lighthouse.
c. It's not how old you are, it's how hard you work at it.
d. He's the kind of bore who's here today and here tomorrow.
e. Hope is the feeling you have that the feeling you have isn't permanent.
f. Home is where the college student home for the holidays isn't.
g. Humor is laughing at what you haven't got when you ought to have it.
h. Here lies old Hank with his guts full of lead. He was only a bag of wind but now he's dead. [gravestone in Dodge City]

[tʃ – dʒ]

§§§ B. SUBSTITUTING OTHER SOUNDS OR CONFUSING THE AFFRICATES

68.   Those whose first language is:
Scandinavian—may substitute [j] for [dʒ].
Jack Jones [dʒæk dʒonz] becomes *Yack Yones* [jæk jonz]
Review [j] and [dʒ] **How to . . .** material, pp. 108–109 and 141–143, then do these:

    a.   yell–jell   yoke–joke   yellow–Jello
          yo–Joe   yam–jam   yawn–John
          yaw–jaw   Ute–jute   yowl–jowl

Arabic, French, Korean, German, or Spanish—may substitute [ʃ] for [tʃ].
chair [tʃɛr] becomes *share* [ʃɛr]
Review [ʃ] and [tʃ] **How to . . .** material, pp. 138–139 and 141–143, then do these:

    b.   Shaw–chaw   wash–watch   shop–chop
          Schick–chick   bash–batch   dish–ditch
          shirk–chirk   cash–catch   hash–hatch

Chinese, German, Korean, Japanese, or Vietnamese—may substitute [ts] and [dz] for [tʃ] and [dʒ].
match [mætʃ] becomes *mats* [mæts]
wage [wedʒ] becomes *wades* [wedz]
Review [t–d], [s–z], and [tʃ–dʒ] **How to . . .** material, pp. 84–88, 134–137, and 141–143, then do these:

    c.   wits–witch   raids–rage
          hits–hitch   cads–cadge
          mitts–Mitch   seeds–siege

German, Korean, Russian, or Spanish—may substitute [ʒ] and [tʃ] for [dʒ].
jail [dʒel] becomes [ʒel]
large [lɑrdʒ] becomes [lɑrtʃ]
Review [ʒ] and [tʃ–dʒ] **How to . . .** material, pp. 138–139 and 141–143, then do these:

    (1) Jealousy is the injured lover's hell.
    (2) Even a flea doesn't jump merely for joy.
    (3) Judge a jest after you've finished laughing.
    (4) If Jack's in love, he's no judge of Jill's beauty.
    (5) There's no life after death. There's just Los Angeles.
    (6) Judge Church told the champ that his chum was a victim of injustice.

GRAB BAG: PRACTICE MATERIAL FOR THE FRICATIVES AND AFFRICATES

Fricatives and affricates are important to your speech, and when they are handled with precision, exactness, and sensitivity, they needn't sound like vocalized belching, exaggerated hissing, or buzzing.

69. The drill material contains all of the fricatives and affricates in a variety of positions and sound combinations. Remember that these consonants have often been described as the ugliest sounds in the English language. None of them has to be offensively noisy or unpleasant. Nip and snip these windy sounds. Be stingy!

   a. A bee is a buzzy busybody.
   b. I plan on living forever. So far, so good.
   c. Happiness is having a scratch for every itch.
   d. A brain is that with which we think we think.
   e. Commercial television does it best to do its worst.
   f. Arthritis is nothing more than twinges in the hinges.
   g. He who hesitates is probably right.
   h. Remember this—if you shut your mouth, you have a choice.
   i. Cheese grater: Cheddar shredder. Earthquake: Chasm spasm.
   j. California smog: It's as if God had squeezed a big onion over Los Angeles.
   k. I wasn't on the chess team in college. The coach told me I was too short. [Danny DeVito]
   l. It doesn't take brains to criticize. Any old vulture can find a carcass.
   m. Monday is an awful way to spend one-seventh of your life.
   n. Girls tend to marry men like their fathers. That's why mothers cry at weddings.
   o. I believe five out of four people have trouble with fractions.
   p. A cabbage is a familiar garden vegetable about as large and wise as a person's head.
   q. Bills travel though the mail at twice the speed of checks.
   r. My intuition freely makes up for my lack of good judgment.
   s. Time flies when you're having fun, but it's even more fun when you're having flies. [Kermit the Frog]
   t. In Italy for 35 years under the infamous Borgias, they had government by terrorists, warfare, murder, and butchery. But they also produced the Renaissance: Leonardo da Vinci gave us *The Last Supper.* Michelangelo gave us the Sistine Chapel ceiling, *David,* and *Moses.* In Switzerland, they had 500 years of democracy, brotherly love, churchgoing, and peace. And what did they give us? The cuckoo clock.

Assignment 10: Fricatives and Affricates

Select material that contains many examples of the nine fricatives—[f], [v], [θ], [ð], [s], [z], [ʃ], [ʒ], [h]—and the two affricates—[tʃ], [dʒ]—in a variety of positions. If you have been experiencing difficulty with one or more of these sounds, be sure that your material is loaded with them. Articulate them with as much care and finesse as you can, but avoid excessive noisiness.

or

Part 1: Prepare eight sentences, 12 to 15 words per sentence. Four of the sentences should be loaded with [s–z] sounds in various positions. Four of the sentences should be loaded with the other fricatives and affricates. For fun, toss in a few plosives, glides, and nasals. (It would be hard to avoid them!)

Part 2: Prepare a short, short story, a joke, or a brief anecdote, approximately 50 to 75 words in length. (Drill 69*t* is an example.)

Be so familiar with your material that in performance you can tell it rather than read it word for word.
Suggested Checklist for Assignment 10: See page 281, Appendix B.

SMORGASBORD: REVIEW MATERIAL FOR ALL THE CONSONANTS

Bilabial Sounds: [p]   [b]   [m]   [w]   [hw]

70. This material highlights sounds that are produced by the action of your lips. The lips are more than just two fleshy flaps forming the margin of your mouth. For adept, precise articulation, make their movements spry and perky.

   a. Babies are such a nice way to start a family.
   b. The day will happen whether or not you get up.
   c. Alimony: The ransom the happy pay to the devil.
   d. When you're about to meet your maker, it makes you meeker.
   e. Sign in jewelry store window: Ears pierced while you wait.
   f. There are plenty of other fish in the sea, but they're probably piranhas.
   g. Politics has become so expensive that it takes a lot of money even to get beaten.
   h. One of the quickest ways to learn how to think on your feet is to become a pedestrian.
   i. The world is full of willing people—some willing to work, the rest willing to let them.
   j. Politician's prayer: Yea, even though I graze in pastures with jackasses, I pray that I will not bray like one.
   k. A bank is a place where they lend you an umbrella in fair weather and ask for it back again when it begins to rain.
   l. There was a pious man who went to bed thinking that he had God Almighty by the little finger, but woke up to find that he had the devil by the big toe.
   m. Climate is what you expect, but weather is what you get.

Labiodental Sounds: [f]   [v]

71. This material features sounds made by placing the lower lip against the upper teeth. These two sounds have a tendency to become buzzy; don't inflate them.

   a. Never put off until tomorrow what can be avoided altogether.
   b. Furthermore is much farther than further.
   c. In the future everyone will be famous for fifteen minutes. [Andy Warhol]
   d. Fancy free: A fancy way to say "playing the field."
   e. Fog: Stuff that's dangerous to drive in, especially if it's mental.
   f. Definition of a book: What they make a movie out of for television.
   g. TV: Where you can see movies that you've been avoiding for years.
   h. Have you fifty friends? It isn't enough. Have you one enemy? It's too much.
   i. If all of us evolved from monkeys and apes, why do we still have monkeys and apes?
   j. Don't tell your friends their social faults. They will cure the fault and never forgive you.
   k. Love does not begin and end the way we seem to think it does. Love is a battle, love is a war, love is a growing up.
   l. One of the strangest things about life is that the poor, who need money the most, are the very ones who never have it.
   m. Hear no evil, speak no evil, see no evil, and you'll never be a TV anchorperson. [Dan Rather]

Linguadental Sounds: [θ]   th   [ð]   th̲

72. This material underscores sounds that are formed by placing the tip of the tongue between or against the front teeth. Be meticulous about tongue placement. Don't overpower these sounds.

   a. A closed mouth gathers no feet.
   b. The trouble with alarm clocks is that they always go off when you're asleep.
   c. When birds of a feather flock together, don't get underneath them.
   d. In Beverly Hills, they don't throw out their garbage. They make it into TV sitcoms.
   e. How can birds flock any way other than together?
   f. How do they know that it's time to tune their bagpipes?
   g. Everything is miraculous. It's miraculous that one does not melt in one's bath. [Picasso]
   h. The afternoon: That part of the day we spend thinking about how we wasted the morning.
   i. The marvelous thing about a joke with a double meaning is that it can mean only one thing.
   j. I can give you a six-word formula for success: "Think things through—then follow through."

k. There are two kinds of directors in the theater: Those who think they're God and those who are sure of it.

l. Sending offspring through college is very educational. It teaches both the mother and the father to do without a lot of things.

m. The worst thing about accidents in the kitchen is that you usually have to eat them.

Lingua-Alveolar Sounds: [t] [d] [l] [s] [z] [n]

73. This material accentuates sounds that are shaped by placing the tip or blade of the tongue on or near the upper gum ridge. A deft and dexterous tongue will help. (And don't turn [s] into a hurricane, please!)

a. Television has brought murder into the home—where it belongs. [Stephen King]

b. I never graduated from Harvard. I was there for only three terms: Reagan's, Bush's, Clinton's.

c. Since God made Adam out of dust, he had to make Eve to settle him.

d. If all the cars in the world were laid end to end, some idiot would try to pass them.

e. Never get married early in the morning and spoil the rest of the day.

f. There are three kinds of lies: Lies, damned lies, and statistics.

g. I get my exercise acting as pallbearer to my friends who exercise.

h. The length of a minute depends on which side of the bathroom door you're on.

i. After Chuck Cheney jumped jail, he robbed a church.

j. Jane Jones said she found no joy in eating Jello.

k. California is the only state in the union where you can fall asleep under a rosebush in full bloom and freeze to death.

Linguapalatal Sounds: [ʃ] sh [ʒ] zh [j] y [r]

74. This material emphasizes sounds that are produced by placing the tip or blade of the tongue on or near the hard palate. Check tongue placement carefully.

a. The best car safety device is a rearview mirror with a cop in it.

b. It's not the size of the ocean. It's the motion of the ocean.

c. Show me a good and gracious loser and I'll show you a failure. [Mike Ditka]

d. I'm not here for your amusement. You're here for mine. [Johnny Rotten]

e. If life is surely a big joke on us, it's our mission to figure out the punch line.

f. Nothing beats a cold shower before breakfast except no cold shower before breakfast.

g. Drive carefully! Remember, it's not only the car that can be recalled by its maker.

h. There are two kinds of politicians in Washington: those who grow and those who swell.

i. You have a gambling problem if you buy a paper and instead of believing that your horse lost, buy another paper.

j. On cutting hospital bills: Use less anesthesia by performing operations at night, when patients are already asleep.

k. Two major benefits of yawning: (1) Provides an unusually deep breath of air; (2) lets people know that you want them to go home.

l. Can you name all seven of Walt Disney's dwarfs? Four out of five can't. To refresh your memory: Bashful, Doc, Dopey, Grumpy, Happy, Sleepy, and Sneezy.

m. Some days you're the pigeon. Some days you're the statue.

Linguavelar Sounds: [k] [g] [ŋ] ng

75. This material dwells on sounds that are molded by pressing the back of the tongue against the soft palate or velum. Make muscular sounds of [k] and [g], and don't let [ŋ] do a disappearing act. Remember, [ŋ] is *not* [n]!

a. If you have trouble parking, drive a forklift.

b. Watching most television programs makes you wish that you had a lower IQ.

c. You can't tell which way the train went by looking at the tracks.

d. The best thing about being asleep is not having to make any decisions.

e. About binge drinking: Drink the first. Sip the second. Skip the third.

f. If there's one pitch you keep swinging at and keep missing, stop swinging at it. [Yogi Berra]

g. To think is to speak low. To speak low is to think aloud.

h. If I can't brag of knowing something, then I brag of not knowing it. At any rate—brag!

    i.   Colleges teach the dead languages as if they were buried and the living ones as if they were dead.

    j.   Asking a working actor what he thinks about critics is like asking a lamppost what it thinks about dogs.

    k.   The brain is a wonderful organ. It starts working the moment you get up in the morning and doesn't quit until you get to the office.

    l.   The cure for love at first sight is to take a second look.

Glottal Sound: [h]

76.   The folds are open just enough so that the air in passing through the glottis produces a frictionlike sound. Don't ignore this sound; don't explode it.

    a.   Hell is heaven's junkyard.

    b.   Heaven has no rage like love turned to hatred.

    c.   The ass went seeking for horns and lost his ears.

    d.   Hand: A grappling hook attached to the human arm.

    e.   I like a woman with a head on her shoulders. I hate necks. [Steve Martin]

    f.   Nothing happens to you that hasn't happened to someone else.

    g.   It takes a wise person to handle a lie. A fool had better remain honest.

    h.   We were both in love with him. I fell out of love with him, but he didn't. [Joan Collins]

    i.   The wicked often work harder to go to hell than the holy do to go to heaven.

    j.   I'd rather have them say "There he goes" than "Here he lies."

    k.   Horse sense: That rare intelligence that keeps horses from betting on human beings.

    l.   Handsome Hugo Harrison was horrified when the hurricane hit his townhouse.

WRAP-UP

1.   The articulators interfere with or disturb the outgoing breath stream to produce consonants.

2.   To produce plosives, the outgoing air column is blocked in the mouth briefly. Then the pressure of the lips and tongue is relaxed suddenly, and the compressed air is released with an explosive noise:

[p]	[b]
[t]	[d]
[k]	[g]

3.   Sounds produced by rapid movements of the articulators are glides. They are brief transitions from one vowel to another:

[l]	[w]	
[r]	[j]	y

4.   For the nasals the velum is lowered and the oral cavity is blocked by the lips or the front or back of the tongue. The breath stream exits via the nasal cavity:

[m]	[ŋ]	ng
[n]		

5.   For fricatives the oral cavity is not blocked completely, and these sounds are produced when the air is forced through a small opening or slit under pressure:

[f]		[h]	
[θ]	th	[ð]	th
[s]		[z]	
[ʃ]	sh	[ʒ]	zh

6.   For affricates (combinations of a plosive and a fricative), the tongue blocks the breath briefly, and then the impounded air is released rather slowly.

[tʃ]	ch
[dʒ]	j

VARNISH YOUR VOWELS

. . . About five words in our language contain all five vowel letters in alphabetical order? Two of them are *abstemious* and *facetious*.

. . . One vowel sound is common to almost every language in the world? It's the *a* in *calm*.

. . . The letters ough represent eight different pronunciations? although, enough, through, cough, thought, hiccough, bough, lough (a lake).

. . . The *e* sound that you use in *me* can be spelled 33 different ways in English?

. . . French poet Arthur Rimbaud associated colors with vowels and diphthongs? a, black; e, white; i, red; o, blue; u, green.

VOWELS

Try this short true–false test:

1. There are at least 14 vowels in the English language.   **T   F**
2. All vowels are voiced.   **T   F**
3. Many early languages, in their written form, omitted vowels altogether.   **T   F**

If you answered *true* to all of these items, you're entitled to an A for the day's work.
As stated earlier:

Vowels are made with more or less open mouth and without blocking the airstream.

Like a sculptor working with clay, vowels are molded and shaped. Vowels are a product of resonance. Regional differences in pronunciation are more evident in vowels than in consonants.

POSITIONS FOR ARTICULATION

We may classify vowels on the following bases:

- **Place of articulation.** There are front, middle or central, and back vowels, depending on which part of the tongue is most actively involved in producing the particular vowel.
   Tongue positions are difficult to describe, because the tongue is extremely mobile and flexible, and the main parts are capable of moving independently. But when we refer to tongue positions, we're referring to the *highest part of the main portion of the tongue.*

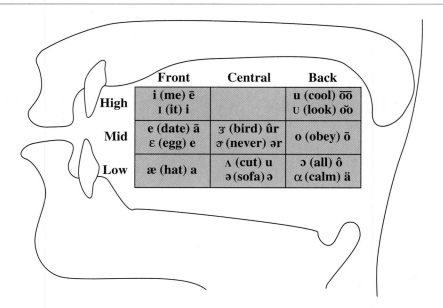

Figure 7.1 Various positions of tongue and mouth for vowel sounds. (Phonetic symbols are placed to the left of the key word. Dictionary symbols are placed to the right.)

And remember that basically it's the size and shape of the oral cavity, *as modified by the tongue,* that determine the nature of the vowel.

- **Height of tongue.** If you say *meet,* you will be aware that the front of your tongue is high in your mouth as you produce the vowel sound. If you say *mate,* the front of your tongue is in a mid-high position on the vowel sound. If you say *mat,* the front of your tongue is almost flat on the floor of your mouth on the vowel sound. Contrast also *feet* with *fate, way* with *woe.*

- **Tension of tongue muscles.** The tongue muscles are more tense for the vowel in *meet* than in *met.* More tension is present for the vowel in *moon* than in *moan.*

Remember that a drawing can only suggest typical, but not exact, positions. The differences in tongue positions from one vowel to another are comparatively slight. Examine Figure 7.1.

The Front Vowels: i ɪ e ɛ æ

To produce these sounds, the tongue is somewhat forward in the mouth, and the front portion of the tongue is most active.

Beginning with the vowel [i], say the front vowels and note what takes place. Your tongue arches high and far forward, but as you go down the list you'll feel the front of your tongue lower, your jaw drop, and your mouth gradually open. Your lips for [i] suggest a narrow rectangle. As you say the other vowels, your lips change from a narrow slit to more relaxed and open positions.

The Back Vowels: ɑ ɔ o ʊ u

To produce these sounds, the back portion of the tongue is most active.

Say the back vowels beginning with [ɑ]. As you proceed from [ɑ] through [u], note how the back of your tongue and your jaw gradually rise. Your lips are relatively open and relaxed for [ɑ], but by the time you reach [u], they're protruded and rounded.

The Central Vowels: ɝ ɚ ə ʌ

To produce these sounds, the middle portion of the tongue is most active.

As you begin with [ɝ], you'll note that your tongue may be arched somewhere between mid-high and high in the middle of the oral cavity. With the other sounds your tongue drops slightly. When you reach [ə] and [ʌ], you'll be aware that your tongue, lips, and jaw are in a quite relaxed position.

FRONT VOWELS: [i] [ɪ] [e] [ɛ] [æ]

Phonetic

each, seed,
he

To practice
your diction,
use the
Pronunciation
Flashcards
on the CD

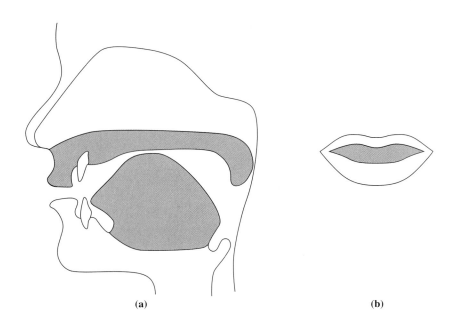

(a)   (b)

VARIOUS SPELLINGS

ae as in AESOP	i as in PIZZA
ei as in DECEIVE	ie as in RELIEF
eo as in PEOPLE	oe as in PHOENIX
ey as in HONEY	

Piddling Pursuit

Phonetic   hwɛn juv sin wʌn ænt, wʌn bɝd, wʌn tri, ju ˈhævnt sin ðɛm ɔl.

Diacritic   yo͞o kant sē t̶h̶ə wo͞odz fôr t̶h̶ə trēz.

How to . . .

    Tongue   Tense your tongue. Arch the front of it high and far forward so that it almost touches the hard palate. Place your tongue tip behind the lower front teeth.

    Lips   Unrounded but spread slightly and stretched back, as if smiling.

    Jaw   Relaxed and slightly lowered.

WARMER-UPPERS

Initial	Medial	Final
eat	beet	see
eke	meet	be
ease	peel	sea
ego	green	ski
Eden	knead	fee
edict	steel	tea
evil	sequel	we
Emil	peon	knee
Egypt	leisure	plea
either	preacher	glee
evening	ravine	Dundee
economic	believe	degree

PLEASE NOTE

If your class has already covered **Consonants,** you may skip the boxed material and jump down to **Faults and Foibles.**

---

§ Indicates sounds that are influenced by dialects.

§§§ **INDICATES SOUNDS THAT MAY BE TROUBLESOME FOR SOME NONNATIVE SPEAKERS OF ENGLISH.**

PLEASE NOTE

For the convenience of ESL students, discussions of specific problems and relevant exercises will be grouped together on designated pages. The material on these designated pages will be particularly helpful to ESL students, but it isn't intended to be exclusive. Non-ESL students will also find many of the discussions and exercises helpful.

Faults and Foibles

§　**A.**　Inserting *uh* [ə]

§§§　**B.**　**SUBSTITUTING [I] FOR [i]**

Now for the details. Choose as needed.

§ A. Inserting uh [ə]

"Did Mr. Kee-uhl stee-uhl your whee-uhls?"

Some southerners and quite a few users of General American dialect—particularly those in midwestern regions—occasionally insert an extra little sound—the schwa [ə]—after the [i], especially if it's followed by [l].

The [ə] is legitimate in words such as *about* [ə`baut], *lion* [`laɪən], *sofa* [`sofə]. But if you stick it in where it doesn't belong, it isn't. Incidentally, many educated people add the [ə] in certain words: *we'll kneel* becomes *we-uhl knee-uhl.* This generally doesn't interfere with understanding. So—to *uh* or not to *uh?* It's up to you.

1. Read these word pairs. You'll have no difficulty pronouncing the [i] in the first word of each pair. Then transfer the same [i] to the second word without inserting [ə]. *Hold your jaw steady on each second word.* If your jaw drops, this means you're stuffing in an [ə] where it shouldn't be.

keen–keel	read–real	eke–eel	veep–veal
peek–peel	seen–seal	teak–teal	need–Neal
feed–feel	dean–deal	heat–heel	creed–creel
mean–meal	wheat–wheel	Zeke–zeal	lean–leal

§§§ *B. SUBSTITUTING [ɪ] FOR [i]*

For discussion and relevant exercises, see page 167.

I Phonetic

ill, quit, penny

Diacritic **i − ĭ**

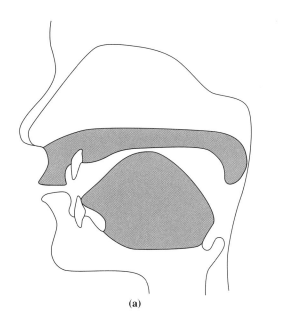

(a)

(b)

VARIOUS SPELLINGS

e as in ENGLISH o as in WOMEN
ee as in BEER u as in BUSINESS
ei as in FORFEITURE y as in PHYSICS
ie as in SIEVE

Piddling Pursuit

Phonetic ɪn ðɪs ˈbɪznɪs ju ˈiðɚ sɪŋk ɔr swɪm ɔr ju dont.

Diacritic igˈnərəns iz no ekskyo͞os′! its t̸hə rēl thing.

How to . . .

Tongue	Say the [i] of m*ee*t. Now relax the tongue and lower it slightly, placing the tip behind the lower front teeth. Then pull your tongue back a bit as you sound [ɪ].
Lips	Slightly parted and more open than for [i].
Jaw	A little lower for [ɪ] than for [i].

WARMER-UPPERS

Initial	Medial	Final
is	Jill	(Note: How about words
imp	chin	ending in *y*—*funny, city?* If
ilk	busy	you say the words in
into	year	isolation, you'll probably
India	guilt	say [ˈfʌni, ˈsɪti]. In normal,
infer	hymn	connected conversation,
idiot	pretty	most of us say [ˈfʌnɪ, ˈsɪtɪ].
insect	squish	There is, however, a
image	syrup	compromise sound that is
invent	dinner	halfway between [ɪ] and [i].
issue	whisper	It is represented by the
innocent	Sierra	phonetic symbol [ɨ].)

Faults and Foibles

   A. Inserting *uh* [ə] or *yuh* [jə]

§ **B.** Substituting [ɛ] or [e] for [ɪ]

§§§ **C. CONFUSING [ɪ] WITH [i]**

Now for the details. Choose as needed.

A. Inserting uh [ə] *or yuh* [jə]

Say *pill:* If you're saying *pi-uhl* [pɪ əl] or, even worse, *pi-yuhl* [pɪjəl], you're adding extra, unwanted sounds. If you've worked with [i], you're already aware of the extraneous *uh* [ə].

2.   Try a negative approach with these word pairs. You'll recall that to insert that extra sound, the jaw must drop. So deliberately let it drop on the first word of each pair. Then say the second word. *Don't let the jaw drop.* If necessary, check the jaw with your hand.

mi-uhlk–milk	fi-yuhl–fill	ma-uhl–male
hi-yuhp–hip	thri-uhl–thrill	whi-yuhp–whip
shi-uhll–shill	li-yuhmb–limb	ga-uhl–gall

3.   Read these. Make your articulators go straight from the [ɪ] to the following consonant, with no intervening sound.

   a.   If you want breakfast in bed, sleep in the kitchen.
   b.   If you drink like a fish, swim, don't drive.
   c.   What kills a skunk is the bad publicity it gives itself.
   d.   No one in this world needs a mink coat except a mink.
   e.   A baby-sitter is not experienced until she knows which kid to sit with and which kid to sit on.
   f.   The Bible on smoking: "Let him that is filthy be filthy still." [Revelation 22:11]

§ B. Substituting [ɛ] or [e] for [ɪ]

In a few sections of the country, notably in the Appalachian area—a region in the eastern United States that extends roughly from southern Pennsylvania to northeastern Alabama—the [ɛ] of *egg* or the [e] of *ale* are occasionally substituted for [ɪ].

> *tin* [tɪn] becomes *ten* [tɛn]
>
> *thing* [θɪŋ] becomes *thaing* [θeŋ]

Elsewhere, careless individuals sometimes make the same substitutions. The tongue positions for the three vowels are somewhat alike, but if you say b*i*t-b*e*t-b*ai*t and m*i*t-m*e*t-m*a*te, you'll discover that the tongue is higher for [ɪ] than for [ɛ] or [e].

4. Say [ɪ–ɛ–e] several times. Don't confuse the three sounds as you read:

a.
Jill–jell–jail	kin–Ken–cane	din–den–Dane
rid–red–raid	hill–hell–hail	lit–let–late
fill–fell–fail	till–tell–tale	bin–Ben–bane

b. Fish and guests smell in three days.

c. Do your kids a favor. Don't have any.

d. Ignorance doesn't kill you, but it makes you sweat a lot.

e. Death pays all debts, but debt is still better than death.

f. To touch this cable means instant death. Violators will be prosecuted.

g. Don't ever take a fence down until you know why it was put up.

§§§ C. CONFUSING [ɪ] WITH [i]

For discussion and relevant exercises, see page 167.

This phoneme is more widely used as a diphthong than a vowel. See Chapter 8.

 Phonetic

Diacritic e – ĕ

end, crept

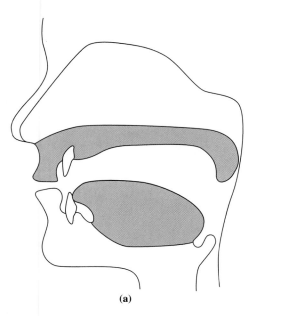

(a)

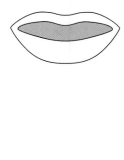

(b)

VARIOUS SPELLINGS

a as in MANY
ae as in AESTHETE
ai as in SAID
ea as in DEAD
ei as in THEIR

eo as in LEOPARD
ie as in FRIEND
u as in BURY
ue as in GUEST

Piddling Pursuit

Phonetic   hi smɛlz bɛst ðæt smɛlz əv ˈnʌθɪŋ.

Diacritic   nev′ər rub yôr īz eksept′ with yôr el′bō.

How to . . .	
Tongue	Relaxed. Front of your tongue is in a mid-high position. The back and the sides touch or are near your upper teeth. The tip should be behind the lower front teeth.
Lips	Lax, unrounded, and farther apart than for [ɪ].
Jaw	Relatively relaxed. Dropped from the [e] position.

WARMER-UPPERS

Initial	Medial	Final
ebb	says	(doesn't occur in final positions)
edge	guess	
etch	thread	
any	strength	
echo	again	
Elmer	heaven	
effort	heifer	
empty	lemon	
ethics	Teddy	
extra	direct	
expect	pelican	
enemy	Greenwich	

Faults and Foibles

    A. Nasalizing [ɛ]

§ **B.** Substituting [e] or [ɪ] for [ɛ]

§§§ **C. SUBSTITUTING [æ] OR [e] FOR [ɛ]**

Now for the details. Choose as needed.

A. Nasalizing [ɛ]

The nasals [m], [n], and [ŋ] are pleasant, congenial sounds, but they tend to spill over into nearby vowels. [ɛ] is one of the most frequently assaulted.

5. Run through these (each contains an [ɛ]) and pause where you see / /.

    e/ /t   e/ /t   e/ /n

    n/ /e/ /t   m/ /e/ /t   m/ /e/ /n

Say them again, omitting the pauses: *net, met, men.*

Is your [ɛ] clear and cloudless—absolutely free of nasality?

    As you practice this material, be sure that the sound isn't nasalized excessively.

  a. Egg: A day's adventure for another hen.

  b. Never depend on anyone except yourself.

  c. The enemy of my enemy is my friend. [Arab proverb]

  d. The heaven of the envied is hell for the envious.

  e. Never contradict; never explain; never apologize; never complain.

  f. Bookkeeping taught in one lesson: Never lend them.

§ B. Substituting [e] or [ɪ] for [ɛ]

"Ayd, don't fergit to git some braid and aigs."

Translation:

"Ed, don't forget to get some bread and eggs."

This is the kind of talk you'll hear now and then in Appalachia and other sections of the country. (I've heard it in southern Indiana.)

If [e] is substituted for [ɛ], *leg* and *dead* become *layg* and *dayd*.

In the Midwest, South, and Southwest, many speakers also tend to switch [ɪ] for [ɛ]. Result: *ten* and *red* become *tin* and *rid*.

(And have you noticed? Of the 285 million Americans, most have trouble with the word *again*. Instead of pronouncing it ə̀gɛn, they pronounce it ə̀gɪn.)

6. Contrast [ɛ] and [ɪ] in the following. Don't shuffle the sounds around.

a. [ɛ] words	[e] words	[ɪ] words
Rear of tongue touches upper molars	*Tongue mid-high; tongue muscles tense*	*Front of tongue high but relaxed*
Ben	bane	bin
den	Dane	din
bet	bait	bit
sell	sale	sill

b. Well done is better than well said.

c. Never face facts. If you do, you'll never get up in the morning.

d. Hell: They should have an express line for people with six sins or less.

e. Country song title: "My Wife Ran Off with My Best Friend and I Miss Him."

f. There's a pinch of the madman in every great man.

g. "As I said again and again in the beginning," remarked Judge Genzler, "anybody who isn't for me is against me."

§§§ C. SUBSTITUTING [æ] OR [e] FOR [ɛ]

For discussion and relevant exercises, see page 168.

Phonetic

ask, trap

Diacritic a — ā̆

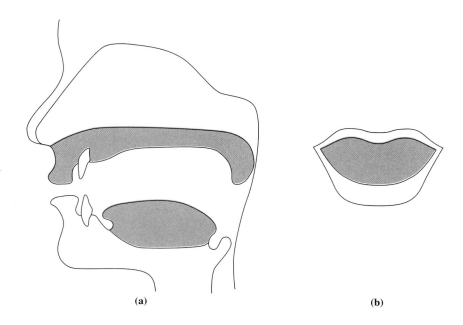

(a)   (b)

VARIOUS SPELLINGS

ai as in DAIQUIRI   i as in MERINGUE
au as in LAUGH

Piddling Pursuit

Phonetic   ˈædəm et ðə ˈæpl̩ ænd aʊr tiθ stɪl ek.

Diacritic   blāk kat, wīt kat, kach mīs, go͞od kat.

How to . . .
   Tongue   This is the lowest front vowel. Your tongue is far forward and should lie almost flat on the floor of your mouth. Place the tip behind the lower front teeth. The tongue muscles should be quite lax.
   Lips   Relaxed, open, unrounded, and drawn back at the corners.
   Jaw   Move it down, substantially lower than for [ɛ].

WARMER-UPPERS

Initial	Medial	Final
apt	calf	(doesn't occur in final positions)
asp	camp	
aunt	gnat	
Abby	snag	
avid	stamp	
actor	plaid	
accent	frank	
amble	lasso	
annex	value	
attic	trample	
actual	perhaps	
appetite	random	

Faults and Foibles

      A. Nasalized and tense [æ]

§ **B.** Substituting [ʌ], [ɛ], or [ɪ] for [æ]

§§§ **C.** **SUBSTITUTING [ɛ], [ɑ], OR [e] FOR [æ]**

Now for the details. Choose as needed.

A. Nasalized and tense [æ]

The most common problem with [æ] is making it with a nervous, tense, and meowlike quality. A couple of decades ago, this taut and unattractive sound was particularly noticeable in some eastern speech. Unfortunately, like the Black Plague, it's spread, and it's now commonly heard in the Midwest, the Southwest, and the Pacific states.

    ask [æsk] is distorted to [ɛ-ask]

    Dan [dæn] is distorted to [dɛ-an]

    band [bænd] is distorted to [bɛ-and]

Or translate this one: "The Hee-am SEEN-wich was absolutely FEE-an-TEE-astic."

This type of bleak, dry, and disagreeable distortion often results from an overtense tongue that is raised too high. A closed and locked jaw also adds to the screechy-scratchy, cat-on-a-hot-tin-roof quality.

Speakers in all sections of the country must be careful with this sound. If [æ] is near a nasal consonant or a plosive, it can easily slip into a tinny, jangling mutilation.

If you're turning *mat* [mæt] into [mɛæt], pull the sound out of your nose and down into the back of your mouth where it belongs.

    7. Try this experiment with the word pairs here.

The negative   On the first word of each pair, deliberately tense your tongue, close your jaw somewhat, and be as nasal as you can. As you pounce on each [ɛ] sound, think of saying the word *egg* between clenched teeth.

The positive   On the second word of each pair, work for a tranquil, almost lazy tongue. Open your jaw. Think of a lamb. Your [æ] should resemble the lamb's gentle *baaaaa*.

    a.

[bɛən–bæn]	[dɛən–dæn]	[mɛəd–mæd]
[fɛən–fæn]	[rɛən–ræn]	[rɛəm–ræm]
[tɛən–tæn]	[hɛəd–hæd]	[tɛəŋ–tæŋ]
[mɛən–mæn]	[fɛəd–fæd]	[grɛənd–grænd]
[klɛəm–klæm]	[sɛət–sæt]	[slɛəŋ–slæŋ]

b. Using the more mellow, relaxed, and pleasant [æ] of the second word in each pair in section *a*, say these rapidly. To reemphasize, pull the [æ] out of your nose and into your mouth.

ban–shan–han–van–can–lamb–tram
jam–jab–sap–tab–Ann–sack–hack
add–mad–scram–bat–map–lass–lab
lag–dad–crab–Nan–and–prance–an
lack–sack–back–wrack–crack–tack–jack

8. As you run through the following, you'll avoid distorting [æ] if you drop your jaw and keep the back of your tongue lowered as far as possible.

a. Laugh and grow fat.
b. Crack down on crack.
c. Happiness is no laughing matter.
d. The fattest of the fat are getting fatter faster.
e. The person who can't dance says that the band can't play.
f. Let the one who hath never had a full bladder cast the first stone.
g. You can and you can't. You will and you won't. You'll be damned if you do, and damned if you don't.
h. There are those who make things happen. There are those who watch things happen, and there are those who wonder what happened.
i. Sleep: Cousin to death and trance and madness.
j. Andy asked Sandy, "What happens if you get scared half to death twice?"
k. A canner exceedingly canny
One morning remarked to his granny,
A canner can can
Anything that he can,
But a canner can't can a can, can he?

§ B. Substituting [ʌ], [ɛ], or [ɪ] for [æ]

"If I Had My Druthers," a popular tune of the 1950s, suggested that Appalachian mountain folk pronounce *rather* as *ruther*. This is possibly true, but folksy mispronunciation is also encountered in other sections of the country.

9. The paired words that follow do *not* rhyme.
Reminder: For [æ]—your tongue is almost flat on the floor of your mouth.
For [ʌ]—raise the center of your tongue slightly.

a. Sam–some   rag–rug
dam–dumb   clack–cluck
fan–fun   ram–rum
bad–bud   cram–crumb

Some people turn *had* into *head* and *can* into *kin.*
For [ɛ]—the back of your tongue touches your upper molars.

b. bat–bet   sand–send
dack–deck   fan–fen
chat–chet   ham–hem
sat–set   lamb–Lem

For [ɪ]—the front of your tongue is relatively high.

c. sack–sick   salve–sieve
mat–mitt   flam–flim
had–hid   dad–did
dapper–dipper   fan–fin

10. Monitor yourself diligently as you read these sentences. Don't let [ʌ], [ɛ], or [ɪ] sneak in and replace [æ].

a. People with tact have less to retract.
b. Ann Thaxter, the actress, pays taxes on taxis in Texas.
c. Hasn't the fine line between sanity and madness grown finer?
d. Never gamble in heavy traffic. The cars may be stacked against you.

e.   Sam Landers once said, "This makes me so mad that it gets my dandruff up."

f.   Mick Jagger had a bad accident recently; one of his pals slammed the car door on his hair.

g.   Anyone who says that rock and roll is a passing fad or a flash in the pan has rocks in his head, Dad. [Sting]

h.   That which you can't do, you can't do—and that which you can do, you also can't do. [Russian proverb]

§§§   *C.*   *SUBSTITUTING [ɛ], [ɑ], OR [e] FOR [æ]*

For discussion and relevant exercises, see page 169.

[i]

§§§ **B. SUBSTITUTING [ɪ] FOR [i]**

If your first language is the tongue of Vietnam, Japan, Spain, France, Italy, Greece, Pakistan, India, Poland, Russia, Korea, some African nations, or China, you may confuse [i] as in b*ee*t with [ɪ] as in b*i*t.

(For speakers of Chinese, a general approach is used because within China at least six languages are spoken, including Amoy, Cantonese, Foochow, Kwangtung, Mandarin, and Swatow.)

If you're making this substitution—

feet [fit] may sound more like *fit* [fɪt]

meat [mit] may sound more like *mitt* [mɪt]

11. For [i], your tongue is high and far forward, but for [ɪ] it's slightly lower and farther back in your mouth. *Feel the difference in tongue positions as you work with these.* Also, can you hear the difference between the slightly shrill [i] and the more velvety [ɪ]?

   a. | reap–rip | sheen–shin | heap–hip | leap–lip |
       |----------|------------|----------|----------|
       | seep–sip | deal–dill | seat–sit | beet–bit |
       | deep–dip | feel–fill | ream–rim | leak–lick |

   b. Sleep faster. We need the pillow. [Yiddish proverb]
   c. I'm on a seafood diet. If I see food, I eat it.
   d. Don't be little. Be big.
   e. Seeing is deceiving. It's eating that's believing.
   f. We joined the navy to see the world. And what did we see? We saw the sea.
   g. Oh, what a tangled web we weave when first we practice to deceive.
   h. Why do we kill people who kill people to show that killing people is wrong?
   i. Whenever I get eager and feel like exercise, I lie down until the feeling passes.
   j. A person always has two reasons for doing anything—a good reason and the real reason.
   k. Some preachers and teachers don't talk in their sleep. They talk in other people's sleep.
   l. We are both great people, but I have succeeded better than you in keeping it a profound secret.
   m. Please, Lord, teach me so that my words will be easy, tender, and sweet, for tomorrow I may have to eat them.
   n. I didn't believe in reincarnation the last time either.

[ɪ]

§§§ **C. CONFUSING [i] WITH [ɪ]**

Individuals from Vietnam may substitute [i] for [ɪ].

Pit [pɪt] turns into *peat* [pit], *fit* [fɪt] into *feet* [fit].

Speakers from some African nations or those whose first language was Chinese, French, Greek, Indian, Italian, Japanese, Korean, Pakistani, Polish, Russian, or Spanish often confuse the [ɪ] of *kill* [kɪl] with the [i] of *keel* [kil].

Result: *feel* and *seat* are changed to *fill* and *sit*.

As you now know, for [i] the tongue is high and far forward, but for [ɪ] it's lower and farther back in the mouth.

12. Read these. Remember that [i] is a rather hard, "tight" sound. [ɪ] is a softer, "loose" sound.

   a. reap–rip   keen–kin   bean–bin   seen–sin
       seek–sick   deal–dill   heat–hit   teal–till

   The Spanish language doesn't contain a vowel sound exactly like the English [ɪ]. Hispanics sometimes have trouble with [ɪ] and substitute [i]. *Gyp* sounds more like *jeep; itch* sounds more like *each*.

   b. As you make the underlined sound in the word columns here—

[i]	[ɪ]
Spread your lips a bit—almost smiling.	Spread your lips slightly, but less than for [i].
Arch the blade of your tongue high in the front of your mouth. The tongue is tense.	Your tongue is lower and more relaxed than it is for [i].

(First read down each column—then across the page.)

greet	grit	leak	lick
Jean	gin	mead	mid
wheel	will	neat	nit
bead	bid	peach	pitch
dean	din	reef	rif
cheap	chip	peel	pill
lean	Lynn	cheek	chick
steal	still	team	Tim
Pete	pit	wean	win
seed	Sid	veep	vip

13. As you read, remember: [i] = tongue high
                            [ɪ] = tongue low

   Monitor yourself carefully as you practice the following. Don't confuse the two vowels.

   a. Honey is sweet, but the bee stings.
   b. Eat to live, but do not live to eat.
   c. He who knows little soon repeats it.
   d. He digs deepest who deepest digs.
   e. It beats as it sweeps as it cleans. [vacuum cleaner slogan]
   f. Eat as much as you wish, but please don't swallow it.
   g. He who lies down with dogs will rise with fleas.
   h. You'd be surprised how much it costs to look this cheap. [Cher]
   i. All that we see or seem is but a dream within a dream.
   j. If the human brain were so simple that we could understand it, we would be so simple that we couldn't.

§§§ C. SUBSTITUTING [æ] OR [e] FOR [ɛ]

If you're from Spain, Korea, Japan, or Vietnam, you may be substituting [æ] for [ɛ].

   bed [bɛd] becomes *bad* [bæd]

   said [sɛd] becomes *sad* [sæd]

If your first language is Chinese, however, you may substitute [e] for [ɛ], turning—

wet [wɛt] into *wait* [wet]

met [mɛt] into *mate* [met]

Before you do the exercises, compare tongue positions.

[æ] Tongue almost flat on floor of mouth.

[e] Tongue mid-high position.

[ɛ] Sides of tongue touch upper molars.

14. Exercise *a* emphasizes the differences in tongue positions.

    a.   (Read across the page.)

can	cane	Ken
sat	sate	set
fad	fade	fed
gat	gate	get
lass	lace	less

Now you're on your own.

    b.   The nail that sticks up gets hammered down.

    c.   A camel makes an elephant feel like a jet plane.

    d.   How long have bacteria been around? Adam had them.

    e.   A dead atheist is someone who's all dressed up with no place to go.

    f.   May you get to heaven a half hour before the devil knows you're dead.

§§§ C. SUBSTITUTING [ɛ], [ɑ], OR [e] FOR [æ]

German, Chinese, Japanese, Vietnamese?

[æ], as we articulate it, doesn't exist in these languages. [ɛ] is often substituted.

tank [tæŋk] becomes [tɛŋk]

French, Spanish, Japanese, Korean, some African nations, Arabic?

(For Arabic, because a variety of dialects is spoken, a general approach is used.)

[ɑ] may be substituted for [æ]

bank [bæŋk] turns into [bɑŋk]

Chinese?

Maybe you substitute [e] for [æ], converting *sack* [sæk] to *sake* [sek].

Do a quick review of the tongue positions:

[ɛ] Sides may touch upper molars.

[ɑ] Low, flat, relaxed on floor of mouth.

[e] Mid-high position, the back near the soft palate.

[æ] Low (not as low as [ɑ]), but front part slightly elevated.

15. Contrast these four sounds as you read across the page. Read them slowly two or three times, then read them rapidly.

wreck	rock	rake	wrack
Bess	boss	bass (singer)	bass (fish)
sex	sox	sakes	Saks
ex	ox	aches	axe
Med	mod	made	mad

In these drill sentences, the four sounds are found in many positions. Work for a pleasant, untarnished [æ].

a. The last straw breaks the camel's back.
b. He who laughs last didn't get the joke.
c. Salt water and absence wash away love.
d. Anger as soon as fed is dead. It's starving that makes it fat.
e. Tax reform means: Don't tax you, don't tax me, tax that man behind the tree.
f. Every man has it in his power to make one woman happy by remaining a bachelor.
g. I knew that I was an unwanted baby when I saw that my bath toys were a toaster and a radio.

BACK VOWELS [ɑ] [ɔ] [o] [ʊ] [u]

 Phonetic

Diacritic ä

 To practice your diction, use the Pronunciation Flashcards on the CD

art, jock, pa

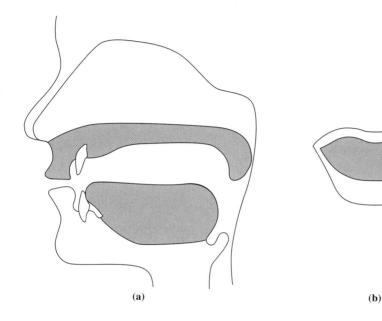

(a)   (b)

VARIOUS SPELLINGS

aa as in BAZAAR   ea as in HEARTEN
ah as in UTAH   ow as in KNOWLEDGE
e as in SERGEANT   ua as in GUACAMOLE

Piddling Pursuit

Phonetic   tʃuz nɑt tu wɑnt hwʌt ju kænt hæv.

Diacritic   wut wē wänt mōst in ə nōō kär iz us.

How to . . .

    Tongue   This is the lowest of the back vowels. Your mouth is wide open. Your tongue should be low, relatively flat, and relaxed on the floor of your mouth. The back of the tongue is slightly raised. The tip is near your lower front teeth.

    Lips   Your lips are quite far apart, in an oval position and unrounded.

    Jaw   Drop your jaw to its most relaxed position.

WARMER-UPPERS

Initial	Medial	Final
on	fox	da
alms	knot	fa
arch	blond	la
aria	guard	ma
honest	stark	Ra
olive	balmy	ha
Arthur	beyond	baa
octane	modern	blah
opera	eggnog	spa
occupy	Harvard	Baha
October	stockade	shah
Ave Maria	positive	hurrah

Faults and Foibles

    A. Nasalizing or distorting [ɑ]

§§§ **B. SUBSTITUTING [o], [ʌ], OR [ɝ] FOR [ɑ]**

Now for the details. Choose as needed.

A. Nasalizing or distorting [ɑ]

Widely used and agreeable, the [ɑ] sound has been described as the most beautiful vowel in the English language. And the most relaxed. Doctors and dentists, peering into your mouth or throat, always have you say "Ah-h-h" [ɑ].

American English has many so-called "short o" words such as c<u>o</u>t, n<u>o</u>t, d<u>o</u>t, h<u>o</u>t, and a majority of us pronounce these words with [ɑ].

Similarly, we have an abundance of common words in which the letter *a* is followed by *r—car, part, large*—and with many of these, too, the [ɑ] is generally used.

If [ɑ] is near [m], [n], or [ŋ], however, there's a tendency to push the vowel through the nose. If you'll remember that the velum must be lowered for the production of the nasal consonants, but not for other sounds, you should be able to avoid an unpleasant quality with this vowel.

Some speakers pull the tongue back and bunch it up in the center of the mouth. This will produce a "choked up" and distorted sound. Don't forget—for [ɑ] the tongue must lie relaxed on the floor of the mouth.

A few self-conscious individuals are wary of opening their mouths too widely as they talk. TV stereotypes suggest that characters with their mouths perennially open in the fly-catching position have IQs in the 70–80 range. To combat this image, some speakers clench their jaws, and a warped [ɑ] results.

16.   As you read these, be certain that for the [ɑ] sounds, your tongue is slack and lowered, your mouth open.

    a.   Absence makes the heart go yonder.
    b.   Half of art is knowing when to stop.
    c.   Wanted: Playpen, cot, and high chair. Also two single beds.
    d.   When you knock, ask to see God—not one of the servants.
    e.   If it's art it's not for all, and if it's for all, it's not art.
    f.   Progress might have been all right once, but it's gone on too long.
    g.   A lot of people who don't do much all day long like to get an early start at it.
    h.   About luck: When you're hot, you're hot. When you're not, you're not.
    i.   People who have what they want are fond of telling people who haven't what they want that they really don't want it.

§§§ B. SUBSTITUTING [o], [ʌ], OR [ɝ] FOR [ɑ]

For discussion and relevant exercises, see page 181.

Phonetic

Diacritic

awe, boss,
draw

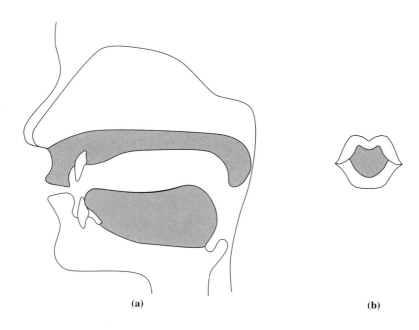

(a)   (b)

VARIOUS SPELLINGS

a as in WARN   oo as in FLOOR
au as in BECAUSE   ou as in OUGHT
oa as in BROAD

Piddling Pursuit

Phonetic   ɑɪ spɪld spɑt rɪˈmuvɚ ɔn maɪ dɔg ænd nɑʊ hiz gɔn.

Diacritic   ə dôr iz wut ə dôg iz ôlˈwāz on t͟hə rông sīd uv.

How to . . .

  Tongue   Your tongue is slightly tense. Raise the back to a mid-high position. The tip is
                      behind the bottom front teeth.
  Lips   Slightly rounded.
  Jaw   A bit higher than for [ɑ].

WARMER-UPPERS

Initial	Medial	Final
all	balk	caw
or	call	claw
off	soft	flaw
ought	wall	gnaw
awl	wrong	jaw
auto	bought	law
often	maul	maw
almost	dawn	raw
author	chalk	Shaw
auburn	Boston	Esau
awning	across	straw
audio	caution	Wausau

Described as a backward *c*, the [ɔ] sound is notoriously fickle. The area of the country in which you live has some influence on your pronunciation of this unstable vowel. Because it's probably heard more often in the eastern states than the rest of the country, [ɔ] has been referred to as a "back East" sound.

To add a little more confusion: If you were to ask each member of the class to say *Paul,* you'd probably hear at least three different vowel sounds. Even within geographical areas, there are differences. Many individuals, particularly in the Midwest and the West, use [ɑ] in place of [ɔ]. A few persons don't seem to use [ɔ] at all. Many cultured, educated people use the two sounds interchangeably.

If you ask a waitperson for a cup of coffee, you'll probably be served regardless if you pronounce it [ˈkɔfɪ] or [ˈkɑfɪ].

Fortunately, [ɔ] causes few problems.

Faults and Foibles

§ **A.** Substituting [o] for [ɔ]

§ **B.** Adding [ɚ], [ə], [ʊ], or [wə] to [ə]

Now for the details. Choose as needed.

§ *A. Substituting* [o] *for* [ɔ]

Some New Yorkers and natives of the Middle Atlantic states have interesting variations on this sound. If speakers round their lips *before* sounding [ɔ], what comes out is *lo-ug* [loəg] for *log. Tall* becomes *to-ul* [toəl].

To eliminate the intruders: If possible check yourself in a mirror. Say *awning.* Are your lips rounded as you begin the word? Do you drop your jaw as you make the first sound? If your answer is yes to both questions, you may be distorting the sound.

17. Read the following without lip rounding or jaw dropping on [ɔ]. If necessary, hold your chin with your hand.
    a. Bumper sticker: I pause for paws.
    b. It's better to have fought and lost than never to have fought at all.
    c. Maud, although cold, sold her fawn-colored coat to Joe Sawyer.
    d. Otto used to go to school with his dog. But one day they were separated. His dog graduated.
    e. The average lawyer is essentially a mechanic who works with a ballpoint pen instead of a ball-peen hammer.
    f. Fall is my favorite season in Los Angeles: watching the birds change color and fall from the trees. [David Letterman]

§ B. Adding [ɚ], [ə], [ʊ], or [wə] to [ɔ]

In certain sections of the East, it's not uncommon to hear [ɚ] added to [ɔ]. This problem is discussed in greater detail in Exercise 32, Chapter 6.

> Result: *law* [lɔ] may become *law-r* [lɔɚ]
>
> *jaw* [dʒɔ] may become *jaw-r* [dʒɔɚ]

Occasionally [ə] or [ʊ] may be added to [ɔ].

> Result: *ball* [bɔl] may become *ba-uhl* [bɔəl]
>
> *daughter* [ˈdɔtɚ] may become a *da-ooter* [ˈdɔʊtɚ]

Those whose speech is Southern may wish to avoid inserting [w] as well as the schwa [ə].

> Result: *tall* [tɔl] becomes *ta-wuhl* [tɔwəl]
>
> *taught* [tɔt] becomes *ta-wuht* [tɔwət]

18. If you use any of these additions and would like to eliminate them, practice the drill material. Have somebody listen to you carefully and tell you if you're deleting unwanted sounds.

draw	shawl	thought	moth
gone	caught	broad	cough
maw	Saul	falcon	morgue

b. To jaw-jaw is better than to war-war.
c. The dog with the bone is always in danger.
d. Adolescence is just one big walking pimple.
e. Dogcatcher: A person with a seeing-dog eye.
f. What is sauce for the goose is sauce for the gander.
g. A good lawyer knows the law. A clever one takes the judge to lunch.
h. I'm against political jokes. Too often they get elected.
i. Arizona epitaph: "Here lies Lawrence Longfellow—planted raw, quick on the trigger, slow on the draw."
j. Many are called but few are called back.
k. Falling in love is awfully simple, but falling out is simply awful.

This phoneme is more widely used as a diphthong than a vowel. See Chapter 8, page 208 oʊ ō.

 Phonetic

Diacritic

shook

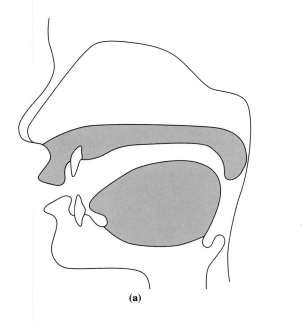

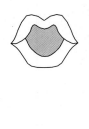

(a)   (b)

VARIOUS SPELLINGS

o as in WOLF   ou as in COULD
oo as in LOOK   u as in PUSH

Piddling Pursuit

Phonetic   ðə ˈbɪgəst ˈsɛlɚ ɪz ˈkʊk bʊks ænd ðə ˈsɛkənd ɪz ˈdaɪət bʊks: haʊ nɑt tu it hwʌt
juv dʒʌst lɝnd hɑʊ tu kʊk.

Diacritic   ī am not ə kro͝ok. ī am ə go͝od ko͝ok′i.

How to . . .
  Tongue   Lax. The back portion is lifted high toward the soft palate. The tip rests near the
lower front teeth.
  Lips   Slightly rounded.
  Jaw   A hairline lower than for [o].

WARMER-UPPERS

Initial	Medial	Final
	[u] doesn't occur in initial or final positions	
	foot	
	full	
	put	
	bush	
	butch	
	your	
	rookie	
	cushion	
	bosom	
	sugar	
	wouldn't	
	Brooklyn	

Faults and Foibles

    A.   Weakening [ʊ] to [ʌ] or [ə]

§§§ **B.** **SUBSTITUTING [u] FOR [ʊ]**

Now for the details. Choose as needed.

A. Weakening [ʊ] to [ʌ] or [ə]

If this occurs *would* [wʊd] may sound something like *wuhd* [wʌd]. [ʌ] is one of the blandest sounds in our language. It's a lazy sound. And because we tend to follow the path of least resistance, we often stick in [ʌ] where [ʊ] belongs. [ʌ], after all, is easier to make than [ʊ].

19.   Give your lips a little workout on the [ʊ] words as you read across the page.

[ʊ]	[ʌ]	[ʊ]	[ʊ]
Lips slightly protruded	*Lips unrounded*		
book	buck	book	book
took	tuck	took	took
could	cud	could	could
stood	stud	stood	stood
hood	Hud	hood	hood
crooks	crux	crooks	crooks

The jaw also plays a part in articulating [ʊ] and [ʌ]. Say these two phonemes rapidly, and you'll be aware of what your jaw is doing:

    [ʊ]–[ʌ]–[ʊ]–[ʌ]–[ʊ]–[ʌ]

Your jaw is slightly lower for [ʌ] than for [ʊ].

20.   As you read, drop the jaw on the [ʌ] words, and differentiate carefully between [ʊ] and [ʌ].
      a.   Brooke said, "Look, I'm in luck."
      b.   Huck Hook bought the book for a buck.
      c.   Hud took a tuck in the hood.
      d.   Could the poor cow chew its cud?
      e.   Luke Root said, "If words such as *hoof* and *huff* bother you, you're in a rut."

§§§ B. SUBSTITUTING [u] FOR [ʊ]

For discussion and relevant exercises, see page 182.

Phonetic

ooze, boot,
clue

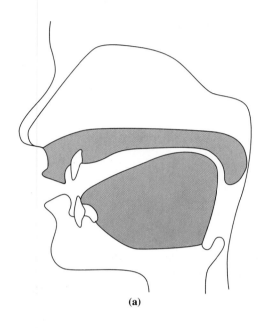

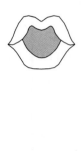

(a)   (b)

VARIOUS SPELLINGS

ew as in BLEW	ou as in SOUP
o as in MOVIE	u as in JUNE
oe as in SHOE	ue as in HUE
oo as in COOL	ui as in JUICE

Piddling Pursuit

Phonetic   ðə dudl̩ ɪz ðə ˈbrudɪŋ ʌv ðə hænd.

Diacritic   do͞o sum′thing. if it duz′ənt wûrk, do͞o sum′thing els. nō ɪdē′ə iz to͞o krā′zi.

How to . . .

Tongue   Slightly tense. Raise the back of your tongue very high toward the palate. The front of your tongue should touch or rest near the lower front teeth.

Lips   Your lips are more protruded and rounded for this sound than any other vowel. Make like a Lifesaver.

Jaw   Lax and slightly lowered.

WARMER-UPPERS

Initial	Medial	Final
[u] rarely occurs in initial	Ruth	blue
positions	goon	moo
oodles	tune	rue
oops	wound	woo
oozy	school	chew
	bruise	sue
	through	view
	shrewd	glue
	fruit	bamboo
	julep	igloo
	duel	voodoo
	approve	ballyhoo

Faults and Foibles

    A. Inserting wuh [wə] after [u]

§ **B.** Substituting [u] for [ʊ]

§§§ **C.** **SUBSTITUTING [ʊ] FOR [u]**

Now for the details. Choose as needed.

A. Inserting wuh [wə] after [u]

Some speakers not only diphthongize [u] if it's followed by a consonant, particularly [l] or [n], but also insert *wuh* [wə]. *Tool* and *moon* become *too-wuhl* [tuwəl] and *moo-uhn* [muwən].

    If you've spent time with [ɔ] and [o], you've been alerted to the sneaky *wuh* [wə]. It has a tendency to intrude where it's unwelcome.

21.   Again, to eliminate the intruder, don't let the jaw drop after you articulate [u] in these words:

    a.   cool   rude   pool   spoon
           boot   boon   rule   spool
           croon   June   ghoul   dune

If you're successful with the single words, you're ready for sentences. Try these:

    b.   Soon learned, soon forgotten.
    c.   Did Sue Boone drool as she pushed the goon into the pool?
    d.   Love rules without rules.
    e.   You booze, you cruise, you lose.
    f.   Calm weather in June sets the corn in tune.
    g.   June's cookbook has a super recipe for prune mousse.
    h.   The sooner you're there, the sooner you'll find out how long you have to wait.
    i.   Dr. Jool, my dentist, said, "It's the matter of the tooth, the whole tooth, and nothing but the tooth."
    j.   Too much truth is uncouth; there is no such thing as too much couth.

§ B. Substituting [u] for [ʊ]

There is some controversy over a handful of *oo* words. How should we pronounce *roof, room,* and *root,* for example?

roof [ruf] or [rʊf]   *room* [rum] or [rʊm]   *root* [rut] or [rʊt]

    The *Random House Dictionary* and *Webster's New International Dictionary* list [ruf], [rum], and [rut] as first choices, and [rʊf], [rʊm], and [rʊt] as second choices. This simply means that both choices are standard. In the Midwest, especially in sections of Ohio and Indiana, the second choices are heard as frequently as the first choices.

22. You'll have to let your own ears serve as your guide. With the following words, try both sounds, but if one of them sounds strange to you, try the other one.

room   roof   root   broom
groom   hoof   coop   hoop
soot   rooster   soon   hooves

§§§ *C.* *SUBSTITUTING [ʊ] FOR [u]*

For discussion and relevant exercises, see page 183.

§§§ B. SUBSTITUTING [o], [ʌ], OR [ɝ] FOR [ɑ]

Students from Russia, Greece, and some African and Asian nations may confuse [ɑ] and [o].

23. *If you're substituting [o] for [ɑ]:*

For [ɑ]: Relax your tongue. Let it lie low and flat in the mouth.
For [o]: Raise the back of the tongue mid-high.
Read across the page:

[ɑ]	[o]	[ɑ]	[ɑ]
calm	comb	calm	calm
shah	show	shah	shah
tar	tore	tar	tar
doll	dole	doll	doll
hod	hoed	hod	hod

24. *If you're substituting [ʌ] for [ɑ]:*

For [ɑ]: Relax your tongue. Let it lie low and flat in the mouth.
For [ʌ]: Raise the midportion of your tongue slightly.

[ɑ]	[ʌ]	[ɑ]	[ɑ]
cop	cup	cop	cop
balm	bum	balm	balm
Tommy	tummy	Tommy	Tommy
lock	luck	lock	lock
cob	cub	cob	cob

25. *If you're substituting [ɝ] for [ɑ]:*

For [ɑ]: Relax your tongue. Let it lie low and flat in the mouth.
For [ɝ]: Retract your tongue slightly and raise its midportion.

[ɑ]	[ɝ]	[ɑ]	[ɑ]
pot	pert	pot	pot
lock	lurk	lock	lock
cot	curt	cot	cot
jock	jerk	jock	jock
hod	herd	hod	hod
Bart	Bert	Bart	Bart

§§§ **B. SUBSTITUTING [u] FOR [ʊ]**

Some foreign-born students, particularly those who speak Italian, Indian, Hindi, Hindustani, Korean, Vietnamese, Spanish, or Russian, may substitute [u] for [ʊ].

full [fʊl] becomes *fool* [ful]

Some Spanish speakers also reverse the sounds:

food [fud] becomes [fʊd]

26. Carefully read the following words across the page:

[ʊ]	[u]	[ʊ]	[ʊ]
Lips slightly protruded	*Lips extremely protruded*		
cook	kook	cook	cook
wood	wooed	wood	wood
pull	pool	pull	pull
look	Luke	look	look
soot	suit	soot	soot

27. Don't substitute [ʌ] or [u] for [ʊ], or [ʊ] for [u], as you do this material. You'll be able to avoid such substitutions if you remember to keep your lips *gently* rounded for [ʊ], but protruded for [u].

   a. A man too good for the world is no good for his wife.
   b. The roof fell in on the poor wolf in Little Red Riding Hood.
   c. It's not the time you put in, but what you put in the time.
   d. The only way to avoid Hollywood—you should live there.
   e. The cook was a good cook, as cooks go, and as cooks go, she went.
   f. One who is good at making excuses is seldom good for anything else.
   g. A poor surgeon hurts one person at a time. A poor teacher hurts a hundred.
   h. Ginger ale: A good sugary drink that tastes like your foot feels when it's asleep.
   i. I just bought an imported car. It's called a Mafia. There's a hood under the hood.
   j. Football coach to player who'd received four Fs and one D: "Looks to me like you're spending too much time with one subject."

[u]

§§§ C. SUBSTITUTING [ʊ] FOR [u]

If you've come to this country from Italy, Scandinavia, Spain or Mexico, China, Japan, Korea, Vietnam, Pakistan, or most sections of India, you may confuse [ʊ] with [u].

> *groom* [grum] becomes [grʊm]; *stool* [stul] becomes [stʊl].

Remember that if your lips are insufficiently rounded or if your tongue is allowed to become too lax, [u] will sound more like [ʊ], the vowel sound in *took*. Your tongue and lips should be relatively tense for [u], but more relaxed for [ʊ].

28.   Try these:

a. [u]	[ʊ]	[u]	[ʊ]
Tongue and lips relatively tense	*Tongue and lips more relaxed*		
fool	full	Luke	look
wooed	wood	pool	pull
stewed	stood	cooed	could
shooed	should	who'd	hood

b.   A fool and his money are soon married.

c.   Never let a fool kiss you or a kiss fool you.

d.   Luke looked at the hood who'd wooed Lucy Cook.

e.   How old would you be if you didn't know how old you were?

f.   Tom Cruise asked me out. I was in his room. [Phyllis Diller]

g.   Most people would sooner die than think. In fact, they do so.

h.   A tutor who tooted the flute
Tried to tutor two tutors to toot.
Said the two to the tutor,
"Is it better to toot, or
Tutor two tutors to toot?"

MIDDLE (CENTRAL) VOWELS [ɝ] [ɚ] [ʌ] [ə]

 and **Phonetic**   **Diacritic** $\widehat{ur}$ and ∂r

early, bird, deter   western, dancer

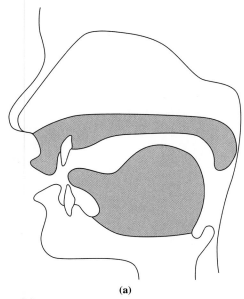

(a)   (b)

VARIOUS SPELLINGS

ar as in HOWARD   or as in WORSE
ear as in YEARN   our as in JOURNAL
er as in TERM   ur as in BURN
ir as in SHIRT   yr as in MYRTLE
olo as in COLONEL

Piddling Pursuit

Phonetic

[ɝ] ðə fɝst θɪŋ ə mæn lɝnz ˈæftɚ hiz ˈmærɪd ɪz ðæt hi snorz.

[ɚ] tʃɝtʃ ɪz hwɛr ju go tu faɪnd aʊt hwʌt jʊr ˈnebɚz ʃʊd du tu lid ˈbɛtɚ laɪvz.

Diacritic

[ûr] thâr är tōō kīndz əv âr travˈəl in tha yōōnītˈəd stāts. fûrst klas and thûrd wûrld.

[ər] nevˈər anˈsər ə kwesˈchən, uthˈər thən ən ôˈfər əv marˈij, bī sāˈing yes ôr nō.

How to . . .

Tongue

For [ɝ] your tongue should be slightly retracted and the central portion raised mid-high toward the palate. The tip should curve up and back a little and point toward the palate behind the upper gum ridge.

[ɚ]—similar to [ɝ], although the tongue position may be lower.

Lips   Very slightly rounded, open.

Jaw   Moderately open.

[ɝ] occurs only in stressed syllables.

[ɚ] occurs only in unstressed positions. A syllable containing [ɚ] is often lower in pitch and softer than a syllable with [ɝ].

Say *murder* [ˈmɝdɚ] and you'll hear the difference.

WARMER-UPPERS FOR [ɝ]

Initial	Medial	Final
irk	bird	her
erg	curl	sir
earl	herd	burr
earn	mirth	cur
err	world	purr
urge	worm	were
Irma	hurry	spur
Irving	gurgle	aver
urban	turtle	defer
ermine	nervous	occur

WARMER-UPPERS FOR [ɚ]

Initial	Medial	Final
[ɚ] seldom occurs in initial positions	surprise	actor
	coward	brother
	eastern	builder
	perfume	dollar
	record	feather
	Amsterdam	junior
	reservation	measure
	sisterhood	quarter
	surrender	runner
	gabardine	satyr

Faults and Foibles

§ **A.** Substituting the schwa [ə] or other sounds for [ɝ] or [ɚ]

§§§ **B.** **SUBSTITUTING [ɛ], [ʌ], [ə], OR [ɑ] FOR [ɝ] OR [ɚ]**

Now for the details. Choose as needed.

§ A. Substituting the schwa [ə] or other sounds for [ɝ] or [ɚ]

If you use General American dialect, the [r] element in your [ɝ] or [ɚ] is apt to be prominent.

If you're from New England, New York, New Jersey, and many southern states, you may use less [r]. In other words, you're possibly substituting the schwa [ə] for the two sounds in question.

rather ['ræðɚ] may come out as *rathuh* ['ræðə]

other ['ʌðɚ] may come out as *othuh* ['ʌðə]

bird [bɝd] may come out as *be-id* [bɛɪd], *be-uhd* [bɛəd], *buh-id* [bʌɪd], or *boid* [bəɪd]

It's only fair to say that, except for *oi* [əɪ], these substitutions seem to be acceptable in some southern and eastern speech. Not all, but some educated and cultured people in these areas use the substitutions.

29. Review the mechanics (**How to . . .**) of making [ɝ] and [ɚ] sounds. Then try the following drills.

    Let somebody help you determine the nature of your sounds. You may swear that you're articulating these sounds with the appropriate "r-coloring." Even your ears confirm it. But a careful listener may hear something else. Take it from there.

    a. First come, first served.
    b. If you choke a Smurf, what color does it turn?

c.   Sore loser: Bitter quitter.
d.   Who never makes an error never plays ball.
e.   There is never enough time unless you're serving it.
f.   Urban sprawl: What you get from eating too many urbs.
g.   To err is human. But to really louse it up takes a computer.
h.   I wonder what kind of a prayer turkeys say on Thanksgiving.
i.   Early to bed, early to rise. Work like hell and advertise.
j.   In the spring a young man's fancy turns to thoughts of love, while the middle-ager wonders if the power mower will start.
k.   Sometimes all the early bird gets is up.
l.   Early marriages all too often prove that the early bird gets the worm.

§§§   *B.   SUBSTITUTING* [ɛ], [ʌ], [ə], *OR* [ɑ] *FOR* [ɜ˞] *OR* [ɚ]

For discussion and relevant exercises, see page 190.

 and **Phonetic**   **Diacritic**

under, mother   about, probably,
Ilama

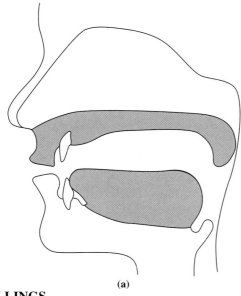

(a)

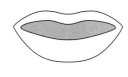

(b)

VARIOUS SPELLINGS

[ʌ]
a as in WASN'T
o as in LOVER
oe as in DOES
oo as in FLOOD
ou as in TROUBLE
u as in UTTER

[ə]
a as in ADULT
ai as in MOUNTAIN
e as in APARTMENT
eo as in STURGEON
i as in BEAUTIFUL
ia as in SPECIAL
ie as in DEFICIENT
o as in OCCUR
ou as in HUMONGOUS
u as in LETTUCE

Piddling Pursuit

Phonetic

[ʌ] wɝ·k ɪz mʌtʃ mor fʌn ðɛn fʌn.
[ə] tə bi ə'dʌlt ɪz tə bi ə'loʊn.

Diacritic

[u] pēp'əl är fun'i—uth'ər pēp'əl, that ɪz.
[ə] if yōō kant kənvins' t́em, kənfyōōz' t́em.

How to . . .
Tongue [ʌ]   Raise the central portion of your tongue very slightly. Place the tip behind the lower front teeth. Tongue muscles are lax.
[ə]   Formed about the same way, although your tongue may be closer to the floor of the mouth. [ə] is also shorter and weaker than [ʌ].
Lips   Opened slightly, unrounded.
Jaw   Lax and in a mid-high position.

WARMER-UPPERS FOR [ʌ]

Initial	Medial	Final
of	mush	[ʌ] doesn't occur in
us	blood	final positions
other	young	
ulcer	double	
ultra	money	
upper	thunder	
upright	country	
umpire	custard	
umbrage	enough	
onion	discover	
umbrella	jugular	

WARMER-UPPERS FOR [ə]

Initial	Medial	Final
aghast	poem	Cuba
agree	Texas	pizza
alone	method	stigma
announce	Jeanette	delta
around	million	Canada
attempt	apparent	vanilla
avoid	medicine	cinema
escape	official	viscera
obtain	possible	Deborah
opinion	potato	orchestra
amoeba	president	Mona Lisa

[ə] is known as a *schwa*. This odd little word comes from a German word *schwach,* which means weak. Compare the schwa of *ago* [ə'go] with the [ʌ] of *up* [ʌp] and you'll notice that it's weaker and shorter in duration and receives less stress.

The neutral schwa is the most commonly used vowel in our language. It's also the most relaxed sound in English.

English spelling doesn't indicate how often we use it. Take the word <u>about</u>. Even if you say it slowly, you won't pronounce the initial <u>a</u> with the same sound you use in <u>ask</u> [æsk]:[æ'baʊt]. So we say [ə'baʊt].

How do you pronounce the underlined <u>o</u> in welc<u>o</u>me? Again, the unstressed vowel becomes [ə]:['wɛlkəm].

There's a definite tendency for vowel sounds in unstressed positions to lose their individual coloring and identities and become [ə].

Not everybody, however, uses the schwa consistently. Take the word *dais.* Many people say 'de-ɪs instead of 'deəs. Should you have a problem with this? Not at all. They both work.

Faults and Foibles

    A. Substituting [ɪ] or [ɛ] for [ʌ]

    B. Confusing *the* [ði] with *thuh* [ðʌ] or [ðə]

§§§ **C.** **SUBSTITUTING [ɑ] FOR [ʌ]**

Now for the details. Choose as needed.

A. Substituting [ɪ] or [ɛ] for [ʌ]

The lyrics of country and folk ballads are loaded with such lines as "Just lovin' you" and "Just say you'll be mine." And if you listen to a few of them, you'll observe that *just* [dʒʌst] inevitably becomes *jist* [dʒɪst] or *jest* [dʒɛst]. Singer Phoebe Snow has one that goes "If I can jest git through the night."

Rural sheriffs and rednecks are all stereotypes, but these folksy characters still show up quite often on TV shows, and just as often they turn [ʌ] into [ɪ] or [ɛ].

Unfortunately, too many city slickers are also guilty of the same heinous offense. About 85 percent of the politicians in recent elections suffered from this vocal dermatitis. Many listeners didn't object, but to some of us the *jist/jest* substitutions for *just* suggested sheer carelessness.

30. There are many [ʌ] sounds in this material. Be careful to articulate [ʌ] rather than [ɪ] or [ɛ]. It helps to remember that [ʌ] is made by a relaxed tongue, the central portion slightly raised. For [ɪ] and [ɛ], however, the front of the tongue is relatively mid-high.

    a. Judge Jist said that the jest was an injustice.
    b. You can't judge a book by its cover, so why pay for the cover?
    c. Junk is the stuff we throw away. Stuff is just the junk that we save.
    d. Judd Jetson juggled quotations from the Book of Judges.
    e. Rush hour: If all those cars would just move, there wouldn't be such a traffic problem.
    f. More muggings are taking place in broad daylight. Muggers are just afraid to be out at night with all that money on them.
    g. Does fuzzy logic tickle?

B. Confusing the [ði] with thuh [ðʌ] or [ðə]

The most common word in the English language? *I*. The second most common? *The*. Few of us have trouble with the pronoun. Quite a few of us get addled with the article. If you say "*Thee* higher you get in *thuh* evening, *thee* lower you feel in *thee* morning"—your *thee* and *thuh* are reversed.

The rules are simple.

The is pronounced *thuh* [ðə] if it's followed by a consonant: *thuh* girl, *thuh* book, *thuh* zebra. *The* is pronounced *thee* [ði] if it's followed by a vowel: *thee* apple, *thee* Indian, *thee* onion.

How about the article *a*, as in "*a* boy and *a* girl"? No rules are necessary. In most conversational speech, the article is rarely pronounced as [e]. Use the schwa [ə].

31. Read these:
    a. It's a small world, but it's a long wait.
    b. Cigarette: A fire on one end and a fool on the other.
    c. It's often the last key on the ring that opens the door.
    d. The emptier the pot, the quicker the boil—watch your temper.
    e. You can't tell a millionaire's son from a billionaire's.
    f. It's not the ups and downs that bother the average man. It's the jerks.
    g. Juvenile delinquency starts in the high chair and could end in the electric chair.
    h. The only thing certain about a watch with a lifetime guarantee is that you'll lose it.
    i. The expressway is a highway with three lanes—the right lane, the left lane, and the one you're in when you see the exit.

§§§ C. SUBSTITUTING [ɑ] FOR [ʌ]

For discussion and relevant exercises, see page 191.

[ɝ] and [ɚ]

§§§ B. SUBSTITUTING [ε], [ʌ], [ə], OR [ɑ] FOR [ɝ] OR [ɚ]

[ε] Substitutions

earth [ɝθ] and *burn* [bɝn] become [εrθ] and [bεrn].
Who? Speakers of German, Greek, Italian, Russian, Arabic, and some African languages.

[ʌ] Substitutions

earn [ɝn] and *herd* [hɝd] become [ʌn] and [hʌd].
Who? Speakers of Arabic, Chinese, Japanese, and Korean.

[ə] Substitutions

teacher [ˈtitʃɚ] and *hovered* [ˈhʌvɚd] become [ˈtitʃə] and [ˈhʌvəd].
Who? Speakers of Chinese and Korean.

[ɑ] Substitutions

part [pɑrt] and *runner* [ˈrʌnɚ] become [pɑt] and [ˈrʌnə].
Who? Speakers of Chinese, Japanese, and Korean.

32. Contrast and compare your tongue positions:

[ε]	[ʌ]	[ɑ]	[ɝ]–[ɚ]
Back touches upper molars	*Raise central portion very slightly*	*Low, relatively flat*	*Slightly retracted, center raised mid-high*
head	Hud	hod	herd
get	gut	got	Gert
pet	putt	pot	pert
peck	puck	pock	perk
pep	pup	pop	order

33. These drills are saturated with [ε], [ʌ], [ɑ], and [ɝ]–[ɚ] sounds. Read them slowly. Try not to juggle these sounds around. Then try reading them at a relatively rapid rate.

    a. Two heads are better than one.
    b. Great spenders are bad lenders.
    c. We all of us live too much in a circle.
    d. Being over the hill is better than being under it.
    e. You have to get up early if you want to get out of bed.
    f. If you want to live, you must first attend your own funeral.
    g. The early bird gets the worm, but the early worm also gets eaten.

[ʌ]

§§§ C. SUBSTITUTING [ɑ] FOR [ʌ]

If your first language is one of the following, you may be substituting [ɑ] for [ʌ]: Spanish, Italian, Slavic, German, Arabic, Chinese, Japanese, Korean, Vietnamese.

love [lʌv] becomes [lɑv]; *sun* [sʌn] becomes [sɑn].

Remember: [ʌ] is a relaxed vowel, but the central portion of the tongue should be slightly raised. For [ɑ] the tongue should be relatively flat on the floor of the mouth.

34. Don't confuse [ɑ] with [ʌ] as you read:

    a. calm–come   dock–duck   shot–shut
        knot–nut   mock–muck   log–lug
        sop–sup   got–gut   rock–ruck
        cob–cub   hot–hut   cop–cup

    b. Trust everybody but cut the cards.
    c. It's always darkest just before it becomes totally black.
    d. The perils of duck hunting are great, especially for the duck.
    e. One does not get a headache from what other people have drunk.
    f. The dog dug in the sod and gnawed under the palm before Don was done.
    g. So many people are taking drugs, it's no wonder they believe the Martians are coming.
    h. Middle age occurs when you're too young to take up golf and too old to rush up to the net.
    i. The chances of getting eaten up by a lion on Main Street aren't one in a million, but once would be enough.

SMORGASBORD: REVIEW MATERIAL FOR ALL THE VOWELS

Front Vowels

[i] ē   [ɛ] e
[ɪ] i   [æ] a
[e} ā

35. This material emphasizes vowels in which the front portion of the tongue is most active.

    a. Sleeping at the wheel is a good way to keep from getting old.
    b. Fill what's empty. Empty what's full. And scratch where it itches.
    c. A real friend will tell you when you have spinach stuck in your teeth.
    d. A problem in this country: Too many adults believe in Santa Claus. Too many children don't.
    e. If you think a seat belt is uncomfortable, you've never tried a stretcher.
    f. Germs attack the weakest part of the body, which is the reason for head colds.
    g. How many seconds are there in a year? Twelve. January second, February second, et cetera.
    h. If nothing ever sticks to Teflon, how do they make Teflon stick?
    i. The difference between a king and a president is this: A king is the son of his father. A president isn't.
    j. Some people say that the squeaky wheel gets the grease, but others point out that it's the first one to be replaced.
    k. Bette Midler's ten favorite dinner guests from all history: "I realize that I might have a seating problem with this creep heap, but on the other hand, the table chitchat would be a blast." Ivan the Terrible, Jack the Ripper, John Wilkes Booth, Adolf Hitler, Lizzie Borden, Nero, Joe Stalin, Dracula, Lady Macbeth, Charles Manson.
    l. Only in show business could a guy with a C − average be considered an intellectual. [Conan O'Brien]

Back Vowels

[u]	o͞o	[ɔ]	ô
[ʊ]	o͝o	[ɑ]	ä
[o]	ō		

36. This material emphasizes vowels in which the back portion of the tongue is most active.

    a. Modern art: oodles of doodles.

    b. Adam: Do you love me? Eve: Who else?

    c. Never go to a doctor whose office plants have died.

    d. Go for the moon. If you don't get it, you'll still be headed for a star.

    e. A fool and his money are soon partying.

    f. Why is life so tough? Perhaps it was cooked too long.

    g. What goes ha-ha-ha-thump? A man laughing his head off.

    h. It takes more hot water to make cold water hot than it takes cold water to make hot water cold.

    i. Kissing is where two people get so close together that they can't see anything wrong with each other.

    j. Some people are so dry that you might soak them in a joke for a month and it would not get through their skins.

    k. Yesterday I was a dog. Today I'm a dog. Tomorrow I'll still be a dog. There's so little hope for advancement. [Snoopy]

    l. "Does anyone prefer mono over stereo?" "Yes, me." [Vincent Van Gogh]

    m. Any boy anywhere can be a basketball star if he grows up, up, up, up.

    n. Aunt Olive said, "Art, love is like a full moon in June. It doesn't last."

Middle (Central) Vowels

[ɝ–ɚ]		ûr–ər	
[ʌ]	u	[ə]	ə

37. This material emphasizes vowels in which the central portion of the tongue is most active.

    a. Rubber bands last longer when refrigerated.

    b. Love your enemy. It will drive the person nuts.

    c. Good luck is a lazy person's estimate of a worker's success.

    d. If you're a surgeon, never say "Oops!" in the operating room.

    e. A dog is the only thing on earth that loves you more than it loves itself.

    f. Everyone is crazy but me and thee, and sometimes I suspect even thee a little.

    g. We are hurried and worried until we're buried, and then there's no curtain call.

    h. For three days after death, hair and fingernails continue to grow, but phone calls taper off.

    i. We must have respect for both our plumbers and our philosophers, or neither our pipes nor our theories will hold water.

    j. Telephones—did you ever wonder why wrong numbers are never busy?

    k. The early bird gets the worm, but who wants to eat that stuff so early in the morning?

    l. A coward dies a hundred times, a brave man only once. But then, once is enough, isn't it?

Assignment 11: Vowels

Prepare material containing many examples of the vowels that you have found troublesome. As a reminder, here is a key:

Front Vowels	Back Vowels	Middle (Central) Vowels
[i] ē as in be	[u] o͞o as in moon	[ɝ–ɚ] ûr as in fir;
[ɪ] i or ĭ as in hit	[ʊ] o͝o as in look	ər as in ever
[e] a as in cake	[o] ō as in omit	
[ɛ] e or ĕ as in led	[ɔ] ô as in all	[ʌ–ə] u as in cup;
[æ] a or ă as in ask	[ɑ] ä as in alms	ə as in idea

or

If you have no major problems with the vowels, why not work for a little finesse and polish?

A suggested format:

Part 1: Prepare eight sentences, 12 to 15 words per sentence. Two of the sentences should emphasize front vowels; two, back vowels; two, middle vowels. The last two sentences should be saturated with all the vowels.

Part 2: Prepare a short, short story, a joke, or a brief anecdote, approximately 50 to 75 words in length. Be so familiar with your material that in performance you can tell it rather than reading it word for word.

Suggested Checklist for Assignment 11: See page 283, Appendix B.

WRAP-UP

1. A vowel is a vocal sound produced by relatively free passage of the breath stream through the vocal tract. Changes in the size and shape of the oral cavity help to make one vowel different from another.

2. To produce these front vowels, the front portion of the tongue is most active.

[i]	ē
[ɪ]	i or ĭ
[e]	ā
[ɛ]	e or ē
[æ]	a or ā

To produce these back vowels, the back portion of the tongue is most active.

[u]	o͞o
[ʊ]	o͝o
[o]	ō
[ɔ]	ô
[ɑ]	ä

To produce these middle or central vowels, the middle portion of the tongue is most active.

[ɝ]	ûr
[ɚ]	ər
[ʌ]	u or ū
[ə]	ə

DISCIPLINE YOUR DIPHTHONGS

WOULD YOU BELIEVE THAT

> . . . Contrary to popular belief, only a small percentage of New Yorkers pronounce *girl* as *goil?* A colleague recently spent a week in New York taping casual interviews with about 300 native New Yorkers: waiters, cops, reporters, cab drivers, concierges, bankers, doormen, maitre d's, and bus drivers. Only 5 out of 300 used the *oi* diphthong in words such as *learn* (loin), *thirty-third* (toity-toid), *burns* (boins), and *pearls* (poils).

DIPHTHONGS [ɑɪ] [ɑʊ] [ɔɪ] [eɪ] [oʊ]

As previously stated, *a **diphthong** is a rapid blending together of two separate vowel sounds within the same syllable. In other words, when two vowels marry, a diphthong results.*

Say eye: What you're really articulating is [ɑ] + [ɪ]. Connect them and say them rapidly, and you have eye. Say ouch. What you're articulating for the underlined sounds is [ɑ] + [ʊ]. Say them rapidly, add the ch, and you have ouch.

To practice your diction, use the Pronunciation Flashcards on the CD

 **[ɑɪ]** or **[aɪ]** Phonetic

Diacritic **ī**

ice, file, cry

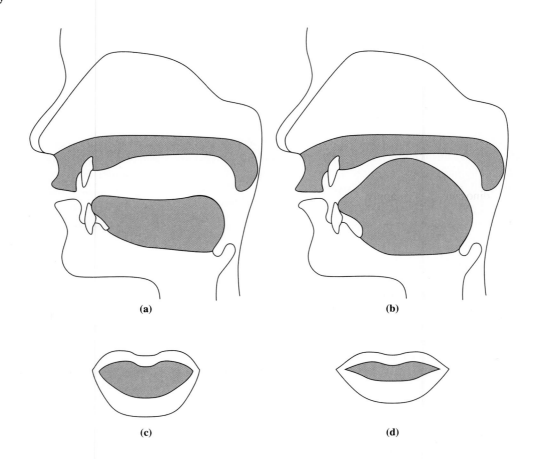

(a)   (b)

(c)   (d)

NOTE
Both [ɑɪ] and [aɪ] are used by educated speakers in all parts of the country.

VARIOUS SPELLINGS

ai as in CAIRO	igh as in MIGHTY
ei as in HEIST	ui as in GUIDE
ey as in EYE	uy as in BUY
i as in CRIME	y as in JULY
ie as in TIE	ye as in LYE

Piddling Pursuit

Phonetic   ɑɪ lɑɪk lɑɪf. ɪts ˈsʌmθɪŋ tu du.

Diacritic   "nō t͡hīself'"? if ī nōo mīself', īd run əwā'. [bil gāts]

How to . . .	
Tongue	Lax. Start out with [ɑ] or [a]. Lower your tongue to a flat position. Now move it to the relatively high-front position for [ɪ].
Lips	Open, unrounded. Retract slightly as you move into the [ɪ] position.
Jaw	Lower your jaw for the [ɑ] portion, then raise it for [ɪ].

WARMER-UPPERS

Initial	Medial	Final
Ike	rile	dry
I'll	wild	fie
aisle	right	guy
icy	spice	high
idle	blight	rye
icon	height	shy
Ima	silo	sigh
item	preside	why
ideal	disguise	deny
island	diary	belie
Ireland	dinosaur	apply
ivory	dialysis	reply

Faults and Foibles

§   **A.**   Substituting *ah-uh* [ɑə] or *ah* [ɑ] for ɑɪ

§§§   **B.**   **SUBSTITUTING [ɑ] FOR [ɑɪ]**

Now for the details. Choose as needed.

§ A. Substituting ah-uh [ɑə] or ah [ɑ] for [ɑɪ]

You don't have to be a United Nations interpreter to translate the following sentences, but it would help.

Ah fahnally opened mah ahs.

He fahred his rahfle at the lah-uhn.

The qwahr sang qwah-uhtly Frahday nah-ut.

Puzzled?
Try them again. Wherever you see *ah* or *ah-uh,* substitute [ɑɪ].
Southern? Southeastern? Southwestern?
Many speakers in these areas linger so long on the first vowel component—the [ɑ]—that they cheat on the second one, turning it into *uh* [ə].

like becomes *lah-uhk* [lɑək]

dine becomes *dah-uhn* [dɑən]

In more extreme cases, the second vowel component—the [ɪ]—is allowed to evaporate completely. We hear *lahk, dahn* [lɑk, dɑn].

1.   Remembering that the tongue shifts from a relatively flat to a mid-high position, try these slowly a few times, pausing as indicated:

ɑ / / ɪ   ɑ / / ɪ   ɑ / / ɪ   ɑ / / ɪ

Now repeat. No pauses.

Depending on your geographical locale, you may or may not wish to modify your [ɑɪ] diphthong. If you do, avoid overstressing or dropping either element of [ɑɪ] as you practice this material.

a.

sign	admire	buy	china	geyser
height	biceps	lie	style	rhyme
kite	fly	isle	eye	pie

b. Hired, tired, fired.

c. Of all my wife's relatives, I like myself the best.

d. When you buy, use your eyes and your mind, not your ears.

e. Exercise daily. Eat wisely. Die anyway.

f. In Frankenstein, a mindless scientist tries to create life from a pile of bones.

g. Don't wait for pie in the sky when you die. Get yours now with ice cream on top.

h. The ties that bind always find time to unwind.

i. My interest is in the future because I'm going to spend the rest of my life there.

j. "I mourn death, I disperse the lightning, I announce the Sabbath, I rouse the lazy, I scatter the winds, I appease the bloodthirsty." [Inscription on old bell]

k. You must remember this: A kiss is but a kiss, a sigh is just a sigh. The fundamental things apply, as time goes by. [Popular song, 1930s]

l. Today I will gladly share my experience and advice, for there are no sweeter words than "I told you so."

m. The only time I made four A's in college was when I signed my name. [Alan Alda]

n. I read Shakespeare and the Bible. I like Beethoven's Ninth Symphony and I can roll dice. I'm a true liberal, right? [Kathy Lee Gifford]

§§§ *B. SUBSTITUTING* [ɑ] *FOR* [ɑɪ]

For discussion and relevant exercises, see page 212.

 · [ɑʊ] **Phonetic** **Diacritic** ou

ouch, down, allow

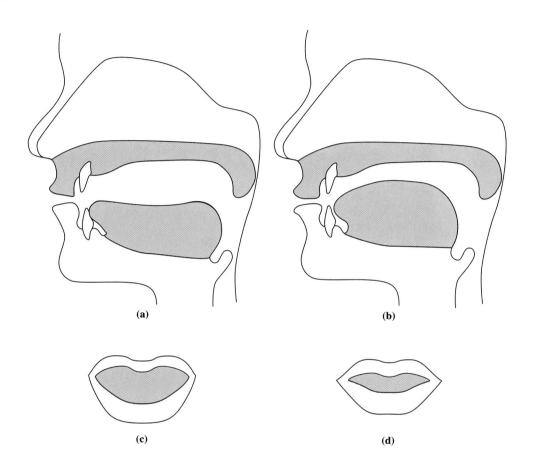

(a)   (b)

(c)   (d)

> **NOTE**
> Both [ɑʊ] and [aʊ] are used by educated speakers in all parts of the country.

VARIOUS SPELLINGS

au as in MAUI   ough as in DROUGHT
ou as in POUT   ow as in POWWOW

Piddling Pursuit

Phonetic   hɑʊ mʌtʃ ˈbɛtɚ ɪt ɪz tu bi ə mɑʊs ɪn ə kæts mɑʊθ ðən ə mæn ɪn ə ˈlɔjɚz hændz.

Diacritic   wen in dout, dōnt stärt out.

How to . . .

Tongue	Start with the [a] or [ɑ] position. Your tongue should be relaxed and low in the mouth. Then elevate it to the high-back position for [ʊ].
Lips	Unrounded, but as you move toward [ʊ], round and tense them.
Jaw	Lowered for [ɑ]; raised for [ʊ].

WARMER-UPPERS

Initial	Medial	Final
ounce	clout	ow
oust	loud	brow
owl	douse	now
outer	clown	pow
outdo	ground	prow
outfit	about	scow
outlaw	tower	chow
outlet	flower	thou
outgrow	astound	plough
output	mountain	avow
outrage	sauerkraut	endow

Faults and Foibles

§   **A.**   Substituting [æ] or [ɛ] for the [ɑ] part of [ɑʊ]

§   **B.**   Nasalizing and distorting [ɑʊ].

§§§   **C.   SUBSTITUTING [ɑ] FOR [ɑʊ]**

Now for the details. Choose as needed.

§ A. Substituting [æ] or [ɛ] for the [ɑ] part of [ɑʊ]

[ɑʊ] too often turns into an extremely piercing, screechy sound. Instead of using [ɑ] or [a] as the first vowel element, some speakers articulate the [æ] of *and* or the [ɛ] of *egg*.

Not too many years ago, this aberration was apparently confined to the East Coast, notably the New York, New Jersey, Philadelphia, and Baltimore areas. Unfortunately, in the past decade or two, [æʊ] and [ɛʊ] have, like killer bees, infiltrated other sections of the country. So much so that one expert has decided that these distortions are now "standard," therefore acceptable.

Your author heartily disagrees. These deviations are to many listeners extremely unsavory sounds that have been likened to the "meow" of an irritable cat.

If you're interested in combating diphthong abuse and producing a diphthong that is free of this vinegary edginess, here are a few *don'ts*.

DON'T

- raise your tongue too high or allow it to get tense.
- tighten your jaw.
- spread your lips into a smiling position.

2.   In the following, pronounce

ah as [ɑ]

oo as [ʊ]

ow or *ou* as [ɑʊ]

Read across the page. Don't forget: Your jaw *must* drop on [ɑ].

(Stretch the *ah* sounds)	(Say slowly)	(Say rapidly)
dah	dah-oo	down
clah	clah-oo	clown
mah	mah-oo	mound
sah	sah-oo	sound
hah	hah-oo	hound
nah	nah-oo	noun
pah	pah-oo	pound

3. As you read the following material, painstakingly avoid [æ] or [ɛ] as the first vowel element of the *ou* or *ow* blends. Always start with that relaxed and open-jawed [ɑ].

   a.
scout	tower	outrage	chow	bough
ow	louse	scowl	rouse	bower
devout	county	foul	wow	tout
dowel	gout	cowl	glower	fountain

   b. The rush hour is the only hour when all the cars downtown are laid end to end.
   c. The pioneer of stereophonic sound was a politician who talked out of both sides of his mouth.
   d. This hound is worth $25,000, but nobody can figure out how he managed to save that much.
   e. It's easier to stay out than to get out.
   f. Better to be a devout coward than a corpse.
   g. A mousetrap—easy to enter but not easy to get out of.
   h. Live around wolves, and you'll soon learn how to howl.
   i. By the time you know what it's all about, it's about all over.
   j. Some men have a den in their house, while others just growl all over the house.
   k. Howard Powers fell out of the tree and hit every branch on the way down.
   l. Holding down public office is like dancing on a crowded dance floor. No matter how you move around, you're bound to rub someone the wrong way.
   m. The gum-chewing student
   And cud-chewing cow
   Look quite alike,
   But they're different somehow.
   And what is the difference?
   I see it all now.
   It's the intelligent look
   On the face of the cow.

§ *B. Nasalizing and distorting* [ɑʊ]

Substituting the brittle [æ] or [ɛ] for the [ɑ] portion of [ɑʊ] produces an ugly, fingernails-on-the-chalkboard sound, but there's another complication. The vowels [æ] and [ɛ] are often nasalized, especially if a nasal sound [m], [n], or [ŋ] precedes or follows them. Add excessive nasality to [æʊ] or [ɛʊ] and a metallic and tense diphthong results.

4. Practice this material, avoiding [æ–ɛ] variations or exaggerated nasality in *ou* or *ow* words.
   a. When down in the mouth, remember Jonah. He came out all right.
   b. No doubt Jack the Ripper excused himself on the grounds that it was human nature.
   c. How does the guy who drives the snowplow get to work?
   d. One thing about being president: Nobody can tell you when to sit down.
   e. When you're down and out, lift up your head and shout, "I'm down and out!"
   f. There's a big difference between good, sound reasons and reasons that sound good.
   g. I swapped my cat and got me a mouse. Its tail caught fire and burned down the house.
   h. Each of us should have personal sounds to listen for. The wind outside is one of my sounds—a lonely sound, perhaps, but soothing. One of the greatest sounds of all—and to me it is a sound—is utter silence. [Emily Dickinson]

§§§ *C. SUBSTITUTING* [ɑ] *FOR* [ɑʊ]
For discussion and relevant exercises, see page 212.

 **Phonetic**

Diacritic

oil, Boise, toy

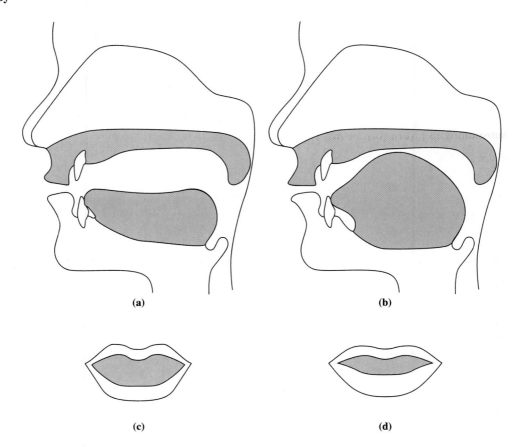

(a)   (b)

(c)   (d)

VARIOUS SPELLINGS

eu as in FREUD   oy as in BOY
oi as in COIL

Piddling Pursuit

Phonetic   gɑd əˈpɔɪnts, bʌt mæn ˈdɪsəpɔɪnts.

Diacritic   wun boiz ə boi, to͞o boiz är haf ə boi, thrē boiz är nō boi at ôl.

How to . . .
   Tongue   Relaxed. Start the sound from the mid-high position of [ɔ] as in *awe*. Then pull the tongue back a bit and let it glide effortlessly to the high-front position for [ɪ] as in *it*.
   Lips   Change from slightly rounded to unrounded.
   Jaw   Begin in an open position, then raise it slightly.

WARMER-UPPERS

Initial	Medial	Final
(except in *oil-* and *oyster-* prefixes, the sound rarely occurs in initial positions)	coin	coy
	Boyd	soy
	poise	poi
oilcloth	roil	cloy
oink	Floyd	Troy
ointment	doily	ploy
oyster bed	goiter	ahoy
	invoice	alloy
	rejoice	annoy
	soiled	deploy
	adenoid	enjoy
	hoity-toity	employ

Faults and Foibles

    A. Inserting [ə] or [jə] between [ɔɪ] and a following consonant

§ **B.** Substituting [ɝ], [ɛɪ], [oɪ], or [ɑɪ] for [ɔɪ]

Now for the details. Choose as needed.

A. Inserting [ə] or [jə] between [ɔɪ] and a following consonant
If you say something like

> *Boy-uhd Hoy-uhl poured oy-uhl on the coy-uhl*

you're inserting an unwanted *uh* or *yuh*. Why? Because you're letting your jaw drop after the [ɔɪ].

5.   Using negative as well as positive practice, try these:

Negative (Drop the jaw)	*Positive* (No drop)	*Negative*	*Positive*
boy-uhl	boil	boy-uhl	boil
joi-uhn	join	joi-uhn	join
roi-uhl	roil	roi-uhl	roil

(*Negative*) Did Lloy-uhd Coy-uhn toi-uhl in the soi-uhl?
(*Positive*) Did Lloyd Coyne toil in the soil?

As you read these sentences, don't let your jaw drop after the [ɔɪ] diphthong.
  a.   Don't boil oysters in olive oil.
  b.   Earl Boyd hurled the moist oilskin at Doyle.
  c.   He anointed the pork loin with Hoyle's sauce.
  d.   In Detroit, Joyce Royal was employed to broil sirloin.
  e.   Moira Freud was foiled in her attempt to steal the Rolls-Royce.

§ B. Substituting [ɝ], [ɛɪ], [oɪ], or [ɑɪ] for [ɔɪ]
Stand-up comic's one-liner: "Annoys is defined by some New Yorkers as the lady who checks your pulse in the hospital."

    This is a stereotype, of course. One frequently hears beautiful speech in the New York–New Jersey area. And the "beautiful goil with the poils on toity-toid street" is by no means as common as non–New Yorkers like to think. But it *does* show up. And some citizens of the Big Apple pronounce girl without an [r]: *ge-il* [gɛɪl].

And the same beautiful *goil*—with or without the *poils*—may drive her car into a *soivice* station to have her *erl* [ɝl] checked. Her cousin, a Dallas debutante, may ask the attendant to check the *all* [ɔl] in her Ferrari.

In some provincial, regional speech [ɑɪ] replaces [ɔɪ]. The friendly mountain folk of West Virginia, for example, may readily ask you to *jine* [dʒɑɪn] instead of *join* [dʒɔɪn] them.

6. If you've been told that your [ɔɪ] is quaint, rustic, or otherwise attention-getting, rehearse this drill material. For comparison and contrast, read the following words across the page. Most problems with [ɔɪ] result from too much lip rounding. Remember that as you say [ɔɪ], your lips should move from a slightly rounded to a relaxed and un-rounded position.

[ɔɪ]	[ɝ]	[ɑɪ]	[ɑ-ɔ]	[ɔɪ]
boil	Burl	bile	ball	boil
foil	furl	file	fall	foil
loin	learn	line	lawn	loin
poise	purrs	pies	paws	poise

As soon as you feel that you have a stable and unblemished [ɔɪ], read these:

a.
loiter	point	destroy	gargoyle
toyed	soy	foist	Roy
doily	void	choice	loin
voice	envoy	toil	poignant

b. Satan has no unemployment problem.
c. Than an oyster, there's nothing moister.
d. What kind of a noise annoys a foiled oyster?
e. Your greatest desire is your path to joy, but don't let it destroy you.
f. The biggest difference between men and boys is the cost of their toys.
g. Many have pointed out that boys will be boys, but they don't have to be the James boys.
h. If oil spoils water, perhaps the answer to oil spills is to paper train the oil tankers.
i. There's many a boy here today who looks on war with great joy, but, boys, it is all hell.
j. There is no way to avoid the birds in the air, but the pilots can avoid being where the birds are.
k. In Boyne, Bill Moyer had a choice of dining royally at the Burger King or the Dairy Queen.
l. We know where olive oil and corn oil come from, but what about baby oil?

 **[eɪ]** **Phonetic**   **Diacritic** **ā**

ache, pale,
Kay

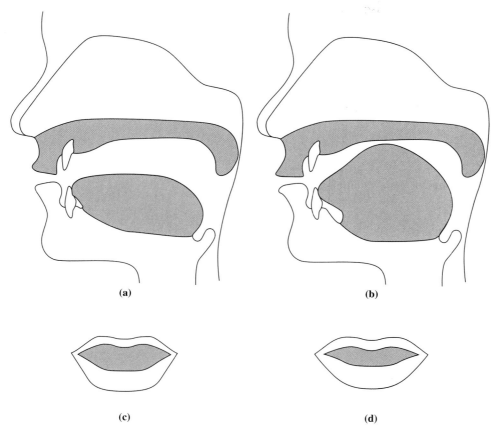

(a)   (b)

(c)   (d)

VARIOUS SPELLINGS

au as in GAUGE   ei as in FREIGHT
ay as in HAY   et as in FILET
ea as in STEAK   ey as in GREY
ée as in ENTRÉE   ué as in RISQUÉ

Piddling Pursuit

Phonetic   ɪf keɪn wʌz ɪnˈseɪn, wʌz ˈeɪbl ʌnˈsteɪbl?

Diacritic   t͟hā sā t͟hat rok iz hēr tə stā, but t͟hā nevʹər sā wâr.

How to . . .

Tongue   A mid-high position, but pulled back a bit. The tongue muscles are quite tense. The
                        tip should be behind or near the edges of the lower front teeth. To make the diphthong,
                        raise your tongue tip quickly from the mid-high position of [e] to the higher position
                        of [ɪ].

Lips   Spread, relaxed, moving from unrounded to slightly rounded.

Jaw   Mid-low, but for the diphthong close it slightly as you glide into the [ɪ].

WARMER-UPPERS

Initial	Medial	Final
Abe	Cain	Fay
ale	jade	hey
aim	game	ʾlei
aids	Dave	way
Amy	maim	clay
age	reins	they
amiable	wage	Klee (artist)
angel	stain	buffet
agency	gravy	today
ancient	chain	defray
aorta	vacate	sachet
aviator	whale	matinee

[e] or [eɪ]?

Ray mailed the plate to Kay.

Some of you sounded the *ay/ai* as a pure vowel—a monophthong.

[re meld ðə plet tə ke.]

Probably most of you sounded the *ay/ai* as a diphthong—a rapid blending of two vowels.

[reɪ meɪld ðə pleɪt tə keɪ.]

[e], as a pure vowel, is used infrequently in American English. You'll likely use it if it occurs in unstressed positions: ch*a*otic [keˈɑtɪk], v*a*cation [veˈkeɪʃən].

[eɪ] is used in most stressed positions: aw*ay* [əˈweɪ]; b*a*by [ˈbeɪbɪ].

If, however, you use [e] where [eɪ] is preferred, your speech may sound somewhat stunted. Actor Sly Stallone, both on- and off-screen, is a notable example. Most of the street toughs who inhabit such TV shows as *NYPD, Homicide: Life on the Streets,* and *New York Undercover,* are unaware of the existence of [eɪ].

Faults and Foibles

    A. Nasalized [eɪ]

§ **B.** Excessively prolonged [eɪ]

§§§ **C. SUBSTITUTING [ɛ] FOR [eɪ]**

Now for the details. Choose as needed.

A. Nasalized [eɪ]

A common fault is a tendency to nasalize [eɪ] in words in which it's preceded or followed by [m], [n], or [ŋ]. If you've studied the three nasals, you already know that these three sounds are directed mostly through the nose. Thus the soft palate (velum) must be lowered to divert the airstream through the nose. For all other sounds, including [eɪ], the velum is raised.

Say [eɪ–m] several times, and you'll feel the action of the velum.

7.   Carrying this feeling over into these word pairs, you should be able to produce an [eɪ] in the second word of each pair that is as free of undesirable nasality as the [eɪ] in the first word.

    a.

day–dame	fray–frame	gay–game	lay–lane
ade–made	Kay–came	pay–pain	ail–nail
ape–nape	ray–rain	shay–shame	say–same

Guard against excessively nasalized and strident [e] sounds as you practice this material.

b.   Filet mignon: An opera by Beethoven.
c.   Myth: No pain, no gain. Fact: Train! Don't strain.
d.   *Two Dames and a Dane* is a maimed version of Shakespeare's famed *Hamlet.*
e.   To say "Keep changing" is not a cliché. When you're through changing, you're through.
f.   An expert is a man who has made all the mistakes that can be made in a very narrow field.
g.   The other day by a little lake,
    James Gaynor was bitten by a snake.
        What was the sequel?
        Needless to say,
    The snake, not Gaynor, passed away. [Adapted from Voltaire]

§ B. Excessively prolonged [eɪ]

If excessively prolonged, this sound may become a three-vowel production.
    Result: *fate* becomes *fa-i-uht* [feɪət].
    This isn't uncommon in some southern speech, and is used quite often by educated people in the South. If your speech is nonsouthern, you're probably producing a relatively pure diphthong.
    Some speakers let [eɪ] drop and shorten to [ɛ] if it comes before [l].
    You'll go to jail, Dale, if you fail turns into *You'll go to jell, Dell, if you fell.*

8.   Are you converting this sound into a triphthong or shortening it to [ɛ]? Then correct as necessary.

a.
fate	sale	wail	pail
mail	bathe	slain	kale
came	bale	same	rein

b.   The pain goes away on payday.
c.   Make haste slowly. Haste makes waste.
d.   The ideal neighbor is the one who makes noise the same time you do.
e.   A person should work eight hours and sleep eight hours, but not the same eight hours.
f.   About encores: "It's better that they should want and we don't play than we should play and they don't want." [Isaac Stern]

§§§   C.   SUBSTITUTING [ɛ] FOR [eɪ]

For discussion and relevant exercises, see page 213.

 **Phonetic**

Diacritic

ode, coal, toe

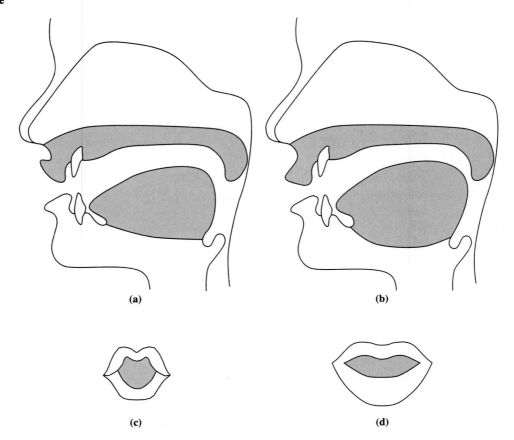

(a)

(b)

(c)

(d)

VARIOUS SPELLINGS

eau as in TABLEAU   oo as in BROOCH
ew as in SEW   ough as in DOUGH
oe as in DOE

Piddling Pursuit

Phonetic   ðɛrz noʊ ˈbɪznɪs lɑɪk ʃoʊ ˈbɪznɪz.

Diacritic   yo͞o drīv fôr shō, but put fôr dō.

How to . . .

   Tongue   Somewhat tense. For the vowel [o], the back of your tongue is raised mid-high toward the palate. The tip is close to the lower front teeth.
For the diphthong [oʊ], the tongue shifts to a high back position to form the [ʊ] sound.

   Lips   Rounded, lax, and protruded.
For the diphthong, the lips tense slightly, round even more, and come closer together.

   Jaw   Half-lowered.
To make the diphthong, raise the jaw for [ʊ].

The pure vowel [o] is most often found in unaccented or lightly stressed positions: *obey, omit*. Occasionally it's heard as a simple vowel if followed by a voiceless consonant, as in l*o*tion and c*o*ach, or if followed by [r] as in d*oo*r and c*o*re.

In stressed syllables, the diphthong [oʊ] is heard more often than the vowel [o].

To be honest, a majority of speakers, if they're aware of it or not, probably use [oʊ] much more frequently than [o]. And certainly anyone striving for a bit of extra finesse and polish will be more comfortable with [oʊ] than [o].

WARMER-UPPERS

Initial	Medial	Final
omen	pose	foe
old	soul	flow
oval	doze	go
ogle	clone	throw
odor	froze	toe
oleo	zone	Poe
Owen	grown	beau
ogre	moan	Jell-O
Ozark	moment	although
Olympic	boulder	yellow
overrate	woman	swallow
ozone	shoulder	vertigo

Faults and Foibles

    A. Substituting [ə] for [oʊ] in unstressed syllables

§ **B.** Distorting [oʊ]

§§§ **C. SUBSTITUTING [ɑ], [ɔ], OR [ʌ] FOR [oʊ]**

Now for the details. Choose as needed.

A. Substituting [ə] *for* [oʊ] *in unstressed syllables*

Is it *uhvation* [əˈveʃən] or *ovation* [oʊˈveʃən]? The latter is preferred. Nevertheless, good speakers in *rapid conversation* often turn initial unstressed [oʊ] into the schwa [ə]. Not preferable, however, is turning a final unstressed [oʊ] into [ə].

If you say *pilluh* [ˈpɪlə] instead of *pillow* [ˈpɪloʊ], you'll bother some listeners.

9.   In the following, the letter *o* occurs as the vowel [o] in some words and as the diphthong [oʊ] in others. To be on the safe side, sound a recognizable *o* in this material.

    a.   Obese Milo yelled olé out the window.
    b.   Did Ophelia follow the swallows to Shiloh?
    c.   On some occasions it's okay to omit the word *obey*.
    d.   The notorious fellow from Ohio played the hotel piano.
    e.   Othello and the widow ate the yellow Jell-O in the oasis.
    f.   Otto, the piano player with the bolo tie, practices his solo while watching polo through the open window.

§ B. Distorting [oʊ]

This is an annoying little mannerism.

Instead of "Don't smoke to cure an old cold," the speaker says, "Do-*wuh*n't smo-*uh*k to cure an o-*wuh*ld co-*uh*ld."

The speaker is inserting an unwanted *wuh* [wə] or a simple schwa [ə] after the [oʊ]. When we talk about the so-called southern "drawl," this [wə-ə] sound tacked onto [oʊ] is one of the reasons for the drawl.

[ɛoʊ]?

Very commonly in the East and in the Middle Atlantic section of the United States, this diphthong becomes a triph-thong. A sound something like [ɛ] is inserted before the [o], and the resulting distortion is [gɛoʊ rɛoʊ ðə ɛoʊld bɛoʊt].

If it's accompanied by too much nasality and tension—and it generally is—it becomes an extremely jarring sound.

10. Work for simple, uncluttered [oʊ] sounds as you read this material. Round your lips. Although the back of the tongue is raised, the front of the tongue must be low. Use a relaxed approach and don't let that undesirable *wuh* [wʌ] or [ə] sneak in before [oʊ]. And don't let the sound go through your nose.

   a. snow   hold   over   onus   beau
       soul   owe   gold   bowl   Joe
       foe   no   poll   Rome   ego
       coat   cold   toe   oak   sew

   b. Polo: Ping-Pong with ponies.
   c. If you don't know, simply say so.
   d. Oboe: An ill woodwind that nobody blows well.
   e. Talk low, talk slow, and don't say too much. [John Wayne]
   f. It's better to know nothing than to know what ain't so. [Jay Leno]
   g. A folk singer is a joker who sings through his nose by ear.
   h. One who knows only one's own side of the case knows little of that.
   i. If you don't go to other people's funerals, they won't go to yours.
   j. What I know about work. Live by this code: You can't have bread and loaf.
   k. In Wyoming rodeos they say there's never been a horse that can't be rode, and never been a rider that can't be throwed.
   l. Gravestone in Dodge City: Here lies Lester More. Four slugs from a .44. No Les, no more.
   m. New movie rating—NOOO: No violence, no sex, no audience.

§§§ C. SUBSTITUTING [ɑ], [ɔ], OR [ʌ] FOR [oʊ]

For discussion and relevant exercises, see page 213.

THE "TWILIGHT ZONE" DIPHTHONGS [ɛr] [ɪr] [ɔr] [ʊr]

(Also known as off-glides, falling diphthongs, and minor diphthongs)

That chameleonlike [r] again!

Your primary address may strongly influence your pronunciation of this rather promiscuous sound. And to add to the general merriment, the experts don't always agree about the precise nature of the sound that you articulate.

Take, for example, such a simple word as *hair*. You may pronounce it as (1) hɛr, (2) heɚ, (3) hɛɚ, or, as heard in some southern and eastern regions, (4) hɛə.

If you prefer pronunciation 4 to the more widely used 1–3, does this mean that you're wrong? Not at all! And how about

near?	1. nɪr	2. nɪɚ	3. nɪə
ford?	1. fɔrd	2. fɔɚd	3. fɔəd
sure?	1. ʃur	2. ʃuɚ	3. ʃuə

Remember: When you combine the two sounds, the vowels and consonants color and modify their neighbors. For example, the [ɛ] that you articulate in *hair* is not an identical twin to your [ɛ] phoneme in *egg*.

For obvious reasons, a specific group of exercises cannot be provided for each of these variants.

Anyone who needs more homework with these "Twilight Zone" sounds should review sections in the text dealing with the individual components of each diphthong or blend.

11. In the meantime, if you need a tune-up, here are a few Internet gems that might interest you.
    a. A few beers short of a six-pack.
    b. Never wear a backward baseball cap to an interview.
    c. Wanted: Hair cutter. Excellent growth potential.
    d. Wanted: Man to take care of cow that doesn't smoke or drink.
    e. Never take a job where winter winds can blow up your pants.
    f. Although in poor health, the patient refused an autopsy.
    g. The patient expired on the floor uneventfully.

[ɑɪ] or [aɪ]

§§§ B. SUBSTITUTING [ɑ] FOR [ɑɪ]

Those whose first language is Vietnamese may say *ahs* [ɑs] for *ice* [ɑɪs], *sah* [sɑ] for *sigh* [sɑɪ]. Now and then, speakers of other Asiatic languages also lapse into this substitution.

[ɑ] is simply a relaxed, tongue-on-floor-of-mouth position. But for [ɑɪ] don't forget to raise your tongue to a mid-high position on the second half of the sound, and raise your jaw slightly.

12.   Practice these word pairs.

spot–spite   dock–dike
Todd–tide   God–guide
trot–trite   Tom–time
cot–kite   blond–blind
job–jibe   lot–light

Now review the drill sentences in Exercise 1.

[ɑʊ] or [aʊ]

§§§ C. SUBSTITUTING [ɑ] FOR [ɑʊ]

Japanese, Korean, and Vietnamese students sometimes have a problem with this one.

doubt [dɑʊt] sounds more like [dɑt]

scout [skɑʊt] sounds more like [skɑt]

As you now know, [ɑ] is easy. To form the diphthong, start from the tongue-on-floor-of-mouth position and rapidly raise the back of your tongue, gliding into the [ʊ] position.

13.   Read these pairs. Check your tongue position on the second part of the diphthong.

bond–bound   prall–prowl
clawed–cloud   prod–proud
crotch–crouch   Roddy–rowdy
fond–found   shot–shout
Kant–count   spot–spout
plod–plowed   trot–trout

[eɪ]

§§§ C. SUBSTITUTING [ε] FOR [eɪ]

Do you say *met* when you mean *mate, get* when you mean *gate?*

    If your first language is Arabic, Chinese, Japanese, Korean, or Vietnamese, you may be substituting [ε] for [eɪ].

    For [ε]—let the back of your tongue touch your upper molars. Your tongue tip should be behind the lower front teeth.

    For [eɪ]—your tongue should be in a mid-high position. The back of the tongue should be close to the soft palate. Then it moves into the [ɪ] position.

14. Don't confuse the two sounds as you work with the following:
    a. Go ahead. Make my day.
    b. Great hopes make great men.
    c. Heads I win. Tails you lose.
    d. Death is the great leveler.
    e. Tell the truth and shame the devil.
    f. The pepper taster tested the paper as he read Ray's letter.
    g. I hate housework. You make the beds, et cetera, and six months later you start all over again. [Roseanne]

[oʊ]

§§§ C. SUBSTITUTING [ɑ], [ɔ], OR [ʌ] FOR [oʊ]

Arabic, Spanish, Russian, Japanese, Chinese, or Vietnamese your first language?

Perhaps you pronounce *stone* as [stɑn] or [stɔn].

Korean language background?

Do you say *dunt* [dʌnt] for *don't* [doʊnt], *sup* [sʌp] for *soap* [soʊp]?

15. For comparison, try these. *You must be able to feel the difference in tongue and lip positions.*

[ɑ] or [ɔ]	[ʌ]	[oʊ]
Tongue low, relaxed. Lips unrounded.	*Tongue on floor of mouth, but center slightly raised. Lips unrounded.*	*Back of tongue raised mid-high. Lips rounded.*
mall	mull	mole
hall	hull	hole
Gaul	gull	goal
doll	dull	dole

SMORGASBORD: REVIEW MATERIAL FOR ALL THE DIPHTHONGS

16. Practice this material.

    a. Playboy: A plowboy with a Rolls-Royce.
    b. If love were oil, I'd be about a quart low.
    c. How is it that they can announce power outages on TV?
    d. The devil doesn't know how to sing, only how to howl.
    e. Small children, small annoys; big children, big annoys.
    f. I went to a fight the other night and a hockey game broke out.
    g. Why are there interstate highways in Hawaii?
    h. Enjoy money while you have it. Shrouds don't have pockets.
    i. Apply moisturizing cream, and you'll be oily to bed and oily to rise.
    j. When a person is down and out, an ounce of help is better than a pound of preaching.
    k. How do they get deer to cross at that yellow road sign?
    l. It takes the average person 2 years to learn how to talk and about 60 to learn how to shut up.
    m. How can you rejoice if you've never joiced? How can you reconnoiter, if you've never connoitered?
    n. How to win in court: If the law is on your side, pound on the law. If the facts are on your side, pound on the facts. If neither is on your side, pound on the table.
    o. Prayer of high school senior: Please lead me out of this constant coma. And give me a chance at my diploma. Let others fight about church and state. I pray only to graduate.
    p. The tourist stopped his car on a road and asked a boy how far it was to Mountainville. With a twinkle in his eye, the little boy smiled and said, "It's about twenty-five thousand miles the way you're going, but if you turn around, it's about four."
    q. The more liquid a man pours down his throat, the less chance there is of drowning his voice.
    r. If you say, "I'll hate myself for this in the morning," you're probably right.
    s. The best rule about driving through the five o'clock traffic is to try to avoid being part of the six o'clock news.
    t. When you're traveling so fast that you can't stop quickly enough to avoid knocking down a pedestrian, honk the horn. This is known as a warning.
    u. Drive carefully and don't insist on your rites.
    v. How to solve traffic problems: Pass a law that allows only paid-for cars to use the highway.

Assignment 12: Diphthongs

Prepare material containing many examples of those diphthongs with which you particularly need work. As a reminder, here is a key.

[ɑɪ] ī as in my   [ɑʊ] ou as in cow   [oʊ] ō as in go
[ɔɪ] oi as in oil   [eɪ] ā as in pay

(Twilight Zoners: [ɛr] as in hair; [ɪr] as in leer; [ɔr] as in board; [ʊr] as in tour)

or

Use the optional format suggested for Assignment 11: Vowels. This time, of course, emphasize diphthongs in your material.

Suggested Checklist for Assignment 12: See page 285, Appendix B.

WRAP-UP

1. Diphthongs are smooth blends of two different vowel sounds within the same syllable. A diphthong changes quality during production. The first vowel receives greater stress than the second.

[ɑɪ]	ī
[ɑʊ]	ou
[ɔɪ]	oi

2. [e] and [o] in stressed positions are almost always sounded as diphthongs: [eɪ] and [oʊ].

3. Diphthongs and blends, especially those in which the first part, the vowel, is followed by the letter *r*, are not always consistent and are strongly influenced by regional differences.

chapter 9

BE VARIED AND VIVID— EXPRESSIVENESS

... You can get an excellent response from an audience even if you're talking to them in a language they don't understand? Helena Modjeska, a great Polish actress, was once asked quite unexpectedly at a dinner party to do one of her favorite scenes from Shakespeare. She performed in Polish for about 10 minutes before an English-speaking audience. Her performance was so emotional that she had her listeners in tears. Later she confessed that she had merely recited the Polish alphabet over and over again!

... Great careers have been demolished because of voices? In silent films, John Gilbert was one of the most passionate screen lovers of all times. Shortly before talking pictures came along, Gilbert signed a five-year contract with MGM for a million dollars a year (megabucks in those days). Then he made his first sound film. His scrawny, high-pitched voice cracked up audiences, and Gilbert's career soon ground to a halt.

... *Castrati* (emasculated male singers) were the rock stars of the 17th and 18th centuries? The cruel operation was done when a boy was between 7 and 12 to prevent his soprano or alto voice from changing. As an adult, however, he had all the physical power and strength of a grown man. When *castrati* sang particularly well in an opera, Italian audiences liked to shout, "*Viva il coltello!*" ("Long live the knife!")

... If you tell a lie the pitch of your voice tends to rise? This is according to voiceprint experts who work with courts of law.

... "The Star Spangled Banner" is the world's most unsingable national anthem? It's more often mangled than spangled. The range—an octave and a half—is beyond the capabilities of 9 out of 10 Americans. The melody, an old English drinking song, had been "borrowed" for 26 other songs before Francis Scott Key stole it for "The Star Spangled Banner."

VOCAL MONOTONY

Now I lay me down to sleep,
The lecture dull, the subject deep;
If he should quit before I wake,
Give me a poke, for heaven's sake!

That three-word phrase at the beginning of the second line—*The lecture dull*—is a key to what this chapter is about.

Table 9.1   Criteria for Rating Instructors

General Ratings of Instructors	Reasons or Comments
Superior, excellent, good	Enthusiastic delivery, alive, brisk, peppy, alert, vocally animated, dynamic way of talking, has warmth and rapport, vivid, positive
Fair, inferior	A "moanatone," drones and chants, bored, ho-hum, wooden, burned out, monotonic, exciting as a roll of soggy toilet tissue

Recent surveys at 50 colleges and universities gave 2,500 students the opportunity to evaluate their instructors on "teaching personality" and to explain or comment briefly on their ratings. Table 9.1 is a simple breakdown of some of the most typical, unedited responses.

Warning: Monotony may be hazardous to your social health. Communicating with your listeners in a voice in which rigor mortis has set in may easily convince them that your feelings toward them are negative.

Vocal monotony is a plague that strikes clergy, lawyers, nurses, legislators, astronauts, homemakers, butchers, bakers, candlestick makers, and—you knew this was coming—*students!*

Actually, the identities of these vocal bores—let's call them *drones*—are less important than why they are the way they are. Every time they say something, they pound coffin nails into their remarks. Vocal monotony has its roots in

- Personality characteristics.
- The purpose of the speaker, including the subject matter and the general nature of the material.

Each factor has its own Drones' Gallery.

PERSONALITY CHARACTERISTICS

Are you bashful?

Do you tend to think, move, and talk slowly?

Have you ever been told that you have a "cold" personality?

An important word from your sponsor. There are surely hundreds of Bashful Beths around us, but it would be wrong to think that all shy, modest, or reserved people are drones. Beth may be excessively bashful in her everyday relations with friends and classmates, but she may suddenly become supercharged and emit sparks on a speaker's platform or on a stage. Likewise, not all slow-paced people—the slow movers and speakers—are bores in front of audiences. Frigid Freddy, too, and his "cold" colleagues are sometimes able to catch fire in performance situations.

Paradoxically, warm, outgoing people can sometimes turn into icicles. They may suddenly find themselves communicating or performing in an unfamiliar environment (classroom, large auditorium), and they're intimidated by this strange atmosphere. Their immediate reactions? Vocal gridlock. Monopitch.

PURPOSE OF THE SPEAKER

Some individuals don't try very hard to communicate with their listeners. They're unimaginative. If you have no fire in yourself, you certainly can't warm others.

A former colleague—the students nicknamed her Repetitious Rita—teaches Economics 101 and has been teaching it for almost as many years. As the students put it, "She makes us feel numb on one end and dumb on the other." She's slowly slid into the wrong kind of groove without being aware of it. Her argument is that it's impossible to sound lively in something you've been saying over and over again, year in and year out. In reality, she's no longer interested in what she has to say. She's stagnant. She needs her batteries recharged! (It is only fair to add that academia has more than its share of Repetitious Roberts.)

FACING THE PROBLEM

Do *you*, by any chance, belong to the Drones' Gallery? Suffer from too much of a muchness? Maybe you're just a part-time monopitch. Be honest. No one likes to be tagged as drab, colorless, or cadaverous. The world's second worst crime is boredom. The first is being a bore.

Make a realistic attempt to face the problem head-on. The old saw "A leopard can't change its spots" is quite true—for leopards. If you're receptive as you work on the material in this chapter, you'll remove yourself from the Drones' Gallery (and enjoy yourself in the process!).

Typically, many drones use a range of only two, three, or four tones as they speak. The singsong drone may use many more, but his or her up–down–up–down vocal pattern is just as monotonous as the voice of the three-note drone. The trained voice is capable of using tones within a range of an octave and a half or more. Almost everyone should be able to develop and use effectively a range of at least one octave. Before you can work on specific techniques that will help you achieve greater vocal flexibility, you should consider the interesting subject of pitch.

PITCH

The legendary tenor Enrico Caruso was singing an opera in Philadelphia. Before the performance started, the bass complained of laryngitis. There was no understudy. The show had to go on. The bass was particularly worried about his big aria in act 4. Caruso told him to do the best he could, but if he felt his voice giving out, to alert him with a stage whisper. The bass struggled through the opera and finally got to the big solo. His voice disappeared, and he frantically signaled Caruso. The performance wasn't stopped. Caruso sang the bass aria in a deep voice, while the stricken singer simply mouthed the words. Not a soul in the audience knew the difference, and the aria was greeted with tremendous applause.

Caruso, with that 24-karat voice, had built a reputation as a tenor and not as a bass. He looked like a tenor, acted like a tenor, sang like a tenor, and had the vocal equipment of a tenor. We all understand that a tenor voice is higher in pitch than a baritone and that an alto is lower in pitch than a soprano. But what, specifically, does *pitch* refer to?

Pitch *refers to the highness or lowness of tone or sound.* The slower the vibration cycles of the vocal folds, the lower the pitch; the faster the vibration cycles, the higher the pitch. Find middle C on the piano and hum a corresponding pitch. Your vocal folds are meeting and separating in vibratory cycles of approximately 262 times per second! Strike the lowest key on the piano and the string vibrates approximately 27 cycles a second. The highest key: the string does approximately 4,096 vibratory cycles.

What Determines Pitch?

As a youngster, did you ever indulge in a little hero or heroine worship? You may have modeled your speech after a teacher; a TV, movie, or sports celebrity; or a parent. If your model had a well-pitched voice—fine and dandy! If the model didn't, you may have copied his or her problems.

Some movie critics have found Tom Cruise's voice too thin and high-pitched. Sensitive to such criticism, the actor has insisted that a new recording system be used in his most recent movies. The device, known as a "voice enhancer," apparently makes his voice sound lower and richer.

Age, sex, and general emotional states are the most obvious factors that determine pitch, but you must also reckon with three other relatively subtle factors: the length, thickness and mass, and degree of tension of your vocal folds.

- *Length.* Pitch is lowered if length is increased. A man's larger vocal folds produce lower tones than a woman's smaller vocal folds. (The longest piano strings produce the lowest bass tones; the shorter strings produce the highest treble tones.)

- *Thickness and mass.* Pitch is generally lowered by greater weight—that is, greater thickness and mass of the vocal folds. (The strings on a bass viol are thicker and heavier than the strings on a violin.)

- *Tension.* Pitch is raised as tension of the vocal folds is increased. (As a guitar string is tightened, the pitch is raised.)

In general, pitch is largely the result of variations in tensions and of changes in pressure beneath the vocal folds.

The most important thing for you is to use a pitch level that is suitable for *your* voice. To do otherwise is like squeezing a size 10 foot into a size 8 shoe.

Voices, like musical instruments, have a range or span of tones in which they sound their best. For example, strike two keys at the top and bottom of a piano keyboard, and you'll immediately realize why composers rarely write music calling for the use of those particular keys.

You've heard individuals who speak in an inky bass—a sort of glottal gargle. They're probably using the lower extremes of their vocal range. More irritating are the persons who habitually use the upper extremes, producing squeaky, Barbie-doll voices.

The Optimum Pitch Level

The optimum pitch level (it's also known as the natural pitch level) is simply the most desirable and serviceable level of pitch for the individual voice.

Your voice functions most dynamically and efficiently at this level. Young people are often interested in cultivating relatively deep voices. Many radio, TV, movie, and stage personalities massage our ears with sultry bass rumbles. James Earl Jones, Mel Gibson, and Whoopi Goldberg own voices in which deep bells ring.

The late Tallulah Bankhead, a flamboyant stage and movie actress with a *basso profundo* voice, once received a telephone call from Earl Wilson. Wilson, a well-known New York gossip columnist, had a shrill, high-pitched voice.

Wilson: Tallulah, have you ever been mistaken for a man?

Tallulah: No Earl. Have you?

There is surely nothing wrong with a mighty Wurlitzer bass or a smokey contralto voice. At the same time, there's nothing wrong either with a well-used tenor or soprano voice. A large number of successful speakers or entertainers—Tom Selleck has already been mentioned—have voices that are relatively high pitched. Being tall and macho doesn't guarantee you a deep, plummy voice. One of the most satiny, lush bass voices I've ever heard came from a young man who stood 5′4″ and weighed 135 pounds!

One critic said about a certain popular but Munchkin-voiced young movie star that he sounded as though he should be auditioning for the Vienna Boys Choir. Nevertheless, baby-voiced Melanie Griffith and Chris O'Donnell have had relatively prosperous careers in spite of their somewhat immature voices.

> By his own admission, Shock Jock Howard Stern, early in his radio career, had a terrible, piccolo-pitched voice. But he worked on it and dropped it about four tones.

Your business with this section of the chapter is not how to develop an enticing or commercial voice. Your business is *how to make the best of what you already have.*

The Habitual Pitch Level

You'll notice that as you speak or read a few lines of material, the pitch of the voice varies in highness and lowness. The upward and downward inflections, however, seem to cluster about one average or central pitch level. It's the pitch level you most frequently use. You move up and down from it, but you most often return to it. This is your *habitual pitch level.*

Finding Your Habitual Pitch Level

1. Sit comfortably erect in a chair. Inhale deeply two or three times and then sigh. (Vocalize! Don't whisper.) Listen carefully to the pitch level of the sigh. Repeat the process and sigh several times. You'll discover that the sighs are being vocalized at approximately the same pitch level. This level is *close* to your habitual level.

2. Read sentences *a–g* in a normal and relaxed manner. Emphasize the italicized words, but try to concentrate on the nonitalicized words. You'll be quite close to your habitual level on the unemphasized words. (The final syllable or word in a sentence, however, is often pitched lower than the habitual level.)

   a. Life is a camel. It *won't* back up.
   b. Old jokes never *die*. They just smell that way.
   c. *Most* family trees have at least *one* crop failure.
   d. Bees can't *make* honey and *sting* at the same time.
   e. Daniel Boone was born in a log *cabin* which he *himself* built.
   f. I can answer that in *just* two words: im possible.
   g. If I'm not for myself, who *will* be?

3. Read the story in this exercise three or four times. During the first reading, use as much variation as you wish. Then, read it again, gradually working toward a monotone, narrowing and compressing the range until you've eliminated the upward and downward inflections. When you arrive at a level, sustain *ah* at that level, and find the corresponding note on the piano. You're probably at or near your habitual pitch level.

There was a villager whose business caused him to travel every day to a nearby seaport. As his neighbors rarely traveled, he was their newspaper. Each night he told them about some strange sight he had seen until finally the time came when he had exhausted all of the seaport's novelties. As he hated to return without a story, he made up one about a fish so large that it filled the entire harbor. His amazed but trusting listeners were so impressed by the story that they set out to see the fish. On the way they overtook their storyteller who, carried away by his own invention, was also hurrying to see the amazing sight.

4. Starting with the *ah* that you leveled off with in Exercise 3 (and be sure that you check this again with a pitch pipe or piano), sing *one* on the *ah* and then down the scale with *two, three, four, five* to the lowest note you can produce comfortably and with reasonably good quality.

    Repeat this exercise several times. It will be the basis of another exercise to help you locate your *optimum pitch level*—the pitch level that's most desirable and useful.

Finding Your Optimum Pitch Level: Exercises

5. Repeat Exercise 4, singing down the scale to the lowest good note you can produce without scraping. This time sing *one* on that note, and then go back up the scale with *two, three, four, five*. Sustain the *five* for a few seconds. (Actually, you'll be prolonging the *i* sound.) With the help of a piano or a pitch pipe, determine what note you're sustaining. Using this level, say monotonously,
    The day is dark and cold and dreary.
    Repeat the sentence one tone higher and then one tone lower. It's in this general area that your optimum pitch level is located.

6. Hold your hands over your ears and hum up and down the scale several times. You'll notice that one tone has an increased intensity. It sounds richer and fuller. This particular tone should be very close to your *optimum* pitch level. Now, compare the results of this exercise with the results of Exercise 5.

7. Start again at your lowest comfortable pitch, this time singing *ah*. You don't have to cover your ears. Then move up and down the scale several times. Again you'll hear and feel that one particular note seems to be the strongest, richest, and easiest to produce. It should be the same or almost the same tone you discovered in Exercise 6, and also at or very near your most efficient pitch level.

    Another way of recognizing your most congenial pitch level: On a scale of 1 to 12—with 1 representing the lowest comfortable note in your pitch range, 12 the highest—the tones in the vicinity of 3–4 are probably your best. (You may want extra help with this one. A piano or a pitchpipe will come in handy.)

Repeat Exercises 3, 4, 5, and 6 until you're able to tell the difference, if any, between your habitual and your optimum pitch levels.

If you find a difference of approximately one or two tones between the two levels, the pitch level you're using is probably satisfactory.

If the difference is greater, you should try to make your optimum pitch level habitual.

A WORD OF WARNING
As far as optimum pitch is concerned, a large majority of us don't have problems.

Your habitual pitch is, in most cases, also your optimum pitch. If a competent authority tells you that your habitual pitch level is too high or too low, raising or lowering your pitch level a note or two won't result in vocal abuse or damage. Exercises 8–12 will help.

Don't try to lower your voice three or more notes without professional supervision. You'll hurt your voice.

If your habitual level is satisfactory, skip Exercises 8–12, and jump to the section on *range*.

Making Your Optimum Pitch Level Habitual

8. Once again, locate your optimum pitch. A piano or pitch pipe will be necessary. Sing *ah* on the optimum pitch and hold it for approximately six seconds.

9. Chant these words at your optimum pitch level. Practice with maximum controlled relaxation.

dawn	lot	feet	bath
murmur	hope	boat	all
hush	men	match	tip

10. Chant these sentences with deliberate monotony at your optimum pitch level. In other words, concentrate on how you sound as you read the lines rather than what you are reading.
    a. There is no they, only us.
    b. When turkeys mate, they think of swans.
    c. You're no bigger than the things that annoy you.
    d. We had seen the light at the end of the tunnel, and it was out.
    e. Never get into fights with ugly people because they have nothing to lose.
    f. Dream research is a wonderful thing. All you do is sleep for a living.
    g. The lip can slip, the eye can lie, but the nose knows.

11. Read each selection differently, according to this key:

    OLD-HAB=Chant the material *monotonously* at your old, habitual level.

    NEW-OPT=Chant the material *monotonously* at your new, optimum level.

    a. **OLD-HAB**—Most of us hate to see a poor loser—or a rich winner.
        NEW-OPT—Never keep up with the Joneses. Drag them down to your level.
    b. **OLD-HAB**—The only way to stop smoking is to just stop—no *ifs, ands,* or *butts.*
        NEW-OPT—Most children are spoiled because the parents can't spank Grandma.
    c. **OLD-HAB**—A person with a bad name is already half-hanged.
        NEW-OPT—Memory is the thing you forget with.
    d. **OLD-HAB**—What you get free costs too much.
        NEW-OPT—Nothing in fine print is ever good news.
    e. **OLD-HAB**—If you have an excuse, don't use it.
        NEW-OPT—Pigs go through a mud-life crisis.
    f. **OLD-HAB**—Two pints make a quartet.
        NEW-OPT—Better to sit up all night than to go to bed with a dragon.
    g. **OLD-HAB**—If it tastes good, it's trying to kill you.
        NEW-OPT—Does the name Pavlov ring a bell?

12. Repeat selections *a–g*, reading them at your *optimum level,* **but read them with vocal variation.** Don't chant. Work for casual, conversational spontaneity.

    or

    Read this charming little fable at your new *optimum level,* and "talk" it—as though you're telling a joke or an anecdote to a good friend.

    One summer evening, a sentinel who stood leaning on his spear at the entrance to the Han Ku Pass—for this was many years before the building of the Great Wall—beheld a white-bearded traveler riding toward him, seated cross-legged upon the shoulders of a black ox.
         Said the elderly stranger, when he drew near and halted, "I am an old man, and wish to die peacefully in the mountains which lie to the westward. Permit me, therefore, to depart."
         But the sentinel threw himself on the ground and said, in awe, "Are you not that great philosopher?" For he suspected the traveler to be none other than Lin Tang, who was known to be the holiest and wisest man in China.
         "That may or may not be," replied the stranger, "but I am an old man, wishing to depart from China and die in peace."

At this, the sentinel realized that he was indeed in the presence of the great Lin Tang, who had for more than a hundred years sat in the shadow of a plum tree, uttering words of such extreme simplicity that no man in the world was learned enough to understand their meaning.

So the sentinel threw himself in the ox's path and cried out, "I am a poor and ignorant man, but I have heard it said that wisdom is a thing of priceless worth. Spare me, I beg of you, before you depart from China, one word of your great wisdom, which may enrich my poverty or make it easier to bear."

Whereupon Lin Tang opened his mouth, and said gravely, "Wow."

[Quoted in *The Theater Book of the Year* (1946–1947) by George Jean Nathan]

Assignment 13 (*if needed*): Pitch Level

Prepare 9 to 12 lines of material. Mark and practice your selections as follows:

> 1. Read 3–4 lines monotonously at your **habitual** pitch level.
> 2. Read 3–4 lines monotonously at your **optimum** pitch level.
> 3. Read 3–4 lines at your optimum level but with **vocal variation.**

Schedule at least two practice sessions. The first session, use steps (1), (2), and (3).

The second and longer session, use (3) only. And, of course, use this level when you present your assignment in class.

The suggested checklist for this assignment may be useful to you as you practice your material.

Suggested Checklist for Assignment 13: See page 287, Appendix B.

RANGE

Range *is the span of tones from the lowest to the highest that the voice is capable of producing.*

A major general in the front row of a speech communication class? Yes, I had the gentleman as a student in a class at the Pentagon. Why would a major general be in a basic speech course? In his little speech of self-introduction, he confessed all:

> I've been putting audiences to sleep for years. I didn't realize what a turkey I was until I saw myself on film the other day. I look and sound like a zombie. I should be selling embalming fluid. I thought a course like this might help me.

At the end of the course, we "shot" the general once again, and we ran the *before* and *after* tapes for the entire class. His improvement was astonishing.

Not as well known as the Academy Oscar award is Hollywood's Golden Raspberry award, which was recently won by Sylvester Stallone as the worst actor for the third time in five years. The citation read, "For the drone of the century."

The drone typically reads or talks using a skimpy, shriveled range of two to four tones. People with glimmer in their voices have a range of 12 to 14 tones!

(Using your full range will not only make you far more interesting to your listeners, but for some fairly subtle reason, your intelligibility will also be improved!)

The next few exercises will help you remove the cobwebs from the upper and lower extremes of your range. Or they'll show you how to use expressively and flexibly the range you already have.

13. Hum a tone that is easy and comfortable for you. From there, hum down the scale to your lowest safe tone. Don't scrape rock bottom. Then hum back up the scale to your highest decent tone, but don't strain at the top. You'll most likely discover that your range is about 12 tones and possibly more.

14. Do a vocal walk *up* the scale. Say the first word in each line on a comfortably low pitch, and pitch each succeeding word a half or whole tone higher.

   a. Sink or swim.

   b. Long tongue; short friendships.

c. Little things affect little minds.

d. That most knowing of persons—gossip.

e. Cigarettes are killers that travel in packs.

f. A rose by any other name would smell.

g. "Why not?" is a slogan for an interesting life.

h. Horses are what more people bet on than get on.

i. Did the devil really create the world when God wasn't looking?

j. When you've got them by the wallet, their hearts and minds will follow.

k. How awful to reflect that what people say of us may be true.

l. It seems sort of significant that we have two ears and only one mouth.

m. Celebrities are persons who are known to many people they are glad they don't know.

n. If you're going to do something tonight that you'll be sorry for tomorrow morning, sleep late.

Repeat but this time do your vocal walk *down* the scale, starting on a comfortably high pitch and then bouncing down the steps.

INTONATION

As you talk, your voice moves from sound to sound with an almost continuous rise and fall in pitch, touching peaks, plateaus, and valleys. The overall pattern of pitch changes in phrases and sentences is described as *intonation, speech melody,* or *pitch contour.*

Let's consider three aspects of intonation: *key, inflections,* and *steps.*

Key

Key *is the general pitch level—ranging anywhere from high to low—that is used at any given moment in talking or reading.*

High key

If you win your state's $20 million lottery, you'll report your good news to the world in a *high key.* Even if you don't luck out and are simply saying or reading something that is light, humorous, cheerful, or expresses joy, your key will be in the higher part of your range.

Catch a few TV commercials—particularly car salespeople—and you'll note that many of the performers do their stuff in a comparatively high key.

On the negative side, the voices of people in a rage or scared spitless often soar into the upper regions.

> One "cops and courts" TV show has been vastly acclaimed by reviewers. There is a lone dissenter, however, who finds the show "stone-stiff." He complains that the actors deliberately act dull, believing that real cops and lawyers behave in that manner. He accuses the cast of suffering from "dramatic constipation."

Middle key

Informal, casual, and unemotional material—a recent shopping trip, a test, lunch at McDonald's, or a so-so date—work best in the middle range.

Low key

If you're telling somebody about the death of a friend, if you're feeling romantic under a full moon, or you're digging deeply into Nietzsche, you'll use a low key. Quiet, melancholy, or profound ideas tend to seek out the lower depths.

Shakespeare even tells you what key to use when he says, "Speak low if you speak of love."

General Douglas MacArthur's classic speech to Congress in 1951 had the entire nation dissolved in tears. In his closing sentences, he carefully shifted to a low key: "Old soldiers never die; they just fade away. I now close my military career . . . an old soldier who tried to do his duty as God gave him to see that duty. Good-bye."

In a less patriotic mood, Oscar-winning Anthony Hopkins, as Hannibal the Cannibal in *Silence of the Lambs,* delivered many of his venomous lines in a hushed, low key.

15. Read these selections in a *high key.* But don't deliver them in a high monotone. Work for contrast, color, and variation *within* that area.

a. Ye Gods! Now nobody, but nobody, is going to stop me from going straight to your wife and telling her the truth . . . the whole story about you and your carousing. Does she know that you're a philanderer, a swinger, and, to boot, a lecher? Does she know about your ladies, your playgirls? You just wait, you tomcat, until she finds out. All those parties you gave and that I was never invited to. You just wait and see!

b. Love makes you feel special. It changes everyone for the better. It is the one commodity that multiplies when you give it away. The more you spread it around, the more you are able to hang onto it because it keeps coming back to you. Where love is concerned, it pays to be an absolute spendthrift. It cannot be bought or sold, so throw it away! Splash it all over! Empty your pockets! Shake the basket! Turn it upside down! Shower it on everyone—even those who don't deserve it! You may startle them into behaving in a way you never dreamed possible. Not only is it the great mystery of life, it is also the most powerful motivator known to humankind.

c. I'll do the explaining, Sir! When the war began, like the dutiful wives we are, we tolerated you men and endured your actions in silence. Small wonder. You wouldn't let us say boo. We'd sit at home, and we'd hear that you men had done it again—mishandled another big issue with your staggering incompetence. Then, masking our worry with a nervous laugh, we'd ask you, "And did you manage to end the war in the assembly this morning?" And what did you say to us? "What's it to you? Shut up!" Now we women are going to set you right! Inside there we have four battalions—fully armed fighting women completely equipped for war. What did you expect? We're not slaves. We're freedom women, and when we're scorned, we're full of fury. Never underestimate the power of a woman! Into the fray! Smash them to bits! The day is ours! [Aristophanes, *Lysistrata*]

16. Read these selections in a *middle key.* Again, strive for flexibility and variety.

a. When I was a boy of 14, my father was so ignorant I could hardly stand to have the old man around. But when I got to be 21, I was amazed at how much he had learned in seven years. [Mark Twain]

b. The Statue of Liberty: Made by an Italian, presented to the American people on behalf of the French government for the purpose of welcoming Irish immigrants to New York, which was founded by Dutch people who had stolen it from the Indians and in which today's largest ethnic group is Jewish.

c. The crowd cheered lustily as the team trotted onto the field. Eleven mighty and determined men going forth to fight for the old alma mater, to give their all. With them came Charlie. Everybody knew Charlie. On the campus his bubbling personality had won him many friends. He turned and faced the fans. He grinned. There was confidence as well as determination in his grin. He assumed the pose the vast crowd had seen so often. With an assured tone in his voice he barked out, "Peanuts, popcorn, candy!"

17. Read these selections in a *low key,* but don't freeze your voice at one level. Let it rise and fall.

a. Today marks my final roll call with you. But I want you to know that when I cross the river, my last conscious thoughts will be of the Corps, and the Corps, and the Corps. I bid you farewell. [Douglas MacArthur]

b. The day is cold, and dark, and dreary.
It rains, and the wind is never weary;
The vine still clings to the mouldering wall,
But at every gust the dead leaves fall,
And the day is dark and dreary.

c. Yea, though I walk through the valley of the shadow of death, I will fear no evil; for thou art with me. Thy rod and thy staff they comfort me. Thou preparest a table before me in the presence of mine enemies; thou anointest my head with oil. My cup runneth over. Surely goodness and mercy shall follow me all the days of my life, and I shall dwell in the house of the Lord forever. [From the Twenty-third Psalm]

18. Which key—*high, middle,* or *low*—is most appropriate for each of the following? Experiment by trying the selections in more than one key. Be as expressive as you can.

a. I am thy father's spirit, doomed for a certain time to walk the night.
b. If you have to kiss somebody at 7:00 A.M. in front of the camera, you'd better be friends. [Liza Minelli]
c. Good night, sweet Prince. And flights of angels sing thee to thy rest.
d. If I reach for the stars, I might not touch them. But I won't come up with a handful of dirt.
e. Do you ever get the feeling that the only reason we have elections is to find out if the polls are right?
f. We are such stuff as dreams are made of and our little life is rounded with a sleep.
g. Hey diddle, diddle. The cat and the fiddle, the cow jumped over the moon.
h. Why condemn the devil? He's using the same defense many of us are using: "I'm doing my own thing."
i. Life is a tale told by an idiot, full of sound and fury, and signifying nothing.

j.   Is it going too far when the owner puts a lemon slice in the dog's water bowl?

k.   Silently, one by one, in the meadows of heaven, blossomed the lovely stars, the forget-me-nots of angels.

l.   Is death the last sleep? No, it is only the last and final awakening.

m.   If at first you don't succeed—try, try again. Then quit. There's no use being a total fool about it.

n.   Fear death?—the fog in my throat, the mist in my face.

o.   You know what's wrong with an Italian dinner? Seven days later you're hungry again.

p.   Twilight and evening bell, and after that the dark!
And may there be no sadness of farewell when I embark.

q.   What better way to spend an afternoon than reclining in a dentist's chair, listening to a high-speed drill, smelling your tooth enamel burn, and watching clouds of smoke billow out of your mouth?

Inflection

Try these:

> What is this thing called love?
>
> What? Is this thing called love?
>
> What is this thing called? Love?

You probably used different inflections or intonation patterns with each one. *Changing pitch within a syllable, word, or group of words is called an* **inflection.** *A* **rising inflection** *is an upward gliding of the voice from a low to a high pitch.*

Say

The upward inflection indicates **questioning, hesitancy, curiosity, suspense, surprise,** and **perplexity.**
It leaves your listeners waiting.

    To be avoided: "Up-talk," currently fashionable with some individuals. It happens if the speaker turns a simple statement into a question:

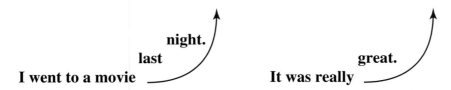

A **falling inflection** *is a downward gliding of the voice from a high to a low pitch.*
Say

The downward slide denotes **certainty, command, emphasis,** and **finality.**
This inflection leaves few if any doubts in your listener's mind.

A **double inflection** *combines the upward and downward gliding of the voice. It sounds like a siren.*
Say

The double inflection signifies **uncertainty, sarcasm, evasion,** or **double** or **hidden meanings.**
In some listeners, the double inflection may trigger a defensive attitude or it may lead to further questioning.

19. Read each of these words three times using a falling, a rising, and then a double inflection. Exaggerate your inflections.

    a. hey   c. well   e. please   g. maybe
    b. ah   d. yes   f. no   h. don't

20. Experiment with the inflections. And say *oh,* suggesting the following meanings. Remember—there isn't necessarily just *one* right way to do these. Several different ways might work convincingly.

    a. elation   d. sarcasm   g. indifference
    b. fear   e. anger   h. amazement
    c. pity   f. disgust   i. curiosity

21. Try each of these words, using a suitable inflection. The sentence in parentheses suggests a specific meaning for the word, but don't read the sentence aloud.

    a. So (We've caught you at last, you rascal!)
    b. So (What's it to you?)
    c. Stop (Here?)
    d. Stop (At once!)
    e. Please (Don't hurt the puppy.)
    f. Please (This is the last straw!)
    g. Why (I've never heard of such a thing.)
    h. Why (I'll tell you why.)
    i. Yes (I'm not so sure.)
    j. Yes (I'm positive.)
    k. Well (This is just what I expected.)
    l. Well (Have you made up your mind yet?)
    m. Ah (The poor thing.)
    n. Ah (I'm tired.)
    o. Hey (I dropped a button.)
    p. Hey (I flunked three courses.)
    q. Wow (Isn't it a beauty?)
    r. Wow (I've had it!)
    s. Really (Did it actually happen?)
    t. Really (Don't ever speak to me again.)
    u. Help (I'm drowning!)
    v. Help (Why should I?)
    w. Jim (Is that you tiptoeing upstairs?)
    x. Jim (What do you mean by coming in at this hour?)

Steps

A **step** *is a pitch change between words or syllables. The voice leaps or springs from one pitch to another, either up or down. Only one tone is used per word.*

22. Read each phrase twice, placing a slight pause between the two words: Use a higher pitch on the second word than on the first. Repeat, using a lower pitch on the second word than on the first.

a. He didn't.　　　　d. How much?　　　　g. They're here.　　　　j. Not now.
b. She did.　　　　　e. Who's there?　　　　h. You again.　　　　　k. You'll see.
c. I'm melting.　　　f. Oh, no.　　　　　　i. Which one?　　　　　l. Die, die!

23. In sentences *a* and *b*, given as examples, the position of the word indicates the location of the step and the relative size of the jump or skip. Read them in an exaggerated manner.

　　　With sentences *c–n*, however, you're on your own. Exaggerate these, too, working for maximum variety in steps, jumps, and skips.

a.　　　　　you　　　　　　　　　　　　　　　　scream.
　　　　　　　　say
　　　　　　　　　　that
　　　　　　　　　　　　again,
　　　　　　　　　　　　　　I'll
　　If
b.　　　be
　　To　　　　or
　　　　　　　　not　　　　　　　　　that
　　　　　　　　　to　　　　　　　　　　　is the
　　　　　　　　　　be,
　　　　　　　　　　　　　　　　　　　　　question.

c. I won't answer now and I won't answer tomorrow.
d. Speak now or forever hold your peace.
e. Smile when you say that, my friend.
f. I'm tired of telling you to get out.
g. Karen, will you marry me?
h. Oh, Mike, you and I would never get along.
i. Gee, it's spooky in here. Let's get moving!
j. I told you that would happen, didn't I?
k. What a party, and darn, am I tired.
l. I don't think he fell. I think you pushed him.
m. Careful! They're getting nearer. Oops! It's too late.
n. I'm not lying, but you certainly are.

24. Look over these sentences and experiment with a pattern of keys, inflections, and steps that fits the general meaning of the line. Then read the material aloud. Again, you'll discover that there may be three or four different ways to read a line, each of them effective.

a. Mark, I hate to do this. Here's your ring.
b. I have never liked him, and I never will.
c. Our son is dead. And Martha doesn't know. I haven't told Martha.
d. Strange—that I should run into her everyplace I go.
e. John, darling, don't try to pull the wool over my eyes.
f. If you're not responsible for this disgusting mess, would you mind telling me who is?
g. I was afraid this would happen; I kept telling you it would.
h. Rodney, is that lipstick on your shirt collar?
i. Darling, we've got to stop meeting like this.
j. Just you wait! You'll get what's coming to you!
k. Oh, Kevin, a Porsche? It's just what I wanted.
l. I'm tired, I'm sick, I'm disgusted, and I'm boiling mad.
m. Helen, is that you? Why, Mabel, what are you doing here?
n. It can't possibly flood here. Where's all that water coming from?
o. All right, I'll go. Wait a second. Why are you so anxious for me to go?
p. Judy? Didn't you know? She died more than three years ago.
q. Who stole my billfold? Oh, here it is on the desk.
r. He's such a wimp—how much money did you say he inherited?

STRESS AND EMPHASIS

Stress *is the degree of prominence of a syllable within a word or a word within a phrase or sentence.*

The syllable or the word is generally made louder, longer, and higher in pitch than neighboring syllables or words.

You stress syllables because English is a subtle language, and by doing this you increase intelligibility. There are obvious differences between *con*vict and con*vict,* between *pro*ject and pro*ject.*

You stress words to make meaning and feeling clear.

25. Read these aloud, stressing the underlined syllable.

    a. li·brary   con·<u>clu</u>·sive   dis·<u>crim</u>·i·<u>na</u>·tion
        re·<u>bel</u>   <u>ev</u>·i·dence   va·<u>ca</u>·tion·ist
        <u>re</u>·bel   <u>prob</u>·a·bly   <u>Mis</u>·sis–sipp·i·an
        <u>cav</u>·al·ry   <u>po</u>·di·um   re·pub·li·<u>ca</u>·tion

    Read these sentences, observing the differences in meaning as you stress underlined words.

    b. Is <u>that</u> the creep you wanted me to date?
    c. Is that the <u>creep</u> you wanted me to date?
    d. Is that the creep <u>you</u> wanted me to date?
    e. Is that the creep you wanted <u>me</u> to date?
    f. Is that the creep you wanted me to <u>date</u>?

Emphasis *is the degree of prominence given to a phrase or thought grouping.* An important phrase, or one containing a key idea, can be made louder, higher-pitched, and faster than neighboring words. Sometimes it works if you speak softer, lower the pitch, and use a slower rate on the phrase you wish to emphasize.

Read this sentence. When you get to the underlined phrase, turn up your volume, raise your pitch, and read the phrase rapidly.

I forgot to call you. <u>I refuse to apologize.</u>

Repeat. This time, read the underlined phrase softer, with a lower pitch and slower. Which one works better?

Remember: The key or idea words that most truly reveal the meaning and thought of a passage are the nouns, verbs, adjectives, and adverbs. The shorter words—pronouns, prepositions, conjunctions, and helper verbs—are generally skimmed over. You'll find important exceptions to all of the foregoing, however.

26. Read the drill sentences twice. The first time, emphasize the underlined sections. The second time, emphasize a different section.

    Suggestion: Don't hit or punch certain words so that they stand out like Shaquille O'Neal in a chorus of Munchkins. Emphasis should be restrained and subtle.

    a. <u>Even though a number of people have tried</u>, no one has yet found a way to drink for a living.
    b. If you haven't got any socks, <u>you can't pull them up.</u>
    c. <u>There are worse things in life than death.</u> Have you ever spent an evening with an insurance salesperson?
    d. On Thanksgiving Day <u>all over America</u>, families sit down to dinner at the same time—halftime.
    e. <u>If marriage were outlawed,</u> only outlaws would have in-laws.
    f. <u>Don't worry about avoiding temptation.</u> As you grow older, it starts avoiding you.
    g. You can fool some of the people all of the time, and all of the people some of the time; <u>but you can't fool all of the people all of the time.</u>
    h. Marriage is a lot like the army; <u>everybody complains</u>, but you'd be surprised at the large number that reenlist.

27. Your best friend has just starred as Ophelia or Hamlet in a campus production of *Hamlet.* After the performance you go backstage and say to the person, "You were great! What a performance!" with these suggested meanings:

    a. Your friend was outstanding.
    b. Your friend was outstanding. The others in the cast were atrocious.
    c. Your friend was fair.
    d. Your friend was awful.
    e. Your friend was outstanding, and you didn't think he or she could do it.
    f. Your friend was a fine actor—several years ago.
    g. You slept through the entire performance and you're asking your friend how effective he or she was.

Gimmicks

Anybody can say *I'm the happiest person in the world!* choosing the proper key, the right inflections, emphasis, and the most effective steps. The sentence might be coldly correct, and yet the overall effect would still be mechanical, bland, or false. Gimmicks are helpful, but they're not quite enough. If you're inhibited, all the gadgets and gewgaws in existence won't add one iota of color and flash to your voice.

28.   As an interesting venture, read these one-liners twice. In your first reading, ignore the obvious emotional nature of the material. *Deliberately* give a flat and cold reading.
        In your second reading, respond with as much sincerity, vitality, and animation as possible.

a.	I'm frightened.	m.	They're going to run me for president! Me? Me?
b.	Am I happy!	n.	I can't stand it another minute.
c.	She's dead! You're sure?	o.	You're too late—he just died.
d.	I hate him.	p.	This is the strangest thing that ever happened to me.
e.	I'm sad.	q.	That's disgusting.
f.	I'm suspicious of her.	r.	Go ahead! I dare you!
g.	My, how eerie it is.	s.	I'm getting sick and tired of your nagging.
h.	I guess I'm in love.	t.	I passed math? You must be kidding.
i.	Get out of here.	u.	Fasten your seat belts. We just ran out of fuel!
j.	Please don't leave me.	v.	Who could be knocking at the door at this hour of the night?
k.	You're the murderer!	w.	You won't believe this! I've just won the $20 million lottery!
l.	Frankly, my dear, I don't give a damn!		

Assignment 14: Vocal Variation

The ideas suggested next have proven most effective in helping individuals whose reading and speaking tend to be somewhat dull and monotonous. They're also quite enjoyable, and the shy, reserved type of person will find any one of them conducive to "letting go."
   Suggested Checklist for Assignment 14: See page 287, Appendix B.

Short, Short Story

Select narrative prose that contains conversation. A short, short story, or a paragraph or two taken from a short story, is suggested. Choose material that is exciting or dramatic. Analyze it carefully in terms of *key, inflections, steps,* and *emphasis.* In your performance before the class, however, concentrate on the story you're trying to tell and the ideas and emotions you're attempting to get across.

or

A Fairy Tale

If you've ever been exposed to preschool-age children, you've discovered that a favorite phrase is "Tell us a story!" Delicate nuances and shadings may be too subtle for such a young audience, so the experienced storyteller generally uses a somewhat exaggerated melody pattern with considerable pitch variation.
   Prepare a fairy tale, folk tale, children's story, or a myth. It can be a straight or a "fractured," satirical version. If you have a creative flair, make up your own story. Exaggerate when you present it—as though the age level of your audience is approximately three to five years.

> Whichever assignment you choose, be so familiar with your material that you don't have to read it word for word from your script. *Tell your audience. Don't read to them.* Inject as much spontaneity and animation as you can into your performance, and enjoy yourself while you're doing it.

RATE

Don'tspeaktoorapidly.

But on the other hand

d o n ' t   s p e a k   t o o   s l o w l y .

Here are two questions and answers that will help you win the next time you play Trivial Pursuit:

1. In what popular "classical" music selection does the composer change tempos (rates of speed) 77 times—approximately two contrasting rates of speed per minute?

2. In what popular "classical" music selection does the composer maintain one tempo all the way through the composition?

THE ANSWERS

1. Tchaikovsky's Piano Concerto No. 1.
2. Ravel's *Bolero.*

Time and rate variations are as essential in reading and speaking as they are in music. In other words, if you want to compare yourself to a composer, pick Tchaikovsky as your role model, not Ravel.

It's only fair to point out, however, that Ravel was a brilliant genius who could make a one-tempo piece of music irresistibly mesmerizing.

For the rest of us, unless you're also a brilliant genius, it's all but impossible to make even a short oral performance exciting if the tempo never varies.

Rate *includes the speed at which a person speaks, the length or duration of sounds, and the length and number of pauses.*

Most of us tend to think that *our* speaking rates are normal. Others may talk too rapidly or too slowly, but we don't. And even if we recognize the fact that our speaking rates are ineffective, we don't do much about it, because the process of changing speaking rates is a difficult one.

Measuring rate by counting the number of words read or spoken per minute (wpm) isn't entirely accurate, because words vary in length. But it can give you some idea.

Speaking rates, of course, are almost always slower than reading rates.

120 to 140 wpm

A speaking or reading rate of 120 to 140 wpm can irk your listeners even more than the "faster-than-a-speeding-bullet" rate some hyperkinetic individuals use. Not only does it suggest that the speaker is unsure of the information, but it hints of illness, timorousness, or stupidity. (Actors playing not-too-swift characters often speak at a tortoise crawl.) Tom Hanks, in *Forrest Gump,* frequently used a very slow speaking rate.

On the less ominous side, it should be noted that laid-back individuals with less outgoing personalities often tend to use slower speaking rates.

People can listen faster than you can talk, and if your rate is draggy or funereal, you'll not only bore your listeners and lose their attention, you'll soon lull them into a catatonic state.

On the other hand, if your local Sesquipedalian Society invites you to give an after-dinner speech on "A Comparison of the Myoelastic–Aerodynamic and the Neurochronaxic Theories of Voice Production," you'd be wise to talk at 120 to 140 wpm. *Complex, technical, sad,* or *profound* matter works well at this rate.

29. Even though you'll rarely have an occasion to read or speak in slow motion, get the feel of it. The selection below contains exactly 140 words. The number of words up to the diagonal lines is 120. A maximum and a minimum are established. Practice, timing yourself, until it takes you close to a minute to reach either terminal point.

All of you who live on after us, don't harden your hearts against us. If you pity wretches like us, maybe God will be merciful to you on Judgment Day. You see us here, five or six of us, strung up. As for the flesh we loved too well, it's already devoured and has rotted. And we, the bones, now turn to ashes and dust. Don't mock us or make us the butt of jokes. The rain

has rinsed and washed us; the sun dried us and turned us black. Magpies and crows have pecked out our eyes and torn away our beards and our eyebrows. Never are we at rest. The winds keep swinging us—now here, now there. / /
Lord, keep us out of hell! There's nothing for us to do there! Friends, don't jeer! May God forgive us! [Villon, *Ballad of the Hanged*]

180 to 200 wpm

A rate of 180 to 200 wpm may exhaust your listeners. Burning up the road tells the world that you're highly nervous, unsure of yourself, or emotionally rattled. Faster speaking isn't necessarily better speaking. And have you noticed? We tend to be suspicious of fast talkers; we pigeonhole them as slick operators, shady lawyers or politicians, or high-pressure used-car salesmen.

Looking at it positively, people with exuberant, effervescent personalities are frequently, if not always, fast talkers.

> The late Danny Kaye sang a show-stopping number in *Lady in the Dark,* a Broadway musical, in which he rattled off the names of 54 Russian composers (including such jaw-poppers as Balakirev, Mussorgsky, and Shostakovich) in 38 seconds!

Unlike cigarettes, which carry warnings that smoking may be hazardous to your health, excessively fast talking won't destroy you physically. But a 190-words-per-minute speaking rate is apt to pulverize sounds and is certainly not conducive to sharp articulation and intelligible communication. A few professionals get by with it. But most of us who speak with greased lips turn our sentences into mush. As one colleague tells her classes, "When a speaker is rushed, many of his or her skills are flushed." And this is almost an understatement.

A fast rate, however, is proper for some humorous material, elation, excitement, fear, or anger. Even then—use it sparingly.

30. The selection will give you a general idea of this rate. It contains exactly 200 words. The diagonal lines are placed after the 180th word.

What is it, then? What do you want? What have you come for? What do you mean by this flightiness? Bursting in all of a sudden, like a cat having a fit! Well, what have you seen that's so surprising? What kind of an idea has gotten into your head? Really, you know, you act like a three-year-old child and not in the least like what one would expect from a girl of 18. I wonder when you'll get more sensible, and behave as a well brought-up young lady should and learn a few good manners? Oh, your head's always empty! You're copying the neighbor's girls. Why are you always trying to be like them? You've no business using them as models. You have other examples, young lady, right in front of you—your own mother. I repeat—your own mother! That's the model you ought to imitate! There, now you see—it was all because of you, you silly child, that our guest was on his knees in front of me—proposing—then you blunder in.//
You come snooping around, just as though you'd gone completely out of your mind. Just for that, I refused him! [Gogol, *The Inspector General*]

140 to 180 wpm

The most tolerable and useful all-purpose rate is 140 to 180 wpm. If you have to handle material that expresses sorrow, gravity, or meditation, or material that is technical—aim for the lower end of the range: 140 wpm.

If your material expresses happiness, humor, or, on occasion, wrath, target the upper end of the range: 180 wpm.

Purely conversational situations? 150 to 180 wpm is excellent.

Have to deliver a speech? Our best public speakers find that 160 wpm is a congenial and efficient average.

> Recent studies of 200 students showed that about 80 percent of the ones with relatively strident voices tended to be very fast talkers. About 70 percent of those with breathy or throaty voices tended to be slow talkers.

31. This selection contains 180 words; the diagonal lines are placed after the 140th word. Practice at different rates until you feel natural and at ease.

Just how different are college students of today from students of the Middle Ages? Not much. They complained much more about food than we do. For a five-year period at the University of Paris, however, a lot of students discovered they could eat well and cheaply. Near the campus were the shops of a pieman and a barber. The pieman specialized in meat pies. Students could chip in and buy one and have a filling, delicious, inexpensive meal. The barber had the sharpest and fastest razor in Paris. So skilled was he that a client coming into his shop at the end of the day never felt the blade that shaped his beard until it slit his throat. The body was then dropped through a trap door into a cellar which connected with that of the pieman.//
You've guessed the rest. But one day a neighborhood dog got into the baker's backyard and dug up human bones. He took them home; his owner was a constable. The two men were caught and burned alive at the stake.

32. Look over the selections here and decide on a general rate that fits the mood of the material. When you read aloud, however, be sure that you vary the rate: accelerate, decelerate, hold steady.

    a. One dark and stormy night, a ship struck a reef and sank. But one of the sailors clung desperately to a piece of wreckage and was finally cast up exhausted on an unknown beach. In the morning he struggled to his feet and, rubbing his salt-encrusted eyes, looked around to learn where he was. The only thing he saw that could have been made by man was a gallows. "Thank God!" he shouted. "Civilization!"

    b. A majority of gunslingers from the Wild West weren't too bright. A bad man named Wes Hardin was determined to shoot it out with Wild Bill Hickok. Hardin was extremely jealous of Wild Bill, because Bill was rated as number one gunman, but Hardin was only number two. Hardin heard that Wild Bill was in El Paso, so he rode there, went into a popular bar and was given the corner seat—in those days, the best seat in the house. He sat in the corner for three days, staring into the long mirror behind the bar so that he could instantly see anybody who came through the door. And on the fourth day, who should enter the bar with gun drawn? Wild Bill Hickok? No! The sheriff. And guess what Hardin did. He shot the mirror instead of the sheriff. The sheriff then shot Hardin. You can visit his grave in El Paso today.

    c. Tell General Howard I know what is in his heart. What he told me before, I have in my heart, I am tired of fighting. Our chiefs are killed . . . The old men are all dead. It is the young men who say yes or no. My brother, who led on the young men, is dead. It is cold and we have no blankets. The little children are freezing to death. My people, some of them, have run away to the hills, and have no blankets, no food. No one knows where they are—perhaps freezing to death. I want to have time to look for my children and see how many of them I can find. Maybe I shall find them among the dead. Hear me, my chiefs, I am tired. My heart is sick and sad. From where the sun now stands I will fight no more, forever. [Chief Joseph to the Nez Percé Indians]

    d. There is one contemporary artist who refuses to go along with all the wild and weird "modern" art—square-faced ladies with three ears and a nose sprouting from the middle of the forehead. Phil Ernst insists on realism. "Tell it like it is" is his motto. One day Ernst decided to paint a picture of his backyard and garden. There were eight rather large trees in the yard, but the artist decided that if he included all eight of them, it would clutter his painting, so he painted only seven. His wife came out to look at the completed work of art. "But Phil, darling!" she said. "Where's that missing tree? There are eight trees, but you painted only seven." And what did Phil do? Paint in the missing tree? No! He took an axe and cut down the extra tree!

Assignment 15: Rate

If you're an excessively rapid or slow reader or talker, you may want additional practice in making yourself feel comfortable with a range of 140 to 180 wpm. Choose about two minutes of informal, colorful material, and place diagonal marks after word 140, word 180, word 280, and word 360. As you read, time yourself. Does your performance take approximately two minutes?

or

Prepare three short paragraphs of informal, conversational material.

Paragraph 1: Place marks after the 120th and 140th words. Practice until it takes one minute to read to either mark.

Paragraph 2: Place marks after the 180th and the 200th words. Read it in one minute.

Paragraph 3: Place marks after the 140th and 180th words. Read it in one minute.

Suggested Checklist for Assignment 15: See page 287, Appendix B.

DURATION

Duration *refers to the length or amount of sound.*
Who's suffering the most—A or B?

A.   I <u>feel</u> <u>so</u> <u>cold</u>!

B.   I <u>feel</u> <u>so-o-o-o</u> <u>co-o-o-old</u>!

Obviously, B.

Words and syllables are squeezeboxes. Like accordions, they can be expanded or compressed. When do you squeeze and when do you stretch?

33.   For demonstration purposes, read the following excerpts from two of the most popular poems in the English language:

The curfew tolls the knell of parting day,
The lowing herd winds slowly o'er the lea,
The ploughman homeward plods his weary way,
And leaves the world to darkness and to me. [Gray, "Elegy Written in a Country Churchyard"]

"Now, Dasher! now, Dancer! now, Prancer and Vixen!
On, Comet! on, Cupid! on, Donder and Blitzen!
To the top of the porch, to the top of the wall!
Now dash away, dash away, dash away all!" [Moore, "A Visit from St. Nicholas"]

As you read Gray's "Elegy," you instinctively stre-e-e-etched the words by le-e-e-engthening most of the vowels and diphthongs.

A **prolonged** or sustained treatment of words is appropriate if you're dealing with *awe, reverence, deep grief,* or *calmness.*

But with the Moore poem, you probably attacked the words as though you were touching a hot stove. You didn't linger.

For such brisk, riveting machine attacks, let's borrow the word *staccato* from musical terminology. A **staccato** treatment of words is relevant if you're expressing extreme emotional states: *joy, rage, enthusiasm, fright.*

Now say these: "I'm going shopping. Want to come along?"
"How did you do on your math test?"

Did you compromise between *prolonged* and *staccato?* Probably. You used a **regular** treatment of words, which is ideal for matter-of-fact, casual, routine conversation and speech.

34.   These lines are marked **S** for staccato, **P** for prolonged, and **R** for regular. Read them accordingly, noting the contrasts.

   a.   S: I can't stand it another minute!
   b.   P: The sea is sad and calm tonight.
   c.   R: May I see you later this evening?
   d.   S: If I've told you once, I've told you a hundred times—no!
   e.   P: Death—awful, cruel, and weary—hung like a pall over the grim field of battle.
   f.   R: Never slap a man who is chewing tobacco.
   g.   S: Don't let them kill me. Your Honor! I'm innocent! I swear it!
   h.   P: The silent forest stood there, cool and green and drowsy.
   i.   R: A lawyer explained why he didn't play golf: "I have more important things to lie about."
   j.   S: If that's the way you feel about it, all right.
   k.   P: Even a small star shines in the darkness.
   l.   R: The trouble with the rat race is that even if you win, you're still a rat.
   m.   S: Look out! He's got a gun! Duck!
   n.   P: I have never been so insulted!
   o.   R: Oh, I wish I had that kind of money.
   p.   S: Get out of here and don't ever come back.
   q.   P: Get out of here and don't ever come back.
   r.   R: Get out of here and don't ever come back.

35. Study each of these sentences and then give it the interpretation you think most apropos. Want to be ingenious? "Shift gears" within a line, going from a *prolonged* to a *staccato* or a *regular* reading.

    a. I'm sorry, but he died quite peacefully three hours ago.
    b. This is the last time you'll ever try anything like that, do you hear?
    c. Go ahead! Strike me if you dare!
    d. The Shenandoah inched along, rippling quietly under the cool light of the slowly rising moon.
    e. Excited? Who's excited?
    f. What did you put in this drink? I'm getting so drowsy.
    g. Jill? It can't be you! You're supposed to be dead!
    h. I've never been so humiliated in my life! How dare you!
    i. I'm afraid the news is bad. Your family has been wiped out.
    j. Don't ever let me catch you in that place again!
    k. She was such a decent person . . . quiet, patient, dignified . . . we couldn't have known that she was . . . dying.
    l. I've never heard of anything like this before, have you?
    m. I guess it would be better if we didn't see each other again.
    n. My wife doesn't understand me. As soon as the divorce is final, I promise to marry you.
    o. John (or Mary), I've known all along where you've been spending your evenings.
    p. Know what happens when you play a country tune backward? You get your girl and your truck back, you're not drunk anymore, and your hound dog comes back to life. [Elmore Leonard]

36. In these selections, you'll find that some phrases or lines sound best if you use *staccato* speech. Others work better if you read with *prolonged* tones or tones of *regular* duration. Work for contrast and variety within each selection.

    a. No doubt I now grew very pale. But I talked more fluently and with a heightened voice. Yet the sound increased—and what could I do? It was a low, dull, quick sound—much such a sound as a watch makes when enveloped in cotton. I gasped for breath—and yet the officers heard it not. I talked more quickly, more vehemently, but the noise steadily increased. Oh God! What could I do? I foamed—I raved—I swore! I swung the chair upon which I had been sitting and grated it upon the boards, but the noise arose overall and continually increased. It grew louder—louder—louder! And still the men chatted pleasantly, and smiled. Was it possible they heard not? Almighty God—no, no! They heard! They suspected! They knew! They were making a mockery of my horror! But anything was better than this agony! Anything was more tolerable than this derision! I could bear those hypocritical smiles no longer! I felt that I must scream or die! And now—again! Hark! Louder! Louder! Louder!

        "Villains!" I shrieked. "I admit the deed! Tear up the planks! Here, here! It is the beating of his hideous heart!" [Poe, "The Tell-Tale Heart"]

    b. I tell the story of love, the story of sorrow, the story that saves and the story that destroys. I am the smoke that palls over the field of battle where men die with me on their lips. I am close to the marriage altar, and when the grave opens I stand nearby. I call the wanderer home, I rescue the soul from the depths. I open the lips of love and through me the dead whisper to the living. One I serve as I serve all, and the leaders I make my slaves as easily as I subject their slaves. I speak through the birds of the air, the insects of the field, the crash of waters on rock-ribbed shores, the sighing of the wings in the trees, and I am even heard by the soul that knows me in the clatter of the wheels on city streets.

        I am music. [Anonymous]

PHRASING AND PAUSES

Almost every actor from Lassie to Jim Carrey wants to play Hamlet, one of the reasons being that it's the longest part—1,422 lines—in all of Shakespeare's plays.

Two of the current century's greatest Hamlets were Lawrence Olivier and Richard Burton. Less incandescent were the portrayals by Kenneth Branagh (his breathy "To be or not to be" soliloquy fell a bit flat) and Keanu Reeves (described by one critic as "marble-mouthed").

(Many people who went to Mel Gibson's movie version of the play, expecting to see *Lethal Weapon, Part IV,* were pleasantly surprised. When asked why he didn't continue his career as a classical actor, Gibson replied, "*Lethal Weapon* sells more popcorn than Shakespeare.")

Be Varied and Vivid—Expressiveness   235

Hamlet's most universal moment, of course, is the famous "To be or not to be" meditation on death. Listen to recordings by various actors, and you'll notice curious differences in the length and location of pauses.

A former student of mine played Horatio to the late Richard Burton's Hamlet. Burton delivered a different performance each night! On three consecutive evenings he gave completely dissimilar readings of the soliloquy:

To be   or not to be   that is the question.

To be or not to be   that is the question.

To be or not to be   that   is the question.

Which is the most effective? Probably none is better than the others. Taste alone, not rules, can decide. As long as clarity is preserved and the desired emphasis is achieved, a group of words can be phrased with the accompanying pauses in several different ways.

Nevertheless, something tells us that we might be annoyed at any of these readings:

To   be or not to   be that is the question.

To be or not   to be   that is the   question.

(With no pauses at all) Tobeornottobethatisthequestion.

*A **pause** is a rest stop—a period of silence. A **phrase** is a group of related words expressing a thought or "sense" unit or an idea. Phrases are set off from each other with pauses.*

WHY PAUSE?

To Take a Break and Take a Breath

You have to pause often enough so that you can replenish your breath supply and always keep a reserve amount in your lungs while speaking. Otherwise, you'll find yourself gasping for breath in the middle of a phrase, with the last two or three words of the phrase sounding like a series of strained grunts.

Then, of course, one occasionally hears this criticism of a speaker: "But he never stops to take a breath!" This individual gets wound up in his words and never runs down. Either fault—"gaspitis" or perpetual motion of the jaw—is apt to call attention to itself and detract from what is being said,.

Caution: Punctuation is generally a guide for the eye rather than the ear. True, you sometimes pause where a writer has placed a comma or a dash, but not always. If you pause for every punctuation mark, you'll sound choppy and jerky. Pauses, in themselves, are *silent* punctuation marks.

37. Read the following sentences. Pause wherever you see double vertical lines, but *breathe only when you have to.*
   a. If you think nobody cares if you're alive ‖ try missing a couple of car payments.
   b. Know what it is to be a child. ‖ It is to turn pumpkins into coaches, mice into horses, and nothing into everything.
   c. Advice to political wanna-bes: ‖ Get elected. Get re-elected. ‖ Don't get mad, get even.
   d. You get your cat and you call him Thomas or George. ‖ Then one morning you wake up ‖ and find six kittens in a hat-box ‖ and you have to reopen the whole matter.
   e. The atomic bomb in the hands of a Francis of Assisi would be less harmful than a pistol in the hand of a thug. ‖ What makes the bomb dangerous is not the energy it contains ‖ but the person who uses it.
   f. That old bromide about truck drivers leading you to the good eats was cooked up in the same kettle as the wild tales about toads causing warts, and goats eating tin cans. ‖ Don't believe it. ‖ Follow the truckers and you'll wind up at truck stops.
   g. The most important part of being a salesperson is confidence. ‖ Confidence is going after Moby Dick with a rowboat, a harpoon, and a jar of tartar sauce.
   h. Ground Hog Day has been celebrated only once in Los Angeles because when the ground hog came out of its hole ‖ it was killed by a mud slide.
        Repeat, placing the pauses in different places. Again, don't breathe until you have to.

To Indicate Changes of Thought, Feelings, or Emotions

38. Read the two examples, pausing as indicated.

   a. Americans believe in education. The average professor earns more money in a year than a professional athlete earns in a whole week. ‖ As Dennis Rodman has said, "I think everybody should get a college degree and then spend six months as a cabdriver. Then they'd be ready to face the real world."

   b. Ruth said, "I cannot leave you. Do not beg me to. And wherever you go, I will go. Your people will be my people. And together we will know great joy. ‖ But wherever you die, there will I die, too, and there will I be buried." [The Bible]

39. In the following unmarked material there are abrupt changes of thought, feelings, or emotions. Pause accordingly. Try each one several times, varying the length of the pauses.

   a. The defense tells you that the defendant loves children, flowers, and dogs. He is kind and decent. I tell you that this man is a brutal sadist, a maniacal, ice-blooded slaughterer of five innocent people.

   b. There is so much apathy in the world today, but who cares?

   c. The fights are the best part of married life. The rest is merely so-so.

   d. A man went to Las Vegas in a $50,000 Cadillac and came back in a $500,000 bus.

   e. What we would avoid, we become. What we loathe, we are. [Sophocles]

   f. I have listened to you quietly. I have not interrupted you. But until this moment, I have not been angry. Have you no decency, sir? Have you no decency?

   g. This individual is kind and compassionate. You have said it. I say that killing people in the name of religion goes beyond blasphemy. It is pure evil.

For Clarity

40. Read these twice. The first time, ignore the pause marks. The second time, pause where indicated.

   a. When Ann had eaten | | the dog ran away.

   b. Hank, her date, | | said Bob | | was quite boring.

   c. Kevin | | said the president | | is ignorant.

   d. That that is | | is.

   e. All lingerie put in the washer inside out comes out of the washer inside out. | | All lingerie put in the washer right side out | | comes out inside out.

   Without the pauses, they're confusing. (Ann ate the dog? Who's boring, who's ignorant? That that *what?* Inside out or inside in?)

For Emphasis and Emotional Quality

41. Again read these twice, without pauses and with pauses. There's a vast difference.

   a. We shall fight on the beaches | | we shall fight on the landing grounds | | we shall fight in the fields and in the streets | | we shall fight in the hills | | we shall never surrender. [Winston Churchill]

   b. How do you know love is gone? | | If you said that you'd be there at seven, and you get there by nine, and he or she hasn't called the police yet | | it's gone.

   c. To become great, what does an actor need most of all? | | Physical beauty? Not essential. | | Great physique? Unimportant. | | Expressive eyes, eloquent hands? No. | | What, then? | | Voice, voice, voice, and again, voice.

42. Believe it or not, you can make sense out of the following nonsense—*if you pause in the right places.* You'll need to gulp some air while you're reading, but don't gasp for breath in the middle of a phrase.

Esau Wood sawed wood. Esau Wood would saw wood. All the wood Esau Wood saw Esau Wood would saw. In other words, all the wood Esau saw Esau sought to saw. Oh, the wood Wood would saw! And oh, the wood-saw with which Wood would saw wood. But one day Wood's wood-saw would saw no wood, and thus the wood Wood sawed was not the wood Wood would saw if Wood's wood-saw would saw wood. Now, Wood would saw if Wood's wood-saw would saw wood, so Esau sought a saw that would saw wood. One day Esau saw a saw saw wood as no other wood-saw Wood saw would saw wood. In fact, of all the wood-saws Wood ever saw saw wood Wood never saw a wood-saw that would saw wood as the wood-saw Wood saw saw wood would saw wood, and I never saw a wood-saw that would saw as the wood-saw Wood saw would saw wood until I saw Esau saw wood with the wood-saw Wood saw saw wood. Now Wood saws wood with the wood-saw Wood saw saw wood.

The Pause That Refreshes

"The right word may be effective," as Mark Twain said, "but no word was ever as effective as a rightly timed pause."

The pregnant pause—also known as the dramatic pause—is an understated way of bringing out meanings or emotional content. A handful of televangelists are geniuses with the art of pausing. On a less ecclesiastical level, many stand-up comics and a couple of late-night talk show hosts are equally skilled.

> The greatest pause in the history of radio: Miserly Jack Benny, being held up by a hood who said, "Your money or your life." Benny paused. Impatient, the mugger said, "Well?" After another long pause, the comic responded, "I'm thinking, I'm thinking!"

Polished conversationalists and public speakers understand the importance of the pregnant pause. So do actors. George C. Scott once said that not only is the pause the most precious thing in speech, but it's the last fundamental the actor masters.

The most provocative thing about the dramatic pause, however, is not its frequency but its length.

Solemn, profound, and complex subjects generally need longer pauses than lighthearted, unpretentious, or familiar material.

The longer the pause, the greater the impact of what you have just said or are about to say.

Specifically, a long pause *after* an idea or phrase underscores what has just been said. The long pause has been described as the *amplification* or the *reflection* pause. My students have also labeled it as the "sinker-inner" pause, because it clarifies what has been said and gives you time to think about it.

If God had wanted us to think with our wombs, why did he give us a brain? I don't mind living in a man's world as long as I can be a woman in it. God made man, and then said I can do better than that and made woman. I'm not radical. I'm just aware. | | I've come a long way, Baby! [Jane Fonda]

He knows nothing and thinks he knows everything. | | That points clearly to a political career.

A long pause *before* an important idea or climactic key word heightens suspense. This pause has also been referred to as the *anticipation* pause. Ever-alert students like the two-worder "appetite-whetter," for obvious reasons.

I've just finished correcting your midterms. Every single person in this class | | flunked.

In Hollywood, if an actor's wife looks like a new woman | | she probably is. [Jean-Claude Van Damme]

If you're trying to be funny or humorous, the punch or laugh line can often be pointed up and made funnier if it's preceded by a protracted pause.

Jerry Seinfeld, Helen Hunt, Eddie Murphy, and Dennis Miller are particularly adept at accentuating their punch lines.

As a simple example of how to point up a line, try these:

Rock Magazine recently took a poll to name the best-dressed rock star. | | Nobody won.

A great composer doesn't imitate | | he steals. [Andrew Lloyd Webber]

43. In this material, one diagonal line suggests relatively **short** pauses. Three diagonals suggest relatively **medium** pauses. Six diagonals—relatively **long** pauses. Be flexible. Experiment.
    a. What is the most important thing in the world? / / / / / / Love.
    b. I am ready to meet my Maker. Whether my Maker is prepared for the ordeal of meeting me / / / is another matter. [Winston Churchill]
    c. Money doesn't go to jail / Money doesn't talk. / / / / / / It swears.
    d. Sunday School: / A place where they tell children about God for 51 weeks and then introduce them to / / / Santa Claus.
    e. Any man's death diminishes me, because I am involved in mankind. Therefore, never send to know for whom the bell tolls. / / / / / / It tolls / for thee.
    f. Gertrude Stein, poet, playwright, and wit, lay dying. In her last moments she came out of her coma. / A friend was nearby, weeping, / and asked, / / / "What is the answer?" Gertrude closed her eyes briefly. Once again she came to, a smile on her lips, and asked, / / / / / / "What is the question?"
    g. And there it lay / / / that moldy coffin / ugly in the bloodless moonlight. Six pairs of trembling hands ripped it open. / / / Something / somewhere shrieked. Our eyes pierced the formless shadows inside the casket. / Again a godless scream / and then we knew / / / the evil box was / / / / / / empty.

h. Somewhere on this globe, every 10 seconds / there is a woman giving birth to a child. She must be found and / / / stopped.

i. **Lady Macbeth:** Out, damned spot / out, I say. / / / One, two. / / / Why, then, 'tis time to / do it. Yet who would have thought the old man to have had so much / blood in him? / / / / / / The Thane of Fife had a wife. / / / Where is she now? / / / / / / What, will these hands never be clean? All the perfumes of Arabia / will not sweeten this little hand. / / / I tell you again Banquo's buried / he cannot come out of his grave. To bed, to bed! There's knocking at the gate. Come, come, come, come / give me your hand. What's done / / / cannot be / / / / / / undone. To bed, to bed! [Shakespeare, *Macbeth*]

44. Look over these selections for location and length of pauses. Be venturesome. If you've found a spot that you're convinced needs a long pause, try it that way. Then do it again with a medium or short pause to determine if it makes any difference. Finally, mark according to your best judgment and then read.

a. I don't worry about crime in the streets. It's the sidewalks I stay off of.

b. Why do celebrities always gripe about their lack of privacy? That's like a fighter coming out of the ring and saying, "There's somebody in there trying to hit me."

c. No matter how far we run or how much we deprive ourselves of ice cream, in the long run we're all dead.

d. There is a time for everything. There is a time to be born and a time to die. A time to be silent and a time to speak. A time to love and a time to hate. A time for war and a time for peace. [Ecclesiastes]

e. And I looked and beheld a pale horse. And his rider's name was Death, and Hell followed him. And power was given to them over a fourth part of the earth, to kill with sword, with hunger, and with pestilence. Behold, there was a great earthquake. The sun became black as sackcloth, and the moon became as blood. The stars of heaven fell to the earth, and the kings of the earth, the rich, the mighty, the slave and the free, hid in caves in the mountains. [Revelation]

f. **Macbeth:** She should have died hereafter. There would have been a time for such a word. Tomorrow, and tomorrow, and tomorrow, creeps in this petty pace from day to day to the last syllable of recorded time, and all our yesterdays have lighted fools the way to dusty death. Out, out, brief candle! Life's but a walking shadow, a poor player that struts and frets his hour upon the stage and then is heard no more. It is a tale told by an idiot, full of sound and fury, signifying nothing. [Shakespeare, *Macbeth*]

g. Not only is suicide a sin, it is *the* sin. It is the ultimate and absolute evil, the refusal to take the oath of loyalty to live. The man who kills a man, kills a man. The man who kills himself kills all men; as far as he is concerned, he wipes out the world. [Friedrich Nietzsche]

h. Do you like "modern" art? I do. Even some of the crazy stuff that looks like doodlings by Jason, the psycho in *Friday the Thirteenth, Part 10.* I have some "modern" art at home. When I show it to friends, the comment I most often get is, "What does it mean?" My standard reply is, "What does a tree mean?" Do you want to know what "modern" art is all about? When my son Jeff was six, he had done something wrong and was being punished by being confined to the backyard for a day. He sat on the steps. It was a hot day, and Jeff felt sorry for himself because he had wanted to go swimming. He started talking to himself. I eavesdropped. Said he, "Am I a boy? Why aren't I a chair? What is a chair?" And that's what "modern" art is about.

i. The great box was in the same place. The lid was laid on it, not fastened down. I knew I must reach the body for the key, so I raised the lid, and then I saw something which filled my soul with horror. There lay the Count, but looking as if his youth had been half renewed, for the white hair was changed to iron-gray. The mouth was redder than ever. On the lips were gouts of blood, which trickled from the corners of the mouth and ran over the chin and neck. Even the deep, burning eyes were set in bloated flesh. It seemed as if the whole awful creature was simply gorged with blood. I felt all over the body, but no sign could I find of the key. Then I stopped and looked at the Count. There was a mocking smile on that ghastly face. A terrible desire came upon me to rid the world of this monster. I seized a shovel. I lifted it high. I struck downward at the hateful face. But as I did so the head turned. The eyes fell full upon me, with all their blazing horror. The sight seemed to paralyze me. The shovel fell from my hand. The last glimpse I had was of that hideous face, blood-stained and fixed with an evil grin which would have held its own in the bottom level of hell. [Stoker, *Dracula*]

When Knighthood Was in Flower—or Was It?

(Slightly embellished, the following is based on a true 13th century incident.)

In a cramped, 50-room castle, surrounded by a deep moat and overlooking the Danube, lived the exquisitely beautiful, 17-year-old Teudalinga. Down the road apiece, in a 200-room castle, lived fearless Sir Wolfgang Geek, the bravest but also the silliest knight in the kingdom. Wolfgang had seen Teudalinga only once, but he was mesmerized by her beauty.

She regarded him as a gruz (medieval slang for "wimp"). He was skinny, chinless, and yellow-haired. Seeking her hand in marriage, Wolfgang visited her father. The duke joyfully consented to the union. (He wanted to get rid of Teudalinga anyway.) "By all means," he exclaimed. "She is yours!"

But Teudalinga refused to see Wolfgang. Storming into her chamber, the duke yelled, "Gadzooks! What ails you, daughter? A 200-room castle?"

Teudalinga shouted, "Absolutely not, my lord!"

"What!" screamed the duke. "You dare oppose my will?"

"I'd die," she hissed, "before I'd marry that gruz!" She yelled, "Fie on you, father!"

"You ungrateful wretch!" he thundered, stalking out of the room.

Teudalinga, however, began to have a change of heart. She didn't want to spend the rest of her life in a cramped castle. "Aha!" she purred. "I have a plan!"

She sent for Sir Wolfgang. Wolfgang arrived, giggling. "Sir Wolfgang, you have something to ask me?"

"My lady," he said reverently, "I heg for your band . . . uh . . . I mean, beg for your hand in marriage." He giggled again.

Her tone was imperious. "Sir Wolfgang, I will become your wife on two conditions. One: in the event of your untimely demise, I will inherit your castle."

Bowing and kissing her hand, he replied, "A deed will be prepared at once, my lady. And condition two?"

"To prove your devotion to me, would you be willing to swim across our moat?" (The moat was 40 feet wide and very deep.)

Triumphantly, he said, "Oh-h-h-h, I can do that, my lady."

A week later, Teudalinga, deed in hand, the duke, and the entire court assembled on the battlements overlooking the moat. Wolfgang, clad only in medieval briefs, approached the water.

"Hold!" cried Teudalinga. "I'd forgotten one thing, noble knight. You must swim the moat in full armor."

Wolfgang stiffened. "But, my lady . . ."

"Are you a coward, Sir Wolfgang?"

He trumpeted, "I am fearless, my lady!"

A squire brought 75 pounds of armor and chain mail, which Wolfgang donned. He stuck an armored toe into the water, hesitated, and then jumped in.

He swam two strokes. And disappeared. Forever.

Teudalinga turned to her father and smiled. "Who said that chivalry is dead?" [Elyl Reyam]

45. The following selections are unpunctuated. Study them silently to determine story line and emotional content. Then, using an appropriate rate, phrases, emphasis, and intonation, try them aloud.

a. I put the glass to my lips and drank in one gulp then I reeled clutched at the table and held on staring with bursting eyes gasping with open mouth oh God I screamed and oh God again and again the most racking agonies ground into my bones deadly nausea and a horror of the spirit that can't be exceeded at the hour of birth or death I looked down my clothes hung formlessly on my shrunken limbs the hand that lay on my knee corded and hairy I was once more Edward Hyde a moment before I had been Dr. Jekyll respected wealthy beloved and now I was hunted homeless a known murderer a refugee from the gallows I'm a creature a monster eaten up and emptied by fevers ugly in body and mind the doom that's closing in is crushing me will I die upon the scaffold God knows this is my true hour of death [Stevenson, *Dr. Jekyll and Mr. Hyde*]

b. Marry you no I can't do that we don't agree and we never will so we'll just be good friends all our lives you'll get over this after awhile and find some lovely accomplished girl who'll adore you and make a wonderful wife for your beautiful home yes you will you will I'd be a terrible wife I'm homely and awkward and odd and old yes I am and don't interrupt me and you'd be ashamed of me and we'd quarrel just as we're doing right now you see I'll never marry you I'm happy as I am and love my liberty too well to give it up for any mortal man oh I'll always be fond of you very fond indeed as a friend but I'll never marry you absolutely never and the sooner you believe it the better for both of us so there [Alcott, *Little Women*]

c. The men in their bloody-minded rage were terrible as they poured down into the streets but the women were a sight to chill the boldest beating their breasts tearing their hair and screaming from their children from their aged and sick crouching on the bare ground famished and naked they ran with streaming hair urging one another to madness Old Foulon has been captured seized alive Foulon who told starving people that they could eat grass Foulon who told my old starving father that he could eat grass Foulon who told my baby that it might suck grass when these breasts were dry hear me my dead baby and my withered father I swear on my knees to avenge you on Foulon husbands brothers and young men give us the blood of Foulon give us the heart of Foulon give us the body and soul of Foulon tear Foulon to pieces drag him torn bruised bleeding screeching to the lamppost stuff grass in his mouth and hang him then hack off his head and put it on a pike [Dickens, *A Tale of Two Cities*]

Assignment 16: Duration, Phrasing, and Pauses

Prepare 15 to 20 lines of material. A brief cutting from a short story or a play would be ideal. Try to choose material that contains several contrasting moods.

Analyze your selection. What kind of treatment works best with certain words, phrases, or lines? Staccato? Prolonged? Regular?

Consider phrasing and pauses—frequency and length.

Do a practice session or two, focusing on duration, phrasing, and pauses. Then practice your selection, concentrating on contents. *Forget techniques and gimmicks. Give it a lot of verve and vigor!*

Suggested Checklist for Assignment 16: See page 287, Appendix B.

PUTTING IT ALL TOGETHER

"Take care of the sense," Lewis Carroll wrote, "and the sounds will take care of themselves."

As you work with the next selections, blend and weave together the various elements that have to do with vocal expressiveness. Don't get hung up on devices! What is the general effect you're trying to achieve? Search for meaning and intelligibility.

This may be a relatively new experience for some of you. Try to submerge your own personality into the personality of the character you're playing. *Forget techniques. Forget yourself. Build up a strong desire to communicate with your listeners. The material that you present should do more than reach your audience; it should penetrate them!*

Sniff and snoop. Research your character. What kind of a personality does your character have? What kinds of feelings and emotions are being expressed? What motivates your character? How old? Physical appearance? Relationship to other characters?

Many students have been encouraged to visit a library to acquire and read an entire show. And they've enjoyed the experience.

When you do this assignment before your classmates, project not your old personality but a new and different personality, a character that your audience has not previously met.

Monologues and Dialogues

Choose one of the following selections. Use all the vocal versatility you can muster. Be original.

46. **Female Characters**

a. **Countess:** Oh, I wish she hadn't brought up the Alps, Lucy. It always reminds me of that nasty moment I had the day Gustav made me climb to the top of one of them. Anyhow, there we were. And suddenly it struck me that Gustav had pushed me. I slid halfway down the mountain before I realized that Gustav didn't love me any more. But love takes care of its own, Lucy. I slid right into the arms of my fourth husband, the count. [Boothe, *The Women,* Random House, Inc.]

b.   **Fanny:** Do you mean that? You're not just trying to be polite? Nick, I'm a good friend of yours. And in a dumb way I'm kinda smart. So I'm going to tell you what you ought to do. You ought to marry me. You don't have to, I'm all yours anyway. But the kind of wife I'd be, you wouldn't *believe!* Look at my past record—no errors, no strikeouts, nothing! That means—no bad habits! I'd be learning the part fresh—*your* way! Besides that, I'm lucky! And I'd be lucky for you! What could be better for a gambler than a lucky wife? [Lennart, *Funny Girl,* Random House, Inc.]

c.   **Sally:** Two days ago. Just after we left here. He saw us in the street . . . Mother and me, I mean—and our eyes met—his and mine, I mean—and he sort of followed me. To a tea shop, where he sat and gazed at me. And back to the hotel. And at the restaurant. He had the table next to us, and he kept sort of hitching his foot around my chair. And he passed me a note in the fruit basket. Only Mother got it by mistake. But it was in German. I told her it was from a movie agent. And I went over and talked to him, and he was! Then we met later. He's quite marvelous, Chris. He's got a long, black beard. Well, not really long. I've never been kissed by a beard before. I thought it would be awful. But it isn't. It's quite exciting. Only he doesn't speak much German. He's a Yugoslavian. That's why I don't know much about the picture. But I'm sure it will be all right. He'll write in something. And now I've got to run. [Van Druten, *I Am a Camera,* Random House, Inc.]

d.   **Christine:** I wasn't dreaming, dear. I was outside my room without knowing how I got there. You saw me disappear from my room one evening. Maybe you can explain. I can't. I can only tell you that, suddenly, there was no mirror, no dressing room. I was in a dark passage. I was frightened. It was very dark, except for a faint red glimmer at the far end. I cried out. My voice was the only sound. And, suddenly, a hand was laid on mine—a stone-cold bony hand that seized my wrist and wouldn't let go. I screamed again. I struggled for a while and then I was dragged toward the light. I saw that I was in the hands of a man wrapped in a black cloak and wearing a mask that hid his whole face. My limbs stiffened, my mouth opened to scream, but a hand closed it. A hand that smelled of death. I fainted away. [Leroux, *Phantom of the Opera*]

e.   **Julie:** You don't think I can stand the sight of blood, is that it? Oh, how I'd love to see your brains on that chopping block. I'd love to see the whole of your sex swimming in a sea of blood. The way I feel I could drink out of your skull. I could eat your heart roasted whole! You think I'm weak! My father will come home—find his money stolen! He'll send for the sheriff—and I'll tell him everything. Then there'll be peace and quiet . . . forever. [Strindberg, *Miss Julie*]

f.   **Rachel:** I remember feeling this way when I was a little girl. I would wake up at night, terrified of the dark. I'd think that sometimes my bed was on the ceiling, and the whole house was upside down. And if I didn't hang on to the mattress, I might fall outward to the stars. I wanted to run to my father, and have him tell me I was safe, that everything was all right. But I was always more frightened of him than I was of falling. It's the same way now. [Lawrence and Lee, *Inherit the Wind,* Random House, Inc.]

g.   **Dorine:** If you ask me, both of you are insane. Stop this nonsense, now! You do want to marry each other, don't you? Mariane, surely you don't want to marry the quack—that imposter—your father has picked out for you? So stop fussing and be quiet. You two are like all other lovers—you're crazy. Your father's a tyrant, and he has a plan we've got to stop. He's acting like a dunce. You'd better humor the old fossil. Pretend to give in to him. Tell him you'll marry the man he wants you to marry. Then keep postponing the wedding day. That way you'll gain time, and time will turn the trick. But if everything else fails, no man can force you to marry him unless you take his ring and say "I do." That's the scheme. Now get going! There's no time to chat. Come on, now! Walk! [Molière, *Tartuffe*]

h.   **Crystal:** Now get this straight, Mrs. Haines. I like what I've got and I'm going to keep it. You handed me your husband on a silver platter. But I'm not returning the compliment. I can't be stampeded by gossip. What you believe and what Stephen believes will cut no ice in a divorce court. You need proof and you haven't got it. When Mr. Winston comes to his senses, he'll apologize. And Stephen will have no choice, but to accept—my explanations. Now, that's that! Good night! [Boothe, *The Women,* Random House, Inc.]

i.   **Donna Elvira:** For a man who is used to this sort of thing, you're certainly not very convincing, are you? I'm almost sorry to see you so embarrassed. And now the lies will start again, won't they? Why don't you swear that your feelings for me are the same as ever? Why don't you swear that you love me more than anything else in this world—'til death do us part? Oh, I'm amazed at my own stupidity! I knew what you were doing. Common sense told me you were guilty. But my simple little mind was busy inventing excuses for you. Did a day pass that you weren't with some other woman? No! You're going to be punished for what you've done to me, Don Juan. If God Himself has no terrors for you, then let me warn you. Beware the fury of a scorned woman! [Molière, *Don Juan*]

j. **Muriel:** Oh, I was a fool ever to come here! I've got a good notion to go right home and never speak to you again! You did too kiss her! You're lying and you know it! You did too! And there I was right at that time lying in bed and not able to sleep, wondering how I was ever going to see you again and crying my eyes out, while you—I hate you! I wish you were dead! I'm going home this moment! I never want to lay eyes on you again! And this time I mean it! [O'Neill, *Ah, Wilderness!,* Random House, Inc.]

k. **Ysabeau:** You have gold for your wine and for your friends—the worst rats and cats in Paris. A swarm of thieves. Sewer scum! Pimps! Hired assassins! But I, Master Bad Rat. I wear the same dress you stole for me three months ago. We can't even stay in Paris. There's a price on your head. Jailbird! You have that gallows' look. Do you ever think of our future, François? We live as long as other men have gold you can plunder. You want me to share a life time of filching . . . pilfering? Really, I grow tired of you! [Mayer, *Villon*]

l. **Birdie:** I've never had a headache in my life. You know it as well as I do. I never had a headache. That's a lie they tell for me. I drink. All by myself, in my own room, by myself, I drink. You know what? In twenty-two years I haven't had a whole day of happiness. Oh, a little like today with you all. But never a single, whole day. And in twenty years you'll be just like me. They'll do the same things to you. [Hellman, *The Little Foxes,* Random House, Inc.]

m. **Martha:** My husband—dead? That dear man! Not really dead? Oh, help me—I may faint! Wait! Do you have the evidence I need? I want a death certificate. I want to know where, when, and how that miserable creature died. What did he say on his death bed? Didn't he send anything to me? A few gold coins, perhaps? A ring or two? He deserted my bed and board three years ago. But that dear, sweet man . . . I forgive him. Oh, I'll be a widow for a year—well, maybe not a whole year—then I'll look around for another man. It won't be easy finding one like him. No woman on the face of this earth had a sweeter fool than mine. If only he hadn't roamed around so much. He was never home. And he couldn't resist that foreign wine, not to mention those foreign women. And those damnable dice! He had a passion for rolling them. Why, that wretch! To rob his children and his wife! May his soul rot in hell! [Goethe, *Faust*]

n. **Mina:** There was in the room the same white mist that I had noticed before. My heart sank. Beside the bed, as if he had stepped out of the mist, stood a tall thin man, all in black. I knew him at once. The waxen face; the high aquiline nose; the parted red lips with the sharp white teeth showing between. He placed his reeking lips on my throat! I felt my strength ebbing away. A long time passed before he took his foul, awful, sneering mouth away. I saw it drip with fresh blood. Then he pulled open his shirt, and with his long sharp nails opened a vein in his breast. When the blood began to spurt out, he took my hands in one of his, holding them tight, and with the other seized my neck and pressed my mouth to the wound, so that I must either suffocate or swallow some of the . . . Oh my God! my God! What have I done, what have I done? [Stoker, *Dracula*]

47. **Male Characters**

a. **Sid:** You're right, Lily!—right not to forgive me! I'm no good and never will be! I'm a no-good drunken bum! You shouldn't even wipe your feet on me! I'm a dirty rotten drunk!—no good to myself or anybody else! If I had any guts, I'd kill myself, and good riddance!—but I haven't—I'm yellow, too—a yellow, drunken bum! [O'Neill, *Ah, Wilderness!,* Random House, Inc.]

b. **Volpone:** Ah, Mosca, you clever puppy, what a fool you are, how little you have learned of me! Do you really think you have to let the ducats fly in order to have everything? No, you fool! Let them rest quietly, side by side. Then, people will come of their own accord to offer you everything. Get this through your head: The magic of gold is so great that its smell alone can make men drunk. They only need to sniff it, and they come creeping here on their bellies; they only need to smell it, and they fall into your hands like moths in a flame. I do nothing but say I am rich—they bow their backs in reverence. Then I make a pretense at mortal illness. Ah, then the water drips off their tongues, and they begin to dance for my money. Ah, how they love me: Friend Volpone! Best beloved friend! How they flatter me! How they serve me! How they rub against my shins and wag their tails! I'd like to trample the life out of these cobras, these vipers, but they dance to the tune of my pipe. They bring presents! Who, I ask you, does a more thriving business here in Venice and has a juicier sport to boot? [Jonson, *Volpone*]

c. **Marius:** If you're sure of getting yourself out of the coffin, I'm sure of getting you out of the grave. The gravedigger is a drunkard and a friend of mine. We'll arrive at the cemetery half an hour before the gates are closed. I'll have a hammer and chisel in my pocket. The hearse stops. The undertakers tie a rope around your coffin and let you down. They leave. I'm alone with the gravedigger. Before he can fill the grave, I invite him to join me at the tavern for a drink. It won't take long to get him fuddled. Being half-fuddled is his natural condition. He'll drink himself under the table. I take his identity card out of his pocket and return to the cemetery. I pull you out of the hole. All will go smoothly. Well . . . unless something goes wrong. Good God! How terrible that would be! [Hugo, *Les Miserables*]

d. **Horace:** I'm sick of you, sick of this house, sick of my life here. I'm sick of your brothers and their dirty tricks to make a dime. There must be better ways of getting rich than cheating poor people on a pound of bacon. Why should I give you the money? You wreck the town, you and your brothers, you wreck the town and live on it. Not me. Maybe it's easy for the dying to be honest. But it's not my fault I'm dying. I'll do no more harm now. I've done enough. I'll die my own way. And I'll do it without making the world any worse. I leave that to you. [Hellman, *The Little Foxes*, Random House, Inc.]

e. **Andre:** Oh, where has all my past life gone to? The time when I was young and clever, when I used to have great dreams. Why do we all become so dull and commonplace and uninteresting almost before we've begun to live? Why do we get lazy, useless, unhappy? People in this town do nothing but eat, drink, and sleep. Then they die, and some more take their places, and they eat, drink, and sleep too. And they indulge in their stupid gossip and vodka and gambling. The wives deceive their husbands, and the husbands lie to their wives, and they pretend they don't see anything and don't hear anything. It's all so stupid! [Chekhov, *The Three Sisters*]

f. **Corbaccio:** I . . . hee, hee . . . like to look at dying men. I've seen so many and I enjoy each one more. I'm eighty-two. I've buried brothers, sisters, friends, enemies, but I'm still alive . . . hee, hee . . . I'll outlive 'em all. I've known many of them in the cradle, and seen 'em grow up and all at once they lie there—blue, cold, and dead . . . hee, hee. And now this one, too! He lived a merry life . . . young, could have been my son—and he's come to die already, hee, hee! I want to take a look at him. Here, stand up, carcass, face an old man. You're younger—you have better legs. Stand up . . . hee, hee! Often you've mocked poor old Corbaccio for being miserly . . . hee, hee . . . who's mocking now, you windbag, you glutton! He'll outlive you all, will old Corbaccio! [Jonson, *Volpone*]

g. **Orgon:** You were a miserable pauper, and I saved you from starvation. I housed you, I treated you like a brother. I gave you almost everything I own. But, just hold on, my friend, not so fast! A little more caution on your part! So you thought you'd fool me? You tried to act like a saint! You're not cut out to be a saint, and you got tired of your little act sooner than you thought you would, didn't you? Trying to marry my daughter, and worse, trying to seduce my wife—right under my nose. I've been suspicious for a long time, and I knew I would catch you in the act. And you've given me all the evidence I need. It's enough! And I don't need any more talk from you. Spare me your lies, and get out of here! [Molière, *Tartuffe*]

h. **Arthur:** I went to Longon as squire to my cousin, Sir Kay. The morning of the tournament, Kay discovered that he'd left his sword at home and gave me a shilling to ride back and fetch it. On my way through London, I passed a square and saw there a sword rising from a stone. Not thinking very quickly, I thought it was a war memorial. The square was deserted, so I decided to save myself a journey and borrow it. I tried to pull it out. I failed. I tried again. I failed again. Then I closed my eyes and with all my force tried one last time. Lo, it moved in my hand! Then slowly it slid out of the stone. I heard a great roar. When I opened my eyes, the square was filled with people shouting, "Long live the King! Long live the King!" Then I looked at the sword and saw the blade gleaming with letters of gold. [Lerner and Loewe, *Camelot*]

i. **Cyrano:** My nose is very large? Young man, you might say many other things, changing your tone. For example—Aggressively: "Sir, if I had such a nose, I'd cut it off!" Friendly: "You'd have to drink from a tall goblet or your nose would dip into it." Descriptive: "'Tis a crag . . . a peak . . . a peninsula!" Graciously: "Are you so fond of birds that you offer them this roosting place to rest their little feet?" Quarrelsome: "When you smoke a pipe and the smoke comes out of your nose, doesn't some neighbor shout 'Your chimney is on fire'?" Warning: "Be careful, or its weight will drag down your head and stretch you prostrate on the ground." Tenderly: "Have a small umbrella made to hold over it, lest its color fade in the sun." Dramatic: "It's the Red Sea when it bleeds!" Countrified: "That's a nose that is a nose! A giant turnip or a baby melon!" My friend, that is what you'd have said if you had had some learning or some wit. But wit you never had a bit of. As for letters, you have only the four that spell out "fool"! [Rostand, *Cyrano de Bergerac*]

j. **Dr. Pangloss:** Well, it's true—they hanged me. They were supposed to burn me, but just as they were ready to roast me, along came a cloudburst. They couldn't start a fire, so for lack of anything better to do, they hanged me. Know what happened? They bungled it. The executioner was superb at burning people alive, but he didn't know beans about hanging. The rope was wet and didn't tighten properly. It got caught on a knot. I was still breathing, but they didn't know I was alive. So along came this surgeon who took me home to dissect me. He made an incision in my belly—all the way up to my shoulders. I yelled so loudly that the poor man thought he was dissecting the devil. He was terrified and he ran away so fast that he fell all the way down the stairs. With the last strength I had, I screamed, "I'm alive! Have mercy! Help me!" He recovered his courage, returned and sewed me up, and in two weeks I was up and about. [Voltaire, *Candide*]

k. **Don Juan:** Aha! And where did this one come from? Did you ever see anything more delightful? Turn just a little, please. What a charming figure! Look up a little. What a pretty little face. Open your eyes wide. Aren't they beautiful? Now a glimpse of your teeth. Delicious! And what inviting lips! And a girl like you is marrying a scrubby peasant? Never! You weren't born to live in the middle of a hell-hole. I've been sent here to prevent you from marrying that dolt. To get to the point. I love you with all my heart. Say the word and I'll take you away and show you the kind of life you deserve. Is my proposal rather sudden? It's your fault. You're much too beautiful. You have made me fall as deeply in love with you in a quarter of an hour as in six months with anyone else. [Molière, *Don Juan*]

l. **The Creature:** I am malicious because I am miserable. I am a wretch. I have murdered the lonely and the helpless. I have strangled the innocent as they slept and grasped to death the throats of those who have never injured me or any living thing. Am I not shunned and hated by all mankind? You, my creator, would tear me to pieces—why should I pity man more than man pities me? But I will revenge my injuries. And toward you, my arch-enemy, my creator, I swear inextinguishable hatred. I will work for your destruction, nor will I finish until I desolate your heart, so that you curse the hour of your birth. [Shelley, *Frankenstein*]

48. **Female–Male Characters**

a. **Magaera:** I won't go another step.
Androcles: Oh, not again, dear. What's the good of stopping every two minutes and saying you won't go another step? We must get to the next village before night. There are wild beasts in this wood. Lions, they say.
Magaera: I don't believe a word of it. We haven't seen a single lion yet.
Androcles: Well, dear, do you want to see one?
Magaera: You cruel brute. You don't care how tired I am or what becomes of me. Always thinking of yourself! Self, self, self!
Androcles: We all need to think of ourselves occasionally.
Magaera: A man ought to think of his wife sometimes.
Androcles: You make me think of you a good deal, dear.
Magaera: Is it my fault that I married you?
Androcles: No, dear, that's my fault.
Magaera: You ought to be ashamed of yourself.
Androcles: I am, my dear.
Magaera: Then why don't you treat me properly and be a good husband to me?
Androcles: What can I do, my dear?
Magaera: What can you do? Your being addicted to animals. You bring in every stray cat and lame duck in the whole countryside. You took the bread out of my mouth to feed them.
Androcles: Only when they were hungry and you were getting too fat, dear.
Magaera: Yes, insult me, do. You used to sit and talk to those dumb beasts for hours, when you hadn't a word for me.
Androcles: They never answered back, darling.
Magaera: Well, if you're fonder of animals than your own wife, you can live with them here in the jungle. I'm going home! I'll make my way through the forest, and when I'm eaten by the wild beasts, you'll know what a wife you've lost. [Lion appears] Oh, Andy! Andy! [Lion roars]
Androcles: Don't you come near my wife, do you hear? Meggy, run! Run for your life! Aw-w-w-w, he's lame. Did him get a thorn in him's footsums wootsums? Well, just one little pull, and then him will live happily ever after! Now it's out! Does him want to dance with Andy Wandy?

Magaera: Oh, you coward! You haven't gone dancing with me for years and now you go off dancing with a brute beast you haven't known for ten minutes. Coward, coward, coward! [Shaw, *Androcles and the Lion*, Copyright 1913 by George Bernard Shaw. Copyright renewed. Reprinted by permission of the Society of Authors, London, on behalf of the estate of George Bernard Shaw]

b. **Martha:** We've got guests coming over.

George: When?

Martha: Now.

George: Good Lord, Martha, do you know what time it . . . who's coming?

Martha: What's-their-name?

George: Who's What's-their-name?

Martha: I don't know what their name is. He's in the math department, blond and . . .

George: . . . and good-looking.

Martha: Yes, and good-looking.

George: It figures.

Martha: . . . and his wife's a mousey little type, without any hips or anything.

George: All right. Well, where are they?

Martha: They'll be here soon.

George: What did they do . . . go home and get some sleep first?

Martha: Hey, put some more ice in my drink, will you? You never put any ice in my drink. Why is that, huh?

George: I always put ice in your drink. You eat it, that's all. It's that habit you have . . . chewing your ice cubes . . . like a cocker spaniel. You'll crack your big teeth.

Martha: They're my big teeth.

George: Some of them. Some of them.

Martha: I've got more teeth than you've got.

George: Two more.

Martha: Well, two more's a lot more.

George: I suppose it is. I suppose it's pretty remarkable . . . considering how old you are.

Martha: You cut that out! You're not so young yourself!

George: I'm six years younger than you are . . . I always have been and I always will be.

Martha: Well . . . you're going bald.

George: So are you.

Martha: I swear . . . if you existed, I'd divorce you. [Albee, *Who's Afraid of Virginia Woolf?* Copyright 1962 by Edward Albee. Copyright renewed. Reprinted by permission of Macmillan Publishing Co.]

Assignment 17: Putting It All Together

For this assignment, three choices are suggested.

1. Present selection(s) from Exercises 46 or 47. Or select a monologue from a play of your own choice. Review the suggestions in the Putting It All Together section, page 241.

2. Select a short scene from a play involving two characters. Choose a climactic moment in the play, one that is intensely dramatic, suspenseful, or funny. *Rehearse with a partner.* Delineate as sharply as possible your characters.

3. The Helena Modjeska gig (see page 217). Choose a partner and contrive a situation that involves some emotional extremes, serious or humorous. Improvise a scene, at first using words. Don't be afraid to ad lib. Then substitute letters of the alphabet—no words.

If you use all the elements of expressiveness with sufficient imagination, your listeners will have little difficulty comprehending the nature of your little "scene."

Suggestions: A lovers' quarrel, a proposal, a bashful fellow asking the homecoming queen for a date, an angry courtroom exchange between two attorneys, a talk show host and a keyed-up guest discussing a controversial subject.

Suggested Checklist for Assignment 17: See page 287, Appendix B.

WRAP-UP

1. What causes vocal monotony?
   Personality characteristics: Lazy, frigid, indifferent, or introverted individuals—also those plagued by stage fright—sometimes tend to be monotonous.
   Dull, technical, repetitious subject matter: The speaker may simply have to try harder to communicate with listeners. If the material isn't animated, the speaker *must* be.

2. Pitch is the highness or lowness of tone or sound. It is determined by age, sex, and general emotional attitudes as well as by length, thickness, mass, and degree of tension of the vocal folds.

3. The optimum (natural) pitch level is your most desirable and efficient pitch level.

4. The habitual (average or customary) pitch level is the one that you use most often. It isn't always the same as the optimum pitch level. If the habitual level is more than two tones higher or lower than the optimum level, an adjustment should be made.

5. Range is the span of tones from the lowest to the highest that the voice is capable of producing.

6. The overall rise and fall of the voice or the melody of pitch changes is known as intonation.

7. A pitch level, ranging from high to low, used at any given moment in speaking is known as the key. A low key often fits material that is quiet, thoughtful, or sad. Excitement, rage, joy, and humor are compatible with a high key. A middle key is used in routine conversation.

8. Changing pitch within a syllable, word, or group of words is called an inflection. A rising inflection indicates questioning, doubt, incompleteness of thought. A falling inflection indicates certainty or completeness of thought. A double inflection registers uncertainty, hidden meaning, and complexity of thought.

9. A step is a pitch change between words or syllables. It is more emphatic than an inflection.

10. Stress is the degree of prominence of a syllable within a word or a word within a phrase or sentence. Emphasis is the degree of prominence given to a phrase or thought grouping.

11. Rate is the fastness or slowness of speech.

12. A rate of 120 to 140 words per minute is useful if you're dealing with material that is complex, technical, or profound.
    A rate of 180 to 200 wpm is sometimes used to convey humor or if the situation calls for elation, excitement, fear, or anger.
    A rate of 140 to 180 wpm will accommodate most speaking situations.

13. Duration is the length or amount of sounds.
    Staccato: vowels and diphthongs are cut short. Often used for expressing extreme emotional states.
    Prolonged: vowels and diphthongs are stretched. Particularly suited for less extreme emotions—peacefulness, awe, reverence, sadness.
    Regular: vowels and diphthongs are not attacked briskly, cut short, or lengthened. Appropriate for casual, matter-of-fact conversation and speaking.

14. A pause is an empty space, a period of silence. A phrase is a thought unit. Phrases are set off from each other with pauses.

15. Phrasing is used to underscore the exact meaning of a thought, to prevent confusion between adjacent phrases, and for emotional effect.

16. Pauses are often a natural place to take a breath. Pauses indicate changes of thought, feelings, and emotions. Pauses help the speaker achieve emphasis and clarity.

Assignment 18: Spontaneity

Your final performance should be your pièce de résistance, which the dictionary defines as a "main dish of a meal" or a "noteworthy achievement."

Prepare approximately three to five minutes of interesting and varied material. Choose material that excites you and that you genuinely want to share with your classmates.

In your presentation to the class, some of your material may be read, but at least half of it should be told from memory, as you might do if you were giving an impromptu talk. Please don't memorize verbatim the material you choose for this section of your performance. Work instead for *conversational, unforced spontaneity.*

For a practice session or two, rather than concentrating primarily on certain aspects or problems, try to think of the many phases of voice and speech that you have dealt with in this course as being integrated and blended together.

Then try a few practice sessions, forgetting about faults and foibles, techniques and tricks. Can you build in yourself a strong desire to communicate? When you perform, do everything that you can to *relate to your listeners so that they can relate to you.*

Suggested Checklist for Final Oral Performance: See Appendix C.

PRONUNCIATION AND VOCABULARY

WOULD YOU BELIEVE THAT

. . . The longest word in the *Random House Dictionary* (45 letters) is *pneumonoultra-microscopicsilicovolcanoconiosis* (a lung disease)?

How do you pronounce it? Simple.

noo′ mə nō ul′ trə mī′ krə skop′ ik sil′ ə kō′ vol kā′ nō kō′ nē ō′ sis

or

[ˈnu mə no,ʌltrə ,mɑɪ krə ,skɑp ɪk ˈsɪl ə ,ko val ,ke no ,ko ni ˈo sɪs]

. . . The two words most widely understood all over the world are *okay* and *Coca-Cola?*

. . . Americans' favorite top 10 words of endearment: *honey, baby, sweetheart, dear, lover, darling, sugar, pumpkin, angel, precious?*

. . . American's favorite top 10 words of contempt: *jerk, moron, fool, idiot, airhead, dimwit, bozo, slimeball, scuzzbag, knucklehead?*

. . . The 10 most commonly mispronounced words are *Arctic, athlete, athletics, library, February, escape, surprise, recognize, genuine, hundred?*

. . . *Aquadextrous*, a recently coined word, is legitimate? Means? The ability to turn the bathtub faucet on and off with one's toes.

STANDARD PRONUNCIATION

When Joe tried to swim ACROSST the lake, he DROWNDED.

Is something wrong with the capitalized words? Errors in articulation? Errors in pronunciation?

Technically speaking, these aren't articulatory mistakes. The sounds might be clearly and distinctly produced, and articulation, of course, refers to sharpness and crispness of speech.

Something more than articulation is involved: It's pronunciation.

Pronunciation *includes the correct production of sounds, but it also includes saying them in the right order (and without omitting any of them or adding extra ones), and with the appropriate stress on syllables in words.*

In this section the word *standard* is used to indicate that the listed pronunciation is frequently used by educated and cultured people. The term *nonstandard* indicates that the listed pronunciation is used less frequently by educated and cultured individuals. A nonstandard pronunciation, however, isn't necessarily always incorrect.

How should we pronounce *advertisement?*

ad ver **TISE** ment or ad **VER** tise ment?

Both are standard.

How should we pronounce *preferable?*

PREF er able or pre **FER** able?

The first is standard.

How should we pronounce *cache* ("hiding place")?

CATCH or **CASH?**

The second is standard.

Now and then we become involved in arguments about pronunciation. Somebody will say, "Let's look it up in the dictionary." If we know how to use a dictionary and don't regard it as divinely inspired, this is an excellent suggestion,

> Editors of good dictionaries are quite specific in stating that their volumes simply attempt to describe and record what people say. They do not try to dictate, command, or prescribe standards of pronunciation. Nevertheless, the *Merriam-Webster Dictionary* specifically states that it stresses showing the English language as it *is* used. The *American Heritage Dictionary,* on the other hand, stresses the language as it *should* be used.

Dictionary makers are aware that our language isn't embalmed or frozen in time and space. English is a dynamic language—forever developing and changing. It is, in short, a gutsy language.

There are more than 1 million words in the English language. No one actually knows how many there are. And no dictionary can possibly keep up with the latest trends, changes, or fads in words. For example, if one explains that most of the hippie jargon of the 60s and 70s has disappeared in the 90s, somebody may ask what the word *hippie* means.

To keep up, publishers would have to put out a new dictionary each year. *Couch potato* and *televangelist* appeared for the first time in some 1989 dictionaries. *Dweeb, date rape,* and *technobabble* appeared for the first time in the latest edition of the *Merriam-Webster Dictionary.*

> Two major dictionaries disagree over the word *ain't.* One, although disapproving, says that the word is acceptable. The other declares the word to be unacceptable.

Walter Cronkite, for many years an outstanding newscaster, once received considerable mail from irate listeners taking him to task for his mispronunciation of *February.* He omitted the first *r* and said *Feb-yoo-ary.*

Cronkite has an interesting defense: "I say *Feb-yoo-ary* [with only one *r*] and to hell with it."

How do new words originate? Who invents them? One example: Popular TV and movie star George Clooney, appearing on a talk show, was asked how he handled the *paparazzi,* the ubiquitous photographers who haunt celebrities.

He replied, "The only way to avoid the *stalkarazzi* is to stay poor and unknown."

Within the week, three entertainment-show hosts picked up on the word. Within the month, five magazines and newspapers quoted Clooney's "new" word.

Will the first dictionary published in the new millenium include *stalkarazzi?* We'll see.

The pronunciations listed in a dictionary tend to be formal. Words are considered in isolation. In connected and rapid speed and especially in informal situations, pronunciations of words are influenced by other words that precede or follow them.

Is there really a standard pronunciation? No. There is, however, a standard of pronunciation. It's this: *Pronunciation that is standard does not attract undue attention to itself.*

If it does, either the speaker is guilty of affectation or of "putting on airs," or the speaker is trying out a pronunciation in an unfavorable environment.

Acceptable pronunciation, like good articulation, is always desirable. If someone occasionally mispronounces a word, the person won't be labeled as a barbarian or automatically consigned to purgatory. But consistent and frequent mispronunciations definitely stamp an individual as careless, lacking in culture, refinement, and know-how. It bothers some people the same way fingernails scraping on chalkboards do.

How may your pronunciation be improved?

- **Be a good listener.** Listen carefully to the speech around you, and especially to the speech of educated and cultured individuals. As often as opportunity permits, listen to recordings of your own speech. Compare your pronunciation with that of established, successful speakers and leaders in your own general region.
- **Have access to a good dictionary,** and learn how to use it properly.

DEFINITIONS

Many words, of course, have more than one meaning.

Fred Astaire, the late, remarkable dancer, made a popular movie in the 30s titled *The Gay Divorcée.* If the movie were to be remade today, the chances are Hollywood would change that title!

Dink is a drop shot in basketball **or** a double-income couple with no kids.

One dictionary lists 179 definitions for *run* and 200 for *set,* the hardest-working word in English.

Where does all this put you?

Dictionaries generally list definitions in one of two ways:

1. *The earliest known meaning of a word is placed first.* More recent or current meanings of the word follow. In other words, the order of definitions is historical.

    doodle: (1) a foolish or a silly person. (2) scribbling aimlessly or absent-mindedly.

    This format is used by *Webster's New Collegiate Dictionary* and *Webster's New World Dictionary.*

2. *The most common definition with the most basic and central meaning is placed first.* Less common meanings and older definitions follow.

    doodle: (1) to draw or scribble idly. (2) a fool

    This format is used by the *Random House Dictionary* and the *American Heritage Dictionary.*

Having a problem using an unfamiliar word in a sentence? Check the unabridged dictionaries—those two-ton tomes in your library. (An unabridged dictionary isn't condensed or shortened. It may contain 500,000 or more entries. Your abridged paperback, or even hardback, dictionary is condensed. It generally contains 150,000 to 200,000 entries.) The unabridged dictionaries give many examples of how to use difficult words in phrases or sentences.

PRONUNCIATION

Why are there five syllables in the word *monosyllabic?*

In this book I have provided you with standard pronunciations of 149 different words. But suppose you want to do a little snooping yourself. What do you do when you look up a word and find not one but two varying pronunciations?

In most dictionaries both of the pronunciations are regarded as standard. In some cases, however, the first pronunciation shown is considered to be the one most frequently used. But let me emphasize that *the second choice is also widely used by educated speakers.*

There's one small fly in the ointment. No doubt, by now you've noticed that your knowledge of the International Phonetic Alphabet (IPA) won't necessarily help you determine a standard pronunciation of a word.

For example, look up the word *chic* (stylish, elegant) in the *Random House Dictionary.* Its first pronunciation is given as

shēk

This bears little resemblance to the phonetic transcription

[ʃik]

As a matter of fact, the majority of popular dictionaries do not use the IPA.* They use dictionary symbols (diacritics). This means that a mark, a sign, or a symbol may be attached to a certain letter to designate one of several sounds for which the letter might stand. This system is known as the Diacritical Marking System (DMS).

---

*The *Pronouncing Dictionary of American English,* by John S. Kenyon and Thomas A. Knott, uses phonetic symbols exclusively. No definitions. This dictionary has become the bible of many speech authorities. Even the Gospels, however, have been revised recently. The Kenyon and Knott work is more than a third of a century old and desperately in need of updating. It is nevertheless still a valuable dictionary.

Are dictionary symbols easier to master than phonetic symbols? This is a matter of endless controversy, and it seems to me that it's six of one and half a dozen of another. Dictionary symbols, however, are certainly not as precise as phonetic symbols. With the IPA, you have a one-to-one relationship between the symbol and the sound itself. A majority of instructors in speech communication areas prefer the IPA. It's traditional.

Dictionary symbols are neither uniform nor consistent. Look up the word *abdomen* in four popular dictionaries, and this is what you'll find:

ab′ də mən   ăb′ də mən

ˋab-də-mən   AB.duh.mun

In spite of the discrepancies among the dictionary symbols, you should be reasonably familiar with at least one system. Whatever your choice of career, and regardless if your personal library contains 6 books or 6,000, a dictionary will probably be one of them. A dictionary for most people is an inescapable fact of life.

Dictionaries aren't a luxury. They're a necessity.

A brief introduction to dictionary symbols will help you better use and understand most dictionaries. The system presented here (Table A.1) is derived largely from the *Random House Dictionary,* the *American Heritage Dictionary,* and *Webster's New World Dictionary,* which are three superior and widely used dictionaries. There have been a few minor simplifications and changes. In each case, the IPA symbol is also listed. The comparison is interesting.

In most dictionaries, the principal stress or accent of a word is indicated by a heavy mark (′) placed after the syllable that receives the greater stress.

A stressed syllable is generally louder (es CAPE, not ES cape), *longer* (a-a-a-agile, not agi-i-i-ile), *and higher in pitch* (sa$_{\text{dist}}$ not sa^{dist}) *than an unstressed syllable.*

The secondary stress or accent, which is given medium emphasis, is indicated by a lighter mark (′) after a syllable.

In IPA transcription, the mark (ˈ) above the line and before a syllable indicates that this syllable receives the greater stress. The mark (,) below the line and before a syllable indicates that this syllable receives lesser or weaker stress.

The following three words are transcribed with dictionary symbols and phonetic symbols:

	Dictionary Symbols	Phonetic Symbols
fever	fē′ vər	ˋfivɚ
aware	ə wâr′	əˋwɛr
party	pär′ti	ˋpɑrtɪ

Each diacritic has a name:

—is a macron.

^ is a circumflex.

¨ is an umlaut.

˘ is a breve.

/ is a slash.

Table A.1   Comparison of Dictionary and Phonetic Symbols

Dictionary Symbols	Key Word	Phonetic Symbols	Key Word
Consonants			
1. b	bib (bib)	[b]	bɪb
2. ch	church (chûrch)	[tʃ]	tʃɝʃ
3. d	dud (dud)	[d]	dʌd
4. f	fife (fīf)	[f]	faɪf
5. g	gag (gag)	[g]	gæg
6. h	hope (hōp)	[h]	hop
7. hw	while (hwīl)	[hw]	hwɑɪl
8. j	jig (jig)	[dʒ]	dʒɪg
9. k	cake (kāk)	[k]	kek
10. l	lull (lul)	[l]	lʌl
11. m	mate (māt)	[m]	met
12. n	nun (nun)	[n]	nʌn
13. ŋ/ng	ring (riŋ)	[ŋ]	rɪŋ
14. p	pipe (pīp)	[p]	pɑɪp
15. r	rip (rip)	[r]	rɪp
16. s	sass (sas)	[s]	sæs
17. sh	shall (shal)	[ʃ]	ʃæl
18. t	tot (tot)	[t]	tɑt
19. th (voiceless)	thin (thin)	[θ]	θɪn
20. th̸ (voiced)	then (th̸en)	[ð]	ðɛn
21. v	vat (vat)	[v]	væt
22. w	won (wun)	[w]	wʌn
23. y	yell (yel)	[j]	jɛl
24. z	zip (zip)	[z]	zɪp
25. zh	azure (azhʹər)	[ʒ]	ˈæʒɚ

Syllabic [l]: If [l] forms a syllable by itself, as in *apple*, *buckle*, and *whittle*, it is printed or written [l̩]: ˈæpl̩, ˈbʌkl̩, ˈhwɪtl̩.

Dictionary Symbols	Key Word	Phonetic Symbols	Key Word
Vowels and Dipthongs			
1. a	at (at)	[æ]	æt
2. ā	way (wā)	[e]	we
3. â	hare (hâr)	[ɛ, æ]	hɛr, hær
4. ä	calm (käm)	[ɑ]	kɑm
5. e	let (let)	[ɛ]	lɛt
6. ē	eat (ēt)	[i]	it
7. ê	dear (dêr, dēr)	[i]	dir
8. i	is (iz)	[ɪ]	ɪz
9. ī	ice (īs)	[ɑɪ]	ɑɪs
10. o	odd (od)	[ɑ]	ɑd
11. ō	ode (ōd)	[o]	od
12. ô	dawn (dôn)	[ɔ]	dɔn
13. oi	oil (oil)	[ɔɪ]	ɔɪl
14. o͞o	too (to͞o)	[u]	tu
15. o͝o	book (bo͝ok)	[ʊ]	bʊk
16. ou	cow (kou)	[ɑʊ]	kɑʊ
17. u	cup (kup)	[ʌ]	kʌp
18. û	burn (bûrn)	[ɝ]	bɝn
19. ə	<u>a</u>bout (əbout′)	[ə]	əˈbɑʊt
	vi<u>o</u>lent (vī′ələnt)		ˈvaɪələnt
	rump<u>us</u> (rum′pəs)		ˈrʌmpəs

PRONUNCIATION AND VOCABULARY LISTS

The word lists, which follow this section, contain 149 words that are commonly mispronounced. Most of these mispronunciations result from one of five reasons.

In the following examples, dictionary symbols are unbracketed and phonetic transcriptions are bracketed.

SUBSTITUTING SOUNDS

Chef is not pronounced the way it looks. It is often mispronounced with the substitution of a *ch* sound for the correct *sh*.

Nonstandard:	chef	[tʃɛf]
Standard:	shef	[ʃɛf]

OMITTING SOUNDS

Arctic is often mispronounced because the third sound is omitted.

Nonstandard:	är′tik	[ˈɑrtɪk]
Standard:	ärk′tik	[ˈɑrktɪk]

ADDING SOUNDS

Burglar is often mispronounced with the insertion of an extra sound.

Nonstandard:	bûrg′ ə lər	[ˈbɝɡələ˞]
Standard:	bûrg′lər	[ˈbɝɡlə˞]

MISPLACING STRESS

Abyss is often mispronounced with the stress incorrectly placed on the first syllable.

Nonstandard:	a′bis	[ˈæbɪs]
Standard:	ə bis′	[əˈbɪs]

REVERSING SOUNDS

Larynx is commonly mispronounced because the *yn* is reversed to *ny*.

Nonstandard:	lar′niks	[ˈlærnɪks]
Standard:	lar′iŋks	[ˈlærɪŋks]

Sometimes, of course, persons may pronounce a certain word correctly, but use it incorrectly in their speech. For example, *guile* (trickery, deception) is pronounced correctly by most people as [gīl.] However, many of these same people do not always correctly use the word *guile* as a noun. Instead, they use *guile* as an adjective.

Incorrect:	Henry VIII was a guile ruler.
Correct:	Henry VIII was a ruler who practiced guile.

Obviously, then, pronunciation and usage cannot be completely divorced from each other. An expressive and flexible vocabulary, not to mention correct pronunciation, is the mark of an educated and refined person.

Practice the words in the lists that follow. Consult a reputable dictionary for definitions. Use the words in spoken as well as written English.

> As you're well aware, some words have more than one acceptable pronunciation. In the following lists, however, only one pronunciation is given. Most students find this less confusing. If you hear a pronunciation that differs from any of those listed here, check your dictionary. It's possible that the variant pronunciation is entirely acceptable.

LIST A

The words in the following list are most frequently mispronounced because *one sound is substituted for another.*

Words	Diacritics	Phonetic Symbols
1. abstemious	ab stēm′ias	æb‵stimɪəs
2. ad infinitum	ad in′fənī′təm	‵æd,ɪnfə‵naɪtəm
3. agile	aj′əl	‵ædʒəl
4. alma mater	äl′mə mä′tər	‵ɑlmə ‵mɑtɚ
5. amphetamine	am fet′ ə mēn	æm‵fɛtə,min
6. androgynous	an droj′ə nəs	æn‵drɑdʒənəs
7. aria	är′ i ə	‵ɑrɪə
8. attaché	at ə shā′	,ætə‵ʃe
9. avant-garde	ə vänt′ gärd′	ə,vɑnt‵gɑrd
10. bestial	bes′ chəl	‵bɛstʃəl
11. blatant	blāt′ nt	‵bletn̩t
12. bona fide	bō′ nə fīd′	‵bonə ‵faɪd
13. bourgeois	boŏr zhwä′	bʊr‵ʒwɑ
14. cache	kash	kæʃ
15. censure	sen′ shər	‵sɛnʃɚ
16. charisma	kə riz′ mə	kə ‵rɪz mə
17. chasm	kaz′ əm	‵kæzəm
18. chic	shēk	ʃik
19. chutzpah	khoŏt′ spə	‵khʊtspə
20. coma	kō′ mə	‵komə
21. comely	kum′ li	‵kʌmlɪ
22. connoisseur	kon′ ə sûr′	,kɑnə ‵sɝ
23. crux	kruks	krʌks
24. debauched	di bôcht′	dɪ ‵bɔtʃt
25. deluxe	də loŏks′	də ‵lʊks
26. disheveled	di shev′əld	dɪ‵ʃɛvl̩d
27. et cetera	et set′ərə	ɛt ‵sɛtərə
28. euphoria	yoō fôr′ i ə	ju ‵fɔrɪə
29. exorcise	ek′ sôr sīz′	‵ɛk sɔrsaɪz
30. facetious	fə sē′ shəs	fə ‵siʃəs
31. faux pas	fō pä′	fo ‵pɑ
32. fungi	fun′jī	‵fʌndʒaɪ
33. garrulous	gar′ə ləs	‵gærələs

256   Appendix A

Words	Diacritics	Phonetic Symbols
34. genuine	jen′ yoo ən	ˈdʒɛnjuən
35. gist	jist	dʒɪst
36. heinous	hā′ nəs	ˈhenəs
37. hirsute	hûr′ soot	ˈhɝˑsut
38. in absentia	in ab sen′ shə	ˌɪnæb ˈsɛnʃə
39. indict	in dīt′	ɪn ˈdaɪt
40. longevity	lon jev′ə ti	lɑn ˈdʒɛvətɪ
41. macho	mä′ chō	ˈmɑtʃo
42. malignant	mə lig′ nənt	mə ˈlɪgnənt
43. masochist	mas′ə kist	ˈmæsə ˌkɪst
44. misogynist	mi soj′ənist	mɪ ˈsɑdʒənɪst
45. niche	nich	nɪtʃ
46. ogle	ō′ gəl	ˈogl̩
47. orgy	ôr′ji	ˈɔrdʒɪ
48. penchant	pen′ chənt	ˈpɛntʃənt
49. persona non grata	pər sō′nə non grät′ə	pɚˈsonə nɑn ˈgrɑtə
50. pique	pēk	pik
51. pitcher	pich′ ər	ˈpɪtʃɚ
52. posthumous	pos′ chə məs	ˈpɑstʃəməs
53. prima donna	prē′ mə don′ə	ˈprimə ˈdɑnə
54. propitiate	prə pish′ i āt	prə ˈpɪʃɪˌet
55. pugilist	pyoo′ jə list	ˈpjudʒəˌlɪst
56. recluse	rek′ loos	ˈrɛklus
57. regime	rə zhēm′	rəˈʒim
58. renege	ri nig′	rɪ ˈnɪg
59. sadist	sād′ ist	ˈsedɪst
60. sagacious	sə gā′ shəs	sə ˈgeʃəs
61. schizophrenia	skit′ sə frē′ niə	ˌskɪtsəˈfrinɪə
62. scourge	skûrj	skɝˑdʒ
63. slovenly	sluv′ ən li	ˈslʌvənlɪ
64. suave	swäv	swɑv
65. surrogate	sûr′ ə gāt	ˈsɝˑəˌget
66. taciturn	tas′ə tûrn	ˈtæsəˌtɝˑn
67. Tchaikovsky	chī kôf′ ski	tʃaɪ ˈkɔfskɪ
68. tempus fugit	tem′ pəs fyoo′jit	ˈtɛmpəs ˈfjudʒɪt

Words	Diacritics	Phonetic Symbols
69. tête-à-tête	tāt′ ə-tāt	ˈtetəˈtet
70. titular	tich′ə lər	ˈtɪtʃələ˞
71. unscathed	un skāthd′	ʌn ˈskeðd
72. vicarious	vī kâr′i əs	vɑɪ ˈkɛrɪəs
73. virile	vir′əl	ˈvɪrəl

LIST B

The words in this list are most frequently mispronounced because *one or more sounds have been omitted.*

Words	Diacritics	Phonetic Symbols
1. accelerate	ak sel′ə rāt	æk ˈsɛlə ˈret
2. Arctic	ärk′tik	ˈɑrktɪk
3. asphyxiate	as fik′ si āt	æsˈfɪksɪet
4. berserk	bər sûrk′	bə˞ ˈsɝk
5. environment	en vī′rən mənt	ɛn ˈvɑɪrənmənt
6. February	feb′rŏŏ er i	ˈfɛbrʊɛrɪ
7. idiosyncrasy	id′i ə sin′ krə si	ˈɪdɪəˌsɪnkrəsɪ
8. naive	nä ēv′	nɑ ˈiv
9. picture	pik′ chər	ˈpɪktʃə˞
10. quixotic	kwik sot′ik	kwɪks ˈɑtɪk
11. recognize	rek′əgnīz	ˈrɛkəgˌnɑɪz
12. succinct	sək singkt′	sək ˈsɪŋkt
13. ubiquitous	yōobik′wə təs	ju ˈbɪk wətəs
14. wouldn't	wŏŏd′ nt	ˈwʊdn̩t
15. wunderkind	vŏŏn′dər kind	ˈvʊndə˞kɪnd

LIST C

The words in this list are most frequently mispronounced because *one or more sounds have been added.*

Words	Diacritics	Phonetic Symbols
1. accompanist	ə kum′pə nist	əˈkʌmpənɪst
2. ambidextrous	am′ bə dek′ strəs	ˌæmbə ˈdɛkstrəs
3. anonymous	ə non′ ə məs	ə ˈnɑnəməs
4. athlete	ath′ lēt	ˈæθlit
5. athletics	ath let′ iks	æθˈlɛtɪks

Words	Diacritics	Phonetic Symbols
6. clique	klēk	klik
7. escape	ə skāp′	ə`skep
8. extraordinary	ek strôr′dn eri	ɛk`strɔrdn̩ ɛrɪ
9. forte (strong point)	fôrt	fort
10. grievous	grē′vəs	`grivəs
11. hors d'oeuvres	ôr dûrvz′	ɔr`dɝˑvz
12. prostate	pros′tāt	`prɑstet
13. schism	siz′əm	`sɪzəm
14. scintillate	sin′tlāt	`sɪntl̩ˌet
15. scion	sī′ ən	`sɑɪən

LIST D

The words in this list are most frequently mispronounced because of *misplaced syllable stress* (also described as placing the accent on the wrong syllable).

Words	Diacritics	Phonetic Symbols
1. abdomen	ab′ də mən	`æbdə mən
2. aberrant	ə ber′ ənt	ə `bɛrənt
3. admirable	ad′ mər ə bəl	`ædmərəbl̩
4. amicable	am′ ə kə bəl	`æməkəbl̩
5. applicable	ap′li kə bəl	`æplɪkəbl̩
6. autopsy	ô′top si	`ɔtɑpsɪ
7. barbarous	bär′bər əs	`bɑrbɚˑəs
8. bravado	brə vä′dō	brə `vɑdo
9. chagrin	shə grin′	ʃə `grɪn
10. clandestine	klan des′ tin	klæn `dɛstɪn
11. debacle	də bä′ kəl	də `bak!
12. formidable	fôr′ mə də bəl	`fɔrmədəbl̩
13. hallucinogen	hə lōō′ sə nə jən	hə `lusənədʒən
14. hyperbole	hī pûr′ bəli	hɑɪ `pɝˑbəli
15. ignominious	ig′nə min′i əs	ˌɪgnə`mɪnɪəs
16. impious	im′ pi əs	`ɪmpɪəs
17. impotence	im′pə təns	`ɪmpətəns
18. incomparable	in kom′pər ə bəl	ɪn `kɑmpərəbl̩
19. infamous	in′ fə məs	`ɪnfəməs
20. irreparable	i rep′ ər ə bəl	ɪ `rɛpərəbl̩

Words	Diacritics	Phonetic Symbols
21. libido	li bē′ dō	lɪ ˈbido
22. maniacal	mə nī′ə kəl	mə ˈnɑɪəkl̩
23. mischievous	mis′ chə vəs	ˈmɪstʃəvəs
24. operative	op′ûr ə tiv	ˈɑp ɚətɪv
25. perseverance	pûr′sə vir′əns	ˌpɝˑsəˈvɪrəns
26. placebo	plə sē′bō	plə ˈsibo
27. preferable	pref′ər ə bəl	ˈprɛfɚˑəbl̩
28. respite	res′ pit	ˈrɛspɪt
29. risqué	ris kā′	rɪs ˈke
30. superflous	sōō pûr′flōŏəs	suˈpɝˑfluəs
31. theater	thē′ə tər	ˈθiətɚˑ
32. vehement	vē′ ə mənt	ˈviəmənt

LIST E

The words and phrases in this list are most frequently mispronounced because *two or more sounds have been reversed* (or are often incorrectly used because their meanings aren't clearly understood by the speaker).

Words	Diacritics	Phonetic Symbols
1. ad hoc	ad hok′	ædˈhɑk
2. coup de grâce	kōō də gräs′	kudəˈgrɑs
3. dais	dā′əs	ˈdeəs
4. entrepreneur	än′trə prə nûr′	ˌɑntrə prə ˈnɝˑ
5. e pluribus unum	ē plōō′ri bŏŏs ōō′ nŏŏm	i ˈplurɪbʊs ˈunʊm
6. equanimity	ē′ kwə nim′ ə ti	ˌikwə ˈnɪmətɪ
7. fait accompli	fā′ tä-kôn-plē′	ˈfeta kɔn ˈpli
8. irrelevant	i rel′ ə vənt	ɪ ˈrɛləvənt
9. jihad	zhē hod′	ʒi ˈhɑd
10. laissez-faire	les′ā fâr′	ˌlɛse ˈfɛr
11. larynx	lar′ingks	ˈlærɪŋks
12. oxymoron	oks′ē môr′on	ˈɑksi ˈmɔrɑn
13. pièce de résistance	pē es′ də ri zē stäns′	pi ˈɛs də rɪziˈ stɑns
14. quid pro quo	kwid prō kwō	kwɪd pro kwo

Incorporate the words in these lists into your vocabulary. Use them in conversation, writing, or both as soon as you can. It's been said: Use a word three times and it's yours.

SUGGESTED CHECKLISTS

Name _____ Class/Section _____ Date _____

Suggested Checklist for Assignment 1: Breathiness

As you practice, you may want to work with this checklist. Listen carefully to yourself. If it's feasible, tape the assignment, or get a classmate or friend to listen to you. Your instructor may use the checklist to evaluate you.

Overall Effectiveness

Needs Improvement _____   Satisfactory _____

Faults or Foibles, If Any:

Inefficient breathing habits—shallow or clavicular breathing _____

Overbreathing: takes in too much breath _____

Excessively low loudness level _____

Excessively low pitch level _____

Breath leaks before or after sounds or during pauses _____

Breath leaks on voiceless consonants (s f th–θ h sh–ʃ k p t) _____

Carries over breathy quality from voiceless consonants to adjacent vowels and consonants _____

_____

Other:

Comments and Suggestions:

Name _____   Class/Section _____   Date _____

Suggested Checklist for Assignment 2: Stridency, Harshness, and Vocal Fry

As you practice, you may want to work with this checklist. Listen carefully to yourself. If it's feasible, tape the assignment, or get a classmate or friend to listen to you. Your instructor may use the checklist to evaluate you.

Overall Effectiveness

Needs Improvement _____   Satisfactory _____

Faults or Foibles, If Any:

Stridency

Excessive tensions and constrictions of pharynx and soft palate _____

Shallow or clavicular breathing _____

Excessive or improper loudness _____

Too-high pitch level _____

Harshness and Vocal Fry

Too-low loudness level _____

Too-low pitch level _____

Pulls chin back against neck _____

Excessive relaxation (laxness) of throat _____

Excessive tensions and constrictions of lower part of pharynx _____

Shallow or clavicular breathing _____

_____

Other:

Comments and Suggestions:

Name _____   Class/Section _____   Date _____

Suggested Checklist for Assignment 3: Nasality and Denasality

As you practice, you may want to work with this checklist. Listen carefully to yourself. If it's feasible, tape the assignment, or get a classmate or friend to listen to you. Your instructor may use the checklist to evaluate you.

Overall Effectiveness

Needs Improvement _____   Satisfactory _____

Faults or Foibles, If Any:

Nasality (Too Much Nasality)

General muscular sluggishness _____

Permits tongue to hump in rear of mouth _____

Excessively rigid jaw and clenched teeth _____

Nasalizes vowels before and after nasal consonants _____

Improper pitch level _____

Inadequate loudness level _____

Denasality (Too Little Nasality)

Excessive tension in nasopharynx _____

_____

Other:

Comments and Suggestions:

Name _____   Class/Section _____   Date _____

Suggested Checklist for Assignment 4: Throatiness

As you practice, you may want to work with this checklist. Listen carefully to yourself. If it's feasible, tape the assignment, or get a classmate or friend to listen to you. Your instructor may use the checklist to evaluate you.

Overall Effectiveness

Needs Improvement _____   Satisfactory _____

Faults or Foibles, If Any:

Pulls chin back against neck _____

Excessive tongue humping toward back of mouth _____

Insufficient energy in speaking _____

Too-low pitch level _____

_____

Other:

Comments and Suggestions:

Suggested Checklist for Assignment 5: Glottal Shock

As you practice, you may want to work with this checklist. Listen carefully to yourself. If it's feasible, tape the assignment, or get a classmate or friend to listen to you. Your instructor may use the checklist to evaluate you.

Overall Effectiveness

Needs Improvement ——————————   Satisfactory ——————————

Faults or Foibles, If Any:

Excessive tension or strain in throat or larynx ——————————

Too-high pitch level ——————————

Apparently closes glottis *before* vowels are begun ——————————

Other:

Comments and Suggestions:

Name _____ Class/Section _____ Date _____

Suggested Checklist for Assignment 6: Loudness

As you practice, you may want to work with this checklist. Listen carefully to yourself. If it's feasible, tape the assignment, or get a classmate or friend to listen to you. Your instructor may use the checklist to evaluate you.

Overall Effectiveness

Needs Improvement _____   Satisfactory _____

Faults or Foibles, If Any:

Doesn't Adjust to

    Size and proximity of audience _____

    Size and acoustical qualities of room _____

    Nature of material being presented _____

Loudness unvaried _____

Fades _____

Undue muscular constriction and tension of throat _____

Rigid jaw, clenched teeth, immobile lips _____

Too-low pitch level _____

Too-high pitch level _____

Other:

Comments and Suggestions:

Name _____ Class/Section _____ Date _____

Suggested Checklist for Assignment 7: Plosives

As you practice, you may want to work with this checklist. Listen carefully to yourself. If it's feasible, tape the assignment, or get a classmate or friend to listen to you. Your instructor may use the checklist to evaluate you.

Overall Effectiveness

Needs Improvement _____   Satisfactory _____

Faults or Foibles, If Any:

	Omits	Substitutes	Dentalizes	Other
1. **p** (pop)	_____	_____	_____	_____
2. **b** (bib)	_____	_____	_____	_____
3. **t** (tot)	_____	_____	_____	_____
4. **d** (did)	_____	_____	_____	_____
5. **k** (kick)	_____	_____	_____	_____
6. **g** (gag)	_____	_____	_____	_____

Comments and Suggestions:

Name _____ Class/Section _____ Date _____

Suggested Checklist for Assignment 8: Glides

As you practice, you may want to work with this checklist. Listen carefully to yourself. If it's feasible, tape the assignment, or get a classmate or friend to listen to you. Your instructor may use the checklist to evaluate you.

Overall Effectiveness

Needs Improvement _____   Satisfactory _____

Faults or Foibles, If Any:

	Omits	Substitutes	Weakens	Other
1. **w** (wit)	_____	_____	_____	_____
2. **hw** (why)	_____	_____	_____	_____
3. **l** (lull)	_____	_____	_____	_____
4. **j** (yet)	_____	_____	_____	_____
5. **r** (rare)	_____	_____	_____	_____

Regional [r] _____
Intrusive [r] _____

Comments and Suggestions:

Name _____   Class/Section _____   Date _____

Suggested Checklist for Assignment 9: Nasals

As you practice, you may want to work with this checklist. Listen carefully to yourself. If it's feasible, tape the assignment, or get a classmate or friend to listen to you. Your instructor may use the checklist to evaluate you.

Overall Effectiveness

Needs Improvement _____   Satisfactory _____

Faults or Foibles, If Any:

	Omits	Substitutes	Weakens	Other
1. **m** (mum)	_____	_____	_____	_____
2. **n** (nun)	_____	_____	_____	_____
3. ŋ (sing)	_____	_____	_____	_____

   Adds ŋg-click _____

Comments and Suggestions:

Name _____ Class/Section _____ Date _____

Suggested Checklist for Assignment 10: Fricatives and Affricates

As you practice, you may want to work with this checklist. Listen carefully to yourself. If it's feasible, tape the assignment, or get a classmate or friend to listen to you. Your instructor may use the checklist to evaluate you.

Overall Effectiveness

Needs Improvement _____   Satisfactory _____

Faults or Foibles, If Any:

	Omits	Substitutes	Overemphasizes	Other
1. **f** (fife)	_____	_____	_____	_____
2. **v** (van)	_____	_____	_____	_____
3. **θ** (thin)	_____	_____	_____	_____
4. **ð** (the)	_____	_____	_____	_____
5. **s** (sass)	_____	_____	_____	_____
6. **z** (zone)	_____	_____	_____	_____
7. **ʃ** (shy)	_____	_____	_____	_____
8. **ʒ** (beige)	_____	_____	_____	_____
9. **h** (home)	_____	_____	_____	_____
10. **tʃ** (chin)	_____	_____	_____	_____
11. **dʒ** (gem)	_____	_____	_____	_____

Comments and Suggestions:

Suggested Checklist for Assignment 11: Vowels

As you practice, you may want to work with this checklist. Listen carefully to yourself. If it's feasible, tape the assignment, or get a classmate or friend to listen to you. Your instructor may use the checklist to evaluate you.

Overall Effectiveness

Needs Improvement _____   Satisfactory _____

Faults or Foibles, If Any:

	Distorts	Substitutes	Nasalizes	Other
Front Vowels				
1. **i** (eat)	_____	_____	_____	_____
2. ɪ (ill)	_____	_____	_____	_____
3. **e** (ale)	_____	_____	_____	_____
4. ɛ (egg)	_____	_____	_____	_____
5. æ (ask)	_____	_____	_____	_____
Back Vowels				
6. ɑ (alms)	_____	_____	_____	_____
7. ɔ (all)	_____	_____	_____	_____
8. **o** (ode)	_____	_____	_____	_____
9. ʊ (cook)	_____	_____	_____	_____
10. **u** (do)	_____	_____	_____	_____
Central Vowels				
11. ɝ (earn)	_____	_____	_____	_____
12. ɚ (actor)	_____	_____	_____	_____
13. ʌ (up)	_____	_____	_____	_____
14. ə (sofa)	_____	_____	_____	_____

Comments and Suggestions:

Suggested Checklist for Assignment 12: Diphthongs

As you practice, you may want to work with this checklist. Listen carefully to yourself. If it's feasible, tape the assignment, or get a classmate or friend to listen to you. Your instructor may use the checklist to evaluate you.

Overall Effectiveness

Needs Improvement _____   Satisfactory _____

Faults or Foibles, If Any:

	Distorts	Substitutes	Nasalizes	Other
1. ɑɪ (isle)	_____	_____	_____	_____
2. ɑʊ (owl)	_____	_____	_____	_____
3. ɔɪ (toy)	_____	_____	_____	_____
4. eɪ (ale)	_____	_____	_____	_____
5. oʊ (go)	_____	_____	_____	_____
6. ɛr (dare)	_____	_____	_____	_____
7. ɪr (dear)	_____	_____	_____	_____
8. ɔr (lord)	_____	_____	_____	_____
9. ʊr (poor)	_____	_____	_____	_____

Comments and Suggestions:

Suggested Checklist for Assignment 13–17: Expressiveness

As you practice, you may want to work with this checklist. Listen carefully to yourself. If it's feasible, tape the assignment, or get a classmate or friend to listen to you. Your instructor may use the checklist to evaluate you.

Overall Effectiveness

Needs Improvement _____   Satisfactory _____

Interpretation of Material:

On a scale of 1 to 5 (5 being excellent), how successfully are these qualities conveyed?

Emotions, feelings	1 2 3 4 5
Specific meanings	1 2 3 4 5
Overall comprehension of material	1 2 3 4 5

Faults or Foibles, If Any:

Pitch

Unsuitable level _____ Ineffective range _____

Unvaried _____ Patterned _____ Other _____

Rate

Excessively fast _____ Excessively slow _____

Unvaried _____ Inappropriate _____ Other _____

Pauses and Phrases

Too few _____ Too many _____ Unvaried _____

Inappropriate _____ Other _____

Comments and Suggestions:

VOICE AND SPEECH PROFILE AND ANALYSIS CHARTS

Name _____   Class/Section _____   Date _____

Voice and Speech Profile

(All information on this sheet will be kept confidential.)

Classification: F   S   J   S Graduate Unclassified

_____

Reasons for taking this course: (required) _____

(recommended) _____   (elected) _____   (other) Specify: _____

Place of birth: _____
               city   state or country

How long did you live there? _____

Other cities or countries you have lived in for more than one year: _____

_____

_____

Parents' origins: _____

If your parents primarily spoke languages other than English, please list them: _____

What are your major or career goals? _____

_____

If you think that you speak with a dialect (accent), describe it: _____

Other than dialect (accent), evaluate your voice and speech problems (breathy, nasal, mumbling, high-pitched, monotonous, etc.): _____

_____

Possible causes of vocal problems (physical, dental, allergies, negative conditioning): _____

_____

What changes would you like to make in your voice and speech? Be specific. _____

_____

List other speech communication courses that you have taken or are currently taking: _____

_____

Name a celebrity whose speaking voice you particularly like and tell why you like it: _____

_____

Name a celebrity whose speaking voice you particularly dislike and tell why you dislike it: _____

_____

Hobbies: _____   _____

_____

If you have any comments or questions regarding this course, please state them here:

Name _____   Class/Section _____   Date _____

If evaluating another individual, subject's name: _____

Analysis Chart 1

Overall Effectiveness

1 = Needs Improvement   **2** = Good   **3** = Excellent

Quality   1   2   3

Was the voice pleasant to listen to?

Why or why not?

Loudness   1   2   3

Was the voice easily heard?

Why or why not?

Articulation   1   2   3

Was the speech clear, distinct, and easy to understand?

Why or why not?

Expressiveness   1   2   3

Was the voice varied and flexible? Was the material meaningfully interpreted?

Why or why not?

Unobtrusiveness and Appropriateness   1   2   3

Did the voice, speech, and pronunciation seem to be natural, unaffected, and generally acceptable?

Why or why not?

Comments and Suggestions:

Name _____   Class/Section _____   Date _____

Analysis Chart 2

Overall Effectiveness

1 = Needs Improvement   **2** = Good   **3** = Excellent

Quality   **1 2 3**

(Check applicable terms)

Breathy _____   Nasal _____

Glottal shock _____   Denasal _____

Strident _____   Throaty _____

Harsh _____   Hoarse _____

Vocal fry _____

Loudness   **1 2 3**

Too loud _____   Unvaried _____

Too soft _____   Lacks emphasis _____

Articulation   **1 2 3**

General inaccuracy _____

Sounds omitted or dropped _____

Sounds substituted _____

Sounds added _____

**Unobtrusiveness and
Appropriateness**   **1 2 3**

Arty (overly precise articulation) _____

Affected pronunciation _____

Mispronunciation _____

Regional dialect _____

Foreign dialect _____

Interpretation of Material   **1 2 3**

(Check applicable terms)

Emotions, feelings inadequately expressed _____

Specific meanings not always clear _____

Overall comprehension inadequate _____

Pitch

Too high _____

Too low _____

Monotonous _____

Patterned _____

Rate

Too fast _____   Hesitant _____

Too slow _____   Jerky _____

Monotonous _____   Poor phrasing _____

Patterned _____   Lack of pauses _____

What is your best vocal attribute?

In which aspects of voice and speech do you need to make the most improvement?

Name _____ Class/Section _____ Date _____

Analysis Chart 3: Quality

Present material orally before the class or listen to a recording of your voice. If you listen to a recording, you may use the one you recorded at the beginning of the course, or you may make a new one. With the aid of your instructor and classmates, analyze your voice quality as candidly as possible. Use this chart as a guide.

Overall Effectiveness

1 = Needs Improvement   **2** = Good   **3** = Excellent

If my voice quality needs improvement, the following term(s) most accurately describe(s) the sound of my voice:

Breathy _____   Nasal _____

Glottal shock _____   Denasal _____

Strident _____   Throaty _____

Harsh _____   Hoarse _____

Vocal fry _____

If my quality is unpleasant, it may be due to:

Excessive tension _____   Inefficient breathing habits _____

Inadequate loudness _____   Improper pitch level _____

Lazy lips, jaw, and tongue _____   Tongue humping _____

Rigid jaw _____   Excessive relaxation of soft palate _____

Burying chin in neck _____

Comments and Suggestions:

Name _____   Class/Section _____   Date _____

Analysis Chart 4: Loudness

Present material orally before the class. With the aid of your instructor and classmates, analyze your loudness as candidly as possible. Use this chart as a guide.

Overall Effectiveness

1 = Needs Improvement   **2** = Good   **3** = Excellent

In general, my voice is:

Easily heard _____   Difficult to hear _____

If my loudness needs improvement, the following term or phrase most accurately describes my problem:

Too loud _____   Lacks emphasis and contrast _____

Too soft _____   Patterned _____

Unvaried _____

If my loudness is unsatisfactory, one or more of the following factors may be responsible:

Inadequate openness of mouth _____   Unsatisfactory voice quality _____

Improper pitch level _____   Sluggish articulation _____

Excessive muscular
   constrictions of throat _____   Insufficient
   energy and animation _____

Improper control
   of breath pressure _____   Too rapid rate of speaking _____

Comments and Suggestions:

Name _____ Class/Section _____ Date _____

Analysis Chart 5: Articulation

Present material orally before the class or listen to a recording of your voice. If you listen to a recording, you may use the one you recorded at the beginning of the course, or you may make a new one. With the aid of your instructor and classmates, analyze your articulation as candidly as possible. Use this chart as a guide.

Overall Effectiveness

1 = Needs Improvement   **2** = Good   **3** = Excellent

In general, my speech is:

Clear, distinct, and accurate _____   Overly precise _____

Sluggish and indistinct _____

If my articulation is unsatisfactory, it may be due to:

Sluggish tongue activity _____   Rigid jaw _____

Immobile lips _____   Inactive velum _____

Inaccuracy of tongue position and movement _____

Specific errors:

Sounds omitted: _____   Sounds distorted: _____

_____   _____

_____   _____

Sounds substituted: _____   Sounds inadequate: _____

_____   _____

_____   _____

Sounds added: _____

_____

_____

Mispronunciation: _____

Foreign dialect: _____

Regional dialect: _____

Comments and Suggestions:

Name _____ Class/Section _____ Date _____

Analysis Chart 6: Expressiveness

Present material orally before the class or listen to a recording of your voice. If you listen to a recording, you may use the one you recorded at the beginning of the course, or you may make a new one. With the aid of your instructor and classmates, analyze your expressiveness as candidly as possible. Use this chart as a guide.

Overall Effectiveness

$$1 = \text{Needs Improvement} \qquad 2 = \text{Good} \qquad 3 = \text{Excellent}$$

In general, my voice is:

Varied and flexible _____ Unvaried and monotonous _____

If my vocal expressiveness needs improvement, the following terms or phrases most accurately describe my problem:

Interpretation of Material

Emotions, feelings inadequately expressed _____

Specific meanings not always clear _____

Overall comprehension inadequate _____

Pitch

Too high _____

Too low _____

Monotonous _____

Patterned _____

Excessive variation _____

Rate

Too fast _____   Hesitant _____

Too slow _____   Jerky _____

Monotonous _____   Poor phrasing _____

Patterned _____   Lack of pauses _____

Comments and Suggestions:

Name _____ Class/Section _____ Date _____

Final Oral Performance

Overall Effectiveness

1 = Needs Improvement   2 = Good   3 = Excellent

Quality

Satisfactory improvement _____

Needs further improvement _____

Specific comments: _____

_____

_____

_____

Interpretation of Material

Satisfactory improvement _____

Needs further improvement _____

Specific comments: _____

_____

_____

_____

Loudness

Satisfactory improvement _____

Needs further improvement _____

Specific comments: _____

_____

_____

_____

Pitch

Too high _____

Too low _____

Monotonous _____

Patterned _____

Excessive variation _____

Articulation

Satisfactory improvement _____

Needs further improvement _____

Specific comments: _____

_____

_____

_____

Rate

Satisfactory improvement _____

Needs further improvement _____

Specific comments: _____

_____

_____

Comments and Suggestions:

Unobtrusiveness and Appropriateness

Satisfactory improvement _____

Needs further improvement _____

Specific comments: _____

_____

_____

_____

Glossary

abdominal breathing A type of breathing that is regulated by controlled movements of the abdominal muscles. Most of the expansion–contraction activities occur in the abdominal area.

accent The stress, or the degree of prominence, given to a syllable in a word or to a word in a phrase or sentence. The stressed syllable or word is made louder and is generally higher in pitch than adjacent syllables or words.

Adam's apple See *thyroid cartilage.*

affricate A single consonant sound that results from a plosive and a fricative closely and rapidly blended. The underlined sounds are affricates: <u>ch</u>ild, lo<u>g</u>ic.

alveolar ridge The gum ridge or the tissues behind the upper front teeth. The alveolar ridge is used in the underlined sounds: <u>T</u>om, <u>s</u>eem, rai<u>s</u>e, aw<u>l</u>.

articulation Movements of the lips, the jaw, the tongue, and the velum (soft palate) to form, separate, and join speech sounds.

articulators The organs of speech used to produce speech sounds. The most important are the lips, the front teeth, the jaw, the tongue, and the velum.

arytenoid cartilage A pair of small, pyramid-shaped, and movable cartilages to which the vocal folds are attached. They have to do with the opening and closing of the vocal folds.

assimilation Occurs when a sound in a word is changed or modified as the result of the influence or overlapping of neighboring sounds (for example: "Jeat?" for "Did you eat?")

assimilation nasality The tendency for the production of a vowel to be influenced by a preceding or following nasal consonant (m n ŋ]. Example: Say "man" and "rap," and notice that the vowel in the first word has more nasality than the same vowel in the second word.

back vowels Vowel sounds produced when the back portion of the tongue is most active. The underlined sounds are back vowels: c<u>oo</u>l, l<u>oo</u>k, <u>o</u>bey, <u>a</u>ll, c<u>a</u>lm.

balanced resonance Pleasant, desirable resonance that avoids the extremes of nasality and denasality.

bilabial Sounds produced by contact between the lips. The underlined sounds are bilabials: <u>p</u>ie, <u>b</u>it, <u>M</u>ack, <u>w</u>on, <u>wh</u>y.

breathy A voice quality in which there is an excessive loss of breath while talking—as if the speaker were sighing or half-whispering. A fuzzy, feather-edged sound results.

bronchus Either of the two main divisions of the trachea.

cartilage A firm but flexible tissue related to bone. Gristle.

central–deep breathing Breathing in which most of the expansion–contraction activities occur in the abdominal area.

central (middle) vowels Vowel sounds produced when the middle portion of the tongue is most active. The underlined sounds are central vowels: d<u>ir</u>t, nev<u>er</u>, id<u>ea</u>, b<u>u</u>t.

chest resonance Vibrations in the ribs and chest indicate that this area may contribute to overall resonance.

clavicular–shoulder breathing A type of breathing in which most of the movement consists of raising and lowering the collarbones (clavicles) while inhaling and exhaling.

clusters Two or more consonants side by side in the same syllable, with no vowel between them. The underlined sounds are clusters: <u>dr</u>ink, <u>str</u>eak, <u>cr</u>am, <u>gr</u>oan, <u>tr</u>out, <u>thr</u>ill.

coarticulation The overlapping of neighboring sounds. The process by which one sound influences and colors adjacent sounds.

consonant A sound that can be made by stopping the breath, making it explode, or making it buzz or hum. There are about 25 consonants in American English. The underlined sounds represent a few of them: <u>u</u>p, <u>l</u>ie, <u>r</u>aw, o<u>n</u>, <u>th</u>e, <u>w</u>oe, <u>b</u>uy, a<u>gg</u>ie.

cricoid cartilage The signet-ring-shaped cartilage in the lower and back portion of the larynx. It forms a base, or foundation, for the rest of the larynx.

decibel A unit that expresses the relative intensity of sounds or sound waves. One-tenth of a bel.

denasal A voice quality in which negative or inadequate nasality results in a voice that sounds as if the speaker has a stuffed-up nose. Generally caused by a blockage in the nasal cavity. *Mining* becomes *bidig; thing* becomes *thig; hand* becomes *had.*

dentalization Incorrectly placing the tongue tip on the back of the upper front teeth, producing a slushy sound.

diacritical marking system (DMS) See *dictionary symbol.*

dialect A form of a language differing from other varieties of the same language. A dialect is used by a group of speakers who are set apart, geographically or socially, from others who speak the same language.

diaphragm A tough, double-domed muscle that separates the chest and abdominal cavities. It is the main muscle of breathing.

diaphragmatic breathing See *central–deep breathing.*

diction Refers to accuracy and clarity of speech. For all practical purposes, the word has the same meaning as *articulation* or *enunciation.* (In another sense, it means the choice of words in speaking and the accuracy with which they are used.)

dictionary symbol The Diacritical Marking System (DMS) mark or symbol accompanying a letter, as in ēt (eat), ôr (or), käm (calm), o͞o (to͞ok), which indicates the pronunciation of the letter's sound.

diphthong A rapid blending together of two vowel sounds within the same syllable. The first vowel element receives greater stress than the second vowel element. The underlined sounds are diphthongs: f<u>i</u>ve, j<u>oi</u>n, s<u>ou</u>th.

drone A speaker whose words or sentences are continually pitched at, or very near, one sound level. A dull, monotonous speaker.

duration The length or amount of sound: how long a sound is held.

Eastern dialect A form of American English, which differs from other varieties of the same language and which is heard primarily in the eastern United States.

emphasis The degree of prominence given to a phrase or thought group.

enunciation Accuracy and clarity of speech. Some prefer to use the term in reference to the production of vowels and diphthongs.

epiglottis A thin, valvelike cartilage that covers the entrance to the larynx.

esophagus A muscular tube connecting the mouth with the stomach.

exhalation The expelling of air from the lungs.

expressiveness Vocal variety: the pitch level at which we speak, our vocal movement from pitch to pitch, our rate of speaking, phrasing, emphasis, and contrast.

extrinsic muscles Those muscles that are concerned with movements of the larynx as a whole, as in swallowing.

fading Losing power; excessive drop in loudness at the end of phrases or sentences.

frequency The number of cycles or vibrations of a sound per second.

fricative A frictionlike sound produced when the outgoing breath stream is partially obstructed. The underlined sounds are fricatives: <u>s</u>it, <u>z</u>ap, <u>f</u>in, <u>v</u>im, <u>th</u>in, <u>th</u>us, <u>sh</u>y, rou<u>g</u>e, <u>h</u>ot.

front vowels Vowel sounds produced when the front portion of the tongue is most active. The underlined sounds are front vowels: b<u>e</u>, <u>i</u>t, r<u>a</u>te, b<u>e</u>g, <u>a</u>sk.

fundamental A tone produced by the overall vibration of the vocal folds, which is recognized as the basic pitch of the tone.

General American dialect A form of American English, which differs from other varieties of the same language and which is heard primarily in the Midwest (as far south as the Mason-Dixon line), in the West, and in parts of the Southwest.

glide A consonant sound in which the articulators move or glide from one position to another. The underlined sounds are glides: <u>w</u>in, <u>l</u>ake, <u>r</u>ope, <u>y</u>et.

glottal shock A raspy little bark or a sharp click or pop on vowel sounds, which may result from extremely tense vocal folds.

glottis The space or opening between the vocal folds.

habitual pitch level The pitch level most frequently used by an individual. The pitch may rise or fall, but the person's speech most often returns to this level.

hard palate The dome-shaped, bony roof of the mouth.

harsh A rough, raspy, gravelly, and possibly low-pitched voice quality, which may result from abnormal vibrations of the vocal folds or excessive tension within the larynx.

hoarse A harsh, raw, and strained voice quality that may also be somewhat breathy. It sounds as though the speaker has a sore throat.

hyoid bone A horseshoe-shaped, free-floating bone of the neck. The larynx is extended from this bone; the muscles of the jaw and tongue are attached to it.

hypernasality Excessive nasality.

hypertension Excessive tension, pertaining to high blood pressure.

hyponasality Insufficient nasality; denasality.

inflection A pitch change that occurs within a single, uninterrupted vocal tone or sound. An inflection may be described as rising, falling, or circumflex (a combination of rising and falling).

inhalation The drawing of breath into the lungs.

International Phonetic Alphabet (IPA) An alphabet that uses a special set of symbols to represent the sounds of languages. Each symbol represents one sound. The underlined sounds in the following words are shown with their IPA equivalents: <u>th</u>e = ð, <u>e</u>gg = ɛ, ic<u>er</u> = ɚ, si<u>ng</u> = ŋ; su<u>ch</u> = tʃ; c<u>a</u>t = æ; <u>u</u>p = ʌ.

intonation The overall pattern or melody of pitch changes in phrases or sentences.

intrinsic muscles Relatively tiny muscles attached entirely to various points within the larynx itself. They are directly concerned with the process of making speech sounds.

key The general pitch level—ranging anywhere from high to low—that is used at any given moment in talking or reading.

labial Pertaining to the lips.

labiodental Consonant sounds that are produced by placing the lower lip against the upper teeth. The underlined sounds are labiodentals: <u>f</u>og, <u>v</u>at.

larynx The voice box. The structure for producing voice. It includes the vocal bands, and it is the uppermost part of the trachea.

lingua-alveolar Sounds that are produced with the tongue touching or near the gum ridge. The underlined sounds are lingua-alveolars; hi<u>t</u>, <u>d</u>o, <u>l</u>ip, <u>s</u>o, <u>j</u>azz, <u>n</u>ick.

linguadental Sounds that are produced by placing the tip of the tongue against the upper front teeth. The underlined sounds are linguadentals: <u>th</u>in, <u>th</u>ey.

linguapalatal Sounds that are produced with the tip or the blade of the tongue on or near the hard palate. The underlined sounds are linguapalatals: <u>sh</u>all, plea<u>s</u>ure, <u>y</u>et, ro<u>ck</u>.

linguavelar Sounds that are produced by raising the back portion of the tongue against the soft palate or velum. The underlined sounds are linguavelars: <u>k</u>ill, <u>g</u>et, si<u>ng</u>.

loudness The power or intensity (sound level) of the vocal tone; volume, projection; force.

lungs The two large, saclike organs of respiration in the thorax. Spongy and cone-shaped.

monotone (or monopitch) Lack of pitch and rate variation; sameness; boring.

nasal Pertaining to the nose.

nasal consonants Consonants produced as the oral cavity is blocked off at some point, the velum is relaxed and lowered, and the breath stream is directed through the nose. The underlined sounds are nasals: hi<u>m</u>, <u>n</u>ot, ri<u>ng</u>.

nasality A nasal twang, as if talking through the nose. The voice has a foghorn (and sometimes a whiny) sound.

nasal resonance Amplification and reinforcement of sounds in the nose.

New England dialect   A form of American English, which differs from other varieties of the same language and which is heard primarily in Massachusetts, Rhode Island, Connecticut, Vermont, New Hampshire, and Maine.

optimum pitch level   The most desirable and serviceable level of pitch for the individual speaker. It is the level at which a person can produce the best vocal quality and the loudest voice with the least effort.

oral cavity   The mouth.

oral resonance   Amplification and reinforcement of sounds in the mouth.

overlapping speech   See *assimilation.*

overtones   Tones produced as the vocal folds vibrate in small parts or segments. Overtones are generally higher in pitch than the fundamental tone. See also *fundamental.*

pause   A period of silence. Pauses are used for expression (to achieve clarity, emphasis, meaning, contrast, and variety) and for taking breath.

pharynx   The throat.

phonation   Vocal tones or sounds produced by the vibration of the vocal folds as breath is forced between them.

phoneme   The basic sound unit or sound family; a group of closely related sounds. The *t* sounds in tip and pit are not exactly alike, but are recognizable as member sounds of the phoneme *t.*

phonetic symbols   See *International Phonetic Alphabet (IPA).*

phrase   A group of words expressing a thought unit or an idea. A phrase need not be a complete sentence.

pitch   The highness or lowness of a tone or a sound.

pitch pattern   A fixed melody pattern of speech used over and over again.

plosive   A consonant sound made by blocking the outgoing airstream. The tongue is dropped or the lips opened suddenly, and the built-up air is released in a little explosion. The underlined sounds are plosives: pop, bib, fit, hid, lake, rug.

projection   Controlled energy that gives impact, precision, and intelligibility to spoken sounds. Similar to *loudness, strength,* and *volume.*

prolonged duration   Lengthening or stretching sounds, particularly vowels and diphthongs. Appropriate for relatively serious material.

pronunciation   The correct production of word sounds in the right order without omissions or additions, and with appropriate stress on syllables.

quality   The texture of a sound or a tone that distinguishes it from other tones having the same pitch, duration, and loudness.

range   The span of tones from the lowest to the highest that the voice is capable of producing.

rate   The number of words spoken per minute: the fastness or slowness of speaking, which includes the quantity or duration of sounds and the length and number of pauses.

resonance   The process by which sounds produced at the vocal folds are amplified, modified, and enriched by the cavities of the head and chest.

resonators   The main human resonators: the cavities of the mouth, throat, nose, and larynx (voice box).

respiration   The inhalation and exhalation of air.

rib cage   The cagelike structure of the body formed by the ribs and their connecting bones.

septum   A dividing wall separating the two cavities in the nose.

soft palate   The velum: a soft, flexible, and muscular flap of tissue attached to the hard palate and located in the rearmost portion of the roof of the mouth.

Southern dialect   A form of American English that differs from other varieties of the same language and that is heard primarily in the states of the Old South. It is used as far west as Arkansas and in parts of Texas.

staccato duration   Slashing or shortening sounds, particularly vowels and diphthongs. Appropriate for relatively extreme emotional states or material.

step   An abrupt pitch change between words or syllables. A step is also known as a shift or a jump.

stress   The degree of prominence given a syllable within a word or a word within a phrase or a sentence. The stressed syllable or word is made louder and is often higher in pitch than its neighbors.

strident   A voice quality that is offensively metallic, tense, hard, and strained. It is often relatively high-pitched.

thorax   The chest.

throaty   A voice quality that is hollow, muffled, and dullish—voice-from-the-tomb quality, which is often relatively low-pitched.

thyroid cartilage   The Adam's apple. The large, butterfly-shaped cartilage that rests upon the cricoid.

timbre   The characteristic tone color or texture of a voice, regardless of pitch or loudness; quality.

trachea   The windpipe.

triphthong   Three vowels blended together in the same syllable as in [hɛɑʊ] for *how.* Generally considered unacceptable.

uvula   The small, fleshy tip of the velum that hangs downward.

velum   See *soft palate.*

vocal folds   Two small, tough bands of connective tissue located in the larynx. Voice is produced when the folds are set into vibration by the airstream from the lungs. Also known as vocal bands, vocal cords, or vocal lips.

vocal (glottal) fry   A noisy, growling, or "bacon-frying" voice quality that closely resembles harshness. It usually occurs when the pitch of the voice is dropped at the end of a sentence.

voiced consonant   A consonant on which the vocal folds vibrate. The underlined sounds are voiced: the, dip, azure, or, way, his, video.

voiceless consonant   A consonant on which the vocal folds do not vibrate. The underlined sounds are voiceless: thick, pal, should, cat, chin, sill.

vowel   A relatively open and continuous sound that is sonorous and free of friction noises. In normal utterance (nonwhispered speech), all vowels are voiced. They result from vocal tone created by the vibration of the vocal folds. There are about 15 vowels in American English. The underlined sounds represent a few of them: be, end, had, curl, cup, fool, took, old, calm.

windpipe   The trachea.

Index